Apprentice to the Masters

Adventures of a Western Mystic
Part II

Peter Mt. Shasta

Church of the Seven Rays
P. O. Box 1103
Mount Shasta, California 96067
U.S.A.

Third Edition by Church of the Seven Rays, February 2016
Second Edition by Church of the Seven Rays, August 2010
First Edition by AuthorHouse, March 2010

Copyright 2010-2016 by Peter Mt. Shasta. All rights reserved.

No part of this book may be reproduced, stored in a retrieval system, or be transmitted by any means without the written permission of the author.

ISBN: 978–0692570449 (Third Edition, February, 2016)

Original Library of Congress Control Number: 2010902624

Front cover photo: Mount Shasta 2009, by Sequoia Petengell, www.sequoiaphotography.com. Image enhancement by Dana Bainbridge, roundhouseagency.com

Back cover photo: Peter Mt. Shasta, City Park, Mount Shasta, California, May 2010, by Linda Held

Also by Peter Mt. Shasta:

"I AM" The Open Door

"I AM" Affirmations and the Secret of their Effective Use

I Am the Living Christ: Teachings of Jesus

Search for the Guru: Adventures of a Western Mystic, Part I

My Search in Tibet for the Secret Wish-Fulfilling Jewel

Lady Master Pearl, My Teacher

Step by Step, Ascended Master Discourses

Website: www.i-am-teachings.com

Dedication

To Pearl

* * * * * * *

About the Cover

The image of the author on the cover is an illustration of the *tantric* transformation of an ordinary being into Manjushri, the Bodhisattva of Wisdom, wielding the sword of discriminating intelligence. In the Western tradition this sword may also be visualized as that of Archangel Michael. This transformation of mundane reality into higher awareness is accomplished through the power of attention for *As a man thinketh in his heart, so is he* (Solomon, Proverbs; 23:7). This process is made visible here through digital enhancement.

By realizing completely the cosmic mirror principle...and by invoking that principle utterly in the brilliant perception of reality, a human being can become...living magic. This is how one...becomes a master warrior....

What distinguishes such leaders of humanity and guardians of human wisdom is their fearless expression of gentleness and genuineness—on behalf of all sentient beings.

—Chögyam Trungpa, *Shambhala, The Sacred Path of the Warrior*

The Master Saint Germain, shown here as he frequently appeared in the courts of Europe in the eighteenth century, and as he often appears on the inner planes. However, he often manifests other personae as the occasion requires, and is the one assisting humanity's transition into the new age of self-empowerment through the knowledge of the I AM.

Contents

Illustrations
    Saint Germain 4
    Peter Mt. Shasta 20
    Pearl Dorris 51
    El Morya 208
    Kuthumi Lal Singh 209
    The Lord Maha Chohan 210
    Madam Blavatsky and Three Masters 211
    Peter Mt. Shasta 404

Prologue 9
Foreword 11
Preface 21

Part I: In the Footsteps

1. Rendezvous in Muir Woods 25
2. Sent to Mount Shasta 31
3. Meeting Pearl and Making a Vow 41
4. A Pearl of Great Price 53
5. Above Mount Shasta 61
6. Gaining Faith in the Master on the Job 65
7. Meditation with Pearl 71
8. A Midnight Visitor 79

Part II: Living the Law

9. By This Word—I AM 85
10. To Manifest, or Not… 91
11. The Uncreated Restaurant 97
12. Love, Sex, and a Vow 103
13. Thy Will, Not Mine 111
14. Obeying the Law 117
15. A Test 121
16. The Man in the Denim Jacket 127

Part III: In the Material World

17. Descension 139
18. The Man in the Brown Shirt 149
19. Slumlord 155

Part IV: Learning to Trust

20. Cheesecake Guidance 163
21. The Atomic Accelerator 167
22. Rendezvous at Lake Louise 177
23. Finding the Rainbow 187
24. Calgary Connection 199
25. Meeting the Masters in Israel 213
26. Trial in Athens 227
27. Sued 239
28. The Last Leaky Pipe 243
29. Teleported in San Francisco 251
30. Million Dollar Affirmation 257
31. You Are Ready 261

Part V: Direct Engagement

32. Saint Germain on the Battlefield 269
33. One with God Is a Majority 275
34. Saint Germain in Madrid 277
35. Mission in Grand Central Station 287

Part VI: Through the Open Door

36. Partings 295
37. A Greater Service 311
38. Face to Face with the Master 317
39. The Good Karma Café 323
40. The Indigo Volvo 329
41. Gold Venture 335
42. The Battle for Hollywood 343
43. Starting Over 365

44. With Shirley MacLaine on Rodeo Drive 369
45. Return to Shambhala 375
46. Released 381
47. Empowerment at Lake Titicaca 387
48. I Am With You Always 399

Postscript 403
Acknowledgments 405

Appendices
    Appendix I: Who Are the Masters? 407
    Appendix II: The Seven Rays and Their Chohans 411
    Appendix III: Recommended Reading 415

Prologue

This is the second part of *Adventures of a Western Mystic,* the autobiography of Peter Mt. Shasta's spiritual awakening and training by both masters of the East and those known in the West as Ascended Masters.

The previous volume, *Search for the Guru,* describes his spiritual awakening in the materialist culture of New York during the decades leading up to the '60s. This culminated in his journey overland to India in 1971 and encounters with former Harvard professor Richard Alpert (later known as Baba Ram Dass) and his guru, Neem Karoli Baba. He also describes his transformational experiences with Anandamayi Ma (the "Bliss-Permeated Mother") and Sathya Sai Baba, as well as other beings that, although unknown to the outer world, had transcendental wisdom and extraordinary powers.

These experiences all led to the same realization—that the guru for which he was seeking was within himself. On returning back to the States and his farm near Woodstock, New York, he felt the pull of his Inner Presence to journey westward. Piling his few belongings in his old Dodge van, he had further encounters with remarkable beings, among them Joseph Sunhawk, in Taos, New Mexico, and a Tibetan Lama, Chögyam Trungpa Rinpoche, who he met first at the Lama Foundation and then again in Boulder, Colorado. Finally, in California, he met another Tibetan Lama, Chagdud Rinpoche, through whom he realized the essential unity of the Dzogchen teachings of spontaneous realization with the "I AM," the consciousness of one's own higher self, on which he had been directed to meditate by Sathya Sai Baba.

Search for the Guru ends with the author's desire to leave physical embodiment, as the materialistic quest of Western society no longer holds any allure. As he drives from Berkeley, California, across the Golden Gate Bridge, he little dreams that his journey is just beginning, and that in Muir Woods he will soon meet the fabled Ascended Master known as Saint Germain, who will offer him what he desires.

Foreword

Overview

Peter is a good friend of mine. In fact, we have known each other for almost a decade and live about a mile apart, at the base of sacred Mount Shasta. He is also, spiritually speaking, one of the wisest men I know. What you are holding in your hands is, I believe, something truly special, a book destined to become a spiritual classic in the field of contemporary spiritual memoirs. After all, there are just not that many places one can go to read about Christ, Buddha, Manjushri, Saint Germain, Sai Baba, Francis Bacon, Krishnamurti, Babaji, Anandamayi Ma, Paramahansa Yogananda, Chögyam Trungpa Rinpoche, H.P. Blavatsky, Gurdjieff, Lao Tzu, Godfre Ray King, Swami Vivekananda, Ram Dass, Neem Karoli Baba, Oscar Ichazo, Alice A. Bailey, and other great spiritual teachers, and all under one literary roof!

In this single volume you will find profound teachings taken from the Hindu, Buddhist, Judeo-Christian, Hermetic, Theosophical, and I AM traditions. Most importantly, though, they have all been refined and refracted through Peter's unique and sparkling personality, and his nearly unbelievable adventures all over the world. It is inspiring, educational, and ultimately, if you the reader put even some of these spiritual laws into practice, empowering beyond your wildest dreams. *Adventures of a Western Mystic* provides substantial clues to answering the following important questions:

1) Why are we here on this planet, enrolled as students in the Earth School?
2) What is Self-Mastery, and what does achieving it entail?
3) Who are the Masters of Wisdom, and how do they work with us in the Human Kingdom?

4) What is true guidance, and how do we find and follow it?
5) What are some of the "perils of the path," and how can we avoid them?
6) What is the relationship between our "outer guru" or spiritual teacher, and our inner guru, our own source of guidance and grace?

There are many real treats, or perhaps I should say "pearls," in this autobiography. Here I will mention only four. First off, there is Peter's great and vulnerable honesty, as he remembers and shares his personal triumphs and setbacks on the spiritual path. Such ruthless self-reflection and self-disclosure can serve as a model for the next generation of would-be mystics and initiates.

Secondly, there is his sense of humor and perspective, something often sorely lacking in accounts of psychological growth and spiritual transformation. The Tibetan lama Chögyam Trungpa Rinpoche said in *Cutting Through Spiritual Materialism* that having a sense of humor "means seeing both poles of a situation as they are, from an aerial point of view. There is good and there is bad and you see both with a panoramic view as though from above." He goes on to note that "a sense of humor is not merely a matter of trying to tell jokes or make puns, trying to be funny in a deliberate fashion. It involves seeing the basic irony of the juxtaposition of extremes, so that one is not caught taking them seriously, so that one does not seriously play their game of hope and fear." Peter, often seeing and writing from the etheric vantage point of the Masters, understands quite well the ironies and paradoxes on the spiritual path, and finds the humor (at least after the fact!) in situations that were undoubtedly highly stressful and initiatory at the time.

Thirdly, and no doubt related to the previous point, Peter makes it clear that he was neither looking for, nor trying to have, these sorts of outrageous metaphysical experiences. In fact, at certain points the narrative begins to resemble an old Pink Panther movie, with Peter Sellers as Inspector Clouseau bumbling his way from one (mis)adventure to another, barely making it out alive! This is important to ponder, because so many seekers believe that they must drop out of daily life and spend years looking for the Masters. In reality, when the time is right, and the *chela* or pupil is ripe, the Masters contact him or her, often unbidden and without due warning.

Fourthly, there are the detailed, lively, and useful accounts of Peter's years studying with Pearl, a legendary but relatively unknown teacher residing in the town of Mount Shasta. As he puts it at the beginning of Chapter 4, Pearl was not exactly the teacher he had anticipated. Instead of looking like a materialized photo of one of H.P. Blavatsky's mentors, she was instead an "elderly housewife…who sat with her knitting in her lap." This was truly a case of "not being able to judge a book by its cover," and another good lesson for latter-day Seekers after Truth—that teachers come in many guises.

To Function as a Soul

> …true freedom does not exist except where the individual is linked with the rhythm of his soul, for it is only from the strength of that centre that he can cope with the rather powerful forces that move through the physical and emotional and mental realms.
>
> —David Spangler, from *Towards a Planetary Vision*

French philosopher Henri Bergson once remarked that in order to really understand what a teacher or great thinker is trying to communicate, one needs to find and explore what Bergson called his "central intuition," the focal point and guiding light for his entire system of thought. For example, the great Catholic mystic and paleontologist Teilhard de Chardin extensively explored the idea of "evolution." For Jung it was probably "individuation," and for Freud the discovery of the "unconscious." I recently had the chance to ask Peter what he felt his central intuition was, and perhaps continues to be, and he responded immediately that it was the reality and power of the I AM Presence. This probably requires some explanation.

Who, or what, is this mysterious I AM Presence? I don't want to say overly much here because Peter himself does such an admirable job of defining and ultimately experiencing it. Moreover, he is clearly concerned with how we, too, can become one with our own I AM Presence, and with understanding all the obstacles along that path. Rather, my concern is how this understanding and realization differs from the famous Atman = Brahman formulation of the Hindu Upanishads. To my mind, the latter, as it is generally applied in religious exegesis and yogic practice, is more impersonal and philosophical, without any necessary reference to a real, human individual, someone striving to be fully embodied and to integrate spirit and matter within his or her own Soul. Atman usually refers to the Spirit or light within, but I feel the I AM Presence is something more personal and loving.

It is important then to understand why we need to contemplate, invoke, and even declare "I AM," and not just "I." The latter refers to the ego and on a higher register to the Atman or Pure Spirit, but "I AM" is both more personal and more empowering. Pearl explains the difference in her own inimitably clear and simple way: "I AM is the Christ, meaning God in form and action." And elsewhere: "Whenever you say 'I AM,' you are calling forth the Source, the Inner Light, and whatever follows those words is what you are calling into being. The greater your realization of the I AM, the greater your acceptance of the great God Presence that you are, the quicker will be the manifestation of whatever you call forth. This is your God given power to create." This concept can be found in numerous places in world spiritual literature. To give just one possible example, in the Old Testament Moses asked the Lord at Mount Sinai by what name He should be known, and the response was *Ehyeh Asher Ehyeh*—"I am that I am." And since, according to the Book of Genesis, we are all made in the image and likeness of God, by implication this is our true name as well.

Why is this distinction between "I" and "I AM" so important? Because of one word—Love. A few years ago I had the good fortune to hear legendary spiritual teacher and raconteur Ram Dass speak at a conference in Palm Springs. In his lecture he noted that "The medium of a fish is water, the medium of a human being is air, and the medium of a soul is Love. The soul literally swims in an ocean of Love." Not only that, the substance of a soul is ultimately Love, and Love is creative—and quite powerful. So powerful, in fact, that much of Peter's text has to do with his learning how to access and transform oneself into the loving, intelligent, and powerful I AM Presence without getting badly burned in the process. Needless to say, readers will find the passages having to do with the right use of will and intention highly instructive—and highly entertaining!

Spiritual Bypassing

Peter mentions the term "spiritual bypassing" in Chapter 28, but I want to add a few quotes and comments to better prepare readers for what is to come. The idea that we often use spiritual ideas and practices to delay dealing with, or avoid altogether, our psychological "unfinished business" may be new to some, but it has been explored and written about since at least the early 1970s when Chögyam Trungpa Rinpoche, again in *Cutting Through Spiritual Materialism,* wrote, "The problem is that the ego can convert anything to its own use, even spirituality. Ego is constantly attempting to acquire and apply the teachings of spirituality for its own benefit. The teachings are treated as an external thing, external to 'me,' a philosophy which we try to imitate. We do not actually want to identify with or become the teachings."

More recently, it was transpersonal psychologist John Welwood who invented and then popularized the actual term. In an online article entitled "Embodying Your Realization: Psychological Work in the Service of Spiritual Development," he writes about how spiritual bypassing involves unconsciously using spirituality to "shore up a shaky sense of self, or to belittle basic needs, feelings, and developmental tasks, all in the name of enlightenment.… In a society like ours, where the whole earthly foundation is weak to begin with, it is tempting to use spirituality as a way of trying to rise above this shaky ground. In this way spirituality becomes just another way of rejecting one's experience. When people use spiritual practice to try to compensate for low self-esteem, social alienation, or emotional problems, they corrupt the true nature of spiritual practice. Instead of loosening the manipulative ego that tries to control its experience, they are further strengthening it.…When people use spirituality to cover up their difficulties with functioning in the modern world, their spiritual practice remains in a separate compartment, unintegrated with the rest of their life."

I mention this because Peter, in mapping out and generously sharing his own life journey for our edification, demonstrates some of the many ways we can, if we are not careful, incorrectly apply the great Wisdom Teachings. Time and again the Masters force him to integrate the profoundest spiritual teachings into daily human life—often with hilarious and/or poignant results. For example, there is Peter's whole relationship to work and money, described in Part III: In the Material World. A Master appears to him in a dream and says, "We want you to get into real estate." Peter of course interprets this to mean that he is going to ascend into his *real estate,* but unfortunately, or fortunately, the Masters mean business (pardon the pun!). What follows makes for great theater as Peter ends up as a sort of slumlord, dealing with difficult and unsavory characters and learning to apply the teachings in trying circumstances. In the process he develops compassion for self and others, and is able, eventually, to see all these tests as learning experiences of the highest order. If it is true that, as John Welwood writes, "spiritual practice can become co-opted by unconscious identities and used to reinforce unconscious defenses," then it is all the more reason for the world to have first-hand accounts of those who have not thrown the baby out with the bath water, but instead have integrated the best of psychology and spirituality to good effect.

Saint Germain, the Seventh Ray, and the New Age

> *I see the new age as an added dimension to our daily, ordinary living. It is a sense of empowerment and enthusiasm arising from the presence of the unexpected in our lives. It is the inner power to imagine and give birth to something new which complements the power to nurture and assist the maturation of what already exists…it is a metaphor for being in the world in a manner that opens us to the presence of God—the presence of love and possibility—in the midst of our ordinariness.*
>
> —David Spangler, from "Defining the New Age"

One reason Peter asked me to write this foreword is that in the 1980s I lived for over two years at the acclaimed New Age intentional community of Findhorn in Northern Scotland, and Mount Shasta and Findhorn have long shared many spiritual similarities and connections. One that comes immediately to mind has to do with the teaching that our world is truly entering a new era astronomically and spiritually speaking, the Age of Aquarius. However, few are aware that with this understanding also comes, to those who are ready, knowledge of the Seven Rays and their associated Masters. Again, I don't want to say too much here because Peter has brilliantly summarized the basic information about them in Appendix II, and the Tibetan Master Djwhal Khul has set forth a near complete exposition of the rays in the Alice A. Bailey corpus, written between 1919 and 1949. One can also find materials on this subject in H.P. Blavatsky's *The Secret Doctrine* and *Isis Unveiled,* Helena Roerich's *Agni Yoga* books, and online through the University of the Seven Rays. But I do want to cover a little ground so that Peter's book is adequately contextualized within the larger set of New Age teachings.

To begin, it has been my observation that this information is still not that well known to the majority of spiritual seekers. So then, one of the most important tasks of *Adventures of a Western Mystic* may be to spread more widely, and in an easily readable and highly enjoyable form, the Ageless Wisdom teachings on the Seven Rays, and especially knowledge of the Seventh Ray and its associated Master, Saint Germain. Next, in order to really understand and appreciate what is happening on our planet today, we have to reflect upon and understand what is meant esoterically by the "theme of Freedom." According to Theosophical teachings, the previous Piscean Age was ruled by the Sixth Ray of Love and Devotion, which has as its shadow side the mindless devotion to given forms. In other words, one potential effect of this ray is to create attachments to the people and places, ideas and ideals, religious, political, and economic institutions to which a person is devoted. Unfortunately, the end result is often ideology, fanaticism, and even violence. Relating this to the book at hand, although the guru-disciple relationship remains intact in the New Age, emotional devotion to the Master must eventually be transmuted into unselfish service to humanity. Peter's apprenticeship to the Masters beautifully demonstrates the need to listen to and heed the advice of the Great Ones, while at the same time avoid being caught up in the glamour of the contact—not easy when a fully embodied Saint Germain ends up sitting next to you and chatting with you for several hours on an airplane from New York to San Francisco, as Peter recounts in Chapter 38!

The incoming Seventh Ray is a world-changing phenomenon. It is known as the ray of ordered activity or ceremonial magic. It is rhythmic, dynamic, relational, and a builder of new forms to host Spirit in new and more evolved ways. It brings a breath of fresh air and sense of freedom and possibility to an often rigidified and oppressed world. In the words of David Spangler, "The keynote of the New Age is the ability to utilize change creatively and not to be frightened by it." One of these changes, and a point of Peter's book, is that people can now have access to spiritual truths and transformative practices without committing to mainstream religious traditions, with all the baggage they carry forward from past centuries.

The Seventh Ray is also the ray of birth on a physical level, and its function is to literally bring Heaven down onto Earth. In this regard, it is interesting to note that the official slogan of Peter's place of residence (and last name!) is: "Mt. Shasta: Where Heaven and Earth Meet." Some of the many new forms that this ray has helped to build since the end of WWII are: The United Nations, various important service and philanthropic organizations and foundations, such as Doctors without Borders and Global Initiative, and innovative, more self-empowering ways of creating, organizing, and running small groups, large businesses, and intentional communities. The Seventh Ray also governs the manifestation of the sexual impulse, which is why we see such confusion and experimentation going on in the fields of sexuality and committed relationship. On the one hand, we see a general increase in the commercialization of sexuality and also sex crimes, but on the other hand, we are witness to an ever greater appreciation for the mystery, beauty, and sacredness of sexual polarity on all levels of existence. Thus, the reader will not be surprised to find our protagonist struggling with the desire for romantic relationship, and trying to figure out how to integrate spirituality and sexuality while keeping his head above water!

Finally, it remains to note that although Peter freely mentions other members of the Hierarchy or Fifth Kingdom, Great Ones such as Masters Morya, Koot Hoomi, and Sai Baba, his primary relationship is still with Saint Germain (at Findhorn we called him simply, with all due respect, "The Count"). To quote from a 1938 edition of the periodical *Theosophy*, "One of the most mysterious characters in modern history is the famous Count de St. Germain, described by his friend Prince Karl von Hesse as 'one of the greatest philosophers who ever lived, the friend of humanity, whose heart was concerned only with the happiness of others.' Intimate and counselor of Kings and Princes, nemesis of deceptive ministers, Rosicrucian, Mason, accredited Messenger of the Masters of Wisdom— the Count de St. Germain worked in Europe for more than a century, faithfully performing the difficult task which had been entrusted to him." What was this task, according to most scholars? Nothing less than the co-creation of post-revolution, modern and democratic, Europe and America. The work he did then helped to lay the foundation for what is written on the Masonic Great Seal on the back of our own dollar bill: *Novus Ordo Seclorum*, a "new world order." I find it highly synchronistic that Peter's book is being published soon after Dan Brown's latest spiritual thriller, The Lost Symbol, which is primarily concerned with disclosing to the general public the esoteric origins of the founding of America. I can only hope that *Adventures of a Western Mystic* finds similar success, in terms of both widespread distribution and its impact on global consciousness.

Carl Marsak, M.A.
April 25, 2010
Mount Shasta, California

Carl Marsak is a teacher, writer, and spiritual counselor, who lives in Ashland, Oregon. He is also the founder and director of the Enneagram Centers of Mount Shasta and Ashland, and can be reached through his website: www.ashlandenneagram.com.

Peter Mt. Shasta, 2013 (photo by Sequoia Petengell)

Preface

In 1972, after returning from a pilgrimage to India, where I had spent time with Ram Dass at the feet of his guru, Neem Karoli Baba, I was contacted by an etheric being on the slopes of Mount Shasta in northern California, who claimed to be as familiar with my future as he proved he was with my past. Although I had met many saints and great yogis in India, I did not believe in the existence of "higher beings" who interceded in human affairs, so my mind discredited even this experience with one of the legendary Masters known in the East as a *Bodhisattva*. Yet, his predictions proved true, and a year later he appeared before me again, this time in a physical body, and instructed me to return to Mount Shasta. There he offered apprenticeship under his all-seeing eye, which I gratefully accepted, little realizing at the time the consequences of that decision. For the next three years I was put through severe tests and training, and then served years of probation under this and other Masters. This book is an account of those adventures, the rigorous training I received, and the consequent spiritual awakening—which took me beyond what I could have imagined.

Some of these events were not written down until years after they occurred, so may be out of order in the text, which however does not alter their veracity. Also, many of the names have been changed for the sake of privacy. However, despite the seemingly miraculous nature of these contacts with omniscient Masters, who can and do materialize at will in whatever form is required, unless otherwise indicated these are real experiences which took place on the physical plane between 1971 and 1983.

These Great Ones, who dwell in the etheric realms, fully conscious of their Source, are unlimited in their ability to render assistance. Even though we are usually not aware of them, they are nonetheless already working with us according to our readiness and capacity. What invokes their direct assistance, however, is the individual's heartfelt dedication to work ceaselessly for the liberation and enlightenment of other sentient beings. May all who read these words be inspired to find the Master within, and so be raised into the consciousness, activity, and dominion of their own I AM Presence forever.

Part I:

In the Footsteps

Chapter 1

Rendezvous in Muir Woods

I was lost. The trail I'd taken through the giant redwoods of Muir Woods just north of San Francisco was shrouded in heavy ground mist, and I'd wandered far from the well-trodden path that led through the forest. Not knowing what direction to take, I hiked uphill, my view limited to what lay a dozen paces ahead of me, beneath the towering sentinels that stretched up towards the heavens. Communing with the ancient trees, which I felt might possibly hear my thoughts, my heart yearned for contact with some enlightened soul who would tell me why I was here on Earth. I had gone to India seeking such beings but had not found one—or, if I had, he remained silent. I had not discovered any personal God, nor did I believe that beings on other planes, if they were aware of Earth, even knew of my existence.

The year was 1973 and at age 28, my life had been full. I had obtained all the material things the world had told me were worth pursuing, yet none had brought me lasting happiness. In fact, life's temporary pleasures had left me feeling empty. I had been on a journey to the East, hoping to find the meaning of life, and although I had seen miracles and experienced moments of expanded consciousness, the holy men of India had not answered my question: *Why am I here?*

Now I no longer wanted to live this material existence, and I thought about ways I could leave my body and journey to a higher realm, one of those blissful realms I experienced in meditation where beings lived in love and harmony. But I didn't want to arrive in Paradise and be told that I had to go back, perhaps as an animal, for having taken my own life.

I had lived in the Himalayas with Gangotri Baba,[1] a disciple of Hariakhan Baba, also known as Babaji, the famous Indian yogi written

---

[1] R.D. Laing (1927-1989), the ground-breaking British psychiatrist, had lived with Gangotri Baba for three weeks several months prior to my arrival, and been initiated by him into tantric Kali practices. See: R.D. Laing, *The Divided Self: An Existential Study in Sanity and Madness* (Harmondsworth: Penguin, 1960).

about by Paramahansa Yogananda, who had maintained the youth of his body for hundreds of years. When Gangotri Baba first met his guru—who had been visiting him in dreams for years—on a street in downtown Delhi, Babaji put his arm around him and transported him in his physical body to the Himalayas. Now Gangotri Baba was getting ready to consciously leave his body and join his master, who was no longer in a physical body—and I, too, longed for the same freedom from the cares of the world. For most of my life I had felt like a stranger in a hostile and unfamiliar place. *Let me leave the Earth and go back to the place from which I came, I prayed.*

As it began to rain, I sought shelter inside the trunk of a redwood that had been hollowed by fire, forming a natural cathedral in which I could sit and meditate. Practicing the *Vipassana* method I had learned, eyes open and softly focused on the ground, I watched the clouds of my breath arise before me. As I began to meditate, I observed the rise and fall of my chest, the in-breath and out-breath, a silent mantra Siddhartha had used to become the Buddha—*one who is awake.*

I felt the silent rhythm carry me into the stillness, where limitation dissolved as my consciousness expanded. The sense of *I, me,* and *mine* disappeared, thoughts slowing, and I began to dwell in the space between thoughts, where one had ended but another had not begun, a timeless lapse into unconditioned awareness.

Then, like a bubble rising to the surface of a still pond, a thought came to the surface—the thought of the Ascended Masters I had read about while a guest of the Theosophical Society in India. I especially thought of the "Wonder Man," the Master Saint Germain, who was active in the affairs of Europe for over one hundred fifty years, and whom Voltaire described as *the man who knows everything, but never dies.* I had read about him in *Unveiled Mysteries;*[2] however, being skeptical by nature, I had dismissed Godfre Ray King's experiences with the Masters as too fantastic to be true. I now pleaded,

Saint Germain, if you are real, and if you hear this prayer, tell me why I am here. Otherwise, I will find a way to leave my body....

I had been sitting inside the cathedral of the tree for some time, watching my breath and the rain dripping on the pine needles of the forest floor, when I became aware of a powerful current flowing through my

---

2   Godfre Ray King, *Unveiled Mysteries* (Saint Germain Press, 1982).

Rendezvous in Muir Woods

body. The energy increased and I felt I was dissolving, everything seeming to shimmer around me.

Two feet suddenly appeared in front of my half-opened eyes, and I became aware of a figure standing before me. How long he had been there, I didn't know. I hadn't seen anyone approach. Because of the cold rain, the woods were deserted, and no one could have walked toward me without my hearing a twig snap. Yet, here was a man standing in front of me wearing blue jeans, a suede jacket, and tennis shoes. It was the white tennis shoes I saw first, planted firmly on the brown forest floor at the spot where my eyes were focused.

"Do not be startled, Peter," the stranger said with a calmness I found comforting. "Your prayer has been answered."

I looked into the face of someone I took to be a hiker in the woods like myself, who now gazed steadily into my eyes. Although it was raining, I noticed that neither his hair nor his suede jacket showed any sign of dampness. I was about to comment on this peculiarity when he spoke again.

"I am the part of the Godhead that has responded to your call. Know that the call compels the answer, and all sincere prayers are heard. You have prayed so earnestly and for so long, this response could no longer be withheld. The answer to your question is *yes,* you may leave the Earth if you wish. I offer you liberation, for you have cleared sufficient karma and advanced spiritually to the point where you can leave the realm of humanity without ever having to return, if that is your wish. The choice is yours. However, before you give me your answer, there is something I wish to show you."

Before I could recover from the shock, that in spite of his common appearance this was no ordinary man, the stranger touched my forehead between my eyes, and I found myself free of my body. Standing now in my etheric form, I looked back at my denser body, still cross-legged within the tree trunk. Then, before I could express delight at my new freedom, the stranger put his arm about me and we soared above the Earth.

In a moment we reached a place in the heavens where I saw luminous clouds, and in those clouds were nestled orbs of light. These were the higher selves (Monads) of beings who had once lived on Earth, I was told, now liberated from the physical plane forever. Like translucent pearls a couple of feet in diameter, each glowed with scintillating rainbow colors that changed with the meditation in which they were absorbed.

Apprentice to the Masters

"Here, in the Great Silence, you can remain in eternal bliss," my guide said, as though I were already a resident of this heavenly place. "In the Great Silence you will be one with God, resting here until some far distant eon when you will again come forth into another cycle of activity."

I envied these blissful beings, nestled in the clouds of eternity, and felt that at last I had found home—a Paradise. About to accept this offer to remain, I heard a wailing below me, the anguished cries of innumerable voices crying out in pain.

"Where is that terrible sound coming from?" I asked my guide.

Pointing to the blue sphere below, from which arose sounds of such suffering and pleading for help that I felt my heart wrench in my chest, "Earth," the stranger said. "The Masters hear these cries and prayers for help continually. This is the condition of humanity, the suffering caused by their separation from the knowledge of God." He watched me closely to see the effect his revelation was having.

"You may either stay here or return to Earth," he said. "The choice is yours."

I was so moved that I now felt there was no choice. My own liberation could wait. I could not turn away from those heart-rending cries, and I had to return. In a moment I was back in the forest, within the body in the tree, the masterful stranger standing before me.

"You have made the right choice, my boy," the mysterious guide said in a caring voice, as though he had known me for an eternity. "If you had stayed in the Silence you would not have seen me again for a long time, but because you have chosen to serve humanity and place the happiness of others before your own, we will be working together. But before you can be of assistance to me you will need training, which you will receive in Mount Shasta."

Mount Shasta? I recalled my visit to northern California the previous year. I'd heard a commanding voice while meditating high on the slopes of the Mountain. The voice had told me of a mission that at the time I had failed to comprehend. Was this the presence who had spoken to me then?

He took a few steps backward and, with a twinkle in his eye, said, "Now I will reveal to you who I am...."

He stood motionless before me for a moment, then transformed from a young hiker to a white-robed Master, whose dark, penetrating eyes sparkled with the love and wisdom of God made manifest. I began to realize that this was the face in *Unveiled Mysteries,* the one to whom I had just prayed—none other than the Ascended Master Saint Germain!

"Return to Mount Shasta," he said, "where your instruction will begin. The first person you meet there will tell you what to do next."

With that final instruction, the form of the white-robed Master began to dissolve, then faded completely from sight, leaving me in a state of exhilaration impossible to describe.

Chapter 2

Sent to Mount Shasta

With heart racing, and barely conscious of where I was, I found my way back to the parking lot where I had left my van. I got into my vehicle and began driving, almost automatically, sensing that in some profound way my life had changed, that I'd made an irrevocable decision and nothing would ever be the same. It was years later when, as a student of Tibetan Buddhism, I took the Bodhisattva Vow to attain enlightenment for the benefit of all beings, that I realized the significance of the choice I had made that day—to choose service to humanity over immediate freedom. Paradoxically, I found that happiness does not always reside where we anticipate it, and freedom is often found in commitment.

I did not remember getting on the freeway, being oblivious of time. Perhaps two or three hours later, I found myself on the Interstate passing the town of Red Bluff. I saw straight ahead, surrounded by evergreen forests, the glacial peak of Mount Shasta looming on the horizon, glistening in the distance like a beacon of light pulling me forward—a sight that took my breath away.

As I drove, the Mountain emanated an energy that filled my heart, and I recalled how I'd first heard about the mystical Mountain from Christar, an American I'd met the year before at the *Kumbha Mela* in Allahabad, India—a festival where millions of spiritual seekers gathered, seeking to find a guru. We had both been spending time with Ram Dass and his guru, Neem Karoli Baba. Maharaji (Sanskrit: Great Ruler), as his devotees called him, had given Christar an Indian name, that of a great yogi who had consciously left his body a century before. We had all assumed that Christar was the reincarnation of that yogi, but on returning to the West he had taken his current name, invoking the Christ Star that is the Source of being.[3]

---

3 This yogi had been reported to have consciously left his body in a stream when he felt his earthly work was done. Many years after I had met Christar on the street in India, on a hot, summer day I went for a swim

Maharaji had told us that it would be very auspicious to attend the *Mela* and drink the water from the confluence of the three sacred rivers, the Ganges and Yamuna which were physical, and the Saraswati, an invisible river. What he had not told me was that by drinking this polluted water I would almost die from amoebic dysentery—which suited the ancient name of this city: Agra, place of sacrifice. However, in order to heal myself I was led to study the healing arts, which would eventually lead to a career that would bring benefit to others. This sacrificial act of drinking this sacred poison bonded me with the suffering of humanity, and awakened compassion—the essence of all spiritual practice—and requisite for a healer.

Christar had told me that Mount Shasta was a focus of the Great White Brotherhood, a group of enlightened beings who, despite the name, was composed of races of all colors, and of both males and females, who had once lived on the Earth and Ascended into a higher octave where they worked unceasingly to guide the destiny of humanity. Inspired by this vision, I made a visit to Mount Shasta when I returned to the States, and camped just below snow line in an open meadow, fasting and meditating in the hopes of meeting a Master or at least of receiving guidance in a vision. Every day I plunged naked into a pool of icy, glacier-fed water, and then sat in the sun, focusing my awareness on my breath in meditation.

Though exhilarated by my austerities, I didn't see one of these fabled Ascended Masters of which Christar had spoken, or have the vision I sought—or so I thought. There was no flaming sword in the sky

---

in Castle Lake, a frigid glacial tarn high in the mountains near Mount Shasta. I had been fasting, and halfway across I ran out of energy. I called out to someone on the float for help. To my surprise, when I looked up into the face of my rescuer, I saw it was Christar. When he said, "I guess your work on Earth isn't finished yet," I said, "Yes, I still need to write a book about my experiences with the Masters, one that conveys the reality of the I AM Presence."

Sitting in the presence of one who had probably left his body in a stream almost a century before, who had now returned in physical form to do further work, and still partially in shock over almost losing my own body in the icy water, I had an overwhelming realization of the preciousness of human birth and the need to get on with my own mission in the world.

accompanied by a booming voice telling me where to go and what to do—nothing like Godfre Ray King's meeting with Saint Germain on the slopes of the Mountain that I had read about in *Unveiled Mysteries.*

In my reading, I had learned that Saint Germain was not a saint in the Catholic tradition, but rather the name by which this great soul, a guiding force for the upliftment of humanity, chose to be known. He had appeared first during an earlier Golden Age, when people still remembered their God source, as the ruler of an advanced civilization that stretched across a lush and semi-tropical northern Africa. But as people strayed from their consciousness of the Inner God, Saint Germain and his family dissolved their physical bodies and withdrew back to the higher realms from which they had come, in order to allow humanity to pursue its chosen path of ego development and materialism. In later ages, Saint Germain embodied again and again to impart wisdom and guidance to those who would heed him, succeeding in guiding at least a few here and there back to the light, and planting the seed of wisdom in the hearts of others, that would eventually flower in later lifetimes.

One of these incarnations was as Sir Francis Bacon, the secret son of Queen Elizabeth and the Earl of Leicester, rightful heir to the throne of England, and the veiled author of the Shakespearean plays. Under King James the First, Bacon was the guiding light overseeing the writing of the King James Bible. His literary efforts and later attempts to correct the debauched and corrupt monarchy were rewarded with false accusations and house arrest. Seeing he could do no more in captivity, he feigned death, staged a mock funeral, and disappeared to Europe, where, under an assumed name, he taught and guided various groups of initiates in occult orders.

Continuing in his service to humanity, Saint Germain became a guiding force behind the founding of America when, in 1636 as Sir Francis Bacon, he wrote *The New Atlantis,* a book presenting the possibility of a society based on spiritual principles. His secret writings, including the manuscripts of the "Shakespeare" plays, were buried in a vault in Williamsburg, Virginia, and later exhumed—probably taken, according to the Baconian scholar Marie Bauer Hall, and hidden by agents of those powerful forces from whose influence he had hoped America would remain free.

A true *Bodhisattva* who refused to forsake humanity, Saint Germain returned as an Ascended being, appearing here and there in apparently human forms, to play a role in the courts of Europe during the time leading up to and during the French Revolution. He was regarded as a miracle worker who seemed as familiar with the future as he was with the past, capable of being in multiple places simultaneously, and there are diary entries which show that he appeared in widely separated parts of Europe on the same day.[4] He attempted to awaken the decadent nobility to their responsibility for those less fortunate than themselves and to save those whom he could. This was prior to the great deluge of execution by the guillotine that ended the tyranny of the monarchy in exchange for the tyranny of the masses, the beginning of the rule of bureaucracy, the ascent of mediocrity and socialism.

Today, Saint Germain continues his work of aiding individual spiritual evolution, as well as being a guiding force in the realms of art, science, and politics—where he is known by different names, depending on what the occasion requires. He continues to help all who are sincere in their desire to achieve the mastery and freedom that is their God-given destiny.

In the Ascended Master hierarchy[5] of the Great White Brotherhood, Saint Germain is Master of the Seventh Ray, and his secret quality is *Freedom*. He often works side by side with the Master Jesus, another Ascended Master whose work needs no introduction.

In spite of plunging into icy streams on Mount Shasta and meditating long hours, I felt unable to contact this great Master presence or even feel his energy. About to give up, feeling too insignificant to be worthy of his attention, the prayed-for contact finally happened. I awoke early one morning as the sky was becoming light. Lying on my back and looking into the heavens through the branches of the pine tree under which I had slept, I heard a voice speaking to me. Looking around, I saw no one, yet the

---

4   Isabel Cooper-Oakley, *The Comte de St. Germain* (Kessinger Publishing, 1942).
5   Hierarchy does not mean that one being is superior to another, for the consciousness of God is within all; however, there is a structure inherent in creation where beings are cast in differing roles, depending on their nature and evolution. One need look no further than the human body for proof, for it is the differentiation of various types of cells into a cooperative hierarchy that makes life possible. Nerve, skin, blood cells, etc., all have their specific function.

voice continued with the familiarity of someone who knew me intimately, knew where I had been and where I was going, the voice of whom I now realized was the Master Saint Germain.

But what he told me, I did not want to hear—that from Mount Shasta, I would go east to my farm near Woodstock, New York, and then return to India, the place where I had almost died from drinking the water at the *Kumbha Mela*. Then I would visit the *Avatar*[6] Sathya Sai Baba and finally return to Mount Shasta, which would become my new home.

He ended by commanding me to change my name—a request I stubbornly resisted. I had seen many Americans come back from the East with Hindu names given by their gurus, intended to dissolve the ego, but which often reinforced it with the feeling of specialness—what the Buddhists called *self-cherishing*. I knew old personality traits couldn't be erased by sweeping them under the carpet of a new name, so I rebelled when he requested me to do the very thing I abhorred.

"You will use the name of the Mountain as your last name."

"What?" I said, incredulous at this bizarre idea.

"You will use Mount Shasta as your last name."

"You've got to be kidding!"

"No, I'm not kidding," came his reply.

"A mountain for a name?" Even the Eastern gurus rarely named anyone after a mountain.

---

6   *Avatar* (Sanskrit): full incarnation of God in human form. Although we are all *Avatars* in a sense, for we are all embodiments of Divinity, awake to varying degrees to our God Consciousness, the term refers only to those few who at rare turning points in humanity's evolution incarnate for a specific mission, born with that consciousness fully awake, and capable of demonstrating from birth all divine attributes and powers. Some previous full *Avatars* are Rama and Krishna. Sometimes those who awaken to their divinity later in life are also called *Avatars,* such as Ramakrishna and the contemporary Ammachi (called the Hugging Saint). Anandamayi Ma, who I met on a street in Jaganath Puri, was called an *Avatar* by her followers, yet she said, "Sai Baba is the *Purna Avatar* (complete *Avatar*)." Jesus said early on that he was *sent* by the Father, later on that he and the Father were one—indicating his advancement into the full awareness of his own Divinity. Technological jargon has corrupted the word to mean icon or substitute, devoid of any connotation of innate consciousness or Divinity.

"Yes."

"I won't do it!" I said, rebelliously.

"Yes, you will," the Master said with finality. "Your new name is Peter Mt. Shasta."

"No! I'm not going to be one of those New Agers with a weird name!"

"We shall see," the voice said, with the annoying certainty of a parent who knows that their child will eventually comply with their wishes. Then the voice ceased, and the energy of the invisible being dispersed into the air. I was alone again, watching the sun rise over the ridge of the Mountain. My visit from the Master had been most unsatisfactory, nothing like the event I had craved. I disavowed my visitation, asserting that I would not change my name, relegating the voice I had heard so clearly to imagination, the effect of fasting on my brain. Looking back, I see how ironic my craving for direct guidance was, since I rejected it when it was given. No wonder the Masters do not appear more often and tell us what to do! Like children, we want to become adults, but often reject the necessary discipline and resent being told we have to sacrifice our childish ways.

Now, as I drove north, the white peaks of Mount Shasta, about which there were so many legends, loomed on the horizon against the azure sky. I sped along in my dilapidated '62 Dodge van filled with all my worldly possessions, which consisted of a sleeping bag, foam mat, backpack, and cook stove, and reflected on the events that had pointed me once again towards this Mountain, that was the destination of spiritual seekers through the ages. Despite my argument with him, I was returning as Saint Germain had said I would, to the place for which he had named me—though I had not yet had the courage to tell anyone this seemingly presumptuous title.

The events that followed my encounter with the voice in the meadow where I'd camped on Shasta were as the Master had predicted. I went to the first Rainbow Family gathering on Table Mountain in Colorado and then returned to my farm in upstate New York. From there I journeyed to India a second time, just as I'd been told would happen. In India, I stayed at the ashram of Sathya Sai Baba, known as the Avatar of our age, and sought guidance from him about what do with my life. He did not respond directly, but gave me an answer that at the time I did not understand. As I sped towards the snow-capped volcano that seemed to hold the secret of my destiny, I wondered if the answer Sai Baba had given me that day was about to unfold.

Even though Sai Baba was recognized by millions throughout the world as the full incarnation of God, embodying all the divine attributes like Rama and Krishna of ages past—I was skeptical of these claims, and had avoided visiting him on my first visit to India. But after I'd returned and was living on my farm, a friend sent me a photo of Sai Baba, saying that Baba had told him in a dream to send it to me. Despite my skepticism, as I looked at the picture it seemed to come to life, and Baba waved at me. A surge of love flooded through my heart, such as I had never felt before, and I found myself crying—something I hadn't done since I was a child.

When I calmed down, I again focused on the photo and was amazed as Baba stepped out of the picture into the room. He walked up to me and embraced me, charging every cell of my body with love, raising my vibrating rate, leaving me in a state of God conscious bliss. *Come visit me in India,* he said playfully, before dissolving into light and vanishing.

Two weeks after this divine invitation, despite my mortal fear of returning to India, I walked through the gate of Baba's ashram, Prashanti Nilayam (Abode of Everlasting Peace). As I approached the main temple, over which Sai Baba had his living quarters, he appeared on the balcony and waved. *Is he waving to me?* I wondered and looked around, but no one was behind me. *Soon he will call me in to meet with him,* I thought, expecting a meeting with Sai Baba no less moving than the one Ram Dass experienced with his guru. In that meeting, Neem Karoli Baba revealed he understood every aspect of Ram Dass' life, mentioning the thoughts Ram Dass had been thinking shortly before about his recently deceased mother—all the while holding Ram Dass' head in his lap while the young Harvard professor wept.

But that initial wave of Sai Baba was to be one of only a few moments of outer recognition he gave me for the months I was there. There was no tear-filled meeting. I was only one of thousands at the ashram, all wanting the same attention. I did receive visits from him in my dreams, and at those times, he opened my heart once again to the divine love with which he had showered me in New York. Many said that this outer rejection was so I would find him within, and not become dependent on his outer attention. Nonetheless, I found that I was constantly aware of his attention inwardly pointing out the nature of my mind, where the work needed to be done.

I saw Sai Baba work many miracles during my stay and heard of many more from others, including the healing of the sick and returning a man to life who had been dead for almost an hour. He caused divine nectar, *amrit*, to precipitate directly in my hands, and in meditation gave me a mantra that put me in bliss. I was given a miraculous photograph of him that came to life when I meditated before it, and through which he spoke to me!

But over time, the photograph became just another still image and the mantra ceased to produce any effect. Time passed, yet still Baba never told me how I should meditate, nor did he address the question that was central in my consciousness, of what to do with my life. I was growing spiritually, but at twenty-eight, I still felt lost, not knowing in what direction to turn. I did not have what the world would call a career, and it never occurred to me that perhaps achieving spiritual realization was my career. My mind still clung to the voice of the inner parent that said, *Get a job, and find your niche in society.*

Finally, it was time for me to leave. My visa was expiring soon and my flight was scheduled to depart the next day. It occurred to me at *darshan*—when the guru walks among the devotees—to write Sai Baba a note and try to give it to him when he came by. Since he couldn't stop and talk with everyone, he sometimes took people's notes and later answered them in his own way, frequently in dreams or by simply bringing about the changes people desired.

Baba, please tell me what I should do with my life. Where should I go? What should I meditate on? I scrawled these questions on a sheet of paper and, miraculously—for he usually ignored me when I wanted to hand him a note—Sai Baba walked up to me and took it, touching my extended first finger with the tip of his.

He heard me! He acknowledged my unspoken wish, to have physical contact with him. Before I left, I wanted some sign from him as the bond between us. I had held his feet in my hands while he was talking to the person next to me, but that was on my initiative. I wanted him to touch me, even if just in some small way.

Now, for a second, he touched my fingertip. Then he continued on down the line of devotees, who all wanted something equally special from him. As I bathed in the bliss of that contact, someone ran up to me from behind and thrust a small black book in my hand, which was open to a page with an underlined phrase that jumped out at me: "Meditate on 'I AM God,'" it said, "and all your other questions will answer themselves."

I knew these words were Baba's answer to me, sent by a stranger handing me a book. *Can it possibly be that simple,* my mind argued? I decided to give it a try.

Upon further reading, I discovered that the anonymous author of this book, *The Impersonal Life,* stressed over and over that the ultimate guru was the guru within oneself. No outer guru in human form could teach a person anything until that person found their inner guru first, for one was a reflection of the other. The way to God Realization, the book directed, was to feel the presence evoked by the statement *"I AM THAT I AM,"* and to dwell on that God Presence within one's heart without ceasing. Repeating the words alone, without feeling the heart, would merely make one a prisoner of the ego, trapping one in the delusion of "me" and "mine." It was the "me" that was the limited, selfish, impermanent ego, while the "I" was the eternal I AM Presence, the immortal God Self.

The Impersonal Life went on to say that only when the mind and emotions were stilled through meditation, and the heart surrendered to the presence of the Divine within, could the I AM Presence truly be felt. Then the guidance being sought would come from within a person's own heart as a deep feeling, or simply as spontaneous action.

As I embraced this wisdom, which it seemed Sai Baba had given in answer to my question, my craving for a guru to give me answers about my life began to dissolve. I would find the guru within my own heart.

I left India, embarked on this simple, yet revolutionary, path. But the transformation to relying solely on the I AM Presence did not occur overnight. It would take me many years of meditation to develop that inner Master, of learning to surrender to my own God presence at all times, in all things. Paradoxically, the stronger my connection with my own true self became, the closer I felt to Sai Baba and, later, the Ascended Masters I was soon to meet.

Back in the States, I continued to meditate on this Presence within my heart, letting it guide me where it would, and it led me across the country to San Francisco, to my life-altering meeting with Saint Germain in Muir Woods. Now he was sending me back to Mount Shasta, which Saint Germain had told me the year before would be my home.

I pondered as my van carried me closer to my destination: *Why was I being brought back to this legendary Mountain to which I seemed so inexplicably connected?*

CHAPTER 3

Meeting Pearl and Making a Vow

As I pulled off the freeway and entered the small town of Mount Shasta, I realized a circle was completing. Saint Germain had told me on the Mountain the summer before to return to India. There, Sai Baba had told me to meditate on "I AM GOD," the Divinity within my own heart, and the guidance that came from following that Presence had brought me back to Saint Germain and the Mountain.

After driving all morning, I was hungry and wanted to find a place for breakfast. As I cruised down the main street, I recalled how Mount Shasta was known for its mystical lore of the Masters, Lemurians, and UFOs, but that morning the tiny town at the foot of the Mountain seemed quite ordinary. It was like so many other logging towns in the Northwest at the time, isolated and desperate for business, with neon "open" signs in every shop window. Yet, despite those illumined invitations, I was about to learn that the local inhabitants were not as open as the signs advertised.

I parked my van and walked down the street, aware of the eyes of passersby probing me, as though I had just gotten off a spaceship. My long hair hanging over my shoulders, a *mala* of prayer beads around my neck, and the loose white clothes from India must have put me in the hippie category in the eyes of the local ranchers and mill workers.

Midway down the bleak main street I caught sight of a lurid sign flashing on and off "Breakfast House," and I walked toward it with grumbling stomach. In the door I was accosted by a red-lettered, plastic sign, "We do not solicit hippie patronage."

I had never liked the term *hippie*, for many who used that term seemed to feel that by growing their hair and wearing baggy clothes they were making a leap in consciousness. As a teenager, I had worn a black turtleneck sweater and hung out in Greenwich Village and read Kerouac's *Dharma Bums*, meditating on Zen *koans* such as "What is the sound of one hand clapping?" But I was fourteen then, and now I tried to dissociate myself from both the Beatnik and Hippie labels, and avoid being put in a category of any sort.

Hippie seemed a diminutive of the Beatnik *hip*, but I didn't find out until later that the word comes from an African dialect, meaning *one who is aware.* I could have lived with that if I had known the true meaning, but I had rejected the label and now felt that the sign in the door forbidding hippies didn't apply to me.

I pushed open the door of the restaurant and stepped inside. The packed room became silent, like the scene from the film *Easy Rider* where two freedom-loving bikers enter a restaurant and are confronted by southern rednecks. Standing in the doorway, I was frozen to the floor by a room of icy stares.

Here's the part of the movie where the lumberjacks throw me into the street and cut off my long hair, I thought, knowing how hippies who crossed the line were sometimes treated in rural areas in those days. Driven by my ravenous hunger, however, I moved into the room and sat down on the only empty stool, between two burly guys in flannel shirts and logger boots. I could feel them bristle as they turned their backs when I slid in between them.

"What'll it be, honey?" the waitress said, walking up and standing in front of me with her pad and pencil, ready to take my order, defusing the bomb of hostility that had been close to exploding. I felt a wave of gratitude toward her. Once everyone saw the waitress was going to serve me, they all went back to eating and talking. *Is it really that hard for these people, who no doubt think of themselves as Christians, to show tolerance and compassion to a stranger?* I wondered.

Soon the fear in the pit of my stomach was gone, as I began devouring a large stack of buckwheat pancakes smothered in butter and maple syrup. As I was finishing breakfast, a radiant, blue-eyed fellow about my own age, whom I had not seen in the back of the restaurant, popped up beside me and thrust his hand into mine.

"Hi, I'm Stephen," he said cheerfully. "I own the health food store around the corner. Come on over when you're done." *Was this the one the Master in Muir Woods told me to see, who would tell me what to do next?*

As soon as I paid my bill, I walked over to Stephen's store, where I found him busy filling plastic bags with sunflower seeds. He looked up as I walked in, and without a moment's hesitation looked me in the eye and said,

"You're supposed to see Pearl!"

"Are you sure?" I asked. "Who's Pearl?"

"Someone who knows...."

"Knows what?"

Meeting Pearl and Making a Vow

"Knows what you want to know…just call her, you'll find out."

Following his instructions, I used his phone to call Pearl. "Come right up," a motherly voice spoke sweetly in my ear.

A few minutes later, I was parked at the end of a dead end road, outside what appeared to be the gingerbread house from the story of Hansel and Gretel, complete with a tall hedge and sheltering pine trees. Walking through the rose-entwined trellis in the hedge, I felt as though I were entering a temple. A flagstone path led to the door, which was round at the top, and standing before it, I let the iron knocker fall with a thud. The door was opened by a kindly woman in her sixties with piercing, hazel eyes. She stood in the doorway, peering intently at me like an owl.

"Come in," she said, "I've been expecting you," and stepped aside for me to enter.

"What do you mean, you've been expecting me?" I asked, after being shown to a chair opposite hers in the cozy living room.

"The Master, Saint Germain, came to me this morning and said that he was sending someone to see me," she said in a matter-of-fact way, as though used to the daily appearance of this renowned Master, who had reportedly been guiding the affairs of humanity for centuries, if not longer.

"He did?" I swallowed hard.

"Now, tell me who you are and what brought you here," she said, drawing her chair closer and beckoning me to pull forward, trying to put me at ease. I looked at the *Reader's Digest* on the table beside her and the tapestry of deer wandering in the forest on the wall and wondered how, after all my experiences in India sitting at the feet of dust-covered, often naked, gurus, whose faces were smeared with ash, sandalwood paste, or vermilion, my wanderings in search of spiritual guidance had brought me to this ordinary-appearing woman in an ordinary house in a northern California mill town.

I told her of my experience in Muir Woods and of the mysterious stranger who had appeared out of nowhere and taken me out of my body to the ecstatic realm of the Great Silence, and how I had decided to return to the Earth to be of service, and how the stranger had transformed himself into a being wearing a white robe who told me to go to Mount Shasta.

Without skipping a beat, this little grandmotherly lady, who looked like Yoda from *Star Wars,* asked, a mischievous twinkle in her eye, "And who do you suppose that was?"

I looked up and saw a picture of Saint Germain on the wall and nodded toward it, still hardly daring to speak of my encounter with this legendary being only hours before.

"Yes, and he is very close by and is indicating that he wants to help you."

"What is he saying?" I asked, astonished that Saint Germain was here, too, and showing such a sudden interest in me. *Where has he been all my life, during all my ordeals, and why has he waited only until now to appear?* I wondered. *Where was he in the past, when I prayed to God and no one answered?*

"I cannot tell you what he is saying, because I do not channel the words of the Masters," Pearl responded. "The Masters do not allow their students to channel, except on the rarest occasions, because the Masters—who are God beings—can convey their wishes *directly* to you through your own heart. You may not hear the words they are saying with your ears or your mind—for your mind would only argue with them and seek to interfere. Instead, they convey information to your higher body, which you access intuitively as needed, later perceiving that information to come from yourself."

I remembered now with great embarrassment how I had argued with Saint Germain the year before when he had come to me on the Mountain and told me to change my name—a name I swore to him I would never use! He had spoken directly to my mind, words which I had dismissed because I had not yet met the Master who was their source. Now Pearl was telling me how I could contact that Master and experience his consciousness within my own field of awareness.

She paused and continued, "If you will go within, turn your attention to the center of your being, and send love to Saint Germain—affirming his presence within yourself, knowing that his heart and your heart are one—you will feel his presence, and that will open the way for him to work directly with you through your heart."

I shut my eyes to meditate until Pearl ordered, "Open your eyes! You do not need to close your eyes to meditate. Simply turn your attention within to the center of your being and say silently to yourself, *I AM the presence of Saint Germain!* Feel the sun within your heart, and within that sun feel his presence. You are not claiming to be the Master, but learning to recognize the oneness of the Master's consciousness with yours.

"The Masters are not separate from you," Pearl said. "There is no distance or time for them—wherever you are, they are also. Oneness with

Meeting Pearl and Making a Vow

Saint Germain is possible because the energy of the Seventh Ray, of which Saint Germain is *Chohan*—the master or director of conscious activity—is already within you. That energy is the spectrum of your own inner rainbow you are invoking, the part of yourself to which the Master corresponds.

"Just as daylight is composed of all seven main colors of the spectrum, so, too, are you composed of all seven rays of creation. There is an Ascended Master who is the Chohan, the head, of each ray, though now we are invoking only the Seventh Ray, that of Saint Germain.

"He is watching you, and you should call on him if you want his help, if you want to invoke him in your life. The same way you would invoke Jesus, to contact Saint Germain, you need only go within and open your heart. These two are brothers, working together. The Master sees you not as separate, but as a part of himself, and so you should see him and not hesitate to call upon him. When you say, *I AM here, I AM there, and I AM everywhere,* you touch on his consciousness—the awareness that within the One is the many, and within the many, the One."

I did as Pearl instructed, repeating over and over to myself,

I AM the presence of Saint Germain.

I felt nothing at first, only embarrassing silence. Then, in a few minutes, I began to feel a spring of happiness beginning to bubble up in my heart, accompanied by an electrifying presence in the room, whose atmosphere had begun to fill with violet light.

"That," said Pearl, acknowledging the shift, "is the Master Saint Germain—and he is very happy. He has verve—a word that combines vitality and nerve. Verve means 'Let's get with it!'—but with a sense of humor."

Indeed, I could swear that the Master was laughing, but I questioned incredulously, *Do Masters laugh? I thought they were always serious.*

"Yes, Masters do laugh," Pearl affirmed, hearing my thought, "though, perhaps not audibly."

As I let go of that thought, a stream of energy poured down through the crown of my head into the center of my chest, filling my body with light, and I heard within me the resounding affirmation repeating over and over, "I AM THAT I AM…I AM THAT I AM…I AM THAT I AM"— and the consciousness of that source became anchored in my heart. The violet hue of the room intensified as I continued to look into Pearl's eyes, watching, amazed, as her physical form seemed to dissolve into a luminous ball of golden light. In that timeless awareness there was no past or future, only the eternal now, and I basked in the light of that sun.

As the light faded I again became aware of my body, and of Pearl sitting across from me. It was hard to believe that this transformation had happened sitting with a grandmotherly lady in her quaint living room in the mountains, not at the feet of a saint in India, and I looked at the herd of deer grazing blissfully in the tapestry on the wall, and the wooden elves staring mischievously at me from their perches on the bookshelves. She began to speak, commenting on my inner experience as if she were seeing my mind.

"Even though you heard no words of direction, you have been given guidance, encouragement, and nourishment, which the Master has imparted to your higher mental body in the form of liquid light. As the occasion calls it forth, you will be able to access the information he has given you. For him to give you a more direct message would only cause your mind to question and interfere. Such direct channeling would weaken you, cause you to look outside yourself, when what the Masters want is for you to go within for your answers. In that way, you will become a Master rather than a perpetual follower of Masters."

No wonder they don't tell us what to do more often, I thought, remembering with embarrassment how I had argued with Saint Germain the year before on the Mountain when he had told me to change my name.

Pearl continued, giving me a further explanation of what I could expect if I were to pursue this path of mastery, "Only rarely does a Master say anything to the human self, and then not through channeled intermediaries, but directly to the student. The Masters are all-knowing, all-present, and all-powerful, very able to convey their thoughts to you in your waking or dreaming state without having to go through others. Give them credit for being what they are—literally Gods—well able to communicate to you in a way that you will perceive. But be prepared, for they will not always tell you what you want to hear, rather what you need to hear.

"On rare occasions the Masters have given spiritual discourses through highly developed individuals who have been well prepared over many years, such as my teacher, Godfre Ray King. However, at those times, the Masters were giving spiritual law and imparting a radiation that strengthened the self-awareness of the individuals present, not prophecies that fill people with fear or keep them coming back for ever more information and high sounding initiations that keep them in their heads by making them feel superior to others."

I was astounded that Pearl had known and worked with Godfre Ray King, the author of *Unveiled Mysteries*. This was the book I first saw in India while a guest of the Theosophical Society, and, although skeptical at first, I was later to read this amazing account of the author's inner experiences with the Masters many times, for the energy I felt radiating from its pages was tangible proof of the Masters' existence and a validation of their teachings.

"All true contact with a Master takes a person closer to the source within, leaving one feeling empowered. Only false prophets try to turn attention to themselves, or barrage their followers with a never-ending stream of supposedly essential information and prophesies, addicting them to the need to come back again and again to get the latest message—which is frequently rubbish.

"As for charging money to hear a Master speak through a supposed channel," Pearl went on, "no one who has ever been so graced as to stand in the presence of a Master would ever charge others money for that same privilege, assuming that the privilege was theirs to dispense. That is one way to tell if someone has truly met a Master. To charge others for that which they received by grace would be to fall from grace themselves. When money is charged for spirit, you know spirit is absent. I am not talking about charging for food, lodging, and the need to pay to rent a hall; but when an individual is denied access to the Masters and their teachings because of lack of money, or people are pressured to pay, you know that you don't need to waste your time there, for the Masters are not there either.

"Further, many sincere channels think they are hearing the Masters' voices, but most are merely hearing their own minds at best; at worst they are contacting disembodied spirits masquerading as Masters, that drift about sucking the energy of their followers. Even though the information these channelers give may sometimes be accurate or inspiring, it may also be largely untrue—giving rise to fear, false hopes, mistaken expectations, and often outright harm. These earthbound entities know they will catch more flies with honey than with vinegar, so they often lace misleading information with accurate observations and flattering comments that appeal to the ego, telling you how great you have been in past lifetimes, or how great you will be in the near future."

I didn't realize at the time that this was not merely theoretical knowledge, but that years later, while working in the movie business, I would come face to face with one of these dark beings, not merely a discarnate entity, but a false prophet from another world, seeking to mislead his followers. This encounter, chronicled later in the chapter "The Battle for Hollywood," almost cost me my life.

"Getting guidance through signs, omens, dreams, tarot card readings, and Ouija boards," Pearl continued, "while fascinating, are all practices that are open to various interpretations, due to the subjectivity of the human mind influenced by desire. The highest form of guidance manifests as spontaneous action, free from thought. It flows intuitively from the center of your being, without any mental interpretation. You simply do what is right! You know what you need when you need it and act spontaneously from your Higher Self with no interpretation or intermediary."

Pearl paused, and then continued her explanation of how the Masters work.

"The Masters guide and direct, most of the time without people knowing, allowing their guidance to be perceived as intuition or simply the spontaneous desire to act. This is because you become a Master by learning to tune in to your own Higher Self, the I AM THAT I AM, not by getting information channeled through someone else.

"How do you think these beings became Masters?" she asked, and then answered her own question, "By becoming conscious of their Higher Selves, the same process by which you too become a Master. There is no other way.

"This is not the work of a day," she continued. "People read a book, attend a seminar, or have a channeling, and they think they are Masters and want to give workshops and charge money. No, it is not the work of a day. It takes time and effort to overcome the lower nature, and strict obedience to the Higher Self and to the Masters for the individual to advance on the path of Mastery. Strict obedience is the key. Saint Germain told Godfre Ray King, 'If an individual will give total obedience, I can help anyone—even a shoe shine boy in the train station—clear his karma and achieve liberation in three years.'"

Seeing me sit up in my seat at this offer from Saint Germain, Pearl glanced at me with a knowing smile. "But let me caution you. Once you embark on this path, you will be severely tested—of that you may be sure. You must walk the razor's edge. Woe to the one who once embarks on this path and tries to turn back, for there is no turning back. To begin and to fail would be to regress many lifetimes, because the power you accumulate as you advance amplifies your every thought and feeling, so any discord would be amplified as well, creating negative karma. It is not a path on which to embark lightly."

Pearl finished, and I sat very still in my chair. I knew now why I had been brought here. I had been led around the world to prepare me for this moment. I understood that the Masters were making me an offer. I was being called to the Great Work, that of self-mastery. The seed had been planted when I read *The Impersonal Life;* now I was embarking on the path to which that book had led me, one starting at my own feet. The book says to forget about Masters, who may be a distraction from the real work of becoming a Master, and to meditate instead on the I AM—the very message the Masters proclaim. Replace worship of deities by becoming one.

The words she had spoken resonated so deeply within me as truth that I vowed then and there to make whatever sacrifice was necessary, to discipline myself in whatever way was needed, so I could become a being who could help others—like the magnificent being who had appeared before me in Muir Woods. Little dreaming how difficult this was to be and the startling adventures I would have under the Masters' tutelage, I took a solemn vow to give total obedience to them and to the I AM Presence, through which their guidance would come. Still feeling his presence, I requested Saint Germain to take me as his apprentice in his great service to humanity. I had vowed only that morning in Muir Woods to return to Earth to alleviate human suffering. Now I was being offered the training that would give me the means.

A pristine energy that was the essence of divinity filled the room—and I knew that Saint Germain had heard me. Little did I realize, though, how soon the lessons would begin and how severe the tests were to be, over the next several years. At that moment, sitting in Pearl's living room, I felt only elation that after so many years of searching—for *what*, I didn't even know—I had at last found the sacred path to perfection, and a true Master who had accepted me for training.

I felt a profound gratitude toward Pearl for being a wayshower and opening this doorway for me. I didn't realize at the time that Pearl could have Ascended years before, but had stayed in her body only to serve as a teacher to those whom the Masters would send her. She, too, had made the

Apprentice to the Masters

same decision as I, to stay on the Earth to alleviate suffering and to guide to the Inner Presence all whom the Masters would send her way.

Pearl concluded our meeting by telling me a parable that hinted at the level of dedication that would be required of me:

In the remote mountains, a seeker found the teacher for whom he had been searching his whole life.

"Master, at last I have found you," he said. "I beg you accept me as your disciple and teach me the path to enlightenment."

"Come with me," the Master said, walking to a nearby stream, the seeker following. In midstream, the Master grabbed the seeker and held his head under water. After what seemed an eternity to the would-be disciple, the Master raised him, gasping, to the surface.

"Now, tell me," the Master asked, "when your head was under water, what did you want more than anything else?"

"Air, air," the student gasped, filling his lungs gratefully.

"Then go away," the Master said. "Come back only when you want what I have to teach as much as, when your head was under water, you wanted air."

Pearl Dorris (1905-1990)

Chapter 4

A Pearl of Great Price

Pearl was not the teacher I had anticipated. Far from it. I had wandered around India for half a year, hanging out with renunciates who had achieved a high degree of spiritual realization, many with dreadlocks, their foreheads marked with symbols, and bodies gray with the ash which symbolized the end state of the body, but none had taught me the secret Pearl was to reveal. At the great *Kumbha Mela* in Allahabad, where years before Yogananda's guru had met the immortal Babaji, I wandered among the millions of seekers hoping, like myself, to meet the guru who would open the door to self-realization and liberation from the Earth.

So when the person who opened that door turned out to be an elderly housewife in a town as ordinary as the suburb where I had grown up, who sat with her knitting in her lap, it was not what I expected. I had to get beyond my disappointment with ordinary reality and realize that *ordinary* and *extraordinary* are an interdependent illusion depending on one's awareness. We realize the extraordinary only in the context of the ordinary. Only then did Pearl begin to reveal herself to me as someone of vast knowledge and power. She told me how we had met on the inner planes at the retreat known as the Royal Teton, inside the Grand Teton in Wyoming, many years before I was born. She had been taken in her finer body to a great meeting of the Masters, where many of the souls who were to come into embodiment in the future were introduced to those with whom they would work and be in relationship. She had recognized me from that meeting the moment she had seen me standing at her door.

"This is not where I would choose to live," Pearl said, looking around her living room, as though aware of my puzzlement over the mundane surroundings. "I would be up on the Mountain, camping out with you kids, if it weren't for my hubby, Jerry. He keeps me from going too far one way or the other—he is the guardian the Masters assigned to me. I ran away a couple of times, but he always came and got me, and I now see this is where I belong. If I were wandering around on the Mountain, or going back and forth to India like you people, who would be here to do this work?"

There was silence. Pearl suddenly perked up on the edge of her chair and seemed to shift her shape into that of a five-year-old with pigtails. "What are you staring at?" she asked.

"Why, you turned into a five-year-old girl!" I stammered.

"With pigtails?"

"Yes."

"Well, I used to have pigtails when I was a kid, until people said I didn't look serious enough."

"But how did you just change like that?"

"It just happens. When I feel five years old, my form becomes five years old. What your attention is on, you become. Sometimes people see other forms as well, depending on what I am feeling."

As if to demonstrate her point, she became very serious and her eyes opened wide. Suddenly, a huge, wise owl was sitting before me.

"Hooo…" she said, laughing at my surprise, and then turning back just as suddenly into an elderly woman.

Sometimes she morphed into a beautiful space traveler in a white jumpsuit, a role she had played in a former lifetime, the memory of which she still retained. She shared how she had come to this planet 11,000 years ago in a small scout craft that landed just north of Mount Shasta. She was returning as a teacher to the planet where she had lived eons before, and her mission was to continue assisting the evolution of human consciousness.

After landing and following the directions she had been given, Pearl made her way to a tunnel high on the side of the Mountain, where she was greeted by other fellow space travelers who had been maintaining a base there. Walking through the electronically charged tunnel, her high vibratory rate decelerated to the frequency where she would be visible to those she was to teach. From there, she descended to a small community situated north of the Mountain, where she was assigned to live and teach among the local inhabitants—who were the reimbodied souls of those she had taught long ago.

Remembering subsequent lives, many of which were as a teacher, Pearl told of having failed the high demands of her mission by giving in to human desire. One such fall took place when she was a teacher to young women in an Atlantean temple near present-day San Francisco. She was not only a teacher, but an example of the modesty and chastity that was expected of people prior to marriage in those days. Her role was similar to that of the Vestal Virgins in ancient Rome, who were teachers under the goddess Vesta, herself a visitor from another world, who had been sent to impart the values and teachings of an evolved civilization to a primitive humanity.

Pearl's undoing came through a relationship she had with one of the guards, who she didn't realize at the time was her Twin Ray—the masculine counterpart of her own heart flame. When their liaison became known, her students lost faith in her and in the truth she taught, and the community descended into chaos. The disruption of that sacred focus of energy precipitated a series of devastating earthquakes that left the society in ruins.

For this disobedience, she blamed herself down through time, even to her present embodiment, always feeling haunted by a sense that no matter how much she did for people, it would never be enough. She feared letting people down again, and had to struggle against self-doubt.

Pearl also told of several subsequent embodiments, some in which she seemed quite ordinary. However, no matter how lowly her position, she was always in contact with the God Flame in her heart and was able to help those around her by relaying that inner light to them. In one lifetime, she was a maid in the castle of a powerful king, and even though he had no intimate contact with her, she was able to assist his evolution by her silent transmission of awareness.

In other lifetimes she again encountered her Twin Ray, with whom she was directed to work in close association, as the spiritual outpouring is increased when the masculine and feminine aspects of the same flame are brought in close proximity to each other. Yet again, in some of those lifetimes the desire of the two to be romantically as well as spiritually united, despite the fact that one or both were already married, led to tumultuous results. As an example, Pearl spoke of the disruption of the Knights of the Round Table by the love affair between Queen Guinevere and Sir Lancelot, King Arthur's most trusted knight, showing how this betrayal had far-reaching and destructive consequences, in this case bringing about the end of the Grail Quest—the esoteric search for enlightenment—for an entire society.

In her current lifetime, Pearl was born on a farm in the Rocky Mountains on October 20, 1905, in La Porte, 20 miles west of Fort Collins, Colorado. She had a happy childhood and spent the summers roaming the mountains barefoot with her dog, Queenie. When Pearl was 14, her mother died, and she had to move with her father to Riverside, California, forced to leave behind her beloved Queenie. Eventually, she moved to Los Angeles, where she attended secretarial school.

At the age of 20, she met Sidney, the first love of her life, and after about a year they were married. They had a happy and harmonious relationship and shared many of the same interests, although eventually Pearl's spiritual awakening and her calling to serve the Masters would cause them to separate.

Her spiritual calling took the form of a white dove flying in her window one morning and telling her, *There is someone I want you to meet.* "Don't ask me how that happened," she said, "but it seemed like a real bird. It landed on my shoulder, pecked me on the lip, and spoke to me as if that were the most natural thing in the world."

The next day, while riding in the back seat of a car with friends, she was visited again by the dove, who told her that the stranger in the front seat was the woman it wanted her to meet. At that moment, the woman turned around and told Pearl she had a book for her. When the woman later showed her *Unveiled Mysteries,* the picture of Saint Germain came to life, and the Master winked at her. Pearl recognized him instantly and begged to know more. Shortly after, the woman took her to an auditorium, where she heard Godfre Ray King give a talk about the Ascended Masters and the great laws of life, and she felt an uplifting radiation that she knew could only come from very great beings. She knew immediately that she had found what she was looking for, and she vowed to become a student of the Ascended Masters.

After meeting her, Godfre soon recognized that Pearl had been sent by the Masters, and he involved her in his work of disseminating their teachings. She was appointed head of the San Francisco sanctuary directly by Saint Germain, who precipitated the letter of appointment out of thin air and allowed it to drop on Godfre's desk. Being a shy mountain girl at heart, and not knowing how to relate well to people, let alone large groups, Pearl found this to be a challenge, and during her tenure many opposed her. However, she also had a number of extraordinary experiences, too.

One day, while working in the sanctuary, a strange man came into her office and asked her about the I AM Teachings. She showed him the sanctuary, and as they stood in front of the Unfed Flame (a crystal goblet used to invoke a focus of light), the man asked her if she truly believed in the Unfed Flame. When she said she did, he replied, "When you have overcome your lower nature and all your energy is raised to here," he said, pointing to his heart, "then you will *be* the Unfed Flame, and your real work will begin." After he left, Pearl realized that the stranger, cloaked in a disguise, had been none other than Saint Germain.

On many other occasions, Pearl had further contact with Saint Germain and other Ascended Masters. One time, Saint Germain appeared on Geary Street in San Francisco in the form of a policeman who protected her from kidnappers. Another time, she was in a hotel room with Godfre and Lotus (Godfre's wife and Twin Ray), when Saint Germain walked right through the locked door into the room and talked to them as they sat around a table—telling them of the work he wished them to carry out and imparting a spiritual radiation she would never forget.

Meanwhile, Pearl began to realize that Sidney was more attached to the sensual life than she, and in order to follow Saint Germain's guidance of raising her energy to her higher centers, she needed to end their marriage. Pearl said that Sidney had been her complement, and that through his love she had developed an emotional stability that would not have otherwise been possible. Pearl explained that sometimes we are placed with a complementary soul, as she was with Sidney, and other times with a Twin or even an opposite—depending on what quality we need to develop.

Soon Pearl was brought together with her Twin Ray, Bob. It was 1939, around the time of Godfre's death,[7] and the Masters were hoping that Pearl and Bob could be used as their new messengers in the "I AM" Activity.[8] The Masters hoped to be able to work through these Twin Rays in the same way they had initially worked through Godfre and Lotus, in order to continue their work, as Lotus was not as able to receive the Masters' direct words as her husband.

However, there were dangers in this possibility. The power engendered by the union of the two halves of the flame brought to the surface any latent, negative emotions that had not been purified. So, to facilitate the desired harmony, Saint Germain precipitated an amethyst cube into Pearl's hand and told her to have it cut in half, each piece of the gem to be cut

---

[7] He severed the connection with the physical body on December 29, 1939. Pearl witnessed, during a memorial service held at the Biltmore Hotel in Los Angeles, the raising of his etheric body into the Ascended State through the assistance of angels and the Ascended Masters. She said that Godfre's desire to return and tell his students of the bliss of the higher octaves was so great that Saint Germain had to restrain him from returning to Earth. He now serves from the Ascended octave.

according to a special design and set in a ring of pure gold, with torches carved into the settings to signify their mission as light bearers.

The initial step in the Masters' plan of establishing Pearl and Bob as heirs to Godfre was to publish a book Saint Germain would dictate through them, demonstrating to Lotus and the rest of the organization that Pearl and Bob were to be the next messengers. However, without reading it, Lotus rejected the book, maintaining that she was to be the only messenger, and taking their book as a personal attack on her authority. Seeing that this path was blocked, Saint Germain instructed Pearl and Bob to withdraw from the organization after Godfre's passing. Although Bob and Pearl were never lovers, during the Second World War they were both stationed on the same military base, where they maintained their spiritual connection. Eventually, they were directed by Saint Germain to go their separate ways, and after the war, Bob was guided to marry someone else. Although saddened at first, Pearl was shown that they had different paths of evolution, and each had unique work to carry out that required they be placed in different circumstances and with other partners.

After the war, a small group of former I AM students was brought together by the Masters in Santa Rosa, California, to establish a focus for their work in that area. It was at this point that one of the group, Jerome Dorris, was brought into Pearl's life. When he first met Pearl many years before, he had seen a vision of them ascending a golden stairway together hand in hand, but because Pearl was married to Sidney at the time, and Jerry (as he came to be called) had taken a vow to remain single and focus on applying the Masters teachings, he had kept his vision to himself.

One day, after a meeting of their group at the ranch where the Masters had been giving spiritual discourses through Pearl, Jerry was driving home on the freeway when the Master Saint Germain appeared in front of him and told him he was to marry Pearl. Without a moment's hesitation, he made a U-turn and returned to the ranch. Surprised to see him back, Pearl asked why he had returned.

"We're to be married," the former rancher, who was more used to talking to horses than women, blurted out.

"Says who?" the feisty Pearl retorted.

"The Master Saint Germain."

"Why, that's ridiculous," Pearl said, "I don't love you. In fact, I'm not sure I even like you."

"I know," he said. "I feel the same; nonetheless, it is the Master's wish.

You can have your own bedroom. Now get your stuff. I'll wait here."

Shocked by what he had said, Pearl ran upstairs and sat down on her bed. After she calmed down a bit, she was able to feel Saint Germain's presence and knew that what Jerry had said was true—they were to be together in service to the Masters. She packed a small bag, and they drove to the courthouse in Sonoma, where they obtained their marriage license. For a number of years, they ran a fruit ranch in that area, an experience that Pearl later said was the grounding she needed after her sudden spiritual acceleration with Godfre in the "I AM" Activity.

Years later, they moved to Mount Shasta and bought a small ranch that Pearl said she recognized as the location where she had landed in the space craft thousands of years before. After a while they sold the ranch, bought a house in the town of Mount Shasta, and got jobs managing a downtown motel. For nearly 20 years they led simple lives, ranching, managing motels, fixing up old houses and renting them out, never telling anyone in town of their connection with the Masters or the "I AM" Activity.

Pearl's latest service to the Masters began on her 67th birthday. A friend had thrown a party for her, mostly attended by people of Pearl's age, but the woman had also invited two young men who worked at the local health food store, a bastion of light in the otherwise dreary town. Having heard of the many legends surrounding Mount Shasta, and sensing Pearl's spiritual energy, the two men followed Pearl home after the party and knocked on her door. Jerry was working at the motel at the time.

"We think you know something, and we want to know what it is," they implored, when Pearl opened the door. She invited them in and, cautiously at first, began to share her experiences of the Masters.

Thinking that was the end of it, Pearl went to sleep that night, only to be awakened in the morning by the same two men, now accompanied by two others, wanting to hear more. The following weekend, a car full of young people, who had been alerted by their friends in Mount Shasta about the amazing woman who knew the Ascended Masters and taught people to find their own God Presence, arrived from San Francisco. Gradually, more and more seekers arrived, all coming through word of mouth, until there was a steady stream appearing at her door every day. She never charged a cent for her long hours, though frequently people gave gifts in gratitude for the priceless gift she gave them.

Sometimes there would only be a single person, other times fifty people flowed into the dining room, through the kitchen, and out the back door. Often a dozen people from different parts of town would congregate at Pearl's house within minutes of each other, without any previous appointment having been made, simply by following the inner pull in their hearts that said, *Go see Pearl!* When all arrived and became silent, Pearl would tell them why they had been brought together and describe which of the Masters were in attendance. Often the purpose of their gathering was to invoke spiritual energy to be sent to troubled spots around the world or into the Earth itself to quell an impending earthquake.

Pearl never channeled the Masters, however, as she knew it would weaken people, and that they needed to get their answers by observing their own hearts. Even if they made mistakes, it was better that they did so, because the mistakes were part of the learning process. The radiation of spiritual energy was so strong on such occasions that the human mind became empty, a wordless transmission of the Masters filling one's awareness.

This elderly woman, appearing so ordinary until you looked into her eyes, was a manifestation of the *Pearl of Great Price,* for which, Jesus said, *a wise man sold all that he possessed*—the pearl that is the Christ Consciousness.

Chapter 5

Above Mount Shasta

Still disoriented by this day's experiences, first with Saint Germain in Muir Woods, now with Pearl—and the irrevocable commitment I had made to the Masters in her living room—I found my way back to the health food store, knowing that my life had forever changed. I had wandered the world, seeking this doorway to higher knowledge, finding it only after giving up and returning home. I thanked Stephen profusely for having followed his spontaneous impulse to send me to Pearl. Stephen was one of those who do the Masters' work without any outer show, sometimes unaware of the service they are giving, simply by following their hearts. He was one of those good-natured souls who never spoke ill of anyone and helped others whenever he was able. Often I saw that simply his good-natured spirit was enough to transform someone's day.

Now he offered to help find me a place to spend the night. Because I had just come from India, where I had been a wandering ascetic, he thought his girlfriend, Gayle, who lived in Weed, a mill town ten miles to the north of Mount Shasta, might have a place for me on the floor. The large, ramshackle house had been used as a dormitory for mill workers decades ago and was now mostly abandoned, save for a few rooms that were rented out on the ground floor.

Gayle greeted me and asked me to follow her down the rambling corridors to the rooms she and a few of her friends occupied at the far end of the building. She opened a door, revealing a closet, and pointing towards the back of it, said, "Your room is in there."

"In the closet?" I asked, a bit surprised.

"No! Everything here is not as it seems," she said, laughing, as she gave me a push through a curtain at the back of the closet into another room—like the closet in the *Chronicles of Narnia*, through which children disappear into another world. I, too, had entered a new world that day, and this hidden passage through the back of the closet seemed symbolic. One's life could change drastically when least expected; a walk in the woods or even a trip to the closet could lead to a new life. Mine had changed that day on my walk through Muir Woods, then again on a stranger's insistence that I visit a certain housewife in suburbia. Now it would never be the same.

Apprentice to the Masters

Gayle disappeared back through the closet, leaving me to set up my things on the floor, and I was soon asleep. But my sleep was not to last long. Shortly after I dozed off, I was awakened by the sound of dogs barking, and I noticed that my room was illuminated by a subtle glow. To my surprise, standing several feet away from me was the etheric presence of Saint Germain, in the form he had changed into earlier that day, when he had transformed himself from what appeared to be a casual hiker into the white-robed form of an Ascended Master. Surrounded by a blue-white light, he emanated an ethereal splendor. Though he was obviously speaking to me, I could not hear a word he said, and soon I fell back asleep.

A little later, I was again awakened by two other Masters, their appearance announced by barking dogs, as they arced through the sky and descended into my room. Strive though I might, I could not hear a word they uttered. Though I yearned to hear what they were saying, I realized that the Masters were speaking to my Higher Self, as Pearl had said they would, giving information I would access at a later time when needed. Even without knowing their message, their presence quickened my being, imparting an energy to my subtle bodies and charging me with the reality of those I had previously regarded as mythical beings.

Around midnight, I was awakened again. *This place is as busy as Grand Central Station in New York! Will I ever get any sleep?* This time my visitor was none other than Pearl herself, now garbed in a white robe like the Masters, looking like a beautiful woman of about 30, rather than the grandmotherly 67-year-old I had met earlier in the day.

"Yes, in the subtle form, we can take on whatever appearance we choose," she smiled, noting my appreciation.

"Now, come with me," she said, and without realizing what was happening, I left my dense body behind and stepped forth into a more subtle form that seemed every bit as real. As she took my hand in hers, a force went through me that caused me to become weightless, and we rose from the floor, shooting upward over the house and over the roofs of the town like the angels in a Chagall painting. Dogs barked as we flew above the Earth. Upward we soared into the night sky, untethered by any earthly bonds, and I felt the freedom of the Superman I had wanted to emulate since childhood, who could fly wherever he wished.

"Where are we?" I asked, as we slowed and hovered in space.

"Look down," Pearl answered. Beneath our feet was the dazzling whiteness of Mount Shasta, her shining glaciers reflecting the full moonlight.

"This is your home now," Pearl said. "I have been waiting for you for many years, ever since we were introduced at the retreat in the Royal Teton. I recognized you the moment I saw you. We are part of Saint Germain's family. We have all worked together in many past embodiments, and have much work to do together in this one. Saint Germain has asked me to train you, for you have much to learn about the Law before you can be of service to the Great White Brotherhood of the Ascended Masters."

Pearl took my hand again, and soaring back the way we had come, she returned me to my room. I finally slept for a few hours before the sun rose and the whistle blew, summoning workers to another day at the mill. I was grateful that I had been spared the tedium of a daily routine, and that I was free to go where I wished in the pursuit of wisdom.

CHAPTER 6

Gaining Faith in the Master on the Job

The next morning, I drove back into the town of Mount Shasta and found Stephen busy in his store. I marveled at how he was able to fill a bag with dates, ring a customer's purchase, and churn a glass of carrot juice at the juice bar, all the while conversing with spiritual seekers like me. Perhaps he was more a master than he realized—true mastery often going unrecognized in the outer world.

Those thousands drawn to the store wanted to know about the Masters and the Mountain they used as a retreat, what the Masters looked like, where they could be found, and how they, too, could enter this retreat. When it was discovered that the famed occultist Helena Petrovna Blavatsky had visited the Mountain during her travels, that redoubled public curiosity. In addition, the Mountain was a great center of UFO activity. People wanted to know if the spectacular lenticular clouds frequently stacked like pancakes above the snow-clad summit contained the space ships they resembled. A meeting place for people coming from all parts of the world, Stephen's store became the focal point of the community and an exciting place to hang out.

With so much traffic, it was obvious that Stephen needed help, so I offered my assistance. He couldn't pay me other than with food, but since I had some savings to live on, I accepted his offer. Soon I was working at the lunch counter, squeezing carrot juice, blending smoothies, and making sandwiches, while listening to the stories of what had brought people to the Mountain. Saint Germain had appeared to many. Some had received guidance in dreams or meditation and others had been drawn by an inner pull they seemed unable to resist. Still others found themselves stranded here when their cars broke down, the needed part not arriving for days, after which time they had lost the desire to leave.

Working at the health food store, I was at the very nexus of an unfolding adventure. It was 1973, and an experiment in the Aquarian consciousness was evolving out of the quest by the Flower Children of the Woodstock Generation for freedom and self-knowledge. Many of the people arriving had lived in Haight-Ashbury or traveled to India looking for gurus. They had glimpsed higher consciousness through drugs, but were now looking for the permanent high of sustained God Consciousness, wanting to live permanently in that awakened state. Through such teachers as Ram Dass and Chögyam Trungpa Rinpoche, people were beginning to realize that consciousness is not dependent on the external world, on finding the right conditions, but on one's own awareness which creates the right conditions—and that the world we perceive is the product of that awareness. Mastering the world, most discovered, is not possible on drugs—which only propel one into yet another world with a different set of illusions.

We had seen that the competitive, materialistic world of our parents did not work. The Vietnam War was still raging, and many of us had marched on Washington or protested in other ways. I had met the Secretary of Defense, Robert McNamara, chief architect of the Vietnam War, whose daughter was a friend of mine. I had been shocked that her father could send our high school classmates to die in the jungles of South East Asia, lie to Congress, and years later confess that the war had been a "mistake." We were looking for a new paradigm, a way of being on Mother Earth, and relating to each other with truth and openness. We wanted a place where people could live in freedom and harmony—the principles on which America had been founded.

This was the Aquarian Dream we pursued, which started so innocently and with such high hopes for human perfectibility, but later degenerated into self-promotion, psychic channeling, multi-level marketing, and various other get-rich-quick schemes—the spiritual materialism that Tibetan lama Chögyam Trungpa Rinpoche, newly arrived in the States, decried in his classic book, *Cutting Through Spiritual Materialism*.[8] The vision of an earthly Paradise, the Shambhala of which Rinpoche spoke, was the essence of the New Age before that term became yet another marketing tool.

Although I had met Saint Germain in person and been in the presence of other Ascended Masters in their etheric forms, my active mind still nursed doubts about the nature of these rarely seen beings, about whose nature there were many conflicting theories. I questioned much that was said about these beings, whose names were casually thrown about by the

---

8   Chögyam Trungpa, *Cutting Through Spiritual Materialism* (Shambhala, 1987).

people who came into the store, their information based on the endless, conflicting channelings they quoted. I had gone to college to become a rocket scientist, and my scientific nature prevented me from accepting on blind faith what I had not personally experienced. Perhaps that trait of not wanting to believe in something until I had tested it myself is one reason the Masters chose me to witness and testify to their reality.

While a guest in India of the Theosophical Society—a group of occultists whose express purpose was to inform humanity of the Masters' existence and teachings—I found that even they had grown skeptical of the Masters' reality. This was probably due in part to the revolt of their star protégé, Krishnamurti, who had been trained by the Masters and raised from childhood to be the next World Teacher, the messiah they expected to lead humanity. Rebelling against this messianic role in which he had been cast by the adoring Theosophists, Krishnamurti refused to be the messiah they had trained him to be from childhood. He made his rebellion complete by stating—to the great shock of the Theosophists—that for all intents and purposes, the Masters did not exist. We have to work out our own salvation.

Krishnamurti's rebellion, his insistence that the teachings of all gurus be dismissed, and that everyone pursue their spiritual quest without reliance on any of the previously discovered methods of the great seers throughout the ages, deprived his followers of any external guidance whatsoever. However, he was a great catalyst, whose appearance marked a turning point in the spiritual evolution of humanity, from slavish devotion to religious dogma and authority figures to the acceptance of the responsibility for one's own salvation. Rather than observing others, he recommended his followers pursue self-observation. Regrettably, he never taught how to practice that self-observation. Many said that Krishnamurti's denunciation of the Masters was precipitated by his knowing they were about to subject him to the *Arhat* initiation—where the Masters seem to turn their backs on the disciple, forcing him to put the teachings into practice—and that Krishnamurti reacted by abandoning the Masters first, before they could abandon him.[9]

---

9   Krishnamurti performed a great service for the Theosophists of the world by freeing them from their slavish worship of the Masters, which had practically turned Theosophy into a religion—when its original

Apprentice to the Masters

Having met Saint Germain now, and having taken an oath of apprenticeship to him, I wanted to know first-hand the extent of his powers—to test the Master, as I knew he was testing me. I wanted to know to what degree he was actually there for me and how much I could rely on him. Quite unexpectedly, I soon had the experience that gave me the validating experience I wanted, but through a more painful means than what I would have preferred.

One evening I stayed at the health food store after closing, to finish packaging a new shipment of cayenne pepper in small plastic bags, weighing and pricing them to put on the shelf. As I worked, spilling some of the red powder on the counter, I brushed it off with my fingers. A few minutes later, forgetting that some of the acrid powder still adhered to my fingers, I rubbed my eye and felt as if a hot poker had been thrust into the socket. Blinded, I ran to the bathroom and doused my face with water, but still I couldn't see. The pain worsened, and in a panic I threw more water in my face—*Am I going blind?* The words of Pearl emerged from memory: "The Master Saint Germain is watching you, and you should call on him if you need his help."

But is this being who is guiding the affairs of humanity really watching what I'm doing here in a health food store in California, and will he bother to intercede? Desperate, feeling I had nothing to lose, I called out, "Saint Germain!"—and before I could finish my sentence, the pain had disappeared. My eye stopped watering. I blinked and found I could see perfectly. It was as though the accident had never happened.

This compassionate rescue from the cayenne pepper began to show me that Saint Germain was an omniscient, powerful mentor who took an interest in my well-being—a friend on whom I could rely for practical assistance. Although knowing how busy he was, working on behalf of humanity in so many places simultaneously, I began to feel that he wanted

---

purpose was to study divine wisdom. However, he never said that the Masters do not exist, only that the path to realization lies within the individual, and can be found only by observing one's own consciousness. It is interesting that after using Madame Blavatsky and her colleagues to establish belief in the reality of the Masters, they would later use Krishnamurti to prevent people from worshiping them—perhaps one of the reasons the Masters do not appear in public and demonstrate their powers. They do not want followers, but finders.

me to call on him and that developing this bond of trust was part of my training. I began to turn to him, not only for spiritual illumination, but for protection, guidance, and inspiration on a daily basis. I told him my every concern, even though my human mind sometimes wondered how closely he was listening. I operated on ever-increasing faith and requested his assistance, trusting that what illumination was needed would be forthcoming.

Chapter 7

Meditation with Pearl

A few days after Saint Germain rescued me from my painful encounter with the cayenne pepper, I felt a tug in my heart to again see Pearl, but resisted. My rational mind told me that she had answered all my questions, and I didn't need to take more of her time. There were many people who were coming to see her now, and I had gotten her message—which seemed to be a simple one: Your I AM Presence is God, and can be called into action with the words "I AM." I didn't see what purpose it would serve to go back and visit her again. I was not yet fully conscious of the etheric substance that was imparted to me while in her presence, that beyond her words the Masters were transmitting knowledge directly to me on higher levels.

However, the urge to call her on the phone would not let me alone. After an hour of struggling with myself, I found a payphone outside a grocery store and rang her number.

"Come up," Pearl said.

"When?"

"Right now.

"Now?"

"Yes, I have been waiting for you!"

As soon as I arrived, Pearl said, "What kept you? You were supposed to be here an hour ago. You have kept the Master waiting."

I was crushed. I had let the Master down. I had felt the call, but let my mind get in the way. I realized that I would have to learn a new way of thinking—or rather, not thinking—of acting from my heart without questioning *why*.

Just do it, you don't need to figure out why—you can't figure it out, anyway, I told myself. To know why would be to suppose I knew more than I did, that my mind with its limited data could determine what was right, when frequently what was right was to act contrary to the obvious. I was quickly learning that the Masters didn't work along the lines of human reason. They saw the big picture, and when their guidance was translated into the ordinary, human mind, the message was frequently, *Feel what is in your heart, then act—and don't look back.*

But that was not how I had lived my life up until then. I had been trained to play it safe, to always understand first what I was going to do—to think out what was best, come to a logical conclusion, and then act impeccably. But now impeccability seemed to be in acting without thinking. *With our limited data, limited view, how could we possibly know what was right?*

"Always follow the prompting in your heart," Pearl began, "even if you don't understand why. In the absence of direct guidance, follow common sense, but when the guidance within the center of your being is leading you, forget about common sense. When you first felt the call to come here an hour ago, you should have followed the prompting. You didn't need to phone. The more you meditate on the center of your being, the stronger your reception and recognition of the guidance will become. You will feel the magnetic center of your being, just as iron filings feel the call of the magnet and obey its attraction." *Perhaps this is what the Tibetan Buddhists meant by crazy wisdom,* I thought, *wisdom that transcends human logic.*[10]

"Now," Pearl said, giving me a penetrating look, "would you like to meditate?"

"Sure," I said, starting to slide to the floor and cross my legs to sit in the lotus position I had learned in India.

"Stay in the chair," she said. "Legs straight, feet flat on the floor, hands on thighs. Now turn your attention within. Eyes open!" she commanded, "and just relax. Your mind is like an office. You've got to shut the filing cabinet, lock the office door, and come downstairs into the cathedral," she said, pointing to her heart.

"Turn your attention here, to the very center of your being," she continued. "Now that you are in the cathedral, you and God are alone. But don't have a one-sided conversation, where you do all the talking. Be still and listen to what God has to say back to you."

A throb within my heart confirmed the truth of her instruction, as though to say, *Yes, put your attention here, on me, this soft, vulnerable spot you try to protect. This is where I dwell.* Although we were not staring, our eyes were open to each other, and as we both turned our attention inward to the presence within our hearts, I felt my gaze go out of focus, dissolving

---

10 Trungpa Rinpoche clarified the concept of *crazy wisdom* by saying wisdom comes first, *then* the crazy, not the other way around, as many practiced during the hippie days.

in a golden haze that began to fill the room. The further I dove within, the brighter the light became.

Pearl was doing with me what I had done alone as a child but never dared to tell anyone, keeping secret such magical moments of blissful dissolution, when the world dissolved into timeless awareness. I didn't want my teacher or classmates to think something was wrong with me. Those moments would happen spontaneously at the most inopportune times, such as in the middle of a baseball game Saturday morning, when suddenly I would be gone, not aware of who or where I was. They used to put me in right field, as balls were hardly ever hit there. Once I came back from one of my escapes into timeless awareness to find the right fielder from the other team standing beside me. "Hey, you're at bat," he shouted, and I realized, embarrassed, that I had not seen my team leave the field minutes before. Guys were supposed to be tough, but I had no desire for competition. *Instead of competing, why don't we work together and use that energy to create something useful?*

Another time, in second grade, while hanging my coat on a hook in the cloak room after recess, I suddenly felt myself dissolving, a delicious warmth suffusing through my body, as I lost awareness of who and where I was, and what I was supposed to be doing—dissolving into that blissful state of *no awareness of self*. Perhaps it had been no more than a few seconds, but that joyful expansion beyond the ego had refreshed and renewed me, though I had to shirk the questioning looks of those who had been watching my motionless form.

Now Pearl was leading me back to that receptive, feminine surrender that wanted to pull me inward to my true self—to heal, guide, teach, and empower me. Yet, part of me was afraid to let go, to renounce the control of the rational mind that kept me locked within the protective box of reason. So I forced myself to once again let go, as I had as a child, and surrender to that inner force of silent knowing.

"Now, say silently, *I AM the Living Light!*" Pearl continued. I did as she directed, and the room became brighter, as though someone had thrown a switch on a hidden lamp.

I AM the Living Light! I repeated over and over, keeping my attention on the presence within, as, through half-closed eyes, I watched the light in the room grow in intensity.

Finally, unable to contain my exuberance, I broke my focus and exclaimed, "That's it!"

Apprentice to the Masters

"That's what?" Pearl inquired, amused at my enthusiasm.

"The light! I've heard people say, 'Have you seen the light?' But all my time in India, going from guru to guru, not one of them taught me to see the light. I never saw it until now, sitting here in your living room."

"This is the Inner Light that Jesus said 'lighteth every man that cometh into the world,'" Pearl responded, acknowledging my discovery, then continuing. "Now you must learn to bring that light down into your heart and consciously send it out into the world. That is why your health has suffered, because in your meditation you were going out of your body. Instead, you must learn to bring the Light of God down into your body. To bring that Divine Light down, to qualify it with positive attributes and then send it forth into the world to accomplish good works is true Mastery—what you have been brought here to learn.

"Know that there is no limit to that light—*the Light of God never fails!* You can call it forth at will, to do whatsoever you choose. Its power will be determined by the extent to which you can unify the masculine power of the mind to visualize, with the feminine power of the heart to qualify and bring into manifestation. The union of these two is the secret of creation."

Pearl continued her seemingly simple, yet profound instruction. "This is the great Law of the Masters, the Law of Creation that you have been sent here to learn: Whenever you say I AM, you are calling forth the Source, the Inner Light, and whatever follows those words is what you are calling into being. The greater your realization of the I AM, the greater your acceptance of the great God Presence that you are, the quicker will be the manifestation of whatever you call forth. This is your God-given power to create. It is said in the Bible, 'God made man in his image and likeness.' Since we are the image and likeness, if God can create, so can we.

"Just be sure you create consciously," Pearl warned, "that you create only what brings benefit to the world, for if you miscreate with that light, whatever you bring forth will come back to you to deal with. You will have to suffer the consequences of your creation—which is why we humans are still here on the Earth today. Many eons ago, we experimented with that light, and now we are cleaning up the consequences of those actions. We were like children then, not knowing what we were doing. Now that we are adults, we must clean up the mess and teach others how to use their creative energy for good.

"Remember, energy travels in a circle. It is magnetic and attracts other similar energies to itself, then returns to you, amplified many-fold. Think, feel, and bring into manifestation only that which you want to experience yourself, for that is what you will get. What you give is what you receive, and how you give is how you receive. This is how Jesus created, how all Masters create. The unified focus of thought and feeling, word and action, brings about the release of tremendous power."

I was enthralled by the simplicity of Pearl's words. Why had I never heard any of this before? How could I have gone through years of college and graduate school and not ever heard of this Inner Light—the sustaining power of life, and the great Laws of Creation? I had neither been taught the meaning of life, nor how to earn a living in the world. All those wasted hours spent writing term papers, all that effort and money down the drain!

I realized that I had learned nothing but how to play elaborate mental games. I had been in a sort of nursery school all those years, not learning anything that would be of use to me. Leaving the graduation ceremony, I had walked down the street away from the auditorium, diploma in hand, but desolation in my heart over the sudden realization that I had wasted so many years of my life in the empty pursuit of *academia* that had little bearing on real life.

"If you want peace," Pearl was saying, "say, *I AM PEACE!* Then you will become peace. Peace will flow through you into the world. There is no limit to the peace you can create and send forth to any location on Earth, using the power of your attention focused by your spoken word—again, the combination of thought and feeling, visualization and qualification. The power to visualize is the male aspect; the power to qualify with energy is the female aspect. Thoughts, words, feelings, or actions alone do not work; it is the unified power of them together that brings thought into manifestation.

"If you want wisdom, say, *I AM WISDOM!* If you want abundance, *I AM ABUNDANCE.* If you want love, *I AM LOVE!* What your attention is upon and what you feel, you become. As you think and feel, *so it is.* This is your Mastery, your God-given power to create. Of course, then you need to go out and do something—your action coalesces your inner work and brings your words into manifestation.

"Some say they have tried this great Law and it doesn't work. I ask them, How long did you try? How long did you hold the focus without wavering? What did you think and feel and say later on that day? Did you say, think, feel, or do anything that contradicted and canceled what you were trying to create?

"If you affirm love for ten seconds and then for the rest of the day dwell in your habitual perception that you are unloved, you have more than canceled your positive affirmation. The affirmation is but a seed that must be constantly watered by your attention and kept free of the weeds of doubt by your constant self-awareness. This is not a matter of chance, but the working of a *law* that works without fail.

"You may also have had many lifetimes of doubt, of negative affirmation, of low self-esteem that created the feeling of lack. You may have lived many lifetimes in fear. Do you expect that now, in five minutes, five days, or even five weeks of positive affirmation, you will dispel all those dark clouds with just a few minutes of sunlight? Though it may take a bit longer than you expect, you have to begin somewhere, and now is the best time—in fact, now is the only time.

"The Light of God is emanating from you constantly without ceasing, ever present like the sun—whether you see it or not—creating your life anew every moment. Whatever image you hold in front of that Inner Light, you create in your life. To change your life, change the image by changing your mind. You are constantly recreating your life at every moment. Could you but break free of habitual thought, you could be and achieve anything you want in the twinkling of an eye. God is unlimited. Identify with that Unlimited Self.

"Mastery is freeing oneself of fixed ideas and habitual tendencies, and then learning to create with that light consciously at will. This great law is a tremendous responsibility. Do you think you are ready for that responsibility? The Masters have been guiding you through all the painful experiences of your life, to help you purify yourself for this great responsibility. But you must make the choice.

"'Many are called but few are chosen,' it says in the Bible. What the Masters say is 'Many are called but few *can* be chosen.' You make the choice yourself. That is why you are here, because you have made the choice. You have chosen yourself."

Pearl leaned forward and took my hands in hers, looking into my eyes with a penetrating gaze that emanated a loving wisdom, then rose from her chair, indicating that our meeting was at a close. As I opened the door, I felt I was moving out into a new world, one suffused with light and instantaneously responsive to my wishes, where every thought was an immediate reality. I felt free of all limitation, possessed of a mastery by which I could change the world with no other tool than my mind.

Without realizing it, I had been raised into the consciousness of my Higher Mental Body, the intermediary between the physical body and the I AM Presence. I was raised twenty feet in the air, looking down on my physical body, the roofs of cars lining the street, and the roofs of the houses of the surrounding neighborhood. In this higher body, every thought became an instantaneous reality. As I thought of the Violet Consuming Flame, waves of violet light filled the atmosphere, flowing out through the town, climbing the slopes of the surrounding mountains as waves of light.

I recalled the words of Saint Germain: "One day you will throw open the door of your human creation and stand forth in your Ascended Master Body, a free being in the service of the light." Now his prediction had come true, and I prayed for this reality to be sustained forever.

I lay down that night so energized I had no need to sleep. Free of my lower self, at last I knew what it was to be a Master, and I felt that soon I would join the other liberated ones whose retreat is inside the Mountain. However, when I awoke in the morning, I found that once again I was human, with the same bodily needs and concerns as before. Only, this morning, I was not quite the same, for having once glimpsed that Ascended Master octave, the essence of which is free dominion, I knew I could never again completely succumb to the hypnotic illusion of human limitation that had previously held me in its thrall.

The door had opened, and I had taken the first step through it toward permanent freedom. I knew that as my absorption in that consciousness increased through daily meditation upon it, so too would my grasp of the scepter of dominion that is Mastery.

Chapter 8

A Midnight Visitor

Since vowing total obedience to Saint Germain, I had gotten used to being awakened in the middle of the night by visits from him and other Masters of the Great White Brotherhood. At first, I couldn't understand what they were saying, but as my spiritual practice deepened through meditating on my Inner Light, I became more able to hear their words. Now I could often remember the salient features of their messages on awakening.

However, two nights in succession I awoke to a majestic presence I did not recognize. There was a new, strangely familiar voice speaking to me of past lives and how they had created my present challenges—yet I was unable to rouse myself sufficiently to see this new Master, by whose exquisite radiance I knew was no ordinary being.

Determined to see this nocturnal visitor and know his name, the third night I meditated before I went to bed, and I closed the meditation with a prayer to my Higher Self: *Beloved I AM Presence, protect me from harm and show me who has been visiting me. Not only do I want to know the name, but I want to see this Master face to face.* Then I turned off the lights and went to sleep.

Again I was awakened by a light in the room and the self-assured voice of the same unknown presence. Suddenly I was fully awake and sat up in bed to behold overhead a light brighter than the sun, encircled by concentric rings of rainbow colors. As my eyes adjusted to the brilliance, I saw before me a white-robed being emanating from the light, whose face was so bright I could not look upon it fully—two luminous eyes penetrating me with such power I had no doubt I was in the presence of a vast being beyond what I had ever experienced.

Summoning my courage, I shouted, "Who are you?" There was no answer. I shouted my demand again, gaining confidence. "In the name of God, I demand to know who you are!"

In response, came a reply that shocked me to my core:
"I AM God!...your own God Presence...I AM you!"

Brighter than the sun at midday, the light of God dissolved the limits of the room, the walls and ceiling seeming to disappear as the vibratory rate increased and every cell of my body blazed with inner fire. My body became drenched in perspiration, as if in an effort to keep from bursting into flame. Then I saw the silver cord linking this being's heart to my own, and I realized that truly I was one with God—the Presence above me. I gasped and fell backward on the bed, sinking into oblivion. Not until the sun's rays lit my room the next morning did I awaken from my slumber—still in shock at realizing *I am God!*

My skepticism regarding the artist's portrayal of the "Magic Presence" in *Unveiled Mysteries,* showing the God Presence above the physical body, was now gone. The higher and lower selves were not a metaphor, but a reality. The Higher Self, what the Buddhists call the *Dharmakaya,* projects a ray of consciousness into a body functioning at a lower frequency, the Higher Mental Body or *Sambhogakaya,* and finally into the human self, the *Nirmanakaya*. But in ignorance we claim that spark of consciousness as our own, thinking arrogantly it is completely independent of its Source, the God Self!

Amazing! We think of ourselves as independent beings, self-sufficient, taking independent existence for granted, when in fact we cannot draw a breath without the light from this God Flame. Not a moment passes that this God Presence is not aware of us. Not a human contact occurs, not an event happens that is not directly arranged by this Presence, and not a dollar or a meal comes to us that is not provided by this Presence—the God Consciousness that is evoked every time we feel the *I* within us and that is called into action every time we say *I AM*. It is like the pilot light of a gas stove, which is burning unobserved all the time, but which lights all the external burners.

Now I knew why Pearl had always replied to my questions, no matter what they might concern, by saying, "Talk to your I AM Presence about that." To Pearl, the I AM Presence was a living being, her best friend and confidant she talked to every day, every moment—and someone who conversed back with her. Rather than imagining how God might talk, or channeling an imaginary presence, Pearl actually conversed with her living God Self.

"God is talking to us constantly," Pearl commented, during one of the many gatherings the Masters drew together in her living room. "But how many are listening? To most people, the chatter of their own mind is all they hear. This inability to distinguish God's words from those of their own mind comes from an inability to concentrate. This deficiency begins in infancy with exposure to television and becomes worse the more electronic stimulation it receives, these chaotic signals interfering with the brain's natural currents. With all the electronic devices today, people's minds are scattered everywhere and focused nowhere. In that lack of focused awareness, the mind is brainwashed by the sea of random, electronic impulses.

"Opportunity knocks but once, the saying goes," Pearl continued. "But the Masters say opportunity is knocking constantly. God is trying to beat down your door. But how many hear the knocking? Of those who hear, how few open the door? Most have the volume of the music in their heads turned up too loud. God is the constant, animating presence of our lives, but how many stop to think, for one minute of their entire existence, where that energy, that life, is coming from, or to give a moment's gratitude—let alone talk to that One from whom all blessings flow?

"We are like debtors, taking and spending the loan we received at birth as though we never had to pay that loan back, not realizing that some day we will have to give an accounting of how we spent our God-given energy! What have we done with that energy? Have we squandered it, or have we done something that will make us more conscious, advance us along the path, and possibly benefit others? Will we leave the Earth a better place for our having been here? Will we be able to face our Creator and say, 'I did something good with the life you gave me?' Will we realize that we are that Creator?

"Because of that ingratitude and lack of self-awareness, we re-embody again and again, lifetime after lifetime. At the Day of Judgment, when you pass from this body and review your life and *you are your own judge,* what sentence will you pass on yourself? Where will you re-embody, with whom, and under what circumstances?

"The conditions of our life are not an accident," Pearl emphasized. "Sai Baba, the great Avatar of this age, says that the major circumstances of our lives are already determined by our past actions, our free will being in how we relate to those circumstances—if we choose to blame others for our misfortunes or use those events as a springboard to grow and evolve."

Now that I knew the I AM Presence was the living God, the source of every condition and event in my life, and that my human self was merely an evanescent form into which that Presence was pouring life and consciousness at every moment, I began to realize more deeply the importance of the Laws of Creation Pearl had been teaching. Either we

Apprentice to the Masters

create consciously, or the habitual thoughts of limitation will create more limitation. Day by day, I was being brought into closer proximity with those Masters who are one with their I AM Presence, and as this association increased, I came further under their instruction and testing—and learned to practice and apply those Laws.

Part II:

Living the Law

Chapter 9

By This Word—I AM

My study with Pearl deepened as she continued to instruct me in the Laws of Creation, the great Laws that, combined with the constant observation of the self, lead to Mastery. I had been attending meetings at her house regularly, and during one meeting, she gave clear instruction on the meaning and power of the I AM. These two words, she taught, enable a person to be a conscious creator, rather than a victim of unconscious thought and speech, bringing into reality whatever one's attention is upon. *By this Word was made all that was made,* the book of Genesis said, and I saw now how that word, or rather words—I AM—worked to manifest one's thoughts.

In her living room I sat in rapt attention as Pearl spoke. "Understand who the *I* is, and you understand everything!" she began, pointing to her heart. "We are not talking about the ego, the *me*, the small, finite *I*, but *the infinite I*. This is not your personality claiming to be God. Rather, you are calling forth the limitless God of the Universe that has chosen to manifest as your Higher Self, available to you at every second once you surrender your need to control to that omniscient mind. It is accessible to you now and always through that soft, open spot near your heart.

"Again, ask, *who is it that says 'I'?* When I ask 'Who are you?' where does that question take you for an answer, to your head or your heart? Where do you access that *'I'*?"

I had never thought about it, but as I repeated *"I"* silently to myself and dove into my heart and felt the consciousness and energy that word invoked, I was drawn deeper into the core of my being.

I...
    I...
        I...

"You see?" Pearl said, pulling my attention back into the mundane reality of the room. "The *I* is the Source. Meditating on *I* takes you inward into the heart of your God Presence. That *I* is also an eye, the *Cosmic All-Seeing Eye* that sees all, knows all. By looking into that eye, you, too, can see all, know all.

"That *I* in your heart is the doorway into what is known as your third eye. This is the single, inner eye, of which your two physical eyes are an outer manifestation. It is through focusing on this third eye that great seers—or 'see-ers'—could see the future and the past, and travel in the timeless realm where all reality is accessible.

"Let thine eye be single, and thy whole body shall be filled with light, is written in the Bible. The 'single eye' Jesus was referring to is the same *eye* that is *the light that lighteth every man that cometh into the world*—the light that is the sun of God Within. Yes, you, too, are a sun of God, a *son* of God. *Know ye not that ye are Sons of God?* Jesus said.

"So, what is the I AM?" I asked Pearl. "Why not just meditate on the *I?*"

"Because I AM is the Christ, meaning God in form and action," Pearl continued. "You can meditate on yourself as *I* for eons and live in bliss in the Great Silence. But as soon as you say *I AM God,* you come forth into manifestation, consciousness in action. You begin to create, and whatever you focus on when using I AM, you call forth into existence by the power of your attention. And that attention, God in action, is creating all the time.

"You can withdraw from the world and enter a cave, as many do in India, retreating into the Great Silence, but when you do, external creation ceases and the human world dissolves. You are safe in your spiritual cocoon, but humanity falls into chaos around you. The path of the Masters is not to withdraw, but to come forth and engage with humanity, like all the great *Bodhisattvas* have done, choosing to remain in relative reality to help liberate others.

"Attention is the key. What you put your attention on, so you become. Your words guide your attention, and your attention guides your manifestation. *As you think, feel, and see, so shall it be.* For this reason, be careful what you ask for, what you say, for your words, thoughts, and feelings all bring about your creation.

"Furthermore, know that whatever you create, you are responsible for. Whatever you create comes back to you, and come back to you it will. Then you will have to deal with your creation. That is the Day of Judgment, when you survey all that you have created, not only in this life, but in every past life, and you judge what you have created and you judge yourself. You determine how you have used your free will, this great God Gift.

"How did I use my Divine power? Have I learned the lesson that I came to this dimension to learn? That is the question you will someday have to ask

yourself. That is the question that every human has to ask him or herself when their time is over on this Earth. *Did I learn the lesson I came to learn, and is there still something I don't know for which I want to re-embody?* And this lesson can only be learned in freedom, through the exercise of free will.

"The angels do not have free will. They are one with the will of God. But God created man with the free will to choose, to experiment with that freedom, and you are the living proof of that experiment. Who you are today, all that you encounter daily in your life, is a product of an experiment that you have been carrying on for eons. How long do you want to continue that experiment?

"*So where is my freedom?* you might ask. You don't feel free because you have limited your freedom in this life as a result of your choices in past lives. Consider the child whose mother gives him five dollars to go to the store to buy a loaf of bread, but on the way, before he can buy the bread, he buys candy. By the time he gets to the bakery, he no longer has enough money to buy the bread and goes home empty-handed. Then he wonders the next day at school why he does not have a sandwich. Why was his mother so unkind as not to make him a sandwich? Where was his free will then? He has to suffer the karma which he, himself, created—not as a punishment, but as the result of the cause and effect of his own actions.

"Why do you not live in a palace encrusted with jewels and filled with everything else you desire? It is because you have already squandered that wealth and have to make do with what is left. That is the story of humanity, for what you are experiencing today is the result of your past choices. So choose well what you do with your free will, the free will you have left over from your previous expenditures. At any moment, however, you can *arise and go unto the Father-Mother God*—the I AM Presence—and any perceived limitation can be transcended by that omnipresent power—that is, if you have learned your lesson and it is in your highest interest."

The room fell silent for moment, and I felt I was at a place where anything could be transcended, that my life could diverge into a completely different direction, based on the choice I made. By the use of the I AM, I knew I could change anything.

As if aware of my thoughts, Pearl said, "The Masters are watching you. They are observing your every thought and feeling, and responding to you on a higher level. They are helping you to understand and apply this great Law of Manifestation and to bring about the highest Divine Plan for your life.

"Remember, whatever you say with I AM, you start to create, to bring into the physical realm of existence. It may not happen immediately, but with those words, you set the process of manifestation into motion. It is a seed that needs to be nurtured, to be fed and reinforced. Even a baby takes nine months to create, so do not become frustrated if what you want does not come to pass immediately. It depends on how clearly you can maintain your focus without wavering or counteracting your decree with habitual thoughts, feelings, and words.

"How often I have seen people decree for something, and in the very next sentence say, 'Oh, it probably won't happen, anyway.' Well, of course it won't happen—their doubt just canceled their decree! Or you might make the mistake of telling a skeptical person about what you are trying to create, only to receive that person's negative reaction and begin to doubt yourself. Well, doubt is contagious, and it cancels whatever positive intent it contacts.

"More energy has to go into *creation* than *uncreation* for something to come into being. Even if you write an eloquent letter, if you don't put a stamp on the envelope, don't take it to the post office and drop it in the right slot, it doesn't arrive, does it? It's the same with decrees—you have to follow through and keep your creation moving without canceling the stamp before the letter is delivered."

"How often should I make a decree?" I asked. "I mean, if I'm trying to create something, how much time should I spend decreeing?"

"Not a moment passes that I am not decreeing," Pearl continued. "Jesus said, *'Pray without ceasing.'* Every breath, in fact, *is* a prayer. The inbreath says *I*, the outbreath, *am*. We are saying I AM constantly…God breathing through me, and I add my own creation to that breath: *I AM Love, God's love flowing through me…I AM Peace, God's peace established through me…I AM guided, moving at all times in the right direction…I AM the Healing Presence of God in Action, healing wherever I AM.*

"We are all creating every moment, with every breath we take and every word we say. The creative power of God cannot be shut off. We are creating every moment of our lives by our thoughts and feelings. Jesus affirmed this when he said, 'As ye think and feel, *so shall it be.*'

"But most people are unconscious, with no awareness of what they are creating, buffeted by circumstance, wondering why their lives are out of control. Identified with what they hear or see, reacting along with the mass unconsciousness—they can only decree more of the same into existence.

They are simply reinforcing the status quo, over and over again.

"At some point, when the pain gets too great, they will wake up and question their existence. *Why am I experiencing these things? Why am I suffering? How can I bring about change?* That is the point at which their growth begins, and they begin to take charge of their own creation.

"My daily mantra is *I AM holy, pure, and perfect.* That is what I am saying, thinking, and feeling, throughout the day on every breath, and so that is what I am becoming through the power of my attention: Holy, Pure, and Perfect. When I hear someone in trouble, I say, *I AM going forth to help that person*—meaning, my God Presence is going forth. *I AM God in action. I AM a God free being of love, a being of free dominion, and that is how I chose to exercise that dominion, by helping others.*"

As I strolled home from the meeting that night, I recalled how in India months before, Sai Baba had guided me to meditate on I AM, and since then all my questions had answered themselves.

I understood now why Sai Baba had refused to answer my questions about what to do with my life. Rather than always relying on his divinity, he wanted me to discover my own. That practice—of following my own inner promptings—had guided me to Muir Woods, to Saint Germain, and finally to Pearl's door—all through meditating on the reality behind those two innocent words: I AM.

Grateful for Pearl's patience with our small group, many of whom came down from the slopes of the Mountain several times a week to sit on her living room floor and hear her discourse, I took her teachings to heart. I intensified my practice and began to apply the Laws of Manifestation in my daily life, the consequences of which, though, were not always what I expected.

CHAPTER 10

To Manifest, or Not...

My stay at Gayle's house in Weed had been a temporary arrangement, and now as I accepted Mount Shasta as my new home, I was in need of a more permanent place to live. I decided to use the Laws of Creation that Pearl had been teaching me to manifest the perfect place.

Following what I had learned about attention, I began to visualize a cabin by a stream, with a large garden in which I could grow organic food. The cabin was in a remote mountain valley surrounded by forests, where I could meditate on the I AM, walk in the woods, and bathe in mountain streams. Since I didn't have a job, the rent would be low.

I held this vision of my cabin, thinking about it so clearly that I could see myself there already. I decreed silently, *I AM the Presence of God, bringing me this cabin immediately.* Three times a day, for about ten minutes, I stopped whatever I was doing, sat in a quiet place, meditated on that vision, and made the silent calls to my God Presence. Throughout the day I maintained the feeling that I would soon be living the good life in my mountain retreat—but told no one about my practices.

Two days into this process, a man came into Stephen's health food store where I had been helping out, and after a brief conversation, asked me, "By any chance, do you need a place to live? I'm staying at a ranch in a valley south of town, and there's a cabin by a stream where you could stay. You wouldn't need to pay rent, because the woman who owns the place is offering the place free to anyone who is on the spiritual path. She wants the place to be a spiritual commune."

In the '60s and '70s, that had been a common occurrence, people wanting their land used for a higher purpose, so now the offer of a free cabin seemed perfectly natural. Just as Pearl had taught, I had visualized what I wanted, knew that it was attainable, released the energy for it by my silent words of affirmation, and kept a positive feeling. Now I saw the proof that the Law worked.

The cabin was about an hour's drive from town, over back roads that led through National Forest into a hidden valley. It was small and cozy, just as I had imagined. A screened porch with rocking chairs overlooked a rushing stream. Inside there was a wood stove for cooking and warmth in the evening, and a stone's throw away, a garden had been prepared for planting by the couple that lived in the main house upstream. In my first meditation after moving in, I gave thanks to the great I AM that had brought my vision into manifestation.

All went well for a couple of weeks. Although I felt isolated from the community in town that was forming around Pearl, I couldn't think of a better place to meditate. Strangely, however, my meditations were unsatisfying, and at night my sleep was troubled.

Then one day, Pearl and Jerry paid me an unexpected visit. I wondered why she was there, as she never went anywhere, except under direction. In a roundabout way, Pearl began delivering her message, "I haven't been seeing much of you lately. Are you sure you are happy here?"

"Well, yes. I mean, I think so," I responded.

"You feel this is where you are meant to be? This is where the Masters want you to be?" Pearl asked, peering meaningfully into my eyes.

"Yes, it's perfect. It's exactly what I wanted. How could I find a better place than this?"

"Well, stay tuned in," Pearl said, pointing to her heart. "Something might change. It's awfully remote out here," she said, looking around at the broad valley and mountains that surrounded my retreat.

After Pearl and Jerry left, I thought: *That was strange. Why did she say that? I applied her teachings and got what I wanted. Was she implying now that I shouldn't be here?* But I decided to do as she said, ask what the Masters wanted, and be open to further guidance.

The next morning I woke up feeling suffocated. The cabin was hot and devoid of air. I went outside, but it was no better. The surrounding hills seemed confining, as if they were closing in on me and holding me captive. I couldn't see Mount Shasta from this small valley, and I felt cut off from the Mountain's energy. *I have to get out of here,* I thought, and threw my few possessions into my van and drove down the dirt road. I didn't feel better until I had left the valley and could see the Mountain again straight before me up the freeway.

Why had I been given that place if it was not where I was supposed to be? In a state of agitation, I drove straight to Pearl's house to ask her that very question.

"First of all," Pearl began, after I settled down in her living room in the chair across from her, "before I answer your question, I need you to come down out of your head. Shut the filing cabinet. Close the office door, and come down here," she said, pointing to her heart. "Come downstairs into the cathedral. Now, you and God are alone. Ask God that question, then be silent and hear what God has to say back to you."

I hadn't realized how mentally focused I had become in the ten days since I last meditated with Pearl, and now sighed with relief as my attention sank into my heart. *This is why you need to be in town,* I heard the voice of my I AM Presence say. *You need to be closer to Pearl, so you can receive the teachings for which I have brought you here....*

"Yes," said Pearl, echoing my own I AM Presence. "You need to be here, because the Masters are working through me to help you. Have you forgotten who brought you here, and for what purpose? Have you forgotten your commitment, your apprenticeship to Saint Germain?

"Also, you are part of the new community of seekers that is forming here in town, the Master's family that he is bringing together. They need you—you have a contribution—just as you need them. The Masters are bringing a group of students together here, to work with them in a more direct way, and that can only happen if you are here, part of the community."

I felt crushed. I had displeased the Master who had sent me here, whose direction I thought I was following. I thought he would be happy that I was using his teachings to manifest what I wanted.

"Why did Saint Germain let me have that cabin if it wasn't where he wanted me to be?" I complained, now more focused in my heart, but still confused.

"In the first place, did you ask him where you *should* be, or did you tell him instead where you *wanted* to be?" Pearl asked, a quizzical smile on her face.

As I tried to remember why I had magnetized the cabin retreat to my use, she continued: "There is a difference between *I* and *me*. The *I* is the Higher Self, the God Consciousness that is one with the Masters, and that knows the Divine Plan. The *me* is the lower self, the ego that acts only for its own wants and desires. The *I* is the permanent, eternal God Self. The *me* is the ego sense of self that dissolves at death, yet it is that lower self that runs most people's lives, and whose hold over your attention needs to be dissolved.

"As we attain enlightenment, the lower self begins to dissolve, like a salt crystal thrown into the ocean of eternity. The Higher Self, however, *is* eternal. If it were not so, creation would cease to exist. We are the Gods who are constantly creating and uncreating the universe. The source of everything is within us. If we cease to exist, then so does the universe. At death, it is only the ego that dies. Dissolving the limiting illusions of the lower self is the Great Work of the Ages, the *Alpha* and *Omega*—the beginning and the end of the spiritual path.

"The use of the Great Teachings to serve materialism has perverted the teaching down through the ages. Students of the Light learn the Laws of Manifestation and then are seduced by their power, using them solely to fulfill the desires of their lower nature, forgetting the source from whence everything comes. When those desires are imposed on others, it is called black magic, *the dark side of the Force* (*Star Wars,* Lucasfilm, Ltd.). To use the laws merely to fulfill personal fantasies is not only a waste of energy but takes the student backward along the evolutionary path. That is why the Masters say: *The greatest curse would be for us to let you attain all your desires, for after you get everything you think you want, then you would beg us for relief!*

"In the future, first ask what God wants, what the Masters want, and then use the Law to bring *that* into manifestation. Then I will not have to intervene on your behalf again."

"Intervene on my behalf?" I asked.

"Yes. The Master Saint Germain sent me yesterday to cut you free. There were forces in that valley of which you were unaware, and that were holding you there."

"What kind of forces?" I asked, recalling the suffocating feeling I'd had that morning.

"There were elemental forces of Nature that were using you, magnetizing you to that location. Of course, the greatest force was your own desire to pursue a carefree existence, free from responsibility. Without that desire, the other forces would have had no power. I had to use the *Sword of Blue Flame* to cut you free."

"Sword of Blue Flame!" I exclaimed. "What's that?"

"It's the sword of Archangel Michael—a sword of blue light that cuts through thought forms and severs human attachments. Hold out your hand," she commanded. "Now, ask Archangel Michael to give you his sword. Feel it in the palm of your hand. It is made of blue light, and from it emanates a humming sound like that of high voltage electricity. Grasp it in your hand and swing it over your head three times, cutting away anything that restricts your freedom. Then release it into the air, allowing it to return to Archangel Michael—and thank him for its use. But remember, use it only to bring freedom, for it has tremendous power and can also cause harm when people are not yet ready for that freedom.

I did as Pearl said, asking Archangel Michael for his sword, and instantaneously feeling the sword's energy and power. But I was puzzled.

"Harm me? How could light harm me?" I asked Pearl.

"By causing you to face something you are not yet ready to deal with—to come face to face with your own negative creation. Few realize the extent to which their reality is held together by illusion. If they dissolve that illusion too suddenly, their world falls apart, like taking away the crutches too soon from an invalid just starting to walk.

"Few people are ready to see the darkest parts of their own nature, their own demons, all at once. Better to work on clearing your field slowly. That is why I always use the Violet Consuming Flame first, visualizing violet light around me or around a person or situation, dissolving and consuming all negativity in a harmonious manner. Unlike the Violet Consuming Flame, the Sword of Blue Flame cuts quickly; its action is sudden and unpredictable.

"I still don't understand. How could the Sword of Blue Flame, which is just light, cause harm?" I asked, confused.

"Just light?" Pearl retorted, shocked at my question. "Light is the self-intelligent, conscious substance of which all creation is composed. Your thoughts affect that light, and that light affects seeming matter, which is itself a vibratory rate of the light substance. So your thoughts affect everything around you, even all creation.

"Whatever thought you send out, positive or negative," Pearl warned, "goes through *you* first. It affects your emotions, the cells of your body, your blood, bones, organs, and your entire life, before it goes forth and affects another. What you are decreeing or even thinking about, you are also bringing upon yourself. So, only use the Sword of Blue Flame if you are prepared for it to cut through your world first. You never know what it will bring up, what the final result will be, for the sword's action is to sever every negative structure, sometimes the very structure, whether physical, emotional, or mental, that is holding your illusory existence together. If you are going to liberate someone from what you perceive has been holding them back, make sure they are ready to move forward and can take their new freedom. When Jesus said, 'I come not to bring peace, but a sword,' this is the sword to which he was referring, the sword that brings wisdom and freedom out of chaos. So, use it wisely."

I was beginning to understand that there was no separation between myself and others, since on some level we were all One, and that I needed to be more aware of my thoughts and become less critical of what I perceived as others' shortcomings.

"Do not think you can wield these spiritual tools with impunity," Pearl continued. "As I said, whatever thought and feeling you send out affects you first, then impacts the world around you. But that is not the end of the matter, for that energy has a magnetic quality. It gathers like energy to itself and then returns to its source like a boomerang, amplified ten-fold. Thus, I recommend you only send out what you are ready to receive—for receive it you will.[11]

"Be master of your attention. Some people say it is good to express your anger. Well, that may be true in therapy, but if you go around in daily life expressing anger, you will eventually perceive the whole world as angry. The more you dwell on that anger, the worse it becomes, for what your attention is on, you become. Your own emotions return to you amplified, to the point where anger is all you know. Far better to use the Violet Consuming Flame to dissolve all cause, effect, memory, and record of it—and be free forever. When that flame is working, however, do not be surprised if those negative conditions intensify at first, for when the light is working, all that has been in darkness comes into the light, into your conscious awareness, so that you can learn from it before the illusion dissipates. That is where your meditation comes in, so that you can observe these phenomena, see that they are not real, and free yourself from them.

"There is no shortcut. No one is going to achieve mastery for you. That is why it is called *self-mastery*. You must achieve it yourself. Self-mastery is the only way to be free."

Pearl paused for a minute to let her words sink in, then winked at me and said, "Next time, be more careful when you decide to create something. Welcome home!"

---

11 Those who use this Law to impose their own will for selfish ends are practicing black magic, and will suffer the consequence of seeing their own freedom dissipated.

Chapter 11

The Uncreated Restaurant

I had learned an important lesson. Because I had found the Inner Power and learned to create with it, that didn't mean I *should*. I had magnetized a secluded cabin for my use, yet it had not suited my higher purpose and I had needed to let it go. I now realized I needed to learn to direct that power wisely, to ask for guidance before invoking more phenomena. I remembered the words of F. Scott Fitzgerald: "The victor belongs to the spoils." What we create owns a part of us. As one becomes magnetic, one needs to become ever more careful about the subject of one's thoughts, for they will manifest.

Yet I was still eager, like a fledgling trying its wings for the first time, and I soon forgot Pearl's words of warning. I yearned for the opportunity to work magic again, to create what I wanted, although I knew I should consult my Higher Self before I exercised that power. Were the creative urges coming from my Higher Self or ordinary desire? It takes years of meditation on the Higher Self to develop that inner magnetic sense that guides one infallibly, that distinguishes true from false, inner direction from self-delusion. Before that discriminating flame has been developed, the mental voice of the lower self often misleads—the same lower self that psychic channels often think is the voice of another, higher, being. So, I decided to restrict my efforts to creating only that which would benefit others—and avoid further chastisement.

I soon found an inexpensive place to live in town and continued to help Stephen out at the juice bar in his health food store. One day he confided that he wanted to start a natural food café in the space adjoining the store. Since there was nothing like that in town, I knew it would be an instant success.

"If only I had the money," he said, wistfully, "I'd do it in a flash."

Since Stephen had been the one to send me to Pearl and also knew the Laws of Manifestation, I proposed we create what was needed using the methods of visualization and qualification we had learned. I was excited by the opportunity to again manifest something, this time something that would help others, and besieged him to invoke the Divine Power.

"Why don't we make the calls and do the decrees? I bet we can manifest the money we need in no time," I encouraged.

"Yeah, but we'd also need someone to draw up plans, get a building permit, and find a good carpenter," Stephen replied without enthusiasm.

"I bet we could find people to do that," I said, encouragingly.

"Well, then we'd need waitresses and a lot of other people…."

"What do we have to lose by trying?" I asked, oblivious to his resistance and not taking into account that his reluctance might be coming from his own inner guidance. In my excitement, I could only see the vision of the completed restaurant, how it would be a tremendous benefit to health-conscious people coming to town who didn't want to eat at the local steak houses. I was certain it would be a tremendous success.

"Go for it," he finally said, giving in. "If you want to start decreeing, be my guest."

I had not yet learned to listen to others so that I could hear what they were truly saying, a deafness that would later take many years of being in relationship to begin to remedy. So, without waiting for a second invitation, I went into the adjoining room that would be the new restaurant and entered into meditation. I began to see the restaurant so vividly I could smell the food cooking and see appreciative customers sitting at every table. With my own God Power flowing through me, I began to decree, every charged word going forth through the responsive ethers to do my bidding:

I AM the Commanding, Governing Presence of God, bringing into full manifestation all that is required to start a restaurant at this location, right now.

I continued this decree, not only calling for the money, but also for the architect, carpenters, and waitresses necessary to manifest the restaurant. Then I let the idea go and went back to work, too busy for the rest of the day to think about my visualization again. The next day I was also busy, waiting on customers, making sandwiches, and squeezing carrot juice until late in the afternoon. Then a young man came into the store and walked around for a minute, as if checking to see if he belonged here.

"This feels like a good place," he said, seating himself at the juice bar. "I met Pearl yesterday, and I like this scene. I want to be a part of what's happening in this town. Do you know of any projects I could invest in?" he asked.

I wasn't surprised when his next words were, "You see, I just inherited some money, and I'm looking for a project I can get involved in."

I promptly told him about the restaurant *we* were creating, and he responded with excitement, "That's exactly what I'm looking for! How much do you need?"

"Oh, I guess about $250,000 to get started," I said, pulling a figure out of the air, "Maybe more later on."

"No problem, I can swing that. Sounds like just what I'm looking for." Then he handed me a slip of paper with his phone number and asked me to call him.

That evening when Stephen came in to close up the store, I could hardly wait to tell him the news, "The natural food restaurant is happening—we have the money!"

I told him about the stranger's offer, but he didn't seem happy. "Well, we still need an architect to draw up the plans. Then we need to get them approved by the Planning Commission, find a manager, waitresses, and stuff…" he continued. "It's not just the money; there's a lot of work in starting a restaurant…."

Crestfallen, but still determined, I went home that night and decreed for everything on Stephen's list of requirements.

The next day, all the required personnel came into the store and offered exactly what was needed. A man who had just graduated from architecture school the month before said that designing a restaurant would give him practice and would look good on his resume—so he wouldn't charge. A restaurant manager, who had just left her job in San Francisco to move to the country, said she would love to be our new manager. Two girls came in, and when I told them about the waitress job, said, "Cool…that would be perfect! When do we start?" Finally, at the end of the day, a man pulled up in front of the store with a van full of power tools. When he came inside, he said that since he had just finished a good paying job, he would be happy to donate his time to work on something that would benefit the community. Building a natural foods restaurant was the perfect project, and he was eager to begin. Everyone seemed to feel the excitement of my vision, and wanted to get started.

But my success didn't excite Stephen. Quite the contrary, his face clouded over when I told him what was happening, and he said, "Peter, I hope you didn't think I was serious when I said I wanted to start a restaurant? That takes way too much time. I've got my hands full just with the store. When I'm not running the store, I'm driving places to pick up produce or at home doing bookkeeping. But thanks anyway for trying."

"What!" I exclaimed. I couldn't believe he was turning down his dream that was now coming true, handed to him on a silver platter. "I spent hours decreeing for this; now you don't want to do it?"

"Sorry, guy…but, thanks for trying," he said, as he headed for the door, head bowed in regret over my wasted effort.

Try? I thought. *I didn't try—I succeeded!* In two days, I had brought together everything that was needed to start the new restaurant—and now it was not going to happen. I had brought Stephen's dream into manifestation, but he no longer wanted it. I was forlorn over my wasted effort. But Stephen knew, I later realized, how much work running a restaurant would have been. I was good at creating, but did not want to sign up for a daily routine.

I spent the next two days uncreating the restaurant—trying to free my mind of the vision, releasing the energy I had set in motion and telling those who had volunteered that the restaurant was not happening, and they shared my disappointment. The vision that I thought Stephen shared, that I thought was coming from guidance, I saw now had only been my ego, once again, wanting to flex its new-found abilities.

When I told Pearl how I had tried to help Stephen manifest his dream, she said, "Yes, that's a hard lesson to learn—when to intercede for someone and when to remain silent. The Masters say, *The greatest challenge for us is watching you suffer and not being able to interfere.* Free will is sacred. The Masters must let us experience the consequences of our actions, and not push us into something before we are ready. That is the only way we learn."

Pearl went on to tell me about a woman who had visited her recently, who said she wanted a piano.

"Do you really want a piano? Pearl asked.

"Yes."

"Really? I need a definite answer before I do the decree. I got someone a piano once, and then when it arrived at their door, they said they didn't have a place to put it. Do you have a place to put this piano?"

"Umm…well, I'm just house-sitting for a friend right now. Maybe someday I'll have my own place."

"That's what I thought," Pearl said. "You don't want a piano, and I'm not going to waste my time helping you get one!" Pearl had learned over the years not to be so hasty in trying to fulfill others' ephemeral wishes.

Once again, I learned that just because we *can* accomplish something does not mean we *should*. My experiment with the restaurant, however, was not wasted, for I learned that once the God Power is focused, it can accomplish anything. I had been able to create a cabin in a mountain paradise and now a restaurant, both without needing any money. Neither was inspired by guidance, but from my ego's desire to stay in control of my new spiritual awareness, to usurp the spirit for its own materialistic ends. I was like a child with a new toy. In the bigger scheme, neither of my creations was meant to be, and dissolved back into the void of infinite possibilities—a place that held limitless seductive attractions that could keep one busy for many lifetimes.

Out of these experiences I began to wonder—*Is there a greater plan for my life? Or has my life been a result purely of my own choices?* I thought of my aunt and uncle who had given me the money that financed my trips to India. *Had I consciously invoked their generosity, or were they following an unknown plan that was meant to be?* I pondered on how I had arrived here in Mount Shasta. *Was it through my own efforts that I had met Saint Germain? Hardly.*

No, I had to admit, none of these blessings was the result of my own efforts. It was through following my heart, listening to the calling that I realized now was coming from my I AM Presence, and passing through the doors as they opened that I had arrived here—at this pivotal point in my life. My perceived plans, needs, and desires seemed to have nothing to do with my being here.

Now I no longer wanted to create confusion by using God-given powers to fulfill transitory desires. I wanted to become a conscious, God-directed actor in the drama for which it seemed my role had already been written. The job was to develop the awareness of my magnetic center, the tangible presence of the God Flame within, so that I could follow its direction infallibly. In turning my authority over to the Flame of the Higher Self and maintaining that focus, I knew the ego's hold would gradually diminish.

I thought of the saying in the Bible, *If ye had sufficient faith, ye could move mountains.* But it was also said that if you had that much faith you would know that the mountains were already where they were supposed to be. Why waste energy trying to move them? Why waste energy creating projects that were not meant to be? There are better things on which to focus attention, I concluded, such as dissolving the emotional, reactive

Apprentice to the Masters

memory, and cutting through the ego's illusion that it knows something—following, instead, the path of service the Masters laid out.

We have been given *dominion over the birds of the air and beasts of the field,* the Bible said, but I was now realizing the responsibility that entailed. We are part of a great web of life that is interconnected, and whatever we do to a part of that web comes back to us with often unanticipated, sometimes unwelcome, consequences.

I saw that Mastery consisted not in manifesting personal desires, but in learning to act in accord with Divine Desire, to bring about the Plan in which I was becoming a conscious participant. With this new awareness of the bigger picture, I chose now to heed Pearl's words more closely, *Be careful what you choose to create!*

Chapter 12

Love, Sex, and a Vow

Immersed in meditation one morning, Pearl and I were disturbed by a knock at the door. Gloria, a red-headed girl who had moved to town from New Jersey recently, burst into the living room, threw herself into a chair, and sobbed to Pearl, "What have you done to my husband?"

"What do you mean?"

"I want to know what's going on here—what are you doing that my husband finds so irresistible. What do you want with him?"

"I have no interest in your husband," Pearl replied, "I have one of my own."

"Then why is my husband up here at your house every spare minute? I make love to him every way I can think of, but as soon as he can get out of the house, he comes up here to be with you. What is it that you do?" the girl pleaded.

"Maybe he wants *this,*" Pearl said, pointing to her heart.

"What?" Gloria responded, her eyes widening.

"The Pure Christ Love," Pearl replied, sending a beam of that very love to the girl's heart.

"Give me a break!" the girl exclaimed. "You expect me to believe that? He doesn't believe in Jesus, he's not into religion. You've put some kind of spell on him."

"As I said," Pearl repeated, "what he feels here is the Pure Christ Love, and no amount of romance or sex can replace that. The Christ Light is the energy of the male and female joined together in the heart, the *marriage made in heaven* that depends on no outer condition—the love that is independent of and precedes all outer relationship. Once someone awakens into that love, all human activity becomes secondary. That is why your husband comes here, because he feels that light which nurtures the Christ within him."

Gloria's eyes opened wider, as though she had been hit by a brick. "What!" she exclaimed, speechless. As she began to feel the love Pearl was transmitting, her anger abated and she leaned forward, "How did you do that? Is that love something I can learn?"

"Turn your attention inward," Pearl said, again pointing to her heart.

"Feel in that soft, vulnerable place within you, that is the center of your being, the love that is always there. Feel the love of the Divine Presence that has been waiting, waiting, waiting throughout the ages for you to turn your attention to It, wondering how long you will give energy to outer people, places, conditions, and things—waiting for you to give your obedience to It. That is the Christ Light, and that is what your husband is after."

As Gloria began to feel the spark Pearl had kindled in her heart, she relaxed in her chair and her eyes closed. I watched, amazed, as the girl's breathing softened and her face became radiant as an angel. In a minute, serenely, she opened her eyes, which were filled with tears.

"Now I understand why he's been spending so much time with you," she sighed. "This is what I want, too. I want to know how to do what you do."

"It is so simple," Pearl said with sadness. "But so few want this truth. So few are willing to give up pursuing outer things long enough to calm down, be still, and know I AM God."

Gloria's outburst still fresh in my mind, and curious about the Masters' teaching on relationship, love, and sex, I asked Pearl the next day to tell me more about how these powerful drives affect the spiritual path. Referring to what had happened the day before, Pearl said, "Jealousy is a poison, and it comes from not knowing who you are, of thinking that your Source is in someone else, of not feeling the source of happiness within yourself.

That ignorance of the Presence," Pearl continued, "is what leads people mistakenly to think that through relationship they can find what they lack, rather than finding completion within. Once one has found the bliss of union with God, no sex or outer romance can hold one's attention for long, for the all-consuming romance is with one's I AM, the God Presence.

"Furthermore, the feeling that one's mate is a possession destroys not only the relationship but also obstructs progress on the spiritual path for both. True love can take place only in freedom. Freedom does not mean the liberty to follow your passions of the moment, but the free dominion that comes from following and being obedient to your own God Source. For both partners to support each other in that quest is the ideal human relationship.

"If you only knew how many married people come to me and say,

'Oh, if I could only be single, then I would make such spiritual progress.' And the single ones come and say, 'Oh, if only I had a partner, then I would be happy.'

"You cannot avoid your feelings. You cannot avoid your passions. No matter what you do, they will come to the surface and influence your thoughts, words, and actions. You can be a yogi in a cave for a while, and because you don't see your delusions any more, think they are gone, but when you return to the world, they will reassert themselves. Better to be in the world and face your miscreated energy with the light of conscious awareness. That is why relationship can be the fast path, because your partner is your mirror—to show you where the real work is.

"Sometimes you may be in relationship, sometimes alone," Pearl continued, "both are appropriate for different times of one's development. But either way, you need to take responsibility for your feelings. Only you are responsible for your own thoughts, emotions, and actions, not anyone else. So, the source of your happiness and freedom is not in someone else, but in yourself. You came into the world alone and you leave the world alone. You can walk with another only part of the way. Make that walk be into the light, where you help each other attain self-mastery."

Pearl's brief talk on relationship only partially answered my questions, still leaving me in the dark as to how I should personally relate to the women coming to town for her teachings and who looked to me for guidance. I was spending a lot of time in their company and wanted to know how I should relate to them in light of my recent commitment to attain self-mastery.

I had not thought much about male-female relationships during the past two years, as I had been traveling in India, where traditionally men and women only entered into relationship under the guidance of a guru or family, and then only for the purpose of marriage and raising children. It was refreshing to be around women who, unlike in the West, where women are encouraged to be seductive, did not project their sexuality, where encounters were guided by traditional roles of mother, daughter, sister, and aunt, rather than by unrestrained animal urges. I was grateful for this more traditional system, as it left my attention unencumbered and free, resting in my center, rather than in another's.

Now I discovered abruptly that most women my age seemed to be searching for romance and instant intimacy. It was the '70s, and society condoned sexual freedom and experimentation, but I was reluctant to follow that trend as I had during my days as a poet in New York. I wanted to receive guidance from a source higher than animal instinct.

My uncertainty came to a head when I met Cassie, a direct and energetic girl who came to see Pearl frequently. We hiked on the Mountain and went swimming in glacial streams, becoming good friends as we discussed Pearl's teachings and the Masters. Soon, however, I became increasingly aware of her feminine beauty and vibrant energy which seemed to enfold me—and I wondered how to deal with this rekindled energy that had been so long slumbering during my wanderings as a yogi.

What do the Masters want me to do about sex?

One night, after Cassie and I had been hiking in the mountains all day, we ended up sleeping at Gayle's house in Weed. She gave us the same room that was through the back of a closet, where I had spent my first night in Mount Shasta and Pearl had taken me above the Mountain in my etheric body. Although in separate sleeping bags, I kept finding that Cassie and I had snuggled close. But as we were about to touch, each time there was a flash of light between us that caused us to separate.

Tired from this struggle lasting most of the night, I rose in the morning, exhausted, and left as soon as I could. Confused, I went to Pearl's house, seeking guidance. As was frequently the case, there was a group in the living room, so I went around back and sat on a stone bench in the garden to ponder. I knew that my reluctance to be physically intimate had disappointed Cassie, and I had felt her anger when I left, but now that I was also in relationship with Saint Germain, and accepted as an apprentice, I felt it more important not to disappoint him. I did not want to commit an irrevocable act without his approval, and I asked for guidance. *What should I do about Cassie? Should I go with the flow, as everyone else seems to be doing?*

I had just sat down on the bench when Pearl surprised me, rushing out the kitchen door with an open book in her hand, which she placed in my lap.

"You need to read this," she said, and without another word, turned and went back into the house to rejoin the group she had left in mid-sentence.

I looked at the book, *After the Order of Melchizedek: The Kingly Meditation of Righteousness and Peace,* and instantly recalled that I'd seen that awe-inspiring title once before. It had been in Santa Fe, in the back of a health food store during my journey across the country in my old Dodge van. When I pulled it off the shelf, a violet light had encircled my hand, and I remembered *Unveiled Mysteries,* the book I had encountered at the Theosophical Society in India, which spoke of the purifying effect of the *Violet Consuming Flame.* But I had not been ready for its simple truth. I was sure that anything powerful had to be more complicated. As I was trying to save money, I didn't buy the Melchizedek book. Instead, I went to the library and borrowed a copy of *Unveiled Mysteries,* reading it cover to cover in a single night. I was unable to put it down. When asking Saint Germain to show if he was real and the book true, the room filled with violet light. I took that to mean *yes.* I made a note to go back and get the other book I had seen in the health food store, but never did so.

Now, here it was. Pearl had just put the book I had last seen in Santa Fe in my lap. *But what is the Order of Melchizedek?* This mysterious book's appearance at this moment seemed uncanny. It seemed this book had some part to play in my destiny, as it had been instrumental once before in guiding my path.

Staring at the page to which Pearl had the book open, I could hardly believe the words that seemed an answer to my question. In life there are two orders of existence, the book said: Those of the first, the *Order of Generation,* marry, have children, and serve life through the propagation of humanity; those of the second, the *Order of Regeneration,* conserve their life force and use it for their regeneration and spiritual service. The latter is the work of the Order of Melchizedek, which has two requirements for admission. The first requirement is celibacy, which conserves and circulates the life force to resurrect the body, and the second is unwavering dedication to the upliftment of humanity.

The book went on to quote the Bible, citing Revelation 22:2:

And he showed me a pure river of water of life, clear as crystal, proceeding out of the throne of God and of the Lamb. In the midst of the stream of it, and on either side of the river, was there the Tree of Life, which bore twelve manner of fruit and yielded her fruit every month. And the leaves of the tree were for the healing of the nations. And they shall see his face, and his name shall be in their foreheads. And there shall be no night there, and they need no candle, neither light of the sun, for the Lord God giveth them light, and they shall reign forever and ever.

The book interpreted this passage to mean that every month, the Tree of Life, which is the nervous system of the body, receives energy from the sign of the zodiac through which the sun is traveling that month. By conserving that energy through celibacy, all the organs of the body—the nations—are healed and energized. This conserved energy enables one to be conscious of the I AM, and the light that shines from the forehead through the third eye of an enlightened person—allowing them to perceive truth directly without any external need for illumination.

The book that had just been placed in my hands went on to say that by conserving the life force through celibacy, one can resurrect the body and Ascend, as did Jesus—who was an initiate of this order, of which Melchizedek was high priest. Melchizedek, not born of earthly parents, came to Earth to teach humanity the path to redemption and liberation. The order of righteousness which he established was kept alive through the ages to the time of Jesus and on inner planes to the present day. It was also said that all those who kept the two main precepts—celibacy and the dedication to serve humanity, were similarly initiates of this ancient, sacred Order.

According to this secret doctrine, I was already a member of the Order of Melchizedek, as I had been celibate for two years and dedicated to serve humanity since my encounter with Saint Germain in Muir Woods. But now I made a formal vow to serve the Order of Melchizedek and keep its commandments. I knew that to earn the trust of the Masters, and to continue meriting further teaching by Pearl, I had to adhere strictly to this vow. I could not serve two masters, my human passions and the Masters.

Now I had my answer about how to respond to Cassie's increasing affection, hoping that we could continue as friends. What I did not realize was that my dedication to celibacy would be severely tested, as I tried to adhere to this new requirement. I soon found that when I asked to know the truth of a matter it would soon be shown to me, and that then I was expected to act accordingly. The lesson came first, then the test. Once shown the truth, I could no longer plead ignorance.

The initial test came two nights later, when Cassie, having temporarily forgiven my abstinence, invited me to go camping with her on the Mountain. She took me to her favorite place, a location I later learned was near an etheric entrance to the Masters' retreat inside the Mountain. After arranging our sleeping bags a few feet apart, we drifted off. As during the previous night, Cassie snuggled close to me and I was awakened by an explosion of light that forced us apart. This time, however, rather than struggle all night, I had the sense to move my sleeping bag a few feet away, and slept soundly the rest of the night. In the morning I explained to Cassie what had been revealed to me sitting in Pearl's garden the previous day, and that I had taken a vow of celibacy.

"That's ridiculous! Why would God have created us with those organs if we weren't to use them?" she exclaimed, with near irrefutable logic. As I tried to explain what I had learned about conserving the life force and instead of dissipating it, using it for spiritual awakening, she scoffed, "I've got plenty of life force, for sex as well as spirit. In fact, I think sex is spiritual."

Realizing there was no point in arguing, I confessed that this was the path I had chosen and asked her to respect my vow.

"Another good man out of circulation," she retorted, her face red with anger. Descending the Mountain, I realized that our adventures together were ending. Although we would remain casual friends, it was not for many years that we would become friends again—when she was a married woman.

Celibacy, I discovered later, while being required of me at that time as part of my apprenticeship, is only one path of spiritual evolution and certainly not right for everyone. In the years to come, I would learn that there are other ways that the life force could be conserved and directed within relationship, for spiritual evolution and service—through a path just as difficult in its own way—a discipline thoroughly explored by ancient Taoist and Tantric practitioners. However, feeling I had received the final word that morning in Pearl's garden, I professed my certainty to others that this was the only path to Mastery—a certainty that would be often tested.

Chapter 13

Thy Will, Not Mine

Although the next day started like any other, I became aware all day of an energy building that finally came to a head around midday—that would be a turning point in my relationship to my God Self and my apprenticeship to the Masters.

During my time in India, my path had been one of surrender, seeing life as *maya,* a dream whose dreamer was God and over which I had no control—so I had tried to free myself of attachment to any particular outcome of that dream. As Buddha said, "All suffering comes from desire." *No desire, no suffering.* So I tried to surrender my desires.

After studying with Pearl, I saw the path differently, that I could awake within the dream by realizing that I was the dreamer, the I AM Presence, which was the source of my life and how it was manifesting—and that as I drew closer to that Presence, I could become a conscious, free being, also able to free others.

Such a responsibility was not to be taken lightly. I had learned the laws of creation, but had also seen the discord caused by willfulness—the casual use of that universal force for purely personal satisfaction. There were many teachers in the West giving workshops on how to create whatever you want, but they were not teaching how to discern what that is. *What do you really want—temporary things to amuse, of which you will soon tire and you will want to rid yourself of?* I was beginning to see that very few really know what they want, and *If you don't know what you want, how can you attain it?*

Creating was easy; knowing what to create was more difficult. I felt torn between what appeared to me to be two opposing views: one of learning not to be attached to whatever happened, that everything was all right since life was just the working out of karmic cause and effect; the other view was to dissolve karma through the use of the Violet Consuming Flame, and combined with self-observation, attain a state of freedom where I could use my free will to create the life I wanted. *But how do I know what to create, that what I bring into manifestation will not have karmic repercussions that will come back for me to deal with and again dissolve?*

Sitting at a table in the corner of Stephen's juice bar, it suddenly dawned on me that both views were right, both facets of the same diamond. Like the blind men in the parable, who each examined a different part of the elephant, each unable to visualize the whole being, my confusion was coming from the blindness of trying to think with the limited mind. *Mastery lies in both the passive and active principles working together: surrender, yes, not to karmic inevitability, but to my own I AM Presence, the source sustaining and creating my life afresh every moment—my own all-knowing Master Presence.*

The sword of discriminating intelligence cut through my confusion, and as I felt my Presence draw near in confirmation, I said,

Thy will, not my will, be done!

My path, I saw, lay in learning to tune in to that Presence at every moment, to transcend human error through surrender to that Higher Mind—a solution so obvious that I already knew the answer, but which I saw now with the immediacy of revelation. Why hadn't I realized this before? I don't need to do anything—*the action to take is no action!* All I need to do is watch and wait, and the path I am to follow will emerge.

Feeling immense relief, I leaned back in my chair, breathing deeply, realizing that *there is nothing I have to do.* I vowed not to move so much as a step from the table of my own volition, but to wait until I could feel God moving in me—every step, every word, every action that of my I AM Presence within. I didn't expect God to appear in a whirling cloud or pillar of fire, or to hear His booming voice from above telling me where to go and what to do. But I trusted that if I sat still and focused my attention on my heart, I would feel the Presence guiding me what to do.

Like the characters in Beckett's play, *Waiting for Godot,* I, too, was waiting…except, unlike them, I had already met the Master, and felt the reality of my own I AM Presence that was one with that Master—so at least I knew that what I was waiting for was real. *But what form will the guidance take? Will it come through a person, or simply an inner feeling?* Like Beckett's characters, I, too, wondered if I would recognize what I was waiting for when it did arrive, or would the opportunity pass me by while my mind was absorbed in itself?

Hours went by, people came and went, but nothing happened. No Master arrived to tell me what to do, no person sat down at my table with a suggestion that triggered a response, I heard no inner voice, felt no inner push to pursue any course of action. I just sat and waited, staring at the stain on the table, hoping that like some Rorschach inkblot, some meaning or clue as to what I should do might emerge, but it remained just a stain. I overheard conversations, people talking about events in the area, but nothing inspired me or stirred me to action. I kept asking God to show me what to do, silently repeating over and over to myself,

I AM the Presence of God. I AM God Directed and God Commanded. God within is showing me where to go and what to do—and I AM doing it.

But still, nothing happened. After a few hours, my patience began to give way to despair. *Has God forgotten me? Is he too busy attending to serious events, earthquakes, disasters, saving people seriously in need, to deal with my comparatively petty demand for direction?*

In the midst of my musing, I overheard a conversation that finally sparked my interest. Two people were talking about a Renaissance Fair in Ashland, a town in Oregon an hour's drive to the north. I knew immediately, *that's it!* I felt an energy pulse in my heart and automatically rose to my feet. Though I had no interest in Renaissance Fairs, seeing people dress in medieval costumes, and listening to Elizabethan music, there was an energy propelling me forward which I knew was my long-awaited guidance.

Now my path of surrender and action united in a form—a force pulling me where I knew not, a path which could only be followed one step at a time as it revealed itself—my own unique path which no one could walk for me.

Since that day, I have found that as I follow that path of trust, all doors open at the right time. If not, then it is the wrong door. Although it has not been easy, since that time I've always had the sense of being at the right place at the right time. If I don't know the next step, I do what I did that day in the juice bar—sit down and wait. Patience, Pearl used to say, is a virtue, and the one that I most needed to learn—one that can only be acquired through meditation and self-observation.

As I rose from the table, following my pull toward Oregon, I felt I'd be gone for more than a day and would need a new sleeping bag and futon to replace the old ones that had fallen apart. On my way out of the store, a woman entered the foyer where a "free box" was placed for people to donate discarded items. She was carrying a sleeping bag and a thin, collapsible futon that she was about to donate, but placed instead in my outstretched arms. My journey had begun auspiciously, the two things I needed just given to me—and free! I walked out the door, freeing myself from my self-imposed captivity like a butterfly struggling free of its cocoon, empowered by my insight and curious to see where my new path led. I knew I was beginning a strange adventure, the first of many on which the Masters would send me.

Arriving in Ashland an hour and a half later, as I waited for a traffic light to change, a man who looked like El Morya, *Chohan* (Sanskrit: Spiritual Lord) of the First Ray, dressed in white with a turban on his head, crossed the street in front of the van, and without a moment's hesitation walked up to my open window.

"I don't know why I'm doing this," he said. "It's not something I've done before—but if you need a place to stay tonight, you're welcome at my house." He wrote his address hurriedly on a slip of paper, handed it to me, and crossed to the other side of the street. The light changed and I drove away, shocked that the Masters had provided for me in such an unusual way. *Who could have planned that? But was I really supposed to stay with a stranger?*

I turned left in the center of town to the park where the Renaissance Fair was being held, but found nothing that drew my attention. I kept trying to feel the guidance in my heart, affirming, *I AM God directed and God commanded,* then headed back to my van. Once inside, unsure what to do next, my habitual thoughts and doubts began to haunt me. I couldn't get the thought of that stranger in white out of my mind. *What am I supposed to do, go to the home of someone I met on the street?* It seemed incredible, but I couldn't think of anything else. It was getting dark and I needed a place to stay and didn't have much money, so I decided to trust in what it seemed the Masters had provided. It was like the old days after coming home from India, driving across the country, staying at the communes, where every day I was magically invited.

As dusk settled on the town and the street lights came on, I drove to the address the man in white had written. He and his wife welcomed me warmly, and we sat in the kitchen of their home, drinking hot Red Zinger tea, sharing our lives—trying to figure out what our connection might be. It turned out we had friends in common in Mount Shasta, and the longer we talked, the more we all seemed like family. Over a dinner of rice and sautéed vegetables, I told them about Pearl. When they later went to visit her, they had an experience that changed their lives forever. Perhaps for no other purpose than to connect them to Pearl was reason enough for us having been brought together. Over the next few years I visited them often, and we had many long nights around the wood stove, during which we shared our realizations about the workings of this great law of the I AM.

That night, before falling asleep on their living room sofa, I turned my attention to the Masters and to my own I AM God Presence, and asked to be shown what to do next:

Beloved I AM Presence and Great Host of Ascended Masters, please come forth tonight and reveal to me where I am to go and what I am to do tomorrow. See to it that when I awaken, I know beyond the shadow of a doubt!

During the night, I dreamed of a woman I had met in Mount Shasta many months before. In the dream, she was now standing in front of me, inviting me to her home in Oregon near Mount Hood, saying that she was confused and had many questions she needed answered. Although I didn't remember her last name or have her address or phone number, I trusted that when I got to Mount Hood, if that is really where I was to go, the Masters would guide me to her.

After saying goodbye to my new family in Ashland, I got into my van and headed north. Approaching Mount Hood at twilight, I began to feel the urge to slow down. Pulling off the road to tune in to my heart for guidance, I heard, *Go back*.

I turned around and headed south again. Feeling better, I knew that was a sign I was headed in the right direction. Then I heard, *Drive slowly*, and a short way down the road, *Stop!*

At a dirt road joining the main road a car was stopped, waiting for an opening in the traffic. Looking out through the windshield as though waiting for me was the woman by whom I had been summoned in the dream. Our eyes met instantly, and we both got out of our cars.

"I am so glad to see you," she said. "I tried to write you a letter inviting you to visit us but I didn't have your address. We need to know more about the Masters. Pearl got us interested and we read her books, but we're confused about how to apply the teachings. I prayed to the Masters for help and know they have sent you. Please come home and be our guest."

That evening I spent hours by the fireside with her and her family, sharing what I had learned about the Masters, telling them how Pearl had taught me to apply spiritual law in daily life, and that our attention is the key to self-mastery. Never before, they said, had they realized how simple these teachings were, and how easy to apply.

Once again, the Masters had prepared the way and guided me at every step. I was grateful I had not given in to doubt, and had succeeded in following that guidance. Even though I had no plan other than to go where spirit took me, I began to realize that there was a plan for my life more all-encompassing than I could have devised myself, and that my freedom was not in asserting *my* will but in becoming one with the Higher Will—through stilling my mind and simply allowing that Will to manifest through me.

Chapter 14

Obeying the Law

Driving south on the Interstate after leaving my friend and her family in Mount Hood, I felt good that my unplanned journey had been going so smoothly. At every turn, the plan unfolded effortlessly. My only job was to stop and tune in to my heart center. If I was unsure what to do, I pulled off the road to meditate and waited until I felt a clear direction—which frequently came as a thought or picture, accompanied by a feeling of serenity. As I drove south through Oregon, knowing that I was in God's hands and that I did not have to figure out a plan, I felt a sense of peace I had never known before.

How clear life is when I let go and let God, I mused, but that serenity was short-lived, as my mind soon reasserted its tyranny. Cruising down the freeway, looking forward to being back in Mount Shasta that night, the green sign for the Springfield exit loomed in front of me. *Ken Kesey!* it shouted, then whizzed past as I remembered that iconoclastic hero of the '60s.

Kesey was author of *One Flew Over the Cuckoo's Nest* and a character in Tom Wolfe's *Electric Kool-Aid Acid Test,* vestiges of a generation that had sought truth in extremes, that confused movement with freedom and drug experiences with enlightenment. He lived near Springfield now with his wife and kids on their dairy farm, so I decide to pay them a visit for old time's sake.

Although I had not resonated with the aspect of the drug culture that had treated the brain as a chemistry experiment, for I had seen too many burnt out freaks that were only shadows of what they had been, I still felt attracted to visit Kesey as one of the pioneers who questioned "the system" and explored limits and boundaries so others could find their own truth. Evolution rarely goes in a straight path, usually winding between extremes.

I had been a part of that generation and sought now some closure on that confusing time of rebellion. I had lived briefly in a few communes and owned a farm near Woodstock, New York, where I had given refuge to many wandering seekers who had come and gone. I had visited "The Farm" commune in Tennessee, then lived in Berkeley with the One World Family, and had traveled to India and become a part of the Maharaji Sangha with

Ram Dass and Neem Karoli Baba in the Himalayas, so I figured that I was part of that extended family, as we had all felt in the '60s that all the awakened ones were of the same tribe. There had been a feeling of belonging to something greater, part of an awakening humanity, and I thought, naively, that by stopping by to visit Kesey I could recapture that feeling. Surely, he who had been a pioneer would want to know of my experiences with the Masters.

I had a vision that somehow Kesey would invite me to dinner and we'd talk about old times. I'd tell him about my travels in India and my recent meeting with Saint Germain, and he'd let me crash there for the night—the kind of welcome we used to give each other when we recognized each other as family.

Musing on that vision as I sped past the Springfield exit, I realized it would be ten miles to the next exit before I could turn around, so I decided to make a U-turn. I should have taken missing the exit as a sign that I was not meant to pursue this journey into the past—one certainly not aligned with my current path. Had I taken the time to stop and tune in, I would have seen this was only my ego's pipe dream. If visiting Kesey had been the plan, I would have felt some anticipation, an urge to slow down before the exit. But I had not yet done enough self-observation to distinguish the source of all my urges, especially those that came up suddenly out of nowhere.

Pulling to the side of the freeway, I looked in both directions. In some part of my mind, I knew crossing the freeway was probably illegal, but the seductive thought had entered my mind that because I was now an apprentice of the Masters, I could transcend certain minor laws that seemed insignificant and that were an impediment to freedom. I felt I had risen above the need to pay heed to such mundane limitations—a dangerous concept, I was soon to realize. I used a corollary of the old philosophical argument to rationalize my action, that if a tree falls in the forest unobserved, it didn't really fall, *so if I break the law and no one sees, I didn't really break the law, did I?*

At one of those rare places on the freeway where the road was straight for a mile in either direction, I saw nothing coming. I double checked, looking either way again—not a car in sight. So without hesitation I pulled out, turned across the grass divider and sped off in the opposite direction. Colored lights flashed immediately in my rear view mirror—the Highway Patrol. A police car was riding my rear bumper.

Where did he come from? I had looked both ways and seen no one. He must have materialized out of nowhere: *Saint Germain!* Only a Master could appear out of nowhere. I recalled how Pearl had said she had seen Saint Germain appear as a police officer, but always for her protection, not to give her a ticket.

"License and registration," the officer requested, when I rolled down my window.

Wow, he's really playing this role well, I thought. Unless it really is a policeman!

"You realize, I hope, that what you just did was very dangerous, Peter!"

How does he know my name? I wondered. He had said it before he looked at my license, and he emanated a kindness, compassion, and air of ultimate authority unlike any police officer I had ever encountered. As he spoke, a deep love enfolded me, not unlike that of a loving father disciplining his child.

"Yes, I guess it was dangerous," I stammered, looking at his gun and badge. *Would Saint Germain carry a gun?* The books said that Masters never use a destructive force, that they accomplish everything they do with love.

His badge read, "Officer Jack Smith." *Would a Master lie about anything, even his name? No,* I concluded, *Masters always tell the truth.* In either case, the ticket he wrote out was very real. Stuffing the summons into my glove compartment, I realized that I was headed in the right direction, at least, and proceeded slowly to the nearby Springfield exit, where I easily found the Kesey farm.

The scene was not what I'd expected. Far from living in a commune, the Keseys now ran a working dairy. A very urbane Mr. Kesey greeted me in his office while talking animatedly on the phone about legal matters with someone I assumed was his attorney, so I waited outside.

While standing in the barnyard, a young man who seemed to be Kesey's son walked by and gave me a questioning look on his way to the barn. *What do you want?* I could hear him thinking. *Not another one of those hippies from the past who wants to take up my dad's time talking over the old days!*

His gaze said it all, and I realized I had made a terrible mistake. Kesey, the Merry Prankster, had changed, as had I. It was no longer the '60s, and I was simply a stranger imposing on his time—someone his family had to ignore while they did their chores on the farm. I knew he would invite me for dinner if I hung around, but instead I stuck my head in the door

Apprentice to the Masters

and waved goodbye. He was still on the phone, pacing back and forth agitatedly. I didn't regret interrupting his life so much as I mourned the loss of brotherhood, the family feeling of the '60s, where we always had time to hang out with each other. Now it all seemed to be about business, money, and lawyers. Sadly, I got in my van and drove away. Going down the country road it hit me—I had failed a test! The Masters had laid out a path for me, which I had followed impeccably. Now, close to home, my attention had wandered and I had let my mind carry me astray.

As I returned to the freeway heading south, I went over my encounter with the law and realized that, indeed, I had done something dangerous— not the U-turn, but that I had thought I was above the law. It was the feeling of superiority that had invoked humbling, first in the form of the Highway Patrolman, then the visit to Kesey's farm. Tired from days of driving, my mind had slipped into its old habits, and I had needed this reminder to be in the present, not dwell on the past or fantasize about the future.

Still, I wondered, *Was that officer, Jack Smith, really Saint Germain?* Regardless of the argument about the tree falling in the forest, certainly God sees everything, and my breaking of the law had invoked swift justice. Back in Shasta, I wavered for a month about whether to pay the ticket or not. If the Highway Patrol officer had been the Master, as I believed, then it was not a real ticket, and no one in the State of Oregon judicial system would know that it hadn't been paid. *But what if it had not been Saint Germain, and it was a real ticket?* On the last possible day, I decided not to take a chance, and sent in my check. The fine, I concluded, was part of my lesson.

A year later I discovered the truth. I was in Santa Fe, driving back from dinner with a car full of friends, when one of them commented on my full stop at every stop sign, though no cars were in sight.

"Every plane has its own laws," I responded, "Before we can ascend to a higher plane, we need to obey the laws of the plane we are on."

At that moment, Saint Germain flashed through my mind, and I saw him say, with a wink, "Well put, my boy! That *was* me in Oregon last year, the Highway Patrolman who gave you the ticket. You have learned your lesson well, and are ready now for the next stage of your training."

Chapter 15

A Test

I came to learn that when a Master is satisfied with your progress, it does not mean that he is going to reward you. Rather, he is more likely to put you through a test—frequently in an area you least expect. Lessons that in previous ages were given in secret, as described in the old occult books where disciples were summoned often on arduous journeys to remote mountain retreats, are now often given in "dreams" or in the challenges of day-to-day experience. Wherever there is a weakness or area of ignorance, the Masters see it and work to bring it to our awareness—of that I was soon to become painfully aware. Their method is often to bring us into relationship with others who make us acutely aware of our shortcomings.

Her name was Elizabeth, a girl ten years younger than I, with penetrating, dark eyes and long, flowing hair, who arrived in town one clear, fall day. She aroused in me an unusual desire, as though recognizing a previously unknown part of myself from which I did not want to be separated. Infatuated by this mesmerizing angel, I followed her toward the edge of a cliff—facing a leap which I dared not make, so I tried to keep my infatuation a secret even from myself.

While in high school she had read the *Saint Germain Series,* and one day not long after graduation she had piled all her things in her Volkswagen and headed toward Mount Shasta, the place where Godfre Ray King's adventures with the Masters had begun.

As we sat drinking tea one afternoon and discussing these teachings, we gazed into each other's eyes and fell into a meditation—the I AM Presence of each bathing us in its effulgent light. Effortlessly, the energy in the room increased and the atmosphere turned violet. Elizabeth's face changed, assuming the form of who she had been in past lives, many of which seemed familiar—and she saw the same transformations in me as we journeyed back in time to a place where we had been as one. *Surely this is my true love, for whom I have been waiting all my life,* I felt within.

Then the pinprick of reality popped the balloon of my reverie, and the vision dissolved. I recalled the vow of celibacy I had made to the Order of Melchizedek that was a condition of apprenticeship. *Perhaps we are to have a celibate marriage, like Pearl and Jerry, and serve the Masters as brother and sister,* I reasoned, trying to make sense of this attraction that pulled in the opposite direction of the path I had chosen. I had no idea what form our relationship was going to take, but I knew that I could not bear the thought of separation from this ancient love that had now returned.

After this lapse of ordinary awareness, we returned to the physical dimension and realized that our tea was cold. She offered to warm it, but I needed to go before I was swept into a vortex of energy that would make me forget why I was here. I needed to return to the center, re-establish my identity with the Source, and find in that place of knowing a course of action, or inaction. As I left her cabin and walked into the crisp fall air, I felt apprehension at the intensity of this sudden flame threatening to consume my recent commitment.

The oneness I had felt made me think that perhaps we were Twin Rays.[12] Pearl had talked of these male and female aspects of the same being

---

12 Twin Rays (also called Twin Flames) are the male and female aspects of the same individualized God Presence. Spherical in shape, the male is the outer, more mental vehicle of which the female is the inner, heart aspect. They can function either as one, or the female aspect can project outward to function as a separate being. When these Rays descended into gross matter, many of them separated into the two aspects to pursue their own separate evolutionary paths—and hence began creating karma. As they finish their lessons, they again become reunited with their other half, usually only after Ascension. The power of the positive and negative poles coming together on the Earth plane, like the poles of a battery, releases so much energy that discord is often the result of their union prior to each one having purified their latent tendencies. Or even if there is harmony, they frequently become so engrossed in themselves that they lose all interest in any activity outside their relationship. In either case, coming into close association with one's Twin is usually not brought about by the Master, except when there is some special service to be rendered. The case of the romance between Sir Lancelot and Guinevere, King Arthur's wife, is a perfect example of the havoc this attraction can bring about. Modern pairs some cite are John and Yoko Lennon, and Sonny and Cher, although I cannot attest to the accuracy of this statement.

Soul Mates refers instead to souls that have been together frequently in past lives, who are brought together in this life to complete some lesson or act of service. A Soul Mate can be a complement by that split apart ages ago to learn the lesson of individuality, yet which were destined to re-unite once the lesson was complete. I prayed to know the answer and in the meantime, mindful of my vow to the Masters, kept my distance from Elizabeth, feeling that my destiny hung in the balance.

Although I tried to explain this to Elizabeth, since I barely knew what was going on myself, I was not able to articulate the inner struggle without making things worse. On one hand I was cautious, because I knew the Masters demanded absolute impeccability, yet I longed for immersion and renewal in that fountain of oneness I had just experienced in her presence. Weeks passed without clarification, and I began to see that my reluctance wounded her. As though to goad me into action, she began going out with other men, some of whom were friends, flaunting these relationships in my face. For the first time that I could remember, I found myself becoming jealous, and also judging her for seeming to not follow the same path—that of unswerving obedience to the purity the Masters had demanded of me.

Saddened by this separation, I rededicated myself to my meditation and spent more time with Pearl—infuriating Elizabeth all the more, and driving her to avoid the teachings taking place at Pearl's home. Although a recent student, she now withdrew entirely, and I saw her only in awkward moments at community gatherings or passing on the street. Despite the transcendent love, we went our separate ways, the longing in my heart unexpressed.

Knowing of my connection with Elizabeth even before I met her, and aware of the challenge I was now facing, Pearl helped sustain my resolve. She didn't hesitate to tell women she thought were interested in me to remain distant—more distant than I often wished. But I trusted her, as she was the one Saint Germain had assigned to teach me, and I honored her dedication. I never dreamed that this mantle of protection would later become a burden from which I would have to free myself—as does every student have to free themselves eventually from their outer teacher once they have found the teacher within.

> whom one is nurtured; an opposite, who challenges one like a catalyst to induce growth; or a Twin. In any case, to actively seek that "other" is a waste of time, energy, and attention, for the people one is destined to be with alway arrive in and leave one's life at the right time—regardless of one's personal efforts.

Apprentice to the Masters

Because of this protection, I was shocked one morning when, after sitting with Pearl in deep meditation, she broke the silence saying, "I see you and Elizabeth going somewhere together in the near future."

Elizabeth and me together, what is she saying? I could hardly believe what I was hearing. She knew, without my saying a word, of my infatuation—fully aware that Elizabeth no longer came to see her because of my dedication to her as my teacher.

A few days later, Pearl said again, "I still see you doing something with Elizabeth. Do you have any desire in that direction?"

Any desire? When I was not meditating or studying the Master's teachings, despite my efforts to control my thoughts, Elizabeth was constantly on my mind. Now, as Pearl persisted, I began to wonder again if indeed, Elizabeth and I were Twin Rays whom the Masters intended to soon join together. *Perhaps that is why Pearl keeps mentioning Elizabeth?* Or perhaps we were only soul mates—partners in past lives coming together now to continue our work in this life? I prayed to know the truth about our inner connection.

That night my request was answered in a most astounding way, through a transcendent experience that revealed the truth of Twin Rays and forever altered my understanding of the dual nature of the soul.

Awakened by a voice calling my name, I opened my eyes and looked up into a golden ball of light hovering above me. As I became fully awake, I realized that it was Elizabeth—her dazzling I AM Presence!

What should I do?

Enfold me! Came the immediate inner reply.

Enfold you? How do I enfold light?

While pondering this dilemma, I rose upward out of my dense body toward my beloved, and as my heart opened, I enveloped her. Our hearts and minds became one in a sea of luminosity that was the union of bliss and emptiness—no consciousness of self or other, only the One Eternal Reality of God.

Awakening in the morning still permeated with that ecstatic joy of oneness, I realized that the spiritual union I had just experienced so far transcended ordinary human sex that I would never again seek in duality what could only be attained through the union of consciousness. I knew that if every human being could experience that union of polarities within themselves—*that marriage made in heaven*—there would be no strife or war. The bliss that I had experienced that night was similar to what I had experienced in meditation when the male and female currents join within. My heart was grateful to the Masters for allowing this union, an experience that answered my prayer to know the truth of this relationship more eloquently than any words they could have spoken.

Though I had not talked to her for weeks, I impulsively grabbed the phone and dialed Elizabeth's number. I was eager to continue the intimacy of last night's ethereal union and bring it closer to Earth. Although I knew that such an experience could not take place on the physical plane, it seemed that at least we could be in a loving relationship that could only be deepened by closer proximity to each other.

To my utter dismay, not only did she not remember what for me had been a soul-altering experience, but was annoyed that I had phoned her so early.

"What? Did you have a dream?" she asked in a tired voice. I sensed that her resentment over my lack of attention to her was in abeyance, replaced now as she awakened by a mild interest.

"Yes, didn't you?"

"No, I don't think I dreamed at all," she said, sounding bored.

"Oh well," I said, glumly swallowing my excitement. I realized that no matter what I said, she would interpret my experience as a dream, and that it would be a mistake to tell her of our union. So, wisely I felt, I applied the motto of the Great White Brotherhood, and kept my mouth shut. For some reason I could not fathom, it seemed the Masters did not yet want her to know of our connection as Twin Rays, though I was certain that would soon change.

"So, why did you call?" she asked, yawning.

Struggling with the urge to tell her everything, that we were destined to be together, I blurted out, "How would you like to go to Ashland and see a play?"

Unknowingly, I was acting a part in the play of which the Masters are the director.

Chapter 16

The Man in the Denim Jacket

The Oregon Shakespeare Festival brought tourists from all over the world to the picturesque town of Ashland, an hour north of Mount Shasta, and I had been thinking of attending one of the plays.

"Sure, I'd love to go," she replied, probably wondering what had finally brought me to my senses to ask her out on a date after all these months of silence.

Well, didn't Pearl say she saw me taking Elizabeth somewhere?

The next day when I told Pearl I was taking Elizabeth to see a play at the Shakespeare Festival, instead of frowning as I expected, she said, "Perfect!"

"Perfect?" I echoed, "Why perfect?"

"It's the Master's plan," she said. "Jerry and I have tickets to the same play. We will see you there!"

Again, further confirmation that the Masters were blessing our union, I thought. The connection with Shakespeare had not eluded me. It was well known among students of the Ascended Masters that one of Saint Germain's incarnations in the 1600s was Sir Francis Bacon, the secret author of the Shakespeare plays. I was later to write the story for a movie, *The William Shakespeare Conspiracy,* about the intrigue surrounding the play's true authorship. *How perfect it is that the Master is bringing us together at this event!* I concluded.

At home I meditated on discovering what the Master's plan might be for this special evening. I wanted Elizabeth to have the same realization, to know the true nature of our relationship, so we could begin working together as Masters in training, as I felt the Masters intended. *Will Saint Germain show Elizabeth what he has shown me? Will he give us some sign of his blessing?* I began to have the feeling that I would see the Master again soon, that he would be at the play and would reveal his plan for Elizabeth and me in person. As I sat in silence, suddenly the etheric form of Saint Germain appeared before me in confirmation of my feeling, and he said with his characteristic verve, "I will be there."

Although by now I had become used to seeing my mentor on a frequent basis, this time he appeared more vividly than usual, and so I asked, "In what form will you appear?"

"This time in a physical body," he replied, smiling with humor at my intense interest.

"Will I see you, then?" I asked, eager to again meet the elusive being in person who seemed to hold my destiny in his hands.

"That depends on you, my boy," he said, his words ringing with fatherly love and compassion.

"Depends on me?"

"Yes, whether or not you recognize me depends on the consciousness that you are in at the time."

"Well, if you are in a physical body, I will certainly see you—I'll keep a sharp eye out for you."

"We shall see," he said. "Of course, you realize I will be attending the play incognito, not as you are used to seeing me in an indigo cape with a Maltese cross on my chest—for a Master would never be so conspicuous as to draw attention to himself. But I will see *you,* in any case," he said, smiling. Then he vanished as suddenly as he had appeared, leaving me in a state of euphoric expectancy about the coming event.

Keeping a secret of the anticipated meeting was almost impossible. I was excited, not only to have a rendezvous with the elusive Master, but at last to being going on a date with my beloved Elizabeth. I thought it was unfortunate that the play we were going to see was *The Winter's Tale* rather than *Romeo and Juliet,* which would have been far more romantic. To contain my excitement, I kept repeating to myself the motto of the Ascended Masters: *To Know, to Dare, to Do, and to Be Silent.*

I succeeded in telling no one, not even Pearl, that I knew during the coming evening we were going to have a rendezvous with an Ascended Master, a God who would take on a human form for a particular service.[13] I assumed that as far as they knew, we were just going to see a play. Pearl was so intimate with the Masters she may well have known about

---

13   In past ages, when Divine beings appeared to mortals, they were frequently worshiped as Gods; hence, they now usually appear more subtly, so as not to mesmerize humans by phenomena, hoping that individuals will instead seek their own Divinity within. Various spiritual disciplines may require one to bow as a sign of respect to the teacher or teaching, but enlightened beings neither need nor desire feigned humility and obedience, preferring the only true homage, which is a grateful heart.

The Man in the Denim Jacket

Saint Germain's promised appearance, but she was too well schooled in the Masters' insistence on discretion to reveal anything.

The evening arrived, and attired in our finest clothes, Elizabeth and I drove to Ashland in my old Studebaker pickup truck. Although I could do nothing about the appearance of the truck except wash it—it was beyond the waxing stage—I had put on my sole tie and jacket. Once dressed in this finery, I felt immediately raised to a sufficient level of splendor commensurate with my anticipation of meeting the Master and receiving his blessing on our union.

I made sure we arrived with an hour to spare before the performance, hoping to spot Saint Germain as soon as possible. Not wanting to waste a moment of our precious time together, the time I had been longing to spend with her since we had met months before, I took Elizabeth for a walk in the beautiful city park adjacent to the Shakespearean theater. Walking hand in hand, I felt the bliss of our heart flames soaring in unison. As we walked, I felt the grace of God upon us. Though barely aware of the mundane world, I managed to scrutinize every person we met on the path in anticipation of meeting the Master, who I expected would walk up to us at any moment and give us his blessing. *How will he appear, in what form, and how attired?*

I soon realized that unless he gave me some clue, finding him might be more difficult than I had anticipated. Not giving Elizabeth any hint who I was expecting, I continued to bask in the simple joy of her nearness, the rekindling of our long-delayed romance. Had it not been for the promised appearance of the Master, I would have been more than content to continue our walk together, skipping the play for the romance in which we were now the lead actors.

This walk, I felt, was the beginning of our life together. I only waited for the Master to appear and confirm what I felt I already knew. Simply a nod from him would be sufficient, I felt, to bestow his silent blessing and consent. Had I known that the director of this play had different roles for us, that our drama together had not been written as a romance, I would have tried, had it been in my power, to prolong this stroll through the rose gardens forever. But in my slumber I continued to dream.

Soon the bell announcing the play rang with finality, and we entered the theater and took our seats. Far below us in the front row sat Pearl and Jerry, but I did not leave my seat to visit. I was far more interested in keeping a sharp lookout for Saint Germain, who had not yet revealed himself.

Apprentice to the Masters

Not wanting to miss him, as he had hinted I might not see him unless I was sharp, I excused myself to Elizabeth and walked out to the lobby. I stood by the usher taking tickets at the door and thought, *I will see him when he comes in. There is no way he can get into the theater except through these doors, and—no matter what his disguise—he will surely betray his presence by his vibrant, uplifting energy, or perhaps with a wink to me, or a smile.*

I looked for him with an eagle eye, scrutinizing every face, but when the lights dimmed, signaling the beginning of the play, he still hadn't shown himself. To avoid missing the performance, I returned in disappointment to my seat beside Elizabeth. Despite my love for her, not missing my rendezvous with the Master was even more important.

I could not concentrate on the play. *What had I done wrong? Why had he given me the slip?* I felt as abandoned as a young girl waiting for her date who has not yet arrived, wondering why I had been stood up.

Struggling with doubt and disappointment, I tried to concentrate on the play, which was about a king who is so suspicious of his wife's fidelity that he destroys their marriage and banishes their infant daughter, whom he suspects was fathered by another man. Yet, unlike the excitement I felt during many of Shakespeare's other plays, I now felt lulled into boredom by the long monologues.

Even if confined to this seat for a while, my mind is free to roam the universe unrestrained. That awareness of my latent power of consciousness to be anywhere, do anything I wished, roused me to alertness as effectively as the hot coffee I had smelled brewing in the lobby, and I began invoking the Violet Consuming Flame. I did this whenever in a theater or public place to clear out old thought forms[14]—and to my surprise, I now saw the

---

14 For more information, see the book by Annie Besant and C.W. Leadbeater, *Thought Forms* (Quest Books, 1969). Every thought generates a vibration as well as an image which, projected into space, lingers until it is either consciously dispersed or dissipates over time. It is these energies, and the forms in which they manifest, which can be seen by those whose inner sight is open, that cause many types of affliction, discomfort, disease, and aggression. When these forms are constantly regenerated by the renewed attention of large numbers of people, living entities of tremendous power are created, which often create natural disasters such as earthquakes and are the sustaining force

stage fill with violet light. *Is that from the spotlights?* I wondered, looking overhead. But those lamps that were illuminating the stage were white and red, without a hint of blue or violet. That must mean *Saint Germain is here,* at least etherically, and amplifying my invocation. I wondered if the actors and the rest of the audience could feel that energy, but I knew that, regardless, it was purifying everyone as it radiated throughout the theater and town. I now found myself becoming an active participant in the play.

Casting my eye around the theater, I could still not see anyone resembling the Master. *Is he going to be here only etherically? He said he would be here in a physical body, and I can't believe I've missed him. Perhaps if I'm sharp, as he said, I will see him yet.*

Now that I knew the Master's consciousness was focused in the theater, that we were all in the embrace of his mind, the time passed quickly. Soon the first act was over, the lights came up, and Elizabeth and I walked down the aisle to visit Pearl and Jerry. Since they were sitting in the center seats of the front row, I leaned against the edge of the stage to rest my back and stretch my legs.

As I talked with Pearl about the play, a young man in blue jeans with a matching denim jacket walked down the aisle and came up to us. *Well, he's certainly under-dressed—wearing jeans to the theater! At least I'm properly dressed,* I prided myself. Pleased at having followed the programming my mother had instilled in me as little boy, to dress up for the theater, I now took comfort in the tie and jacket which most of the year hung in the back of my closet—and looked with disdain on this seemingly uncouth theater goer. Since Pearl had many students, I was used to their coming up and expressing their happiness at seeing her, but they were always respectful of her person and never intruded on her decorum in any way—least of all physically.

Uncharacteristically, this rude young man in denim now plunked himself down in the seat next to Pearl. Leaning against her, he placed his arm on the rest, touching hers. *What insolence! Who does he think he is?* A lady of the "old school," Pearl never allowed anyone to be familiar with her in public, not even her husband, yet this man leaned against her with

---

behind war. However, they can be dissolved by the Masters and the focused attention of conscious light workers.

no protest from her, nor did she pull away. *Hey, who do you think you are!* I wanted to shout, amazed at my sudden jealousy toward this stranger fraternizing with my teacher. *Don't you know who this woman is? She's a teacher for the Ascended Masters! You can't just lean against her like she's your lover! Wait a minute, what if Pearl's purity is feigned, and this really is her lover?* I was astounded at my mind out of control with doubt and jealousy, negative emotions I thought I had overcome years ago now boiling to the surface. At least I was able to observe my mind, rather than being totally identified with it.

Even if they were lovers, I had never seen her allow anyone to express this level of intimacy in public. Outraged, I wondered, *Why doesn't she at least pull her arm away?* I was her main pupil, the one she was training to carry on her work, and even though I hugged her occasionally out of gratitude or kissed her on the cheek, I would never have presumed to be this intimate in front of everyone.

As if sensing my agitation, Pearl looked me in the eye and said, "Peter, do you know this gentleman?"

"No, I don't believe I do," I said, trying to restrain my indignation, *and I'm not sure I want to know him either.* She had called him a gentleman, but he hardly had the attire or manners of a gentleman. Though wearing jeans, I noticed that they were well tailored and that he did sport a silk shirt with a white ruffle at the collar. Looking more closely, this shirt was more elegant than anything I had ever seen—other than in paintings I had seen hanging in the Louvre, in Paris, that dated from the time of the French Revolution. *I'd love to have a shirt like that,* I thought enviously. *Where does he do his shopping—from a catalog?* I was dying to ask, but didn't want to give him the satisfaction of thinking that I approved of his uncouth behavior. Even though his ruffled silk shirt almost compensated for the rest of his appearance, I could not condone the obvious contempt he was exhibiting toward my teacher.

"Do you like the play?" the insolent intruder asked, fixing me in the eye with a piercing gaze and, I thought, the hint of a faint smile on his lips.

"Yes, I love Shakespeare," I said half-heartedly, thinking, *I like most of his plays, though I would have much preferred* Romeo and Juliet, *and perhaps the play would be more interesting if we weren't sitting so far back in the theater.*

"Would you and your lady like to sit in the front row during the second act?" he replied, as if reading my mind.

"Yes, of course," I volunteered, glancing sideways at Elizabeth, seeing her nod, "Yes."

"Well, these two seats will be vacant," he assured, pointing to the two seats adjacent to Pearl. "You may sit here in front, if you wish."

What arrogance! That these seats that were occupied during the first act would be vacant after the intermission could only be a guess. Well, I'm not going to usurp them and risk being asked to leave as the curtain is rising. Realizing that I should use the men's room before the second act started, I asked Pearl, Jerry, and Elizabeth to excuse me, completely ignoring the presumptive stranger, and walked up the aisle to the lobby.

Pushing open the door to the full men's room, I was shocked to see the young stranger in denim standing in the middle of the room, zipping his fly in preparation to leave. *How did he get up here ahead of me? I just left him beside Pearl a moment ago.* He nodded in recognition as he headed past me toward the door.

I averted my eyes from his gaze, as I had been trained from childhood to avoid engaging strangers in men's rooms, and then slid by him without speaking. The bathroom was crowded, so I had to wait, and when I returned to the theater I saw with relief that Elizabeth had resumed our former seats far up the aisle in the middle of the theater. I was glad that she, too, did not want to risk the embarrassment of being asked to leave someone else's seat.

However, as the lights dimmed, we saw that the two seats next to Pearl were in fact empty, just as the stranger had promised. Elizabeth and I looked at each other and made a dash down the aisle just before the curtain rose, and slid into the seats in the front row. To my surprise, the man in denim and the French shirt was sitting in a previously occupied seat next to Jerry on Pearl's right.

Sitting so close to the actors now, I could finally feel the passion with which they played their parts. I began to feel drawn into the drama taking place on stage, almost becoming a part of the play. The king, Leontes, was about to recover his beloved wife, Hermione, whom he thought had died as a result of his cruel jealousy many years before, and to recover his beloved daughter, Perdita, whom he had abandoned and also thought lost forever.

How modern Shakespeare is, I marveled. *Didn't I feel the same anger, suspicion, and jealousy a moment ago? Isn't Elizabeth my Perdita, my true love I lost ages ago, with whom I am now being reunited?* Filled with gratitude

Apprentice to the Masters

to Saint Germain who, as Francis Bacon, was the true author of the Shakespearean plays,[15] the stage again filled with that violet light, this time even more vivid than before. Again I acknowledged the etheric presence of Saint Germain, Master of the Violet Ray, and in a flash I realized that the Master for whom I had been searching was none other than the man in denim I had so severely judged, now sitting near us in the front row.

This was the chance I had been waiting for, to thank him for his presence in my life and to ask his blessings for my relationship with Elizabeth and guidance for our next steps together as a couple. However, just as I was about to get up and sit beside him, he abruptly rose and walked out of the theater. I wanted to run after him and beg his forgiveness for my judgments of him, but it was too late. He was gone!

No wonder he was acting familiar with Pearl. He is her mentor as well as mine, and knows our most intimate thoughts. We have all been together throughout the ages, perhaps even of the same family. Now my rudeness and impetuosity has forced him to leave. How could I be so rash? No way was he going to remain in the theater and risk my exposing his true identity.

Driving home on the freeway that evening, Elizabeth and I sat in silence, each of us lost in thought. The pickup hummed along on the near-deserted road, its headlights the only light to penetrate the lonely darkness that surrounded us.

"You know," Elizabeth said, finally breaking the silence and turning to me with a quizzical look, "I think that stranger we met at the theater was Saint Germain."

"You do?" I said, shocked at her insight. Even though she was only a year out of high school and rebellious toward the discipline required by the Masters, I saw that she had an awareness of them and an intuitive knowledge of their teachings far beyond what I had expected.

Still feeling guilty, however, that my impatience in wanting to besiege Saint Germain with questions had forced him to leave without bestowing

---

15 The historical Shakespeare, who spelled his name "Shagspeare," was the illiterate son of a butcher, who eventually found work in London as a stable boy at the Globe Theater, where the "Shakespeare" plays were performed, and in which he may have had occasional bit parts. There is no mention of any literary works or manuscripts in his will, which he signed with an "X," as he was unable to write even his name, let alone a play.

the blessing which I was certain he had intended to give, I determined not to further disobey the command to silence, and kept my thoughts to myself as we drove on without talking. But the Master was not going to let me wallow in self-criticism a moment longer, and soon we were enveloped in the Violet Consuming Flame which dissolved all discord, and his sense of humor—his *verve,* filled the truck. Gripped by his mirth, we both broke out laughing. I no longer needed to say a thing. Elizabeth sensed the Master's presence as well as I, and knew that he was confirming her recognition of him. I admired her self-possession with which she retained this knowledge, with no desire for idle conversation. We had received his blessing, though not the one I had wanted, and he never conveyed what he wanted us to do about our relationship. So we drove on in silence, and my mind became active again, dreaming of the next unfoldment of our relationship.

Early next morning, I walked up the hill from my house to see Pearl. Bursting with eagerness, I wondered how much I dared reveal to her. On the one hand, Saint Germain came through her as my teacher, but on the other, he might be testing to see if I would reveal what I knew—and how well I could keep his secret. I was learning the hard way not to try to outguess the Masters, and that if I was in doubt, the best policy was always to remain silent.

"So, how did you like the play?" Pearl asked, not mentioning anything of our previous night's encounter with the young man in denim. *Can it be she doesn't know who the stranger was? Maybe it's a trick, and the Masters are using her to test me! Or perhaps she's merely trying herself to keep the Master's command of silence?*

"Oh, it was okay," I said, waiting for inner prompting to see if I should say more.

"I'm glad that you and Elizabeth got to move up to the front row," Pearl said, looking me in the eye. "It was nice of that man to offer you those seats."

Realizing that she, too, was waiting to see what I knew, I asked, "You know who that was, don't you?"

"Oh, yes, of course."

"Of course? When did you know?"

"I felt him coming down the aisle."

"You did?"

"Then when he sat down next to me, it was a dead give-away."

"Why?"

"By what he said—didn't you hear him?"

"No, what did he say?"

"'I AM here.'"

At those sacred words, the Violet Flame illumined the living room, electrifying us with his presence that was, once again, confirmation of his having been with us at the theater in Ashland the previous night.

I waited until after the energy had subsided, hoping that Pearl would give further guidance regarding Elizabeth, but on the subject of the anticipated relationship, she remained silent. I was going to have to figure out what to do on my own. Later I was to discover that it is often the Masters' practice to guide their students into a relationship or other situation and leave it up to them how best to proceed and later extract themselves. This was all part of the training—a crash course in self-knowledge through immersion in the fires of purification.

Soon life itself, destiny, or intercession by the Masters, whatever name you want to call it, took command of the situation, and Elizabeth was called out of town to be with her mother, who was going into the hospital. When she returned to Mount Shasta I, too, was traveling, having left to visit my own mother. Months later when I saw Elizabeth again, it was at the Thanksgiving dinner put on by our community at the lodge in the city park. She was distant toward me and talked more enthusiastically with other men, and I realized that if the Masters were going to bring us together, now was probably not the time.

Gradually I came to realize that Elizabeth, much younger than I and on her own for the first time, was still experimenting with her freedom, and was not ready for marriage to me or anyone. With heaviness of heart at the coolness that had again come between us, I kept my distance and continued more than before to meditate on the Presence of God within, the wellspring of all love where we were already one—from which center I sent her my silent blessings. Continuing to visit Pearl, I struggled under the watchful eye and rigorous teaching of Saint Germain, as an apprentice of whom was required nothing less than one hundred percent obedience.

Part III:

In the Material World

Chapter 17

Descension

In the summer of 1973, the tiny town of Mount Shasta was deluged by a flood of people seeking to know more about the Ascended Masters. Word of the Masters' unmistakable energy, which people felt abundantly in Pearl's presence, brought hundreds to her door that summer to hear her teachings;[16] and with great simplicity she guided them inward to the fountain of truth they sought—connection with the Higher Self. Like a great magnet of God Consciousness, she was able to transmit that magnetism to others whose hearts were open.

Word had reached San Francisco, and large numbers of former flower children from Haight-Ashbury began arriving in town by the car load. Since they usually came by the health food store on arrival, which was the spiritual nexus of the town, one of those who worked there, such as Stephen, Gayle, Don, or I, would direct them to Pearl's house. Many of these seekers had been involved in spiritual paths during the '60s—Hinduism, Transcendental Meditation, or Buddhism—and had read Ram Dass' *Be Here Now*.[17] Now they were looking for a way, without going to India, without drugs or joining a commune, to bring their spiritual awareness into daily life. Although most had experienced some form of higher consciousness or out-of-body state, they still wanted an answer to the same question I had asked in Muir Woods: *What is the purpose of my existence? If striving after earthly happiness is an illusion, as the great spiritual teachings say, why am I here?* They had heard Pearl knew the answer and could teach them to find their own inner guidance, so they would not have to rely on gurus or be misled by psychics to find their path. Even

---

16 In the course of the 18 years that she saw people in her home in Mount Shasta, and later in Yreka, she saw well over 12,000 individuals, not including the many like me whom she saw on a regular basis. She never charged, nor did she advertise her work in any way.

17 Ram Dass, *Remember, Be Here Now* (Hanuman Foundation; Santa Fe, 1971). Thirty years later, Eckhart Tolle also wrote about being in the now with *The Power of Now: A Guide to Spiritual Enlightenment* (New World Library; Novato, 2004).

Apprentice to the Masters

though many had studied with gurus in India or some of the high Tibetan Lamas who had come to the U.S., few of these guru figures had taught how to find guidance within—a practice to serve as a daily compass. Pearl's instruction on how to find that compass within was unique, bold, and devastatingly simple.

Walking up the street to her house, I would frequently see those who had just left Pearl, reclining on neighbors' front lawns, overwhelmed with the Masters' energy they had just experienced. Or I would see them sitting on the curb of the sidewalk with a "stoned" look on their faces as they tried to digest their mind-altering experiences. Later they would pick themselves up, stumble downhill, and often end up back at Stephen's store. As many were either low on funds or wanted to be close to Nature, they would then camp out under the stars, some erecting teepees on the Mountain.

Many had read *The Aquarian Gospel,* which told how Jesus had accomplished the Ascension. This process of dissolving the human self and its identification with the constituent aggregates,[18] allowing the practitioner to reunite with the Higher Self, is a well-known, thoroughly documented occurrence, known in Tibet as attaining the *Rainbow Body* (Tibetan: *jalus*). In Pearl's living room, where they came in contact with the electrifying radiation of the Masters who had already attained this state, they realized that Ascension was not just a metaphysical concept or a myth of a bygone era, but a practical feat which they, too, could accomplish. When Pearl gave this instruction and people felt the quickening, many wanted to attain the Ascended State immediately.

I was also one of those seekers who longed for this quickening to raise me into that unlimited state, as I felt that I would be of more benefit to humanity as an Ascended Being, and I wondered when my apprenticeship in Mount Shasta would be finished. *Ascension, perhaps, will be the final exam that grants freedom from the bonds and limitations of Earth?*

There were stories about retreats in Tibet where candidates for initiation were walled into a chamber built into the side of a cliff, the only opening being a slit for food for those who still needed to eat. When they had dissolved their physical density and could leave the chamber by that narrow opening, the Lama allowed the wall to be removed, revealing that

---

18 Buddhism classifies the aggregates with which we identify as: form, sensation, perception, volition, and consciousness.

the occupant had literally vanished from the physical plane. In later years I met a Chinese Buddhist monk who witnessed his teacher's Ascension. He reported that his teacher disappeared in waves of multicolored light. All that was left behind were his books and robe, where a moment before he had been standing.

So, why not me? I'm ready, aren't I?

I fasted for several days in preparation, then went up the Mountain to a location where at one time I had seen an etheric temple,[19] and began to recite the decrees the Masters had given for this purpose—powerful invocations of the I AM consciousness. From the center of my being, I repeated,

I AM the Ascension in the Light!

Each time I spoke the decree, there was an unmistakable energy triggered in my body, but to my disappointment, I remained in physical form. Not giving up so easily, I stayed on the Mountain and continued to fast. A week later I tried again, with the same results. At a loss, I abandoned my efforts, descended the Mountain, and threw myself down in a chair in front of Pearl.

"It doesn't work!"

"What doesn't work?"

"Ascension."

As I poured out my heart, recounting my futile efforts to ascend, a faint smile appeared on her face. Unknown to me at the time, Saint Germain had been watching my efforts with amusement. I should have known by now that he was always watching. Now seeing the Master's mirth at my words, Pearl tried in vain to maintain her composure, and finally could not help laughing.

"Maybe you are here for a purpose," Pearl ventured, "and it's not time for you to go yet?"

"Really, do you think so?"

---

19 The etheric temples I have seen resemble the temples of ancient Greece which are established by the Masters at various locations on the Earth, but at a higher vibratory rate. The Masters establish these as foci of light and as schools to which they bring their students for instruction while they are asleep or out of the body.

Apprentice to the Masters

"It's quite possible," she replied, still trying to restrain her amusement. "Do you feel you have learned what the Master Saint Germain sent you here to learn, that you have completed your apprenticeship, and that there is no further service you are to render here?"

"I think so," I said confidently, "I can't imagine what else there is to do. I think I could help the Masters much better as an Ascended being."

"Why don't you go back up the Mountain," Pearl said, giving no indication that she was voicing the Master's wish, "and ask the Masters if there is something else they want you to do here on Earth before you ascend."

"That's a great idea!" I exclaimed. "I'll go back up tonight."

That evening, after reloading my camping gear in the back of my van, I again drove up the Mountain and left my van in the parking lot of the abandoned ski area, whose lift towers had been swept away by an avalanche. Then I hiked to a powerful location where I'd camped in the past. It was a flat clearing between two cedar trees, at the foot of a rock face where Pearl had told me there was an entrance into the Mountain.

After reaching the location and getting my mat and sleeping bag set up, I meditated for a long time, then watched the moon rise over the ridge. I sent out a prayer to the Masters, asking them to show me if they still had any work for me and, if not, to aid me in my Ascension. Then I lay down and fell asleep.

Soon a striking, white-robed Master appeared nearby, beckoning to me. I rose, leaving my denser body behind, and followed toward the rock cliff. As I approached, the rock dissolved to reveal a well-lit tunnel penetrating into the mountain. Entering the tunnel, I noticed that its walls were inscribed with mystic symbols that seemed familiar, yet were undecipherable to me. I sensed another door lay ahead, as if I'd been here before, and that soon a door would open to a council chamber of the Ascended Masters.

It was exactly as I expected. We passed through a door that led into a huge chamber where three familiar Masters in white robes were seated around a massive onyx table streaked with veins of gold. The Masters emanated such love and natural authority of God Dominion that I felt tremendous confidence and was overwhelmed with gratitude simply to be in their presence.

"You have called, and we have responded!" one of the Masters said, addressing me. "You should not be surprised, for by now you have learned the law: *The call compels the answer.* Everything is familiar to you because you have been here many times before, only this time, at Saint Germain's request, we will allow you to retain the memory of your visit." Then, with a gracious motion of his hand, he indicated that I should be seated.

There was a moment of silence, during which I looked in turn deeply into the eyes of each of the three Masters, and each steadily returned my gaze, transmitting their energy and consciousness. Words cannot describe the majesty of their noble bearing and the love each radiated. The question suggested by Pearl earlier in the day now came to mind, *Is there anything you still want me to do on Earth, or am I ready to Ascend?* However, not a word issued forth.

The Master directly across from me smiled, putting me at ease, then gave his reply to the question, which he had obviously heard. His reply was so different from what I anticipated that I thought he must be speaking in riddles—a Zen koan, impossible to decipher logically, but which later would produce a *satori* of sudden awakening.

Gazing steadily into my eyes without wavering, he said, "We want you to get into real estate."

Aha, ascend into my "real estate," I thought, proud that I had so quickly solved his koan, but the Master did not acknowledge my interpretation.

While savoring my momentary victory, a man in a brown shirt was escorted into the room and brought to the chair at the table adjacent mine. I noticed he emanated a sense of worldly power, as though he were used to getting his way. He extended his hand into mine in a perfunctory shake, but failed to make eye contact, and I immediately felt a coldness that put me on guard.

"Not only will you be doing business together," the Master on my right continued, nodding toward this man, "but he is to be your teacher in the next phase of your training. We are sending you to him to attain a certain worldly knowledge that will be of assistance to you in the work we shall want you to carry out for us in the future."

Had I not been among those whose energy was so uplifting that negative feelings are not possible in their presence, I would have been disappointed at this news denying me freedom from the cares of the Earth, that what the first Master had said had not been a riddle for me to interpret, but a literal request. Instead of granting me permission to Ascend, I was being told to descend, commanded to enter deeper into the material world—and in the company of someone toward whom I felt a wary dislike. *Perhaps my feelings are wrong,* I thought. *If the Masters are introducing me to this man, he must be someone I can trust,* I naively concluded, and tried to put my aversion aside.

I soon forgot my concerns, as the two of us were led back through the tunnel and out of the Mountain, down a path to the parking lot where my van was still parked. A limousine was waiting, and one of our escorts slid into the driver's seat and beckoned us to get in.

"Do not be concerned about your vehicle," the Master addressed me, hearing my thoughts. "We have established a protective shield around it," his familiar voice continued, "so that no one can touch it until you return. Your human vehicle asleep in your sleeping bag has been likewise protected."

Soon we were driving down the Mountain and onto the freeway, headed south, my new associate sitting beside me in the back seat. Not the least bit in awe of the majestic beings who were our escorts, he seemed preoccupied with his own thoughts. Soon we left the freeway and entered Dunsmuir, a small railroad town on the Sacramento River, nine miles south of Mount Shasta. The driver pointed out a mini-mart and some old houses owned by the brown-shirted stranger, all of which were run-down and badly in need of repair.

As if aware of my judgments, my new associate looked out the window and boasted, "They all generate good income, and you can raise the rents as soon as you take over."

So, I'm not only supposed to go into real estate, but be a landlord as well?

The Master who was driving looked back at me through the rear view mirror, smiling with compassion, no doubt over the anguish he knew I was soon going to experience in my new profession. I had been a wandering mystic for the past few years, keeping my distance from people, and had never been the least bit interested in business or in making more money than I needed at the moment. As we turned north again and got back on the freeway, I anticipated this change with dread. Soon we ascended the Mountain again, and before long the limousine came to a stop beside my van.

"Now you have your answer," the Master in the front seat announced. "Mastery of the world can only be achieved *in the world.* For you to help humanity you will have to understand humanity. You will have to know how other people live and feel, and develop compassion for them. For this you must face all the same tests and challenges they are faced with—and master them. Remember, we are as close to you as your own heart. Follow your heart and everything will work out."

As I climbed out of the back seat of the limousine and closed the door, I looked back at the Master who had just spoken to me and now realized why he seemed so familiar. It was none other than Saint Germain in his higher body, the more etheric form I had seen only briefly before he had disappeared before my eyes in Muir Woods. I was used to seeing him as the courtier from France, the form he seemed to use more frequently for outer work. Now he winked at me, as the limousine pulled away and disappeared into thin air, leaving me standing in the parking lot alone.

The next thing I knew it was morning, and the sun was prying my eyes open to get me to take command of the human body that lay inert on the ground. My sleeping bag was warm against the chill air that blew down from the glaciers above, so I remained where I was, returning to body consciousness slowly, as I lay looking up at the bright blue California sky. Then I remembered that I had come up here to get an answer and had been taken into the Ascended Master Retreat inside the Mountain, but I did not like the answer they had given. *Perhaps it was only a dream, and all symbolic?* I could not conceive of myself going into real estate, for I was still a wandering mystic at heart, seeking to immerse myself in the ocean of spirit.

I'm here on Mount Shasta, this great spiritual focus. Why would the Masters want me to take my attention off spirit and put it on the materialistic world of business? The memory of last night's visit with the Masters I now dismissed along with the mists rising from the mountain and dissolving in the sun—a dream I chose now to ignore. I would need powerful confirmation before I would so radically alter my life as to descend into the world of marketing houses and land and arguing over the prices of things. Emerging finally from my sleeping bag, I stripped off my clothes and jumped into a frigid stream to rid my mind of that memory, then dried off in the sun. Fully awake, I drove back into town to start my early morning shift behind the counter at the juice bar.

As I worked, I made small talk with the customers—a challenge, because I had been essentially shy my whole life, my main concern every day being to find the best time and place to meditate. My current life in some ways paralleled that of my one-time hero, Kane, in the TV series *Kung Fu,* a show on which my generation had been raised. As an apprentice in a Shaolin Temple, the young disciple Kane had to demonstrate his

Apprentice to the Masters

readiness to leave the temple by accomplishing certain feats of mastery. These included being able to walk on rice paper without leaving a footprint, being looked for but not seen, listened for but not heard. Only when he had mastered these feats could he leave the temple and travel to the West, where, in his wanderings, he would help others.

Like Kane, I was also an apprentice preparing to pass the required tests necessary to leave the temple, only my temple was the juice bar. My main test was not to get angry or become impatient with customers, no matter how impossible their requests. A more symbolic test was to operate the old Norwalk juicer without getting saturated by the spray of carrot juice. The juicer pressed carrot pulp contained in a bag that, because Stephen had stored it in the freezer, had numerous tiny holes through which the juice sprayed in unpredictable directions. Knowing that as an apprentice I must master these feats before moving on, I counted on leaving the temple of the juice bar only when I could complete these tests.

One day a woman came in, perhaps a Master, for Pearl said that Masters would be visiting us unawares, to render services and put us through various tests. This middle-aged woman was a real pain. She watched like a hawk as I worked on her Rainbow Sandwich—our avocado, sprouts, and tomato special. When I mashed the avocado, she wanted it sliced. When I slathered on the mayo, she asked me to scrape most of it off, then put some back on. When I put the sprouts on top, she wanted them replaced with lettuce, and when I started to slice the finally completed sandwich sideways, she asked me to cut it diagonally. Not used to such picky people in our casual hangout, a crowd of sympathizers had gathered around the counter to watch the show, wondering when I would lose my temper. However, remembering that she could be a Master, I decided to treat her as such, and miraculously that transformed the experience.[20]

Finally placing the completed sandwich on a plate on the counter in front of the woman, I smiled with relief, and everyone else at the counter seemed to be relieved as well. But the test wasn't over.

---

20 When we change our consciousness, the whole world changes. This is the essence of the Pure Land teachings of Amithaba Buddha. We are already in the Pure Land if we can only get our limited conceptions out of the way and accept the unlimited nature of what we and others truly are.

"Oh, I want it to go."

She seemed to have thought of every possible correction she could make in my performance. Although there was no hostility in her voice, she was not satisfied with the way I did anything. Maintaining my acceptance of her as a Master, the same Master Presence that was nascent in me, I gladly complied, scooping the sandwich onto a sheet of plastic wrap, folding it, and placing it in a brown paper bag.

She gave me a warm smile, conveying that she appreciated the service, and the conscious equanimity I had maintained while rendering it, as much as the sandwich itself. Then she put some bills on the counter and walked out. When I counted the money I saw that her tip equaled the price of the sandwich, and I knew that I had passed the test. Only one test remained.

CHAPTER 18

The Man in the Brown Shirt

So as not to emerge from the juice bar at the end of the day with orange spots on my white shirt, I practiced *meditation in action*. A revolutionary book by that name, written by Chögyam Trungpa, had been dropped in front of me while I was lying on the deck of a houseboat on the Ganges in Varanasi, India, just before returning to the States.[21] Realizing that a true Master is not spaced out, I tried to be totally present so I would know where to stand to avoid the streams of spraying juice. Finally the day arrived when, after hours of work, I noticed my shirt was still white and free of stains, and I awaited the voice of the Shaolin monk from *Kung Fu*, who would say, "Ahh, Grasshopper, it is now time to leave the temple." I had completed this stage of my apprenticeship and knew that soon I would be entering another. Sooner than I anticipated, someone appeared to open the door to my next adventure, one whom I had only met in a dream and whose reality I had doubted.

At the end of the day a vigorous, white-haired man in work clothes, with a certain unpleasant feeling about him, sat down at the counter and ordered some juice. Unlike most of the customers who came into the store, he inspired my instant dislike, as I sensed the manipulative energy of a scam artist. Since the people coming into the store in those days wore pastel colors, the dark brown of his shirt stood out. Though at first I didn't recognize him, with a shock I realized that my experience had been no

---

21 Chögyam Trungpa, *Meditation in Action* (Shambhala Publications, 1996). Prior to this I had considered meditation to be a passive experience, where individual consciousness dissolved into blissful non-being. For the first time, when reading this book, I realized that enlightenment could also manifest in form and take conscious action using skillful means—which was the essence of Mastery. Trungpa Rinpoche's other books all make one acutely aware of the need for conscious presence—and when near him, one could feel that presence as a palpable force. No matter where one goes, one is still *here*. I heard him say once, "Christianity can also lead to enlightenment, but few spiritual paths (apart from Buddhism) teach you what to do next."

149

Apprentice to the Masters

dream, that he was the man the Masters had introduced me to inside the Mountain. He gave no sign of recognition, but then surprised me when he asked, "By any chance, are you interested in real estate?"

"Why, sort of," I mumbled, still attached to what I considered the spiritual life of ease, making just enough money to get by, and dreading the thought of business, despite the Masters' clear instruction to go in that direction. Still unwilling to surrender to the dream, I was determined to thoroughly test my vision before allowing it to become a reality.

"Then come with me," he said, finishing his drink. As the stranger opened the door, I walked outside into the sun and noticed that my shirt was still sparkling white—and I knew that had been my last day of work there, and that I was finally leaving the temple.

Little did I guess how arduous my new work in the world outside the temple was going to be. I was descending into the world, rather than ascending out of it, as I had wished. This would prove a painful lesson for me, as I knew little about relationships of any kind, let alone business relationships involving attorneys and adversarial parties. I had been an only child, raised by a single mother who herself had been an only child, and I knew little about processing my emotions in charged situations, let alone dealing with those energies directed at me by others. The only training my mother had given me about how to get along with people was, "Be polite, look people in the eye, and always tell the truth." Good advice, as far as it went.

Pearl used to say, "Before you can become a divine man, you have first to become a *hu*man." That meant looking deeply into the source of my own emotions, my own fears and insecurities that conflict brought to the surface. No amount of meditation or decreeing could take the place of that self-knowledge learned through interaction with others.

"My name is Ratz," the stranger said, holding out his hand. "Slobodan Ratz. It used to be Ratzoff, but I shortened it to Ratz when I got into the landlord business. Sort of fits the landlord business, eh? No rats in *my* houses," he said, laughing at what he perceived as his own wit.

As we drove toward Dunsmuir, the little town we had last visited with the Master at the wheel, Ratz made small talk about the great properties he owned. He was offering me a lucrative business opportunity, he said, managing rental properties, and spoke as though buying his business was already a foregone conclusion. Though he never acknowledged our meeting inside the Mountain and seemed skeptical of the Masters' existence, what we were discussing was in complete accord with the plan they had revealed. I was amazed at how someone who did not believe in the Masters could still be under their guidance, and even be their unwitting agent. Later I was to find that these agents were often sent to test us as well as offer support.

When Ratz showed me the houses he owned, I was again shocked—they were the same run-down properties I had seen in the "dream." Becoming a landlord was the last thing on Earth I wanted. *Do I really have to make this dream real?* I wondered, feeling apprehensive.

I couldn't seem to contact the Masters or sense any new guidance from my own I AM Presence, though the Masters' plan revealed in the "dream" seemed to be coming to life before me. *How nice it would be if the guidance was always what I wanted to hear, rather than pushing me to the limit.* It seems that if we always get what we want, our growth ceases. And the reason the Masters don't tell people what to do more often is that when their lives don't go the way they expect, they blame the Masters rather than themselves.

Though apprehensive, I felt I had no choice but to get involved with this man. It was obvious the Masters had sent Ratz to initiate me into a certain aspect of life, but what I didn't realize was that I could also question him, and when the need arose, I could confront him and stand up for myself. It seemed the Masters had put me on a train, and it would be a long way to the next stop. Not until later did I realize that although this was my destined path, I had free will in how to travel that path—what I did with my experience was up to me. My attitude, view, and emotional and spiritual growth could all be altered to the extent I could observe my own mind and act with clear intent *to change myself.* By changing myself, everything else changed.

My financial situation at the time consisted of ownership of stock given to me as a child by a wealthy aunt and uncle, which had been intended to pay for my college tuition. Since my mother had paid for my education herself, I still had most of this stock in a brokerage account, the dividends from which had been enough to pay for my ascetic wanderings. But now Ratz began probing the extent of these finances, as only a skilled con man could, explaining, "I need to know if you're financially qualified, so we're not wasting our time."

Since I trusted the Masters and was sure they would only introduce me to someone who was ethical, I went along with Ratz's proposals and began to purchase his rentals for the price he asked—never thinking that he might be overcharging, that someone who worked for the Masters would be motivated by so crass a motive as personal gain at my expense.

"Why pay all that money for appraisals when I know myself what the properties are worth?" he stated, with seemingly irrefutable logic. And real estate agents and escrow companies were also a waste of money. Though I questioned the wisdom of skimping on third party professional advice, I felt that to argue would show distrust of the Masters. *Isn't this what they told me to do? How can I argue with the man they assigned as my teacher?*

The next day I took my concerns to Pearl, and she suggested I talk to her husband, Jerry, who had been in real estate himself. Jerry was a strong, yet inwardly silent man, who always remained in the background, revealing little about what was going on inside. He worked at the front desk of a motel downtown while Pearl saw people at home, so everyone assumed that he must not be as spiritually advanced as she. When home, he sat in the living room along with the groups that came to the house, appreciating Pearl's teachings and stories more each time he heard them, although he had heard them innumerable times. Or he sat in the bedroom answering the phone and making appointments for Pearl while she was teaching in the living room.

Sometimes Pearl would tell people, "Why don't you go out back and talk to Jerry for a while." Jerry would be doing something practical like oiling a squeaky gate, straightening bent nails, or sorting screws into their appropriate jars. "You can never tell when you're going to need one, and when you do, it's good to know where they are," he told me with irrefutable logic on one of these occasions.

Because he hardly ever spoke unless he was spoken to, and then only with the minimum words required, many thought he was a simpleton. I knew he was far from that, for when I went on the road, Jerry occasionally appeared to me in dreams and gave guidance and support. He was a true warrior who, because he knew his strength, needed to say or do little. A few years later when Jerry passed on, it was no surprise that Pearl said that he had Ascended. One did not need actually to raise the physical body to ascend, Pearl explained. If one had done sufficient inner work and cleared all personal karma, one could make that quantum leap to the next dimension without having to dissolve the physical form.[22]

---

22 There are many spiritual terms which are used somewhat interchangeably,

Now, when I queried him about buying the rentals, he said, "I always used to get appraisals, and I never minded paying a little extra to go through a real estate agent, especially if I knew he was going to look out for my interests."

I would have done well to heed this advice, but it was given so matter-of-factly, without the emphasis of ego, that I did not take his warning seriously and went head-on into the deals with Ratz, a rash decision I would soon regret.

"*That* was your guidance," Pearl said, referring to Jerry's advice many months later, when I complained bitterly about having paid too much for the run-down properties. Unlike Jerry's understated common sense, Ratz's words encouraging me to go ahead had been clever and flamboyant. I had gone ahead, trusting blindly that the Masters would protect me, *for isn't it the Masters who guided me into this tangled web?* I believed they would also get me out.

The next morning, at 8 a.m., Ratz was at my door. He was making a big show of generosity in offering to take me to breakfast—the only "free" thing he ever gave me. After the meal, we signed the purchase contracts for

---

but need to be differentiated. *Nirvana, Moksha, Mukti* are all Sanskrit terms which refer to liberation from delusion and afflictive emotions (Sanskrit: *kleshas*), although their differentiation may be debated by scholars. One may be liberated but still, like the Buddha, retain a physical body, a being known as a *jivanmukti*. Ascension is equivalent to what the Tibetans mean by attaining the Rainbow Body: *jalu*, the spherical body of light emitting the rainbow colors of the particular aspects of consciousness attained. To dissolve the physical body requires a degree of realization; however, the ascension may also be attained from a higher dimension after passing from the physical form, assuming one has already achieved liberation from karmic afflictions and ceased identification with illusion. There are many beings on the Earth plane who may have achieved high states of realization and are called Masters by their followers, but who still may have a partially limited view in certain areas. It is almost impossible to determine how advanced another person is on the spiritual path, for one may be close to Ascension but still retain the appearance of an ordinary person, taking on the illusion of a certain *maya* for the sake of being in the world and benefiting others.

his dilapidated rentals, and I agreed to give him the proceeds my broker had sent me from the sale of my stock.

Well, I'm just following the Master's plan, I mused, after the papers were signed, trying to quell a sense of rising anxiety in the pit of my stomach. *Isn't this what they directed me to do?* Despite my calls to the Masters to stop the deal if it wasn't meant to be, I felt the compulsion to sign the papers and the deal went through—the dream that began inside the Mountain now a reality. I would eventually learn to be the conscious dreamer—that I could influence the dream by the power of my inner awareness and focused attention.

Still a neophyte to the teachings of the Masters, I was not yet fully aware of the God Power I had to alter the illusory *dream world*. From the moment I signed the purchase agreement, I felt that everything was *fait accompli,* that there was nothing I could do to change the outcome of events—as if the Masters had cast me adrift in a shark-filled ocean.

Chapter 19

Slumlord

My first challenge as a landlord came in dealing with Ned, the surly tenant of a mini-mart I had bought; it was a gas station, grocery, and liquor store all in one. *How did I, a student of the Masters, who hadn't consumed a drop of alcohol in years, come to own a liquor store?* Surely a paradox. Over the years, I discovered that such human concerns did not trouble the Masters, only their students.

Ratz told me that he hadn't raised the man's rent in several years, and at $450 a month, an increase was overdue. I had gone into the market intending to talk to the tenant, but when he scowled at me I didn't tell him I was the new owner. Instead, I went home and wrote a letter telling him that the new rent was $500 a month. Time passed, and I didn't get a check in the mail. Finally, by the third month of delinquent rent, I contacted an attorney.

"We'll sue the bastard!" was his response. "I'll write him a letter demanding payment within ten days. Then if he doesn't pay, we'll sue him. Don't worry; I'll get your money for you!"

After the ten days elapsed and there was still no check, my attorney went ahead with the lawsuit and had the tenant served with the appropriate papers, notifying him he was being sued and the date to appear in court.

"There's no way he can get out of paying," my attorney assured me. "He has a lot of fixed assets we can go after, plus you'll get court costs and damages. We'll evict him and get a new tenant. You can easily get $600 a month for that place!" But the attorney's threatened actions did not bring a check.

Driving by the mini-mart one day and needing gas, I decided to fill up my gas tank. I had been praying to the Masters for help in getting the rent payment, but it seemed they had turned a deaf ear.

Walking up to the counter to pay for the gas, I got up the courage to confront the owner. I figured since he didn't know who I was, I had the option to back down and leave without bringing up the subject of rent. The deep furrow in his brow and scowl on his face indicated that his mood hadn't improved. Still incognito, I handed him my money for the gas. As he handed me my change, he looked me in the eye, and for a moment I saw an inquisitive look on his face, a flicker of light that indicated he, too, was a sentient being who wanted to be happy and avoid suffering.

"Hi, I'm Peter, the new owner," I said, with hesitation.

"Well, it's about time," he said, brightening, extending his hand, "I'm Ned. Why did you wait so long to come in? I just wanted to meet you. I don't have any problem with $500 a month—it's reasonable—but I do have a problem with lawyers. If you'd have come in yourself instead of sending that lawyer after me, I would have paid you straight off."

He pulled a greasy check book from his back pocket and wrote out a check for the $1500 due in back rent. He confided that he had diabetes and had to drive down the canyon to Redding twice a week for dialysis. He said the pain put him in a bad mood a lot of the time.

"But don't let that stand in the way of your coming in," he urged as I left. "Don't be a stranger!"

I felt relieved that the situation had been resolved without going to court, but sad that I had not known of this man's constant pain that had caused me to judge him by his outer appearance. Over the next year I stopped in frequently and bought my gas at his mini-mart. After I got used to Ned's dark moods, we became friends. It took a while, but I saw that underneath his sullen exterior, he had a wry sense of humor and a heart of gold.

It would be a long time before I used an attorney again. I found that people usually wanted to be reasonable, and if a dialog could be initiated—which meant listening patiently to their view—differences could often be resolved. I discovered that if I could listen with understanding to the other person's view, only then explaining my own, that patient approach accomplished more than an angry reaction. If given a chance, everyone would rather experience love than fear.

But not all of my attempts at communication worked smoothly. Sometimes, even when I communicated patiently and clearly, people flat out disagreed—they wanted more than what I was willing to give. I learned that sometimes I just had to say *No*, and that firm response was what some people *wanted* to hear—what they needed to hear. My first test in saying *No* was soon to arrive.

"There's this sweet hippie girl, Angelina from Santa Cruz, who needs a place to stay; could you hold one of your rentals open for her and her daughter?" a friend who was also a fellow student of Pearl pleaded to me one day. Even though I would lose a few hundred dollars in rent by keeping the place vacant until her arrival, I wanted to be a "spiritual" person and do the right thing for someone who, I assumed, was also a student of the Masters, so I reserved a little house on the main street for her.

Angelina seemed sweet at first, but soon had attracted a new boyfriend who moved in with her, and every time I drove by, more cars were parked in front of the house. I learned that her boyfriend's friend and his girlfriend had also moved in. Soon the place became a drug crash pad, hosting nonstop rock music blaring into the street from open windows day and night. Neighbors and police began stopping me on the street with complaints, begging me to do something about the noise and sleazy characters coming and going at all hours.

One day I went by to talk to Angelina, but for once there was no one home. The door was wide open, so I stuck my head in. The place smelled bad, as though something had died inside. Cigarette butts overflowed an ashtray, in which there was a half-smoked joint. Dirty clothes, pizza boxes, and empty beer bottles littered the floor. But what riveted my attention was the use of a book sacred to me, *The Magic Presence*,[23] to prop up the front window. It was now snow-warped and faded by alternating rain and sun. Long overdue at the library, I took the book to return it and left Angelina a note telling her what I had done, asking her to call me.

When she phoned, I told her of the complaints I'd been receiving from the police and that the extra people living there was in violation of her lease. She said, "Don't worry, I'll take care of it—everything is going to be better." But things did not get better, and the complaints I was getting became more insistent. *Where is the peace and love of the Aquarian Age? This girl is a hippie, so where is the love and light? And how did I become a slumlord, having to get tough with a girl my friends call a "dear sister."*

Communicating my needs to her was not working, so finally I broke down and hired a lawyer, and served the eviction papers. Then all hell broke loose. Angelina's friends in Mount Shasta, many of them also Pearl's students, called to tell me how unfair I was being, taking advantage of this poor single mom on Welfare who had no place to go. Her friends prepared to picket my house, and people passing on the street hissed nasty comments at me. I received threatening notes in my mailbox, and dreaded having to go into town, where I was known by everyone. I noticed, however, that none of her boyfriends or those who crashed at her house lifted a finger to

---

23   Godfre Ray King, *The Magic Presence* (Saint Germain Press, Inc., 1982).

help her during this time. In fact, they all vanished. Yet, I was the bad guy.

The day before the town constable was scheduled to bodily remove her from the house, Angelina, the "sweet hippie girl from Santa Cruz," moved out on her own, leaving the place a shambles. It took days to clean the place and make it rentable again. Though I was the evil landlord in the eyes of many, I punished myself even more, agonizing over whether I had done the right thing or not. I had felt, when meditating on the Presence within, that I had been following higher direction, but wondered, *Is forcing someone out of their home really what the Masters want me to do?*

My answer came a year later when I ran into Angelina on the street, and she greeted me with a big smile and warm hug. "You will never know what you did for me!" she exclaimed, exuding love and gratitude. "Your kicking me out of that house was the best thing that ever happened to me. I got rid of my deadbeat boyfriend who was living off me and I took a job with the Forest Service, got off welfare, and am completely self-sufficient for the first time in my life. I gave up smoking dope—I'm completely clean. I don't even drink beer anymore. I feel the best I've ever felt in my whole life, and I have you to thank for it. Thank you so much!"

I was shocked at this dramatic turnaround in this now self-empowered woman. She exuded happiness. "What about your daughter?" I asked.

"She's living with her dad now, and is really happy. I see her every few weeks, and we're getting along much better than before."

Evicting Angelina was one of the hardest things I had to do as landlord. Even though it had made me hated around town for a few months, I was heartened to find that by following my inner guidance and saying *No* when it needed to be said, I had done a good thing.

My life as a landlord, however, with the phone ringing day and night, endless confrontations with tenants, and having to fix old appliances that broke down, was starting to wear thin. I was constantly getting calls from people looking for rentals, the only problem being they didn't always have money. Word soon got around that I was an easy mark, that if you pleaded poverty or seemed spiritual enough, I wouldn't require a security deposit or last month's rent. In fact, sometimes I let people move in without paying anything if they had a hard luck story, thinking I was helping. In truth it would have been better to say *No* more often, right from the beginning, and spare us both a lot of wasted energy. After all, they would eventually need to learn the lesson of responsibility, the same one I was learning during this apprenticeship to the Masters.

During this time as a landlord I had to learn to work miracles—opportunities to apply the I AM teachings and call my God Self into action. I saw that the infinite resides in every situation as unrealized potential, waiting at every moment to be realized—an active principle waiting to be called into action to do our bidding, that God is not merely a passive consciousness reserved for "spiritual" contemplation, but an active principle that can be invoked to enhance life.

One morning I got a phone call from a tenant complaining that he didn't have any hot water. I called the plumber and he met me at the rental. He turned on the hot water faucet of the kitchen sink, and cold water gushed out. After hooking his meter to the circuit, he announced, "It's burnt out. You can't even get a new element for models this old. You'll have to get a new hot water heater."

As my bank account was close to zero, and I had a pile of unpaid bills on my desk, I began to sweat. "It can't be burnt out," I insisted.

"Well, it is!" he said, showing me the needle of the meter stuck on zero.

Refusing to accept defeat by the three dimensional logic of his meter, and feeling desperation rising within me, I put both hands on the heater and from the center of my being, demanded silently, *Mighty I AM Presence, come forth and charge this hot water heater with your miracle of perfection right now!* I visualized myself as a Master, beams of light pouring from my hands into the defective unit.

"Now turn on the hot water," I said to the plumber with confidence. Both he and the tenant looked at each other as though I was crazy, but, thinking that it was easier to turn on the faucet than argue with a crazy person, they complied. As hot water began steaming into the sink, neither said a word. The plumber chewed his lower lip for a moment, contemplating this challenge to his normal reality, then packed up his tools in silence and stalked out, saying over his shoulder as he went down the stairs, "You'll get the bill for my time."

Later, when I told Pearl what had happened, she smiled and said, "When you turn your attention to the God Presence within, the response can be direct and without limit, and don't you forget that! The more you accept the miracle-working power of the Presence, the more it can accomplish. But you have to call it into action. Only then will it work."

Pearl had worked more than a few miracles of her own. A friend told me how one cold morning, when the engine of their truck had refused to start, Pearl put her hands on the hood, closed her eyes, and made a silent call to her God Self. Then she told Jerry to turn the ignition key again, and the engine started immediately. "She's got quite a bit of power," Jerry said in his casual, understated way, to my friend who'd been sitting there, open-mouthed, watching Pearl charge the battery with her God Power. Why call a tow truck when you can call God?

Over the years, Jerry had become used to Pearl invoking the Divine Consciousness to solve even the most mundane problems. Though she appeared to be a soft-spoken, elderly lady, through the application of the simple laws which she had mastered, she worked seeming miracles.

A year later I was in Los Angeles and I had the opportunity to apply the same law. I had spent a few nights at the home of a Dr. Leonard, a friend I had met on his visit to Mount Shasta to meet Pearl. He had heard stories of her miracles, and they had made a deep impression on him. While I was staying with him, he lent me his car to drive into town, but when I attempted to start it, the engine refused to turn over. Hearing the coughing of the engine, he came out to the driveway to help. Remembering the stories about Pearl's miracles, he asked, "Have you called the Mighty I AM Presence into action?"

"No, I haven't," I answered sheepishly, as I was usually the one who reminded others of the I AM Presence. Immediately I turned my attention inward to my heart, knowing that above me the God Presence was waiting to fulfill every need.

"Mighty I AM, come forth now and start this car," I commanded, calling my Infinite Power into action as I turned the key in the ignition. As the engine came alive, I smiled at Dr. Leonard and thanked him for the reminder. Although he was a doctor of the physical body, I saw that in putting one in touch with the Source was the ultimate healing.

As I backed into the street and drove away, I was grateful for the reminder of that unlimited assistance that is available at every moment, once we turn to the I AM Presence for everything we need.

Part IV:

Learning to Trust

Chapter 20

Cheesecake Guidance

One night, after a busy day repairing an old house in Dunsmuir and getting it ready to rent, I decided to retire before my usual bedtime. I had to be back at the house early the next morning to meet with the electrical contractor, so I showered and prepared for bed. But no sooner had I sat to meditate, as I always did before sleep, than I heard the inner voice say, *Go have a piece of cheesecake.*

We had a gourmet vegetarian restaurant in town called Friends of the Mountain, and their dessert special was a delicious cheesecake for which I had developed a craving, and from which I was trying to wean myself. Thinking this was the voice of my own desire, I ignored it and tried to turn my attention deeper within. *Have a piece of cheesecake,* I heard again, this time louder.

I began decreeing, *I am free of all desire for cheesecake. Dear God, take out of me all desires for anything less than perfection!*

But instead of going away, the command became more insistent, resembling the voice of Saint Germain: *I told you to have a piece of cheesecake. Now get up, get dressed, and go down to Friends of the Mountain, and I don't want to have to tell you again!*

OK, I'll go, I conceded, still fearing that I might not be hearing the voice of the Master but my own desire masquerading as him. So, I decided to put the voice to the test.

I pulled on my clothes, got in the car, and drove the quarter mile down the street to the restaurant and parked in front, but instead of going in I tested the voice once more. *I AM free of all wrong desires,* I decreed, determined not to go inside unless the guidance was crystal clear.

I thought I already told you what to do, I heard the Master's voice, or what seemed to be his voice, again insisting. *But why would he want me to eat cheesecake, and at this hour of the night?* More in an effort to escape that voice than for any desire for cheesecake, I got out of the car and went inside.

To prove my self-control, I ordered tea and nothing else. I sat there, observing what was going on in the almost empty restaurant. Nothing extraordinary was happening, since it was late and the place was getting

Apprentice to the Masters

ready to close, so I just sipped my tea and waited. It's amazing how simply waiting will allow a situation to clarify.

Now, have your cheesecake, came the command, so I got up and went to the counter where the desserts were shown in a refrigerated display, and at the same moment a man from a table in the corner rose and joined me at the counter.

"What do you recommend?" he queried, in a French accent.

"The cheesecake, without a doubt."

"Well, would you allow me to treat you, and invite you to join my family at our table?" he said, bowing in an Old World manner.

I said that I would be glad and was soon seated at his table with his beautiful wife and daughter, with a piece of the famous cheesecake before each of us. As we began to eat, he explained they were from Marseille, and they came to Mount Shasta every summer to be in the radiation of the Masters.

"We have been observing you ever since you came in," his wife said, "and we are sure that you are under the guidance of the Master Saint Germain, because we keep seeing him standing behind you. Since he is our Master, too, we felt prompted to invite you to our table."[24]

They wanted to know how I had come to know of the Master and what had brought me to the Mountain, and as we shared our experiences we soon realized that we were all apprentices under Saint Germain's direction. We were amazed at the similar trials we had gone through and the kindness the Master had extended, which enabled us to progress so rapidly in this lifetime. Although the motto of the Great White Brotherhood is *To know, to dare, to do, and to be silent,* there are exceptional times such as this when it is permitted to share one's experiences with others. And as we did so, we felt Saint Germain's presence and the elevating radiation of his love.

As we were getting ready to leave, this beautiful family invited me to visit them in France, "Be our guest in Marseille, come and stay as long as you like. Any friend of Saint Germain is a friend of ours."

Walking out into the cool night air, I heard Saint Germain laugh; *I hope you enjoyed your cheesecake, my boy.* I realized then that the radiation in the restaurant had been so beautiful, so far transcending anything

---

24   These people could be called *Ascended Master Friends,* a term discussed elsewhere.

material, that I did not even remember eating the dessert, nor have I eaten cheesecake again, all desire for it having been permanently removed.

I realized that until our minds are purified, God often uses our desires to guide us to fulfill our destiny, leading us to the right place at the right time, where we will make the connections we need. Once purity was attained, I knew that I would perceive guidance more directly.

I left with the feeling of Saint Germain's love and remembered that the Masters had said, "What you humans call 'love' cannot compare to the friendship the Masters feel for each other." Now I felt a glimmering of that Ascended Master Friendship as I bid my new friends *adieu*.

Chapter 21

The Atomic Accelerator

During that first year of training with Pearl, I had many lessons in following inner guidance, often referred to as the *still, small voice within*. I was finding that it was not so much a voice as a *feeling* which the mind converts into words—the accuracy of translation depending on the degree to which the mind has been purified of previous concepts, desires, and reactivity. This inner Presence is always functioning, guiding us in even the most insignificant choices in life, but we only sense it when the mind is quiet, free of attractions and aversions. Without that stillness, without that surrender and acceptance of the Higher Will of the God Self (one with the Will of the Masters), we hear only the chatter of the lower mind vacillating between personal fears and desires. I was developing this stillness through *Vipassana*,[25] the technique used by Siddhartha Gautama to attain enlightenment and become the Buddha, the awakened one. This deceptively simple method is based on the observation of the rise and fall of the breath and the expansion of awareness that may then take place. Although many talk about the *"power of now,"* this is a method for attaining and living in the now.

Once I had attained that basic ground of awareness, I began practicing the meditation Saint Germain gives in *Unveiled Mysteries,* of visualizing the light of the Heart and expanding that light through every cell of the body until one becomes a radiant sun in space, blessing all sentient beings. On emerging from that meditation, one repeats affirmations[26] to call forth the supremacy of that light in all one's activity, finally closing with words

---

25 *Vipassana* meditation is taught in Shambhala Centers around the world. To find a nearby Center, visit www.shambhala.org and click on "Meditation."

26 Affirmations, unlike Sanskrit *mantras,* must be repeated slowly with full consciousness to be effective. In repeating them rapidly, they become a mental, psychic force, devoid of consciousness or connection with the Source. Sanskrit, on the other hand, is a language of great vibrational purity, whose sounds create sacred forms almost regardless of the speed of recitation, as long as pronounced correctly.

of gratitude. Realizing the oneness of that state in one's ordinary waking mind, one then frequently perceives the guidance.

I knew that it was Saint Germain who was testing me over and over, to strengthen my ability to follow that guidance, to learn to distinguish between the subtle prompting of the Higher Self that guided from within the heart and the loud assertions of the lower mind. True warriorship, I was learning, had nothing to do with aggression, or even in taking action according to a preconceived plan, but in being in the stillness and from *there* wielding the Sword of Discriminating Intelligence to cut through the enemy of self-deception. Free of delusion, one then needed to realize the courage to follow wherever the vision led without hesitating, wavering, or questioning. That guidance often came unexpectedly, without warning. At times it began as a subtle thought accompanied by a feeling, which grew in intensity to the point where the vision clarified and I just needed to free myself of preconceptions, fears, and doubts before committing energy to follow through. On other occasions the thought diminished over time and faded away, and I realized later it had been the working of my lower mind, or perhaps someone else's thought which I had taken on as my own.

One Sunday morning I awoke to that inner prompting, which took the form of a persistent desire to take a drive. I'd been feeling the pull to go north for several days, so I was not surprised when I awoke with that feeling stronger than the day before. When I dressed and climbed into the car, it seemed to want to go north of its own accord. As a way of getting my mind out of the way, I would pretend that the car had its own innate intelligence, to which I only needed to be sensitive, like giving free reign to a horse, knowing that it always knows the direction to the nearest water.

Driving over the border into Oregon, I looked forward to taking a break in Ashland, where I always enjoyed strolling among the cafés and bookstores, and relaxing in the verdant park adjacent to the Shakespearean theater. But to my surprise, when I came to the first freeway exit for Ashland, my foot did not want to lift from the gas pedal. *Hey, I want to go into Ashland,* my mind protested, as the car raced past the last exit. Feeling apprehensive, I realized I was again being sent on a mission into the unknown territory ruled by the Ascended Masters. I had no idea that what started as a Sunday morning drive would turn out to be a two-week-long intensive on-the-road training by the Masters—what Pearl called *objective teaching,* the realization of truth that can only come about through lessons in daily life. Being told a truth is not as effective as experiencing it as an objective, tangible reality.

Around noon I reached Central Point and pulled onto a side road. After driving for a quarter of an hour, I stopped to eat the sandwiches I had packed. From a high bluff overlooking the freeway, while enjoying the panoramic view of the valley below, I ate my lunch and contemplated the name of where I was, Central Point. In the objective teaching that was unfolding, this suggested that I had symbolically journeyed to the *central point of my being*, the inner place where the God Flame dwells, the pursuit of which is the purpose of existence. As this realization came upon me, I was flooded by a spiritual radiation that pulled my attention further inward, and I surrendered to a natural, meditative state where time ceased and there was *only being and awareness*.

When I returned to duality an hour later, I realized I had been shown a plan—to not return home to Mount Shasta that day, but to continue north, and that my journey would last for many days. I realized, with a mixture of excitement and apprehension, that another adventure under the Masters' guidance was unfolding. Although I recalled a movie-like vision of the route I was to follow, those details soon faded, and all that remained by the time I returned to the freeway was the memory of glacier-covered mountains far to the north, and the certainty that a plan existed.

Using my favorite decree for piloting my vehicle in unknown territory, I chanted aloud as I drove along:

I AM the Presence of God, driving where I AM meant to go, doing what I AM meant to do.

I imagined my heart as a glowing sun casting rays before me, illuminating the road like a brilliant, unfolding ribbon of light. The words of my affirmation kept my attention so fixed on the center of my being that I took no notice of time, which had evaporated in the acceleration of consciousness. In that stillness I was guided in the serenity and peace of the all-enfolding Presence.

Arriving in Eugene late at night, I came upon Pearl Street, which in my awareness of objective teaching represented the inner path I was following of finding the Pearl of Great Price within—so I followed it to the Pearl Street Hotel. Before I went to bed, I turned my attention inward to my Heart Flame, then upward to my I AM Presence above me, and made the inner decree,

> *I AM the Illumining, Revealing Presence, showing me where to go and what to do. See to it that when I awaken, I have the feeling to go where I AM meant to go, and that I follow that guidance infallibly.*

Then I turned my attention to the Masters and made another inner call:

> *Saint Germain, great host of Ascended Masters, please take complete command of my life and world. Remove from me any imperfection or anything that would interfere with my fulfilling your Divine Plan and raise me into the Consciousness, Activity, and Dominion of my I AM Presence forever. Please see to it that I am invincibly protected at all times.*

In the morning, although I didn't remember any dreams or guidance from my sleep, I again felt the pull to travel north toward the glacial mountains I had seen in my mind's eye the day before at Central Point. As on the previous day, I started driving without a plan, not knowing the destination, but trusting that the Presence would lead in its own inner way according to the Plan of which it was fully aware.

As I neared Portland I wondered, *where to from here?* I kept up my decree:

> *I am God directed and God commanded.*

Maintaining the visualization that my God Presence was driving, I felt the guiding, sustaining energy flowing from my heart, through my arms and hands, to the steering wheel. Seeing a sign for Spokane, Washington, I felt an immediate surge of energy. Despite being distracted by traffic and speeding trucks, when I came to the freeway exit for Spokane my body was pulled in that direction, and giving my steed free reign, I allowed my vehicle to take the next exit and turn east. Turning onto the eastbound freeway I felt uplifted, a confirmation of my choice of *no choice,* that although I didn't know where I was going, it was the right direction. A few miles later, as the traffic thinned, I observed that the high energy that had been with me all the way was still present, a clear sign I was "on the beam" and following the Masters' prearranged path.

As the sun was setting, I found Spokane nearing on the horizon, and it seemed like common sense to spend the night. Even though I felt no direct guidance, I knew that often *doing the obvious is the guidance.* Driving down the main street, I came to an elegant old hotel, The Davenport, which looked like a historical landmark. Again, I felt the flame in my heart signal that I had arrived at that night's resting place.

As I approached the hotel desk to register, I was surprised by the spacious elegance of the lobby. The interior appeared to have been designed by a master architect schooled in the inner mysteries, and I admired the gold-leaf columns reaching to the vaulted ceiling that gave the place the feeling of an ancient temple. Bronze statuary and bubbling fountains complemented the richly upholstered antique furniture. The expansive marble floor was covered by rich Persian rugs, and the soft lighting appeared to be from gas lamps from a previous age. The gracious service I received as I checked in, along with the sense of ease and grace that permeated the environment, again affirmed that I had found the right place—as though I was being admitted to an Ascended Master retreat.

After a sumptuous dinner in the ornate dining room, I returned to my room and filled the claw foot bathtub with steaming water. Silently, I invoked the Violet Consuming Flame to charge my bath water, saying:

I AM the Commanding, Governing Presence of God, charging this water with the Violet Consuming Flame, which dissolves all imperfection, and which raises me into the Consciousness, Activity, and Perfection of my own I AM Presence forever.

To my surprise, a subtle violet light illuminated the sides of the tub and spread to fill the room. Climbing into this light-filled tub, I noticed the water bubbling like Champagne, which reminded me of the retreats of the Ascended Masters that Godfre Ray King had described so beautifully in his series of green books about his inner adventures with Saint Germain. These retreats were often located inside mountains such as Mount Fuji, the Grand Teton, Mount Kailash, Mount Kilimanjaro, Mount Popocatepetl, and Mount Shasta, in addition to many others.

I had read with enthusiasm how Godfre told of being taken to the retreat of the Royal Teton, and bathing in a tub of charged, purifying water before changing into his robe and being taken to the Inner Council Chamber. I sensed that I was at a major turning point in my evolution, that I was being summoned now by the Masters to a new level of awareness, from which I would never again descend.

After finishing my bath, I quickly retired to the bed, where I sat and meditated deeply on my own I AM God Presence before laying my body to rest. No sooner was my outer form asleep than I awoke in my subtle body to find a white-robed, masterful presence awaiting me. This messenger was my escort, he announced, to the Masters' retreat in the Royal Teton.

When we arrived, I was shocked to be led to the Atomic Accelerator, a throne-like device I had read about in *The Magic Presence* that, with the Masters' assistance, accelerates the vibratory rate of the individual into the Ascended state. Saint Germain and two other Masters greeted me, and without a moment's explanation or preparation I was ushered into the throne that appeared to be made of solid gold.

"Relax, free your mind of all thought, and turn your attention to the center of your being," I heard. As I did so, I entered the state of emptiness I practiced so often in meditation. Then an ecstatic energy began coursing through my body, electrifying every cell. Saint Germain, I realized, was standing behind me with two other white-robed Masters, whose names I didn't know, on either side. Rapidly, I felt all attachment to the human self dissolving.

Focus your attention on the God Presence within, continued the inner direction. As I became more absorbed in my own essential nature, the electric force increased, and I felt myself becoming lighter.

Make a powerful decree, the most powerful decree you can think of. Without a moment's hesitation, I uttered a decree that I had never said before, which if spoken in the outer world would have sounded egotistical and sacrilegious, but which, said inwardly, affirmed oneness with the Christ. As my attention focused on that God Presence, I started to become that Presence, feeling lighter and lighter until I began to rise from the throne. Dark blotches that I realized were negative thoughts and subconscious memories that had been stored in my body from childhood flew out from the ascending form and, like shadows, were consumed by the ever-increasing light the Masters were focusing. As I rose higher and the great streams of energy increased, dissolving all sense of limitation, I merged with my Higher Self—conscious only of being a luminous Presence...and the realization,

I AM God.

The next morning I was shocked to find that I had not entirely disappeared from the physical plane, as I had thought. There was a body in the bed, and that body seemed to be mine. *I Ascended in the Atomic*

Accelerator. My body dissolved into light. So, what is this body doing here? Yet, here was what appeared to be my former body, one that responded to my will. I pinched an arm to see if it felt pain—which it did—but it could still be a dream, couldn't it? I had just experienced the most powerful event, the pinnacle of my life, the Ascension, so where was I now? I stumbled to the mirror, and to my surprise, saw staring back at me my own face, blank with shock. *There has been some kind of mistake*, I thought. *The body was supposed to disappear!* I had entered Paradise, only to be sent back to the world of human delusion once more, by those Masters I thought had granted total freedom—at a time when least expected.

Searching for an explanation for how I could have Ascended yet still have a physical body,[27] I recalled Daniel Rayborne in *The Magic Presence*,

---

27 What we call the human being is actually only the lowest of many bodies operating with varying degrees of consciousness, each on its own level or frequency, but with the same life-giving Ray of Light from the I AM Presence extending down through and animating all of them. That light is finally anchored in the center of the chest of the physical body near the thymus gland. During Ascension those lower vehicles are subsumed back into the higher vehicle, like the tubes of a telescope being collapsed back into the single segment from which they extended. In Buddhism these bodies are known as the *Dharmakaya*, *Sambhogakaya*, and *Nirmanakaya*. Prior to complete Ascension, some of these lower bodies may merge with the higher ones, which initiations we may temporarily perceive as "enlightenment." There are also some souls who never fully embody, as some of their higher vehicles are held in abeyance, lest they reveal too much of the higher worlds or exercise too much power before either they or humanity is ready. For example, the Masters stated that the eccentricity of Madame Blavatsky, the great occultist who first introduced the Masters and their teachings to the West, was attributable to some of her higher vehicles being held in abeyance in temples on higher planes. Others may achieve a partial Ascension, yet still maintain some degree of connection with their human form and personality as a means of interacting with the human world. A liberated being may take the appearance of a normal person, called *taking on a maya*, to perform certain roles in the human world that could not be performed by appearing as a Master. Such a being, who is liberated, yet retains an outer human form and personality, is called a *Jivanmukti*.

who had experienced a similar process in the Atomic Accelerator. Taken almost to the point of Ascension, he had been told that he must retain his outer form, as he still had work to complete in the human world. *Perhaps I, too, yet have a mission to fulfill?*

Though I retained my physical body, I did not feel the same. As I sat in bed, orienting myself to this new reality, I began to perceive a blue-white light in the center of my forehead. As I focused my attention on it, my vision expanded and numbers began flashing on this new screen in my mind, each one containing a lesson that revealed some aspect of consciousness manifesting on every level, from the smallest sub-atomic particle to the cosmos—and I saw that all were aspects of the One. Fascinated, I watched as the wisdom contained in these lessons downloaded to my mind like a giant file transfer.

The geometric design of creation unfolded—like a movie projected through the aperture of my all-seeing eye, showing how creation operated with an almost inconceivable, mathematical perfection. The secrets of the universe unfolded in a movie more astounding than anything I had ever imagined. I saw how art, science, and spirituality were but varied expressions of the One—a unified field, a geometric lattice of consciousness underlying the ground of being. The material world was merely a chimera, sustained by the celestial music of a vast intelligence, without which creation would cease to exist.

As the revelations began to slow, I remembered the line of William Blake, *"If the doors of perception were cleansed, everything would appear to man as it is, infinite."*[28] And I realized that the infinite can be perceived in the finite at every moment, that there is no place where God is not.

Eventually the screen in my mind went blank, and I became aware of a sensation in the pit of my belly I recognized as hunger. *How strange to be subject to physical needs,* I thought, still vibrant with the energy of Ascension, a state where there are no needs. *Which dream is real—the one of Ascension, or that I am on the Earth in a physical body? And when will all dreams end?* Still pondering these riddles, I dressed and went downstairs to the dining room, where I ordered a huge breakfast with fresh squeezed orange juice. When I had finished eating, I sat in the splendid lobby and

---

28 William Blake, *The Marriage of Heaven and Hell* (original edition, 1827; facsimile edition, Oxford University Press, 1975).

again took in the elaborate design. Everything I focused on revealed layers of meaning that I had not sensed when I checked in the night before. Now that my "doors of perception" had been cleansed, I saw beyond appearances into the pattern inherent in all creation—how everything is interconnected and interdependent. The patterns visible in the design of the lobby—the elaborate designs in the floor, sculptured columns, and artwork hanging on the walls—were the same patterns of consciousness, aspects of my own mind.

Overwhelmed by my realization of the interconnectedness of everything, I rose to my feet, knowing it was time to leave. I felt the energy of my I AM Presence, the Great Source and Sustainer of my being, surging through me and filling every cell of my body with vibrant life.

Asking at the front desk to settle my bill, I was surprised to see I'd been charged not for one night, but for two.

"No, sir," the clerk said firmly, when I protested the mistake. "You arrived here in the evening two days ago. You can check the calendar on the wall here."

"That couldn't be," I stammered, shocked by the clerk's assertion.

"Sir, here's a copy of your room registration with your signature and date, and here is a copy of today's newspaper," he replied, looking at me oddly, perhaps wondering if I had been drunk, passed out in the room, and lost track of time.

I looked at the date on the newspaper and saw that, incredibly, what he was saying was correct. I had been at the hotel for two nights, though I could only recall one. Had I been at the retreat of the Royal Teton for two days? Although my experience in the Atomic Accelerator seemed to have been brief, after entering the Ascended Master Octave I had no memory of where I had gone or what had transpired next. And why hadn't the maid knocked on my door to make up my room? These questions raced through my mind, as I sought an explanation for this bizarre, missing time. If I had not eaten for two days, that would at least explain my ravenous hunger.

Knowing that for the Masters anything is possible, that in their world, time as we know it does not exist, I did not contest my bill any further and paid the clerk for the two nights he claimed I owed.

Returning to my vehicle, I got back on the open road again, driving east, feeling a sense of euphoria in the surrender to the unknown, the blissful emptiness of *no thought, no plan*. Although I had no idea where I was going, everything seemed perfect beyond belief, and I trusted in the Presence now filling me with the bliss of unqualified being.

So this is enlightenment! I thought, unaware that a new level of awareness is but a prelude to the next, which, when attained, will also seem the ultimate realization. Yet, I basked in that bliss of expanded awareness—consciousness without thought or reference point, speeding along through the vast, empty plains without destination. Blissfully, there was *nothing to do,* just be.

I savored this spacious reality, still feeling that I had arrived at some ultimate level; but, as the horizon kept receding before me, I began to realize that there was no boundary, no end, to awareness. As one summit is attained, another one is revealed in the distance. Even the concept "enlightenment" is an illusion, for the very act of naming is to limit that which, by its very nature, is unlimited.[29]

---

29 Chögyam Trungpa Rinpoche, the great Tibetan meditation master who first brought Buddhist *Vajrayana* teachings to America, when asked to comment on enlightenment, replied, "I don't know anything about it."

Chapter 22

Rendezvous at Lake Louise

As I drove northward, this new consciousness began to stabilize. Accepting that I still had a human body and an ordinary mind, I saw that both were vehicles like my car that I could use skillfully to accomplish my mission, which was as yet unrevealed. I began to see things once again, not as aspects of infinite awareness, but as the finite things-in-themselves they appeared to be. No longer did everything seem symbolic or the portent of some revelation; the crossroads before me was not a turning point in my life, but simply a place where I had to decide to turn left, right, or go straight ahead. And I realized that to be an effective agent in this play of appearances, I needed to accept this relative reality and make it my home.

The subtle energy within continued to provide direction, and I seemed more sensitive to that guidance than ever before. I noticed that at times my energy level would drop, that I would suddenly feel tired or disoriented, usually indicating I had taken a wrong turn. Then I reversed direction until I came back to where I had been, trying the other direction. I would do this until I regained that feeling of a beam of energy going up my spine that confirmed I was going the right way.

I wondered, *Why don't more spiritual teachers show their students how to get this natural guidance from within? Perhaps because they don't know it themselves?* Instead, many channel endless new information, keeping their students perpetually dependent on them, in a state of spiritual infancy where they never learn to make their own decision or take responsibility for their own actions. I was learning that there is no Mastery or freedom as long as one is looking outside oneself, for all answers lie within—readily accessible to those who are willing to do the work of stilling the mind and surrendering the ego. Far better to make a "mistake" by one's own decision than to "do the right thing" channeled through someone else—for it is through the very process of making mistakes that we learn and become strong, while in obeying dictations we learn only submission.[30]

---

30 In the *Bhagavad Gita,* Krishna says that it is better to fulfill your own

I felt grateful to Pearl for putting me in touch with this *inner direction finder* in my heart, a global positioning system that needs no batteries and is ready to be used at all times.

Driving on through the desolate country, I watched the vast expanses as they dissolved into each other. Following that beam of energy that guided me infallibly, I passed into northern Idaho, then Montana. I was headed toward the Canadian border, but in a state where rational thought with its tendency to analyze was suspended, I knew that I could be guided to change direction or even turn around at any moment.

Finally, on a horizon in northern Montana, I saw the gleaming mountains I'd seen in my mind's eye while meditating at Central Point, and found myself driving into Glacier National Park. The air was pure and clear as I drove through an icy citadel whose stark, white peaks knifed jaggedly into the ultramarine sky. The air seemed supercharged with life force, and I drew it in with deep breaths.

Enraptured by the intensity of this beauty, I wanted to abandon my vehicle and run through the snow glittering in the sunlight, up the cliffs into the arms of the God I knew was waiting to receive me. But I stayed behind the wheel, and instead of dissipating that energy, breathed in the *prana* (Sanskrit: life force) and concentrated it with the power of my mind, a manna which nourished every cell of my body. I felt I could live on this pure, ambrosial energy, never again needing any physical sustenance—and I felt once again close to the perfection of the Ascended state.

All too soon, the black ribbon of highway wound out of the mountains, leaving the glaciers behind, and the car descended into the cold, windswept plains of Canada. As I drove, I felt the growing sense that I had been driving for an eternity and would never arrive at a destination. I felt that I was traveling through a *bardo* (Tibetan: transitional state) that was the eternity of the present moment, suspended between the illusion of past and future. There were no reference points. None of the towns I passed had familiar names or meant anything to me. I drove on and on, ascending once again another mountain range. I felt I was entering another world, one that was strangely empty, and I wondered if somehow I'd gone astray. Adrift on an ocean of uncertainty, the inner energy of the Presence was

---

dharma (path of righteous action), however poorly, than someone else's, however well.

my only companion and life raft. Trusting that feeling of *inner rightness,* I knew that if the Masters wanted me to change direction, there would be a shift in that feeling within.

Finally, as it was beginning to get dark, I saw a sign indicating that I was leaving this *bardo,* for on it was written the name of a place I recognized: Banff, a real place in the real world. Numb and exhausted, I stopped at a welcome-looking motel with a pink vacancy sign in the office window, paid for a night, and as soon as I was given the key, I stumbled to the room, where, without taking off my coat, I flopped face down on the bed and sank into oblivion. Minutes later, I was stirred into alertness by a shock of realization: *Something is wrong…this is the wrong place…not where I am to stay!* The longer I lay there the more uncomfortable I became. *Yet, it's dark and I'm exhausted; I'm in the middle of the Rocky Mountains with nothing but miles of snowy wilderness ahead. How can I keep going?* Despite my fear, I had to move on. Though I tried to argue with the *inner voice,* I knew there was no reasoning with what was meant to be. I tried to meditate, thinking that the uncomfortable feeling might go away, but I could not drown out that feeling pushing me onward. Finally, I surrendered and rose to my feet, straightened the bed covers, picked up my bag, and trudged back to the office.

Trying to explain to the girl at the front desk who had checked me in only a short while before, I apologized, "I'm sorry, but I can't stay here tonight."

"Is something wrong?" she asked, bewildered.

"No, it's just that I have to keep going."

Sensing that this young woman with a kind, open face was someone who might understand, I said, "Do you believe in what some people call the *still, small voice*—like the voice of your conscience that warns you when you're about to do something wrong?"

"Yes, I believe I do," she said, thoughtfully.

"Well, that voice is telling me that I shouldn't be here, that I should keep on driving. It's just a feeling, but I've got to follow it. I'm sorry to have put you to all the trouble. I'm glad to pay something for the room."

"That's all right," she said warmly, handing my money back, "I understand."

I thanked her from my heart, appreciative of her kindness and understanding. As I walked out the door, she called out, "I hope you find what you're looking for!"

So do I, I thought, *only I don't know what that is.*

Returning to my car and setting out again into the night on the desolate highway, I wondered, *Why did the Masters send me here to the wilds of Canada? I'm hungry, cold, low on gas, and without an inkling of a destination where to spend the night. Where is my Higher Self now, that Infinite Consciousness with which I was so recently merged?* Having re-entered the world of duality, I felt the desolation once more of being an ordinary human lost in the wilderness. I no longer felt the sustaining current of energy that had been with me throughout my travels, but I also did not feel any pull to turn around, so I kept tenaciously to the last clear guidance I had received, and continued onward. Trying to rouse that uplifting, courageous energy the Tibetans call Wind Horse (*lungta*), I called to the Infinite Source of energy within and above me,

Beloved I AM Presence, come forth! Charge me with your Divine Energy and Consciousness, and take me where you want me to go.

Soon, I felt my God Self respond with a flow of energy. Though driving in darkness over icy roads, I was filled with a sustaining force. Enveloped in the huge, snowy wilderness that wrapped me in its blanket of silence, I felt now strangely serene and protected. I watched with curiosity as the needle of my gas gauge flirted with *Empty* and wondered, still without fear, if I would be one of those who every winter die in their cars, stranded in the wilds. Fifty miles from civilization, the temperature below freezing, this was not a place to run out of gas. But now, after my dynamic decrees, I again felt the guiding energy pulling me to drive on.

Just when I was sure the car would cough to a stop, a wooden sign appeared out of the darkness: "Lodging & Gas—Two Miles." The sign pointed down a narrow dirt road with high snowbanks on either side. I turned down this unlikely path with apprehension. There were no lights or signs of civilization to indicate whatever was down there would be open, and I knew I couldn't afford to make a mistake. *What if the place is only open in summer? They wouldn't find me until the snow thaws.*

I kept driving slowly, however, affirming that it was God in me who was driving, peering into the darkness to see what lay ahead. Finally, I came to a huge opening in the forest and saw an ice-covered lake, the surface illumined by moonlight and surrounded on three sides by jagged, snowy peaks. As I came fully into the clearing, I was relieved to see bright lights, then a huge, palatial chateau that seemed somehow familiar, maybe something I'd seen in travel books as a child. The magnificent dwelling was surrounded by dozens of multicolored flags and lit up by spotlights, as though in anticipation of the arrival of some royal being. It appeared like a French chateau of old, where the nobility spent long, snow-bound winters attending string quartets, elegant balls, and discussing the latest works of philosophy, but I saw no one about. There was not even a car parked in sight.

Is this a real place, or am I in another dimension? Perhaps my body is back at that motel, asleep on the bed, and this is only a dream? I could not believe that I had merely stumbled on such an elegant lodging in the middle of nowhere, and with no one else around.

After parking, I walked up to a huge, wooden door mounted on ornate, wrought iron hasps, like the door of a castle, and pushed it open. I found myself in a tunnel-like passageway leading into a grand foyer, whose stone floor was covered with plush, Persian rugs. I approached the desk, but there was no one there. Just as I was wondering what to do, a young man in a hotel uniform appeared behind the desk. He bowed slightly and said, "Welcome to Chateau Lake Louise."

"Lake Louise? This is Lake Louise?" I asked, incredulous. When I was a child, my grandmother and aunt had visited this famous place on a vacation and sent me a postcard. No wonder it looked familiar. More recently, I had heard that Lake Louise was an Ascended Master retreat, a focus of Archangel Michael. In my tortuous travels I seemed to have stumbled onto it by accident, but, to my growing amazement, I realized that this is where the Masters had been leading me through inner guidance.

"It looks as though you're expecting royalty," I stammered, still numb from the driving I had done that day, and in shock at the unexpected splendor of my destination.

"I was awaiting only you, Sir," he replied, bowing again.

"You mean I can spend the night?" I muttered, for I still had not seen another person, and was sure that the place would not be fully illuminated, with all the flags flying, if the arrival of some important personage had not been expected.

He handed me a key, which he assured me was the best room they had, with a view of the Lake. When I asked if I could pay cash, as I didn't have a credit card, he laughed and said, "Don't worry, we'll take care of that in the morning. Now, have a good night's sleep, Sir!"

Apprentice to the Masters

With that, he walked to an electrical panel, switched off all the exterior lights, and dimmed the chandelier in the lobby. Truly, it seemed he had been waiting only for me to arrive before shutting the place down for the night, as if having received unconscious guidance from Saint Germain. Then he walked to the massive door, locked the huge bolt, and disappeared down a corridor. I still had not seen another soul.

As he disappeared, I made my way down the softly carpeted corridor to the staircase, walked up one flight, and soon found my room. As the clerk had promised, I had been given one of the best rooms in the hotel, with a stunning view overlooking the moon-lit lake below. I was no longer hungry, but suddenly so tired that, after locking the door and turning the deadbolt, I didn't even take my clothes off, but climbed onto the bed and fell into a deep sleep.

I had not been asleep for more than a quarter of an hour when I was awakened by the feeling that I was not alone. I remembered having locked the door when I came in, as I always do when reaching my room, but now it seemed there was someone in the room with me. As I raised my head, I saw a man with short, blond hair, wearing a silver jumpsuit, standing a few feet from my bed and staring directly at me.

Although I felt a moment of surprise, I did not feel threatened.[31] Indeed, soon I recognized his face from the vision I'd had while meditating at the beginning of my journey at Central Point. Now I recalled how in the vision, he had appeared in the same close-fitting silver jumpsuit with elastic cuffs at the wrists and ankles, surrounded by a soft, blue light.

Seeing I was awake, my visitor addressed me. "I am sorry if I startled you, but I have been sent to get you."

"Get me? I don't even know who you are. And how did you get into my room?"

"I regret I do not have time to answer all your questions. Only know that I mean you no harm; if you come with me, there is a great surprise that awaits you," the stranger said, without emotion or any hint of coercion in his voice.

Immediately I turned my attention deep within to my heart, to the Presence I had been trained to seek for the answers to all things, and found

---

31 To be free of fear is the *sine qua non* for contact with the Masters and other-worldly visitors, for they will not usually appear to those who might be unbalanced by the shock.

there no fear, or any other warning emotion to keep me from going with the stranger.

"If you are going to come with me, we must hurry and leave without further delay," the stranger said. "Your friends are waiting."

Friends? What friends could I have waiting for me in a forest in Canada in the middle of the night? In answer to my thought, the man said, "Follow me now, and you will soon see."

I felt a rush of energy that was the affirmation I was waiting for and leapt out of bed, following the stranger out the door. As we trudged through the snow, he turned and said, "You will not be disappointed." As I walked behind him, I noticed again a blue-white glow surrounding him, a sign I took to confirm his purity and that I was right in trusting him.

We emerged from the shadows of the trees near the hotel, and I saw on the frozen surface of the lake a polished, silvery metal disk about twenty feet in diameter. As we approached closer, I saw that it glowed with soft luminosity, hovering a few feet above the icy lake. Once again I felt a pang of apprehension, wondering if I was going to be kidnapped by hostile aliens, and called silently within,

Saint Germain! Come forth, and take command of this situation and show me what to do!

Have no fear, I heard within, and felt a reassuring calmness. But while I continued to follow my guide to the craft, I still maintained all my senses fully alert, ready to run at the slightest indication I was walking into a trap.

As I walked up a ramp to the craft's metallic door, it slid open with a hiss. Soon, I found myself bathed in the light of the craft's interior. There, standing before me smiling, was none other than my dear friend, the Master Saint Germain, a violet cape about his shoulders and the familiar gold Maltese cross on his chest. Never before had I been so glad to see him, nor had I seen him look so magnificent. His radiant energy seemed to charge the very atmosphere with the essence of Mastery and God Dominion, and the others on board obviously deferred to his command.

After I overcame my initial shock, he turned to me and said, "I believe you are also acquainted with our hostess, Semjasse, our space traveler friend from the Pleiades...."

Saint Germain gestured graciously toward the beautiful, long-haired, blond space traveler, who was busy monitoring an instrument panel. I recognized her instantly from our association years before, when, during my sleep, I had experienced many subtle plane contacts with her. The Pleiadians, she had told me then, were not aliens at all, but ancestors of the human race that had originally seeded us on Earth, and were returning now to help their descendants through the difficult time of transition fast approaching.[32] Now, though it had been a long time since I had seen her and I was eager to renew our friendship, she smiled only a brief acknowledgment, for I could see she was very busy with her work.

"You see," Saint Germain said, "there was indeed a surprise waiting for you—which you would have missed had you not been obedient to the God Presence that guided you here to our prearranged rendezvous at the appointed hour. To arrive here, you had to go through many ordeals and receive many lessons, including your perilous drive on unknown roads through the mountains. The purpose of those experiences was to get you to further invoke the light and call forth your own Higher Self into human consciousness. Indeed, the purpose of all experience is to strengthen the light within you, that you may become your own Master. That is your destiny."

"Now, if you will take this seat," the Master said, indicating a contour chair nearby, "we will be off."

With a nod, Saint Germain indicated to Semjasse that we were ready to depart, and suddenly we rose effortlessly, with no sense of motion, up from the surface of the frozen lake. I could briefly see the snow-capped peaks lit by moonlight outside of the craft's windows until we disappeared like a shot into the night sky.

---

32 For more information on Semjasse, her associates, and the Pleiadian message, see: Eduard Billy Meier, *Message from the Pleiades* (Privately Printed, 1988). The dialog between Billy Meier and Semjasse is from the notes from actual physical contacts that took place in Switzerland. I believe in the validity of the notes from the initial six months or so of contacts, as I know Wendelle Stevens, the lead investigator, and discussed these contacts with him at length. Later "contacts," however, did not occur physically, but were "channeled" and contain much false and misleading information, which leads me to believe he was no longer in direct contact. For photos of Pleiadian beamships, see: Wendell Stevens and Lee Elders, *Contact from the Pleiades, Vol.1* (Genesis lll Publishers, Revised edition, 1980).

In less time than it takes to tell, we were over the North Pole, then arcing down through an opening in the Earth's crust, a vast entrance unknown to all but a few, through which we dove into the Earth's interior.

"This undiscovered paradise inside the Earth holds a great secret for the people of the Earth's surface and their future destiny," Saint Germain conveyed to me telepathically. "One day, just as happened prior to the sinking of Atlantis, when human discord becomes too great on the surface, those who have overcome their own negativity will be taken into the interior to live in this place most would call a Paradise. The time is not far off when every person will have to choose who they will serve, their lower or their higher nature. That choice, which humanity is now making, will determine where they go at that time.

"In reality, it is a choice that is being made all the time. But a time will come when there is a parting of the ways, when those who are habitually bound to the negative will remain on the surface to continue experiencing the consequences of their actions—their karma, if that is what you want to call it—while those who have overcome their lower natures will be taken within and live in a world more perfect than they could have dreamed."

I marveled at the beauty of the land I was being shown, thankful to have been given a message for humanity's destiny, but was not allowed to remember anything more of my visit. I awakened in the morning in my bed at Chateau Lake Louise, not remembering how I had returned to my room. As was frequent after an inner journey, I was not allowed to remember any more of my visit to the interior of the Earth than I needed at the moment. However, I did know that when the time of great change for humanity approached, I would know what was required.

My intense journey was now apparently complete, and I felt the prompting to return home. By the end of the week, I was back in Mount Shasta. After a few days of the usual routine, I became more grounded in ordinary awareness—like a regular human being again. However, the amazing events of the past week, the Atomic Accelerator and journey to the center of the Earth, were events etched in my memory—especially the revelation I had been given about the coming great change for humanity.

Chapter 23

Finding the Rainbow

The experience in the Atomic Accelerator made functioning in the physical body difficult for a while, as I would have the dual perspective of both the human world as well as that of the I AM Presence, and would sometimes feel unsteady on my feet. Or I would sit down while interacting with the Masters on other planes, and when I got up later, not realize how much time had elapsed; however, after a while I was able to be more present again and focus on the daily tasks of returning phone calls, buying groceries, cooking, washing dishes, paying bills, and filling the gas tank. Yet, almost everything I did seemed to be from the perspective of an observer, an independent consciousness functioning in multiple dimensions simultaneously. To some degree, everyone has this non-localized awareness, the ability to talk to a friend in a café while reading the newspaper, and at the same time be aware that outside the sun is shining—though my ability to do this was now expanded.

Since it was easier to go places in my mind through projected consciousness, I now had to decide if I actually needed to go someplace physically, or if I could just go there inwardly. Should I actually visit the person in the hospital, or simply go there in a higher body and transmit the healing etherically—or, perhaps, both? The temptation was to sit back and meditate, immerse myself in the awareness of the Universal Self that had no limits, and live entirely in the inner world of thought and energy, ignoring the claims for attention in the outer world. I saw that even though all appearance is illusory in the ultimate sense, I had vowed to enter that world of *maya* for a reason, and must learn to operate in those illusory levels with the skillful means of a Master. Fleeing the world under the excuse that all is *maya* is yet a greater *maya*, for there is no escape from the delusional self, which reappears everywhere one attempts to hide, until one has cut through its snares with the *sword of discriminating awareness*. Absorption in oneness, I saw, did not lead to Mastery in the outer world, for to be able to manifest perfect action in the world of duality, one must develop the means—which requires engagement with, and action in, the illusion of daily life.[33]

I began to observe more closely the origin of my thoughts. *Does this thought originate from my human mind, from my Higher Self, or the mind of a Master; or, does this thought originate from someone else?* Through greater self-observation, I began to see how thoughts entered my awareness and became a reality. Sometimes a brief suggestion by someone, perhaps rejected at first, would lurk in the unconscious and later emerge as my own thought, accompanied by fear or doubt, and exert great influence without my being aware of its seemingly innocuous origin.[34]

I learned to observe and test all aspects of my experience, and where I did not know the source of a thought, vision, or impulse, I would wait and watch, observing everything taking place on the screen of my mind. And this ability to watch and observe my thoughts from outside myself was, I saw, a path leading to freedom from unwanted influences and to self-knowledge and wisdom. Simply shutting out the world and suppressing one's "negative" thoughts in the name of being "positive" only leads to further self-delusion.

To become a Master, one had to not only dwell in Oneness, but also have the tools and skillful means to apply that enlightenment in the world, to make the path accessible to others. In a time of famine, one might own a bag of seed and a plow, but not know how to plant the seed, and everyone would go hungry. So, one might be immersed in Oneness, but still not be a Master.

Through years of meditating, I saw that it was the heart, that subtle feeling of the flame within, that gave the final clue to right action—discriminating among all the many illusory ideas that might present themselves as truth. And when I acted in accord with that subtle inner feeling of confirmation within the heart, everything would unfold perfectly.

---

33 Ramakrishna, the Bengali mystic (1836-1886), called one who realizes that the infinite is inseparable from the mundane a *Vijnani*. *Ati Yoga*, similar to the Tibetan *Dzogchen*, teaches that there is no separation between external and internal phenomena. Once one has found the center within, they realize that the center is everywhere.

34 For more information on the origination of thought-forms and their precipitation down into the astral and physical planes, see: Alice A. Bailey, *A Treatise on White Magic* (Lucis Publishing Company, 1934).

I also began to apply this awareness to sleep, observing my dreams more closely. Often these experiences were more than dreams; although we usually have no recollection of it, we go forth in our subtle bodies while the physical body sleeps, and we act in lives which seem independent of our waking experience. We actually live our lives in this subtle plane prior to their manifesting on the physical plane. The lag time might be days, weeks, or even years before we become aware of where our Master Self has led us. Hence, the experience of *déjà vu,* where we suddenly recognize we experienced an event prior to its present occurrence—because we *did* experience it, only in a finer body at a previous time, perhaps in a "dream," and are now merely recognizing, *I have seen this before!* Eventually the distinction of past and future disappears, as time itself slows down and dissolves into the *ever-present now,* leaving us with the experience that life is a dream always in the process of "coming true."

Discerning which dreams were guidance, which were glimmerings of events yet to be, and which were simply the lower mind following its own karmic desires, was a frequent subject of my meditations. A future step would be to dream consciously in both worlds, a practice taught in Tibetan Buddhism as Dream Yoga, for both the waking and sleeping states are illusory, dreams subject to the workings of our mind—the only question being, *Am I going to be the dream or the dreamer?*

For weeks, I had been dreaming about a rainbow, not one in the sky, but painted on a sign over a driveway. I walked up the long, dirt driveway that led to a house where a small group of people lived communally, and in my dream visits, these people wanted to know about Saint Germain and the laws of life he taught. I didn't know their names, but every night in my dreams I would talk to one or another of them, until after a while, each individual became familiar. Still, I had no clue where this commune was located, or if it even existed in the physical world.

One spring day, I found myself on another adventure which had started from nothing other than an impulse in my heart. I left home, and hours later I found myself driving north through Washington State. Not knowing where I was going, I trusted that the energy I felt guiding me had a purpose and let my inner Presence be my compass. As I drove I affirmed,

I AM the Presence of God driving this car, going where I am meant to go, doing what I am meant to do.

When I came over a hill and sighted the peak of Mount Rainier gleaming in the distance, my heart surged with joy at the sight, a sign perhaps that this sister mountain to Mount Shasta held some special blessing for me. My immediate desire was to head toward this shining beacon, but my mind was soon assailed by doubt, for in the early spring the back roads were often blocked by snow, and I was afraid that I might get stranded in some out-of-the-way place.

If I get off the beaten path, where will I end up? I might get stranded where no one will find me until the snow melts! Fearful thoughts of all that could go wrong flooded my imagination. Nonetheless, I felt my foot want to pull up from the gas pedal, and I pulled off the freeway at the next exit and stopped at the lone gas station to the right of the exit ramp. It wouldn't hurt to take a look at a map, I told myself as I gassed up the car, then sent a silent prayer to the Masters to give me guidance.

Looking at the map failed to alleviate my doubts. Mere data could not replace the living guidance within. So, I turned my attention inward and asked, *Saint Germain, please show me where to go,* and let go of any attachment to any particular direction, remaining open to my heart, whatever it might lead. Before departing, I thought to use the restroom, and as I entered the gas station, I thought, *Might as well play it safe, no point in taking chances*—in the absence of a clear signal I would keep going straight.

I paid for my gas, and as I returned to my car I saw that a white car had pulled up beside mine and that a young man was standing there, gazing up at Mount Rainier, shimmering in the distance.

"Sure is beautiful," he volunteered, as I started to get into my car.

"Yes, it is, but I'm not sure the roads are open," I said. "I'd like to go visit the mountain, but don't want to get stuck on the back roads," I replied, bouncing my doubts off the stranger.

"Oh, you don't have to worry about that," he replied with enthusiasm. "I just came through there and the roads are all clear. You won't have any trouble. It's a beautiful drive," he concluded, looking me in the eye, then smiled and drove away.

That's strange, he didn't buy gas or go inside the station. He simply pulled up and told me what I needed to know. Was it Saint Germain? Or was it someone the Master had sent, that he could work through to give me the guidance I needed? After all, didn't I just ask for the Master's assistance? So, why should I doubt? Whoever he was, I now know the road is clear, and my mind has no more excuses for not following the prompting of my heart.

My doubts evaporated as I headed down the narrow ribbon of road toward the mountain. Coming into the town of Morton, I instinctively made a left turn up a narrow road. I had not gone more than a mile when my van began to slow of its own accord, my foot automatically lifting from the gas pedal. There were few houses, but as I passed them I found myself looking at each one with great interest.

Why am I looking at these houses? I wondered, as though in a dream, *I don't know anyone here, or do I?* Passing a house set back from the road down a long, gravel driveway, for some inexplicable reason I turned in, ignoring the "Private Property, Keep Out" sign, and drove toward the house. A dozen yards up the driveway, I saw the sign overhead—the rainbow of my dream. This was the painted rainbow I had been seeing.

Compelled from within, I walked up to the front door and knocked, although my mind was thinking, *I can't just walk up to a house in the middle of nowhere and say, "I've been dreaming about the rainbow over your driveway." Well, no one who puts up a huge rainbow in their yard should be surprised at visitors.* And I remembered the line from the book of Genesis, well known by hippies during the '60s:

"I set my rainbow in the cloud, and it will be for a sign of a covenant between me and the Earth."

As I stood waiting for the door to open, I tried to figure out what I would say if someone appeared, almost hoping no one was home. Then the door opened and a beautiful young girl in beaded braids welcomed me with a friendly smile, the aroma of what I thought must be baking oatmeal cookies wafting invitingly through the open door.

"Hi, come on in," she said, as if I were the friend she'd been expecting. "We were just making granola—you can help us," she said, escorting me into the kitchen, where several people were busy taking trays of warm toasted oats out of the oven. I was seated at a long, wooden table before one of the granola-laden trays and handed a spatula. Somehow the guys with long hair, the girls in their beads and long, floral dresses, and the smell of fresh granola all combined to make me feel I was back in the '60s again—the feeling of a family to which everyone belonged.

"Just turn it over," the girl said, handing me a mug. "Here's some fresh peppermint tea I just picked from our garden."

As I sipped my mint tea and stirred the tray of fragrant oats sweetened with honey, I seemed to be watching from outside myself and thought, *Only in a dream could this be happening.* A few minutes before, I had been a stranger driving up a desolate road; now I was in a warm, cozy kitchen, part of a family I didn't know, that accepted me as though they'd known me forever. *How strange that one's "real" family could be cold and judgmental, while an acquired family could be so friendly—so much more real.*

Conversing around the table, I soon discovered that I had stumbled into a commune that lived in yurts on land around this main house, and that they owned a health food store in town. The owner, an elderly lady who believed in the ideal of the Aquarian Age and who had welcomed them onto her land, had just died; now the lawyers handling the estate were pressuring them to leave. Ignoring the lawyers, they had gone on about their business of making granola, beeswax soap, candles, quilts, and other things to sell in town, living day to day, never knowing when they would be evicted.

In spite of their difficulties, they seemed happy and invited me to stay with them, offering me the master bedroom upstairs. Over the next few hours, I gradually met the rest of the family as they wandered through the kitchen, helping themselves to pinches of the freshly baked cereal. As I looked into their open faces, I felt that each was in some way familiar.

Zachariah, a tall, bearded guy with a long ponytail, was especially outgoing, and asked if I would like to see the nearby waterfall on the river that ran through the forest behind the house. We walked for about a quarter of an hour, and as we stood by the torrent that was melt water from Mount Rainer's glaciers, he asked me what had brought me here. I found myself talking about following inner guidance and the need to still the mind and feel the flame in the heart—when suddenly I had the *déjà vu* experience that I was having the same conversation I'd had with him in dream time—word for word, it had all happened weeks before.

I told Zachariah that I'd dreamed about this place, even what we were saying, and he said, "Yes, I knew you the moment I set eyes on you, but I couldn't remember from where."

Later in the evening, after a dinner of rice and organic vegetables from the garden, I sat with this rainbow tribe around a wood stove in one of the yurts. As the light grew dim, I began talking about my experiences with Saint Germain, of how I met him in Muir Woods at a point in my life when I no longer wanted to live, and the decision I had made to stay on

Finding the Rainbow

the Earth and help others. I talked of the tests and challenges on the path of Mastery, and how one must constantly choose between listening to the thoughts of the mind or following the heart.

The sun had set, and as the light grew dimmer, no one got up to light a lantern. Only the flickering light from the dying fire in the stove lit the figures in the room, who huddled closer to the fire to keep warm. Feeling inspired by Saint Germain, I talked about the ability we have to change our mind and world through the use of meditation and affirmation, and how the Masters are always there to help—in fact, are waiting for us to call to them. And I explained that rather than expecting their reply in words, we must look within for their guidance and observe the effect of their assistance in our lives.

As I spoke, the space inside the yurt filled with a soft, violet light that penetrated the darkest corner. My audience was rapt, leaning forward to hear every word, asking questions until the last embers died down and they began to leave for their own yurts to sleep.

I retired to the master bedroom that had been offered for the night, but the minute I closed the door I felt uncomfortable, as though I were not alone. As I looked around, it appeared the room had been left exactly as it had been on the day the owner died; even her hairbrush and a photograph of her husband lay undisturbed on the bureau, and I shivered. It seemed eerie that while the main part of the house downstairs was filled with exuberant youth, this upstairs room still held the energy of the old woman. As I reluctantly climbed into her old, four-posted bed, I wondered if the sheets had ever been changed since she had died.

Trying to disregard the feeling that the dead woman was still there, I closed my eyes to meditate, but immediately felt a frightening presence. Opening my eyes, I saw with horror ripples in the bed cover moving toward me, and the imprint of someone invisible getting into bed. I shouted out loud,

"Stop, in the name of the Mighty God Presence I AM!"

"Saint Germain, come forth, take command here!" I begged, and saw that the movement toward me had stopped. Almost paralyzed with dread, I wondered if the old woman was angry at me for sleeping in her bed, and if she had power to harm me. *Or is it only my fear which can harm? Maybe she just needs comforting, but then again maybe she has brought other disembodied spirits with her, who will now pounce on me in my sleep?*

I wasted little time in trying to decide what to do, and called on Archangel Michael to grant me the *Sword of Blue Flame,* which Pearl, warning me of its tremendous power, had taught me how to use. I now held out my right hand to receive this devastating weapon, which Pearl had said to invoke, along with the Blue Lightning of Divine Love, only when necessary. But I figured if there ever was a time to use it, this was it.

Clasping the sword in my hand, hearing the hum of its electric force, I wielded it above my head and swept it about me in a circle three times. Each time, I visualized a sword made of blue light going forth throughout the room, house, and property. Its work done, I then released the sword back into the ethers to return to its owner. Then I visualized shafts of blue lightning shooting out of a sun-like orb above me, striking the house and property, penetrating everywhere. I decreed,[35] *Great host of Ascended Masters, take complete command of this entire situation. Purify this woman, her house and property, and bring about the Perfect Divine Plan here—right now!*

Although I could not see her, I sensed her presence at the foot of the bed, and I addressed her. "You have died, whether you know it or not, and you no longer belong here. You need to let go of this place and these people, and go on in your evolution. Go toward the light. I have called on the Masters, and they have come for you. Follow them into the light and you will be much happier in the place they take you to than you are here where you no longer belong." I visualized Jesus, Saint Germain, and Archangel Michael hovering about her, sending rays of light into the woman's heart, and I felt a powerful, uplifting radiation enter the room.

After a few minutes, I sensed she was gone and that it would be safe to go to sleep. I called for invincible protection to surround me during the

---

35 Our every thought, word, and action has an immediate effect on our environment. A decree is an act of creation brought forth by the spoken word, and should only be used under guidance and for altruistic purposes. An affirmation is more subtle in tone, generally used to bring about a change in consciousness—which in turn affects "outer" reality. Both decrees and affirmations use words to direct energy. They should be said calmly and with full awareness. Repeating them rapidly with mental energy, as is often done by "New Agers," often invokes the opposite of what is desired. "In the beginning was the Word, and the Word was with God, and the Word was God" (John 1:1).

night, visualizing a ring of blue fire blazing about the bed, and as soon as my head hit the pillow, I was asleep.

The next morning, when everyone asked me how I had slept, I told them, "Well, I felt the old woman's energy in the room." They nodded knowingly, and I realized that was why none of them slept in the house. I didn't tell them all I had experienced, or that I had invoked the Blue Lightning[36] and used the Sword of Blue Flame to clear the energy and take the entity off the Earth, knowing that it was better not to mention inner powers that might not be understood.

Sitting in the kitchen and eating a bowl of the granola I had helped make the day before, I listened to Zach, who had been in the yurt that night and was now eating his breakfast beside me.

"You know," he said, speaking slowly and deliberately, "last night while you were talking, you dissolved, and all we saw was Saint Germain, wearing a violet cape with a gold Maltese cross on his chest, sitting where you had been."

I stopped eating and stared back at him, amazed. I had felt Saint Germain's energy flowing through me, pouring out to them, but had not known that they were seeing him, that he had been coming through me that directly.

"It was Saint Germain talking to us, answering our questions," he said. "We had been wanting to know more about him, and had been praying to him for help with the lawyers so we could stay on this land. The previous owner has children, and if the land goes to them, they will let us stay. We know now that he has heard our prayer."

A few others were standing around in the kitchen, nodding in agreement. "Thank you for coming here. If you hadn't, we wouldn't have seen him."

"Yeah," said a few others, "Thanks, man, it was really cool."

I said goodbye to this family who lived under the sign of the rainbow, and got into my van. I felt that their prayers had attracted Saint Germain, who had sent me there to help them, and was grateful for the blessing that I, too, had received. Though at that moment there was no sign of what was soon to come, this visit was yet to have a further, dramatic impact on the community.

---

36 Often called the Blue Lightning of Divine Love, this energy has the same purifying effect as the Sword of Blue Flame.

As I backed down the driveway under the rainbow sign, I remembered again the passage from Genesis, that the rainbow was a sign of the covenant between God and man—as it surely had been now.

Many spiritual groups were using the rainbow as their symbol—representing the seven rays of creation, the seven chakras, and the seven root races of humanity[37] living in harmony. I recalled the first gathering of the Rainbow Family I had attended in 1972 on Table Mountain in Colorado, a gathering of many who felt a greater sense of belonging to the family of humanity than to their genetic families. Those were the days of innocence, celebrating the birth of the Age of Aquarius.[38]

I drove north all that day, going where the spirit led me, and found myself by dusk at another ashram, followers of the Sikh guru Yogi Bhajan, where I was given a delicious dinner and a place to lay my sleeping bag for the night. In the morning, the energy to go north had dissipated, and I felt the pull to return south and stop at the rainbow commune again—to

---

37 Helena P. Blavatsky, *The Secret Doctrine: The Synthesis of Science, Religion and Philosophy* (Kessinger Publishing, LLC, 1999). See also the online edition: www.theosociety.org/pasadena/sd/sd-hp.htm.

38 The Age of Aquarius is the time period of approximately 2,160 years that is 1/12 of the entire cycle of almost 26,000 years caused by the precession of the equinoxes, the apparent shift of the stars in relation to the Earth. The previous age was that of Pisces, characterized by the development of deep feeling, sensitivity, and devotional religion. Most of the events that people cite as heralds of the dawning of the Age of Aquarius, such as Woodstock, the Summer of Love in Haight-Ashbury, and the widespread use of drugs, actually mark the end of the Age of Pisces, a water sign ruled by Jupiter and Neptune. In contrast, Aquarius is an air sign ruled by Saturn and Uranus, an age, not of emotion, but of universal consciousness and instantaneous communication. Since the beginning of every age is symbolized by a social phenomenon or invention, I believe that the symbol of the Aquarian Age is the personal computer and the Internet. The World Wide Web first became available over the Internet on August 6, 1991; however, its roots reach back many years to services such as Prodigy (1984) and CompuServe (1977), which made possible the instantaneous sharing of information by large numbers of people around the globe. Seminars and spiritual instruction can now be given online to anyone who has access to a computer or even a cell phone with data access.

spend one last night with them before heading back to Mount Shasta.

But I had a difficult time finding the house—in fact, it wasn't there. Neither was the driveway with the rainbow where it had been. I was sure I had found the right driveway, but there was no rainbow sign—and no house. Is it another part of the dream? Am I back home, asleep in bed, dreaming again about these people that appear, that seem real, then disappear?

Bewildered, I parked my van near the location I remembered, and walked onto the land where I was sure I had walked. Then I spotted a yurt, a sign that I might not have been dreaming. Coming closer, I saw it was the yurt where we had all met the previous night, gathered around the stove. Inside were two members of the commune I remembered.

"What happened?" I stammered, sticking my head into the yurt. "Where's the house?"

"Fire…it burned to the ground in the middle of the night."

"But where's the foundation?" I repeated, hardly able to believe there wasn't a trace of the two-story building where I'd slept the night before.

"Bulldozed into the basement…and covered over."

"Wow, that's a shock," I said, searching for words, remembering Pearl's warning about the Sword of Blue Flame, concluding there must have been a negative force here that needed to be cleansed, perhaps one of the reasons I'd been sent here by Saint Germain. I had acted in self-defense, but saw that act had invoked more far-reaching consequences than I had anticipated.

"The good part," the guy who'd been talking to me said, "is that without the house, the lawyers can't sell the place so easily now. It looks like the old lady's kids are going to get the property, and they'll let us stay."

The Masters work in mysterious ways. Who would have thought that in acting to protect myself by invoking an aspect of consciousness, I would have been able to free an earthbound entity, dissolve a negative focus of energy, and prolong the life of a commune—all at the same time?

Relieved that I had not been dreaming, that I had really visited this place and met these people, I said goodbye again, climbed into the van, and started the long drive back to Mount Shasta. As I passed the gas station where I had been guided by the young man to drive east toward Mount Rainier, I wondered again, *was that Saint Germain?* Regardless, he had definitely been with me, and I felt great satisfaction that I had been of service, both to him and to the family of my dreams that lived under the rainbow—the reality of which I had at last discovered. I saw once more how we exist on many levels and that, although often unaware, we are active in all of them.

One level we call our dreams, another reality—but these are in fact mere projections and reflections of our own consciousness. Our waking life is no more real than the dream life, both manifesting their reality in different densities. Each moment is malleable, capable of being molded by our thoughts, once we realize that *we are its creators.*

Over the next few years, I spent many hours in meditation realizing the limitless nature of consciousness, bringing that awareness into dreams as well as waking life. It was while traveling and in relationship with others that I would receive the greatest tests and challenges—as there, one is forced to manifest consciousness in action. Soon I was to travel more widely and would need to bring meditation more fully into the mastery of everyday life, which would enable me to be of greater service.

Chapter 24

Calgary Connection

Most of the week, I was overwhelmed by the demands of my building renovation and rental business, but I tried to take at least Sunday off. I found that on that day, if I meditated in the morning and asked the Masters to bring about the highest plan, I frequently had some kind of illuminating experience.

Sundays have a distinctly different energy. As a child, I had observed that frequently if it were cloudy or raining during the week, it would clear up on Sunday. I attributed this to the collective thoughts of the millions of people who were relaxed and enjoying themselves that day, not worrying about work. Now I began to discover that every day of the week was unique, that the conscious intelligences who rule the cosmos release specific energies, so that every day has a different quality, a different note with which one could be in tune if one chose. Ancient civilizations named these daily energies after the various planets of our solar system, Sunday being ruled by the Sun, whose inner quality is self-conscious awareness, manifested outwardly as illumination.[39]

I awoke one particular luminous Sunday with the idea of driving north to visit the Oregon Vortex, a tourist attraction I had heard about north of Medford, a small piece of land supposedly exhibiting various gravitational and visual anomalies. Pearl and Jerry had visited the Vortex and I had been curious about it, but avoided going there, thinking it could only be a hoax operated for profit. However, after finishing my morning meditation, I found the pull had grown stronger.

The Vortex was a fascinating place that challenged one's normal perceptions. It contained various optical illusions, creating the impression that one was in some type of geo-physical anomaly. People appeared to change height, depending on where they stood, and balls seemed to roll uphill. Most of the "effects" of the so-called vortex could be easily explained, though some still remained a mystery, such as a broom that

---

39 Monday: Moon; Tuesday: Mars; Wednesday: Mercury; Thursday: Jupiter; Friday: Venus; Saturday: Saturn; Sunday: Sun.

stood on end without support in the middle of the floor. Disengaging both belief and denial, difficult for someone who habitually liked the mental security of definitive answers, I placed the experience in the mental file of subjects on which to hold judgment in abeyance.

However, that evening when I swung the car onto the freeway and headed south to return home, I had the feeling that I was going in the wrong direction. *Perhaps there's something to the vortex, and I'm disoriented from being in it too long?* I hadn't felt any unusual energy at the location, but now I seemed to be going in the wrong direction and felt depleted. The car seemed to slow down by itself, until after a few miles I pulled off at an exit and parked by the side of the road. I knew from past experience that if I didn't have a clear feeling where to go or what to do, I was better off staying where I was until my feelings clarified. If I waited, the direction always became clear.

I took a few deep breaths, closed my eyes, stilled my mind, and turned my attention to the silence within, asking my Higher Self for assistance. After a few peaceful moments, I still had no answer, at least not verbally. But I noticed that when I asked my Higher Self, *Should I go south, toward home? I felt nothing; when I asked, Should I go north? I felt a faint tremble of excitement. I will see how it feels; I can always turn around,* I thought—and turned onto the northbound on-ramp. Immediately I felt better, and the car surged eagerly in its new direction toward an unknown goal.

Letting my inner guidance be my compass was an exercise I practiced frequently. I used to joke with passengers in my car that if we seemed lost, trying to find a restaurant or some other location, for example, we could always "ask the car." I would tune in to my heart, and using the childhood game of Hotter and Colder, I would steer the car in whatever direction felt "hotter" until we arrived at our destination without ever needing to look at a map.[40]

---

40 The extensive use of electronic Global Positioning Systems can weaken that natural ability. There is nothing technology performs that we cannot accomplish ourselves through natural attributes of consciousness: communicate telepathically and know where to go and what to do— all through attunement with our God Self. Indeed, through the inner God Presence there is nothing we cannot accomplish, even without electricity.

Years later, when I owned a small plane, I would close my eyes and ask my Higher Self to do the flying. Then I'd open my eyes and steer in whatever direction felt right, arriving each time at the correct airport, where often some unusual experience awaited me. Flying on one of these intuited headings, I once found myself approaching a landing strip in Novato, a town north of San Francisco, and heard the Inner Presence say, *Land here.* After taxiing up to the gate and tying my plane down, I was shocked to see someone I had met at Pearl's the year before waiting for me.

"Now I know why I felt pulled to drive out here to the airport," the man said, "I guess it was to meet you. Please come home with me and be my guest." That night he and his wife had a few friends over for dinner. They were interested in the teachings of the Masters, and as we sat around the table, a beautiful radiation poured into the room that everyone felt. I knew then, as I told them of the I AM Presence, that I had been sent there on a mission, though when I had taken off that morning I hadn't had any idea where I would fly that day.

Such unhesitating obedience to the guidance of the Higher Self was a prerequisite demanded by the Masters of all those whom they chose to train for service. Learning to feel that guidance, the silent action of the God Flame located in the center near the heart, was the result of many years of meditation. Eventually, my sensitivity to its subtle movement became developed enough so that even under stress, such as when flying through a storm, I could still feel its directions.

Obedience was not difficult, once I knew the message was from my Higher Self, but such certainty wasn't always the case. At those times, to dissolve my uncertainty and quell my fear and doubt, I visualized myself enfolded in violet light, an energy that dissolved psychic interference and discord and allowed me to feel the Presence within more clearly. I would also chant affirmations—*mantras* in English—that kept my attention steady on what I sought to achieve and bring into being.

Driving north through the night instead of south—opposite the direction common sense dictated—and having no knowledge of the Plan, I trusted that it would unfold perfectly. As I cruised up the freeway, I chanted silently to myself,

I AM free from fear and doubt. I AM God directed and God commanded. I AM going where I AM meant to go and doing what I AM meant to do, for I AM God in action.

The Thin Red Line

The car sped on into the darkness, without my having the slightest idea where I was going, a frequent experience since that day in Stephen's store when I had said, *Thy will, not my will, be done.* As always, the lesson was to trust, then wait patiently for the guidance to emerge.

Around 11 p.m., with my gas tank on empty, I arrived in Eugene, Oregon, and felt that I was to spend the night there. Looking for the right place, I kept my affirmations going until I came upon Pearl Street, and remembered that I had stayed at the Pearl Street Hotel during a previous adventure with the Masters—and now I felt the pull to return there. The price of a room was almost exactly the amount of money I had, $22, with only change left over. *This is going to be interesting. Where can I go from here with no money?*

As if in answer to my thoughts, the clerk handed me a coupon for breakfast in the coffee shop next door and I thought, *at least breakfast is taken care of.* But the purpose of my journey still remained a mystery. I prayed to the Masters before going to bed: *I know you have brought me here for a reason, so please show me what that is. Where am I to go from here? And oh yes, I need money.*

That night in a dream I saw a map of North America laid out in front of me. On the map was drawn a fine red line connecting Eugene to Calgary, Canada. As I looked, a voice said, *Follow the red line.* The direction was clear, the dream providing a kind of internal global positioning system telling me where to go. This form of internal guidance, where I would see a red line connecting two locations, came frequently in dreams when I traveled, giving the answer I sought more easily than any computerized system—for there is nothing technology can do that is not a manifestation of some inner attribute we can use if we are willing to spend the time required for its development.

The question of what to do about money, however, had not been answered in my dream. I had left home with only enough cash for a Sunday jaunt, not for a journey to Canada. Sitting in the coffee shop after using my free coupon for breakfast, I pulled out all the change from the bottom of my jeans pocket, piled it on the counter, and found I had only a dollar and eighty cents.

I went into the first bank I came upon and discovered, fortuitously, that it was connected as a "correspondent" of my bank in California, and that a tenant who owed me three month's back rent had just made a deposit. The sympathetic bank manager expedited a wire of the newly deposited $1,000, and soon I was purchasing a toothbrush, extra clothes, and a small canvas suitcase. Within a few hours I was headed north again, following the thin red line of my dream.

Am I crazy, following just a feeling and a dream? I asked myself, wondering, *Should I turn around and go home? No! I asked for guidance—now I have to trust what I've been given, as ephemeral as it seems.*

Two days later I arrived in Calgary and checked into the famous Palliser Hotel, a historic place with crystal chandeliers and a lobby decorated in red damask. The beautiful energy I felt inside, despite the cost, reinforced my feeling that this was where I was meant to stay. I had found that the Masters often establish etheric retreats at elegant hotels, monuments, or even banks that are stable and whose environments are harmonious—temples that serve as foci to ground a spiritual radiation for the benefit of those whom they guide there. I felt that the Palliser was such a temple.[41]

As I didn't have a credit card, I was asked to pay cash. After signing the hotel register, I decided to admire the rich décor for a few minutes before going to my room, and found a large, overstuffed chair in the lobby where I could absorb the splendor and appreciate the opulent ambiance. I wondered when I, too, would have enough money to have a credit card like everyone else, and not to have to pay cash wherever I stayed. In my present vocation as a landlord, most of my income went into making repairs. Of course, reducing the rent of those who were indigent also cut into any profits—some I even put up for free.

Wondering when I would be able to stay at such opulent places whenever I traveled, suddenly I felt the presence of Saint Germain. I

---

[41] For us to be receptive to and interact with the Masters, we must be in a state of equanimity. To facilitate this sense of peace, the Masters maintain certain foci, often within public buildings, that foster harmony and a feeling of well-being, in which spiritual radiation and guidance can be transmitted. Other hotels where I have experienced the Masters' radiation are: the Ritz Hotel, Madrid (see description later in this book); Shangri-La Hotel, Kathmandu; Mena House, Cairo; the original Brown Palace Hotel, Denver; Plaza Hotel, New York City; Fairmont Hotel, San Francisco; Biltmore Hotel, Los Angeles; and Davenport Hotel, Spokane (see description earlier in this book).

Apprentice to the Masters

sat bolt upright in my chair as I heard him responding to my financial reminiscences, which he had obviously been observing. He replied by saying,

Before you can have the abundance you desire, you must be above all temptation to misuse that wealth. Your weakness in the past has been to give money to those who are not ready for it, or who are transgressing the laws of abundance, those who still need to learn lessons that can only be learned from not having money. Do you think you have overcome that tendency now?

Yes, I have, I replied without hesitation, seeing in a flash how I had squandered much of the money that had been given to me, on the mistaken belief that I was helping others. Actually, I was making them weaker by allowing them to continue in their self-indulgent fantasy that God would take care of them, despite their complete lack of effort on their part or any concern for the well-being of others. In taking care of those well able to take care of themselves, I was denying them the opportunity to achieve mastery through engaging with the world and providing for their own support—which would entail coming to grips with their raison d'etre.

The Master now asked, *Do you mean that if some poor, homeless person came into this hotel lobby this moment and asked you for money, you could resist giving it to him?*

Yes, I think so.

Very well, then, came his final reply…then silence.

As I sat in the chair, mulling over what Saint Germain had just said, a hobo in grimy rags entered the hotel, and without looking left or right, walked directly up to me.

"Say, can you spare some change?" he asked, looking me in the eye.

"Why, no," I blurted out, observing my automatic urge to reach in my pocket and pull out a dollar. *Giving only a dollar wouldn't hurt, would it?* I reasoned.

"Can't you spare anything, even some change? Anything would help," he begged piteously, but I couldn't help noticing his beautiful eyes, which seemed to reveal a depth of soul which belied his appearance.

I shook my head and continued to stare at him, unable to reconcile the man's eyes with his bedraggled clothing.

"Please," he said, thrusting an upturned, dirty palm in my face, a palm which, despite its dirt, seemed soft and finely formed, not in keeping with the rest of him. Again, I shook my head.

As he turned away, I thought I caught a glimpse of a faint smile. Then this strange beggar left by the same path he had entered, not approaching any of the obviously wealthy guests in the lobby. Having neither looked at nor spoken to anyone but me, he disappeared out the front door.

That's strange, I thought. *Why didn't he beg from anyone else? There are people in the lobby who look a lot richer than I.* Then I heard again the voice of the beloved Master.

Congratulations, my boy, you passed the test! And I realized who the beggar had been—none other than the elusive Saint Germain. That is why he had approached only me for money, not the other wealthy patrons of the hotel—because I was the one being tested. *Now, look at the coin in your pocket and read the inscription,* Saint Germain continued.

I reached into my pocket and pulled out, to my surprise, a British Two Pence coin stamped with a crown holding three ostrich plumes, and an inscription that I could read only by carefully scrutinizing it in the light of a nearby lamp: *Ich Dien,* it said in German, "I Serve." I recognized the three-fold flame symbolized by the three plumes immediately,[42] what in the *Vedas* would be called the three *gunas,* or modes of energy that are aspects of the light. The intent of the coin seemed clear, "To wear the crown, one must serve the light."

How this British coin came to be in my pocket without my being aware, I don't know, but Saint Germain knew it was there, or perhaps had put it there to teach me that in service to others I would have all the wealth I required. Wealth was not to be squandered or given foolishly to those who would only be weakened by the false notion of something for nothing. The key to ruling one's dominion was first to empower oneself, for only then could one empower others.

Grateful that I had passed the test, I entered the dining room and enjoyed the first good meal I'd had in days. While waiting for dinner to arrive, I gave thanks to the omniscient being who had taken on the form of a beggar to teach me this lesson, and wondered how many people encountered Masters in their daily lives completely unawares—reason enough to treat all whom we encounter as Masters. I felt honored that

---

42　The *Fleur-de-Lis* (French: Lily Flower), with its three stylized petals, is also a symbol of the Three Fold Flame, used as a symbol of nobility from ancient times in all parts of the world, most notably by the kings of France.

out of the multitude of beings stumbling in darkness, he had singled me out and found me worthy of his attention. Although I knew that I had known this great soul in many past lives, nonetheless I was grateful that he would go to the trouble of downshifting his vehicle into the human density to teach me such basic wisdom. I wondered if he enjoyed these incognito appearances—using innumerable disguises, depending on the lesson required—as much as I. The twinkle I had seen in his eye seemed to say that he did, for I sensed the love and humor that overflowed his every action.

I entered the elegant dining room, and over a sumptuous dinner pondered my next move. *Now that I've followed the thin, red line of my dream to Calgary, what next?* Before I went to sleep, I prayed for guidance, and again had a dream. I saw another map; this time it was a map of the world with another red line arcing east across Canada, crossing the Atlantic Ocean, descending through Europe and the Mediterranean to Israel. I awoke with a start. *What do the Masters want of me?* Driving on faith for a few days was one thing, journeying to another continent without explanation, knowledge of a purpose, or money, required a greater leap of faith than I felt capable of making.

Half the money I had been recently wired was gone, yet a force within, certainly not my own desire, was pushing me to travel without resources. The name Calgary, where I had just arrived, was a variation of Calvary, the hilltop where Jesus was crucified. I felt that my ego was being nailed to the cross of duality, where spirit and matter appear at cross purposes, and wisdom reveals itself only to those who realize the unity of all phenomena and resurrect themselves from this materialistic delusion. But at that moment I did not feel wise, for I could only relive my memories of India, where I had been sick and gone months with barely anything to eat. I felt the Masters were preparing for me a slow, humiliating crucifixion, where I would run out of money in some foreign city.

My faith in the Masters finally won out over my fear of their abandonment, but I was not without immediate challenges. After buying the plane ticket to Tel Aviv I had only one hundred dollars left—which had to last twenty-one days, the minimum time before I could return. Then I remembered I didn't have my passport. *Who takes their passport with them on a Sunday morning drive?* Even worse, when I explained my predicament at the American Consulate, they informed me it had expired. Ready to take this as a sign that the trip was impossible and that I should return home, to my great surprise they issued me a new passport overnight. The next day, almost in shock, I was on the plane to Israel.

I had been able to buy a reduced fare, round-trip ticket, the only requirement being that I could not return for twenty-one days. *How is one hundred dollars going to last three weeks?* One could no longer travel around Europe on five dollars a day, as I had when I was seventeen. Now that I was in my thirties, and the monetary elite had engineered a precipitous drop in the value of our currency, one could easily spend a hundred dollars for a basic hotel room.

The Master El Morya, although then still in a physical body in the Himalayas, appeared etherically to Hermann Schmiechen in London in 1884, to pose for this portrait—as described in The Mahatma Letters. *The original is supposedly still at the Theosophical Society in Adyar, India, where it is regrettably kept from the public.*

The Master Kuthumi Lal Singh, then still in a physical body in Shigatse, Tibet, appeared etherically to the painter Hermann Schmiechen in London in 1884, to pose for this portrait prior to the preceding one of El Morya. As described in The Mahatma Letters, *Madame Blavatsky and other Theosophists were in attendance. The original is supposedly still at the Theosophical Society in Adyar, India, where it is regrettably kept from the public.*

The Lord Maha Chohan presides over the Masters of the Seven Rays.

Photograph of Helena Petrovna Blavatsky (1831-1891), founder of the Theosophical Society, with (left to right) the two Masters who are its spiritual founders, Kuthumi Lal Singh and El Morya. On the far right is the Ascended Master Saint Germain (these images are from paintings later inserted).

Chapter 25

Meeting the Masters in Israel

To relieve the monotony of the nine-hour flight on the jumbo jet, I got up from my seat and walked around the cabin, pacing up one aisle and down another to get some exercise, and also hoping for someone I could talk with to pass the time. I repeated this tour of the cabin several times, but found no one who sparked interest. To make time pass more quickly, I tried to intuit the reasons certain passengers were on the flight, and in this process, became familiar with who was on board. Many of the passengers were rabbinical students, wearing *yarmulkes* on their heads and prayer shawls around their shoulders, making a pilgrimage to the Holy Land. Others appeared to be businessmen or retirees on vacation—no one out of the ordinary.

A half hour before landing, when the pilot announced we would soon begin our descent into Tel Aviv's Ben Gurion Airport, I decided it was a good time to visit the restroom. Fatigued after a long flight, I was not ready for the coming shock, but the moment that we least expect is often the one in which the extraordinary manifests and we awaken. Although some call this the "guru's grace," that unexpected illumination could not occur unless we had already been prepared through purification and self-discipline.

Walking down the aisle, I came to two passengers I hadn't seen before, men of striking appearance I knew from my frequent walks had not been aboard the plane, now occupying seats in front of the bulkhead at the end of the aisle. One was a white-turbaned Hindu with dark, piercing eyes, not a face you would ever expect to see in real life. Here was a *mogul* prince from the *Arabian Nights*. I froze in my tracks as I recognized that I was in the presence of the great Master, El Morya. For a moment, he gazed deeply into my eyes, a faint smile appearing on his otherwise inscrutable face. Sitting beside him, another elegant Easterner in white with long, auburn hair flowing to his waist smiled graciously, and as he nodded I recognized this companion as the legendary Master, Kuthumi Lal Singh. Well known as the initiators of esoteric spirituality in the West in the late 1800s who had helped Madame Blavatsky found the Theosophical Society, they had long since Ascended. Prior to their Ascension, their exploits and service to humanity had been chronicled in the Theosophical literature of the past half-century.

What are you, who can travel anywhere by the power of your mind, doing on this airplane? My mind raced, as it struggled with this unexpected occurrence, for which it had no point of reference. I could not understand why other passengers were not taking note of these remarkable men and their phenomenal appearance out of thin air. Had either of these Christ-like Masters appeared on any street corner in the world, their presence would have drawn a crowd and stopped traffic, as it now stopped me in my tracks. My heart leapt and my mind raced out of control with a multitude of thoughts, every word of which I embarrassingly realized they were fully cognizant.

What are you guys doing here? Shouldn't you be in a retreat in the Himalayas, or an etheric temple in a higher dimension, communicating telepathically with your students? What is this, a vacation? And why go to Israel? You could be immersed in complete God Consciousness, so what are you doing here on a crowded plane?

Suddenly, I was pushed by the person behind me in the line cueing to use the restroom, and I was forced to move forward. *I'll talk to them on the way back to my seat. By then I'll have my mind under control and know what to say.* I felt I'd already made a fool of myself, standing there gaping at them, unable to speak.

In the restroom, I summoned up my courage and decided to talk to them. I combed my hair into place, smoothed my crumpled shirt, and tried to think of something intelligent to say, but my mind was still blank.

A knock at the door, signaling that I needed to leave, galvanized me into action. Despite my lack of preparedness for the coming encounter, I decided to be bold and offer myself in their service. However, walking up the aisle, I was crushed to find that the two seats the Masters had occupied were empty. Determined to find them, I walked up and down the aisles of the plane looking for them, until the stewardess became annoyed and told me to return to my seat, as we were getting ready to land. They had vanished from the plane without a trace, and I was devastated that I had missed the opportunity of a lifetime.

As my seat was only a few rows in front of where El Morya and Kuthumi had been sitting, I kept turning around looking for them as we began our descent. But the only people I saw were the two ordinary-appearing passengers who had originally occupied those seats. The Masters were nowhere to be seen. They had vanished from a jet flying over the Mediterranean at forty thousand feet at a speed close to five hundred miles an hour. After the plane landed, I struggled to be one of the first passengers off and watched the passengers disembark, keeping a sharp lookout, but no one emerged even faintly resembling those two majestic personages.

Waiting Room Encounter

The Masters had clearly shown me that I should go to Israel, but not what to do when I got there. I realized I would have to rely minute-to-minute on my inner guidance, feeling the inner gyroscope in my heart for constant stabilization and direction.

Fighting off taxi drivers who demanded exorbitant fees to drive me downtown, I got on a bus that took me to a small bus station waiting room in the center of the city. It was getting dark, and I was tired from the flight and had no idea where to go. The waiting room was empty. After pacing up and down a few times, I went back outside to see if I could get a sense of a direction, but Tel Aviv was crowded and confusing, and I felt lost.

Not speaking Hebrew, I couldn't ask anyone where to find a cheap hotel, so I called on the Masters,

> *In the name of the Love, Wisdom, and Power that I AM, I call on the Ascended Host of Light to show me where to go and what to do. I AM the Presence of the Ascended Masters and Ascended Master Friends*[43] *raised up before me, bringing about the Perfect Divine Plan here right now!*

Going back into the waiting room, I was shocked to see sitting on the bench that had been empty a moment ago that Christ-like being from the plane—the Ascended Master Kuthumi Lal Singh, and I fought the desire to prostrate at his feet and beg him to take me as his disciple. I remembered Madame Blavatsky's similar test when she saw in a group of men on a London street the Master who had instructed her in dreams since

---

[43] Ascended Master Friends are those aligned with the Masters, whom they may send to be of assistance, often other people not aware of the Masters or the service they may unknowingly be rendering.

Apprentice to the Masters

childhood, and she had fought her desire to run up and greet him. He told her later that if she had betrayed who he was by any sign of recognition or adulation, he would not have contacted her again for a long time—for it would have betrayed an undisciplined ego and emotional immaturity of one not yet ready for advanced training.

Standing in front of him now, having mastered my desire, I got up the courage to speak. "I remember you…you were on the plane." He only smiled and looked at me, a faint look of amusement in his eyes.

Looking around, I saw that we were alone. *Where is your friend who was sitting beside you on the plane?* I wanted to ask, wondering where El Morya had disappeared to and if he would soon reappear. I always thought that if I met one of these Masters, about whom I had read so much, I would have endless questions. But now my mind was blank and no words came to mind. I could not even ask the pressing questions about my journey, *What am I doing here? Why did guys you send me to Israel? How am I supposed to survive without money?* For in his presence I wanted only to bask in the unconditional acceptance I felt from this Christ being—never wanting to be separate from that love again.

Hearing the words in my heart, the Master replied, *There is no separation. Though you do not often see us, we see you, and our love is with you always. There is nowhere you go that we are not also.*

Overwhelmed by the grace and compassion I felt flowing from him, I longed for a way to prolong the meeting. *Please don't go, don't disappear again the way you did on the plane,* I begged. Close to tears, I asked, *How can I be of service to you?* As I knew that these great ones did not take on human form and enter the ordinary world casually, just to impress or fulfill personal desires but only for a definite purpose, I wondered now, *What is that purpose? What is he doing here?*

Standing in front of him, I felt my heart merge with his, and I was filled with the overwhelming desire to serve him and be a part of his work for humanity. Finally, I spoke my desire, "Is there anything I can do for you?"

How strange that I could pray to this Master for years, asking this very question, and that he would finally grant me an audience, not in a temple or on the summit of a mountain, but here in a bus station waiting room in Israel.

"No, there is nothing at this moment, but thank you," he replied, with utmost tenderness. "But what can I do for you?"

"I don't know where to go."
"Go to the Sheraton Hotel."
"I don't know how to get there."
"Get on the first bus that comes along."
"The first bus that comes along?" I repeated, stunned that he would know the local bus schedule so well that he could utter such a cavalier answer.

"Yes, the first bus—and now here it is," he said, as a bus screeched to the curb.

"This is it?"

"Yes, and you'd better go outside and get on. This is Israel—and the buses don't wait."

I nodded to him and he smiled back at me. I wanted to continue our conversation, no matter how ordinary and mundane the topic—anything to remain in his presence—but I knew that I needed to act as he had instructed—for the Masters say,

You take care of the small things, and we will take care of the large things.

Reluctantly I picked up my bag, walked outside, and boarded the bus. I looked back, hoping to see the Master leave, but was drawn into conversation with the driver. He asked me where I was going, and I mumbled, "The Sheraton Hotel," then threw myself into a seat, praying that this was not going to be a test that would put me through another trying ordeal, but would bring me lodging for the night. As the bus lurched along, I wondered how I was going to pay for a room at such an expensive hotel.

"Sheraton Hotel," the driver shouted ten minutes later as we lurched to a stop. The door flew open and he pointed to the hotel atop a hill overlooking the Mediterranean. As I suspected, the Sheraton was a fancy place, and as I walked through the imposing doors into the strikingly modern lobby, I already felt the sinking feeling of rejection.

Nonetheless, I summoned my courage, walked to the front desk, and asked, "How much for your cheapest room?"

"Eighty," the desk clerk answered without looking up, as though it was beneath his dignity to answer such a lowly question.

"Eighty shekels?"

"No, dollars," he fired back, annoyed. *Eighty dollars, that's almost all I have!*

"Thanks, anyway," I said, disappointed.

Why did the Master send me here, to a hotel I can't afford? My worst fear of becoming homeless in a foreign city was starting to take shape. I thought of getting on another bus and returning to the depot. *Was Kuthumi still there? Not likely. If he were, I could ask him what he meant by sending me to the Sheraton. Was I going to be one of those homeless people you see begging for change outside all the bus stations of the world?*

I picked up my canvas suitcase and left the hotel, walking outdoors down the broad driveway that curved to the street below, dragging my feet without any idea where to go or where to sleep for the night after my long, exhausting journey. Halfway down the driveway I looked up and saw a neon sign across the street—I could hardly believe my eyes. The bright letters of the sign read: "Mt. Shasta Hotel."

My heart leapt. *Kuthumi had known what he was doing after all! He knew that there was a hotel with my name across from the Sheraton, but it was simpler for him to direct me to the Sheraton, a landmark I could easily find.*

But does the sign really say "Mt. Shasta?" As I drew closer, I saw that a segment of the neon tubing had burned out, the remaining part of the sign appearing to say "Shasta" from a distance. Painted underneath was the full Hebrew name of the hotel, which had not been visible at first. In any case, I was sure that this old, traditional-looking place was sure to be more affordable than the Sheraton; but did they have a vacancy?

Inside I was greeted warmly by the desk clerk and a young, vivacious woman, obviously his girlfriend. "Of course we have a room," he said, jokingly, "for you we have a room, and such a room—and only $12—such a deal!" *What a difference between this warm greeting and the cold reception at the Sheraton,* I thought, silently thanking Kuthumi for his directions.

The clerk gave me the key to my room and both he and his girlfriend wished me, with genuine concern for an obviously weary traveler, a good night's sleep.

That night I dreamed of yet another map, this time of Israel. But instead of a red line, this time I saw a serpent traveling clockwise around the country, and a voice said, *Follow the path of the serpent,* an instruction which I later realized applied to far more than this journey, as the serpent was a symbol of the life force and the wisdom that results when that force is consciously directed through one's spiritual centers.

The Path of the Serpent

After breakfast, I took a bus to the edge of town to begin my journey. It was not long after the Yom Kippur War, where Israel fought to protect itself from the Syrian and Egyptian armies preparing to invade, and everyone was still jumpy about another war. Frequent atrocities committed by Arab terrorists kept everyone on edge. A few days before, Palestinians had fired a mortar from the Golan Heights overlooking northern Israel into a schoolyard, killing several children. I didn't realize I was being sent to that very location.

I never hitchhiked at home, but everyone was so friendly I stuck my thumb out, and soon people were stopping to give me rides. I was picked up by some passing Israelis, and except for the Uzi rifles they toted, I felt I was in a large family or commune where people helped each other and wanted to live in peace. After I was dropped off, a young man picked me up in a small Fiat and shared some bread his wife had made and a slab of tasty cheese from the local kibbutz, then let me off near Kibbutz Dan. It was here that the mortars had fallen on the schoolyard, and several guards at a checkpoint who seemed my own age frisked me for weapons and asked to see my passport before allowing me to pass.

In this militant atmosphere, I was surprised at the open-hearted welcome I was given, perhaps because so many Israelis had relatives in the States, and they realized how closely our destinies are intertwined. Walking up the road to the kibbutz, I was greeted at the office, where my passport was checked again, and after a brief interrogation to ascertain if I were a terrorist, I was assigned to a bunk in a cabin with a dozen other men. It reminded me of the summer camp I had gone to as a kid.

The next morning in the cafeteria, there was a breakfast of homemade bagels and cream cheese, with ripe tomatoes and cucumbers from the garden. After breakfast, I reported for work and was assigned to the orchard to harvest grapefruit. *I marveled that in the midst of human strife, the luscious fruit grew to perfection, oblivious of the surrounding danger.* It was hot work, but it felt good to close my fingers around the warm, golden spheres offering themselves to be eaten, and to inhale their fragrance as I placed them carefully in the wicker basket. I filled basket after basket, which I emptied into a bin. It felt good to work to feed others like myself, who had come from countries all over the world to participate in this vision, rather than to work for money.

After dinner that evening, I went for a walk to watch the sunset. On the edge of a field at the back of the kibbutz, I sat down on a stone wall and swung my legs over to jump down into the tall grass, when I heard wild honking in the distance. A jeep with a machine gun mounted on it was racing toward me, its occupants shouting wildly and waving their arms.

Why are they making such a fuss? I haven't done anything wrong, have I? But since they were waving so energetically at me, I climbed off the wall and waited for them. As the jeep screeched to a stop in a cloud of dust and gravel, a tough-acting girl in a uniform jumped out and barked in my face, "Where do you think you're going?"

"For a walk," I replied innocently.

"No, you are *not!*" she shouted, grabbing me by the hand, as though I were her child she had caught with a hand in the cookie jar, and pulled me back to the wall where I had been sitting.

"Look down there!" she commanded, pointing along the wall. "Do you see that tower? The guards up there have orders to shoot anything that moves in that field. Believe me, they have very good aim. If I hadn't stopped you, you would be dead now."

She rounded up her comrades, who had been manning the jeep's machine gun, and they all jumped back in the vehicle.

"Don't bother to thank me," she shouted, with a sarcastic attitude of *tough love* I often felt among the Israelis—before throwing the engine into reverse and gunning the jeep back down the dusty road to complete the guard duty.

"Thank you!" I shouted, still astounded by the sudden appearance of this avenging angel, but she was already out of earshot. As it was now dusk, and my desire to walk around the kibbutz had seriously diminished, I went back to the cabin for the night.

As Mount Hermon was nearby, the highest summit in that part of the world and one of the places where historians said the Transfiguration of Jesus might have taken place, I set out early the next morning to climb this sacred mountain and hopefully imbibe the spiritual nectar of the Christ.[44]

---

44 Finding the true locations where events of the New Testament took place was impossible, as every religious sect had its own favorite place, somewhat the way numerous bed and breakfast lodgings in the eastern U.S. claim to have been where George Washington spent the night. Mount Hermon, as the highest mountain in the region and the place

If the report was true, and on this mountain Jesus had become bathed in light—probably the descent of his Higher Self which I had witnessed when Pearl's I AM Presence came through her—I knew that my inner sensitivity would enable me to feel whatever record was left in the *akashic* (Sanskrit: etheric) record magnetically imprinted in space. As Moses and Elijah were also supposed to have appeared during the Transfiguration, I was sure that the atmosphere would be highly charged with that Ascended Master energy.[45] On the slopes of Mount Shasta in the 1930s, Godfrey Ray King had assisted David Lloyd in making his Ascension, leaving a vibrant spiritual imprint that uplifts everyone who comes to the Mountain. So, I now eagerly looked forward to experiencing a similar energy field.

Perhaps I, too, will be transfigured on this holy ground...see Elijah...or have a visitation from Jesus himself? After meeting Kuthumi and El Morya on the plane, associates of Jesus, certainly anything was possible. But as I made my way up the mountain, the ground did not seem so holy. The road wound up through the Golan Heights, now a battlefield littered with burned-out tanks strewn among the boulders on its rugged slopes. Halfway up the mountain I rounded a curve in the road when someone shouted, "Halt!"

A helmet popped from behind a pile of rocks, and the barrel of a machine gun swung toward me.

"Halt!" I heard again, "Hands over your head!"

"Don't shoot!" I shouted, raising my hands, as everything became surrealistic. I felt like a character in one of those grade "B" war movies I'd seen so often as a child, like *Bridge at Remagen,* that had become indelibly etched in my subconscious. Now the movie had come to life, and I was on a real life battlefield stained with blood—and, although it seemed that my life hung in the balance, I felt strangely detached, as though I knew that

---

where Jordan, Syria, and Israel are contiguous, would have been a likely place for a wandering mystic to go in search of a place to meditate and contact his mentors.

45 Elijah, a prophet in the ninth century B.C., is mentioned in the Jewish *Talmud* and also the Muslim *Qur'an* as a great miracle worker who healed the sick, raised the dead, and Ascended into Heaven. Enoch, the great-grandfather of Noah, was another great prophet who either Ascended or was taken up in a UFO: "And Enoch walked with God, and he was not; for God took him" (Genesis 5:24).

Apprentice to the Masters

it was not time to go yet. I did not believe that he would actually shoot. I hoped that the movie I was seeing of an encounter with Christ would prevail over his movie of an encounter with a terrorist.

However, as I heard the safety click off and saw the barrel of the gun level at me, I realized that he was serious, that I was going to die. Fascinated, I watched as a second soldier held the ammunition belt in his hands so the gun would fire smoothly without jamming.

"Don't shoot!" I shouted again, wondering how I could snap him out of his conditioned response.

"Come forward with your hands over your head," he commanded. "Where are you from?

I could see now beneath his helmet that he was about my age.

"I'm an American," I stammered.

"You're not Palestinian?"

"No, I'm an American."

"You don't have a bomb in that backpack, do you?"

"No."

"Come forward, slowly, but keep your hands over your head."

"You're sure your American?"

"Yes."

"Do you know Brooklyn?"

"Yes, of course," I said, feeling a bit more relaxed at this unexpected question.

"It's a good place, huh?"

"Yeah, Brooklyn's a great place."

"My uncle lives there," the soldier said, then looking at my backpack again, "You're sure you don't have a bomb in there?"

"No."

"You're not a terrorist?"

"No."

"You wouldn't lie to me, would you?"

"No."

"Okay, you can put your arms down. So, what are you doing up here in no-man's land? Some of my friends died here. This is a dangerous place to be walking around."

I wanted to visit the holy mountain mentioned in the Bible, I explained. With the mention of that book he gave me a quizzical look, picked up a walkie talkie, and began shouting into it in Hebrew. The safety was reset on the machine gun, and soon a jeep slid to a halt beside me.

"Get in," the young soldier ordered. "I have asked them to give you a ride. It's a hot day, and a long walk…no place to be going for a stroll."

Saying good-bye, I promised I would say hello to his uncle in Brooklyn next time I was there, then climbed in the back of the jeep. Sitting beside two soldiers who were walking arsenals, hand grenades and extra ammo clips on their belts, we sped up the mountain.

At the end of the road, I was surprised to find a ski lift. The fastest way to the summit was to follow the line of lift towers, so I hiked under them, picking my way around the boulders to the summit. There I found a small wooden shack used in the winter by the lift operators, and I sat down inside to meditate.

I had just crossed my legs for a long meditation, when I heard a deep rumbling and felt the ground shaking. I tried to ignore the distraction, as my Tantric Buddhist training said to see all phenomena as manifestations of the Goddess. But as the rumbling drew closer and the ground shook more violently, I gave in to curiosity and lifted the wooden flap covering the window. A dozen tanks churning up a cloud of yellow dust were bearing down on me. *Did they see me? Are they going to fire? Am I caught in the beginning of another war?*

Not waiting to see what country manned these tanks or for them to begin firing, I ran out the door, flew downhill through the thorny bushes, and slid down to the road. There an Israeli Army truck was parked, guarded by a female soldier with an Uzi rifle slung at her side. Since the engine was running, and it appeared they were about to descend, I begged her for a ride, but she shook her head.

"Please," I begged.

"No…back off."

"There are tanks coming," I pleaded.

"Probably exercises."

I refused to leave, planting myself in front of her, and finally her maternal instincts won out over her military programming, and waving the barrel of the gun, she told me to get in.

As we rode down the mountain in the back of the truck, I noticed that her face had softened and that she was quite beautiful. I felt sad that instead of being able to follow her natural desire to give birth to and nurture life, she was being forced to confront and kill.

Despite my longing to experience the same mystical union with God that Jesus was said to have experienced, I felt here only suspicion and fear. In fact, nowhere during my travels in Israel did I feel the energy of the Christ, and I began to doubt, as did many scholars, that Jesus had ever been here. Some felt that many of the New Testament events were fabricated to further the political aims of the church and state, and that many of these events likely occurred, if at all, in India and other parts of Asia.[46] The Bible, compiled from hundreds of scattered gospels that were written long after the death of Jesus by men who never knew him—although inspired—could certainly not be used as an accurate historical reference. Historians writing at the beginning of the Christian Era mention nothing of the events of the New Testament.[47]

In India Jesus is reported to have attended Nalanda, the greatest university of the time. During these "lost years" not reported in the New Testament, Sai Baba says that Jesus traveled widely in the East where he was known as "Issa," and that after studying in India and Tibet became a great teacher and healer who wandered throughout the ancient world. In Persia (Iran) there are records of a great saint by the same name who traveled far and wide and was called in some places by the name Yuz Asaf (translated variously as "a Buddha" and "Son of Joseph").[48]

---

46 Lena Einhorn, *The Jesus Mystery: Astonishing Clues to the True Identity of Jesus and Paul* (The Lyons Press, March 2007), p.175, quotes Jawaharlal Nehru, First Prime Minister of India, in a letter to his daughter, Indira Gandhi: "All over Central Asia, in Kashmir and Ladakh and Tibet and even farther north, there is a strong belief that Jesus or Isa traveled about there. Some people believed that he visited India, also."

47 Ibid., p.24, quoting John E. Remsburg, *The Christ: A Critical Review and Analysis of the Evidence of His Existence* (originally published by The Truth Seeker Company, 1909; republished by Prometheus Books, 1994). "Enough of the writings of the authors named in the foregoing list remains to form a library. Yet in this mass of Jewish and Pagan literature, aside from two forged passages in the works of Jewish author (Josephus) and two disputed passages in the works of Roman writers, there is to be found no mention of Jesus Christ." He goes on to cite over 600 contradictions in the first four gospels alone. See also: Gene D. Matlock, *Jesus and Moses are Buried in India, Birthplace of Abraham and the Hebrews!* (Authors Choice Press; New York, 2000).

48 According to the yogi and Sanskrit scholar Ramamurti Mishra (Swami

In those days, this wandering mystic, whatever his true name, was held to be a great prophet, teacher, and healer. However, to unify his far-flung empire, Emperor Constantine had him declared a God to put him on an equal footing with the other Gods worshiped throughout the Roman Empire. It matters not where Jesus lived or if he was called Issa or Yuz Asaf, for now he is an Ascended Being who responds to those whose thoughts turn to him—just as it matters not what name a child calls when in distress; the parent who is closest responds.

It was in India where I had felt the presence of Jesus, not here in Israel.[49] The dominant energy in Israel was that of the Old Testament patriarchs, who lived by the old law of an eye for an eye, a tooth for a tooth. It was the Law of Forgiveness and inner God Presence represented by the Christ for which these people hungered. And my heart said, *Only when these people find the living Christ Presence within, will there be peace in Israel.*

I continued my serpent's journey around Israel, heading south now along the Jordan River. At a youth hostel on the Sea of Galilee, I connected with a group of students who offered me a ride in their tour bus. Sitting up front between the driver and guide, who was an antiquities scholar, I

Brahmananda), from whom I studied Raja Yoga, the word "Christ" is derived from the Greek "Khristos," which in turn derives from the Sanskrit "Krishna" (Krsn na means *crush not*—that which cannot be crushed: the Inner Light).

49 While in Jaganath Puri with Ram Dass, I saw the akashic record of Jesus on several occasions while walking to the famed temple there. Levi, in *The Aquarian Gospel of Jesus the Christ* (L.N. Fowler, London, 1920), also states that Jesus studied with the Brahman priests at the Jaganath Temple, but when he gave the teachings to the "untouchable" fishermen on the Bay of Bengal, the priests conspired to have him killed. Being warned ahead of time, he escaped to the Himalayas. During my stay there, I was told of a Westerner who had sneaked into the temple and was killed by the priests, as the strict law of the Brahmins forbade entrance to outsiders. I contented myself with meditating outside the temple and was blessed to there meet Anandamayi Ma a second time, the woman saint mentioned by Paramahansa Yogananda in *Autobiography of a Yogi*. Neem Karoli Baba had given us the slip, as he was wont to do, and was actually inside the temple at the time—where, as a renowned yogi, he was welcome.

learned secrets of the area's history—and about how many of the Hebrew names of places and people are variations from the Sanskrit. There was evidence that the Jews had migrated to the Middle East from India after one of the great floods that had ravaged northwest India—which would explain the great similarities I found between the Indians and the Jews who, unbeknownst to most, share a common heritage.

Who were these prophets who roamed this part of the world: Elijah, Enoch, and Jesus, who did not die but were taken up into Heaven? Were these special messengers taken up in chariots that were actually UFOs, as many claim? Are the "Clouds of Heaven" the Bible so frequently mentions that appear in the sky when these prophets disappear, the same mysterious UFO clouds that surround the summit of Mount Shasta on days when the spiritual energy is high?

Disappointed that I had not felt the Christ energy in the "Holy Land," or been visited by any of the Biblical prophets, I returned to the "Mt. Shasta" Hotel in Tel Aviv, where I was again warmly greeted and given my former room. That night in meditation, still determined to know the truth about Jesus and his ministry, I went deep into the center of my being and affirmed silently,

I AM the Living Christ.

And I focused on the Living Light within my heart—the Source of my being. Shortly, I felt that light intensify and start to fill the cells of my body as I continued to affirm the Christ Within—and before long I felt myself become a luminous being, illuminating not only my meager hotel room, but all of the city—rays of light reaching out through all of Israel. And I realized that *who* the historical Jesus was, whatever his real name may have been, and where he lived, was insignificant compared to the reality of the Christ within every person—waiting to come forth in full, conscious dominion. And no historical argument should get in the way of discovering *that truth.*

My circular journey around Israel completed, I wondered where to go next. I could not use my return ticket back to Canada for another eleven days, and I had just cashed my next to last traveler's check to pay for the night's lodging, so I was in a bit of a predicament—but one which, under the Masters' guidance, would soon be resolved. Before lying down for the night, I sent out a prayer to my Christ Self and the Masters, with whom I knew *I am One,* and asked to awaken in the morning with the consciousness of that guidance clearly manifest in my feelings.

Chapter 26

Trial in Athens

In the morning, despite the lack of any graphic dreams, I awoke with the feeling that I was to go to Greece. There was simply a clear, distinct feeling that grew stronger with every passing minute. In meditation, I asked that this feeling be removed if it was not the Plan, as the idea of crossing the Mediterranean to Greece seemed bizarre in view of my lack of funds. However, meditation not only reinforced the idea, but impelled me to find the airline ticket office as soon as possible and make whatever changes were necessary.

To my surprise, the airline office was across the street in the lobby of the Sheraton Hotel, where ten days ago I had begun my journey in this country. As I had a premonition that the airline might be reluctant to change my ticket, I asked for Saint Germain to go before me to the ticket office and render whatever assistance I might require, following my request to him by invoking my own I AM Presence:

I AM the Commanding, Governing Presence of God in Action, going before me, taking complete command of this entire situation.

No sooner had I entered the small office which was staffed by a woman getting ready to close early and go home for the Jewish Sabbath, when a young man walked in behind me and took one of the two chairs facing the desk.

What nerve! Doesn't this guy realize that I was here first? Does he think he can just push in here ahead of me? Apparently he did, as he pushed his chair close to the desk, so I cleared my throat as if to say, *Hey, I was here first!*

"Excuse me, I want to change my ticket," I said loudly, putting my ticket on her desk, and the woman turned her attention to me, ignoring the pushy young man also sitting in front of her.

"You can't change that ticket!" the woman snapped, glancing briefly at the ticket, eyes flashing like daggers.

"Oh, yes he can," said the young man who now was taking my side as an ally. He leaned toward the agent, and said with the authority of one

Apprentice to the Masters

who knows, "It's a Q fare. Look on page 154 of your manual, the footnote at the bottom of the page. You'll see."

It suddenly flashed through my mind that this assertive stranger was none other than the one whose assistance I had requested ten minutes before, the Ascended Master Saint Germain, once more traveling incognito. He had taken command of the situation, just as I had requested, and I risked a sideways glance. He could have been any self-confident young man on vacation, wearing slacks and a sports shirt. Around his neck a brilliant gold Star of David seemed to say, "I'm Jewish."

My emotions were calm until, as I looked at him, he winked at me; then I had to fight back laughter at the absurdity of the situation, hoping that the agent who was perusing the manual did not notice my struggle. To keep under control, I bit my tongue and clenched my fists so tightly that the nails dug into the palms of my hands.

Is that really you? I asked mentally, knowing he could hear my thoughts, *What should I do to keep from making a fool of myself?*

Just act natural...make conversation, I heard him reply.

I tried to be natural, but it was all I could do to keep from guffawing out loud. Finally, I tried to make conversation, as he had suggested, saying what seemed the stupidest thing imaginable to one whom I knew to be a liberated being beyond space and time, "So, what brings you here?"

"Oh, I'm here on vacation," he replied, nonchalantly.

"Really. And where are you from?"

"New York."

"Do you come to Israel often?"

"Now and then."

I was grateful for his suggestion to make conversation, for as I talked and began to play my role as he was playing his, I calmed down and began to enjoy the drama of duality, knowing we were Gods merely pretending to be Earthlings.

"Well," the agent said, lifting her head from the manual and addressing Saint Germain. "You are right. I can change the ticket."

Then she turned back to me. "There will be twelve dollars for the airport tax."

As I handed her my last $20 traveler's check, she gleefully rose from her desk, waving the check in my face. "We don't take traveler's checks. If you don't have cash or a credit card, I can't change your ticket. It's late, and I'm going to close up now and go home for *Shabbat!*"

"Just one minute," Saint Germain, interjected. "The bank next door will cash the check."

"But they are just now closing," said the agent, obviously annoyed, waving my check in the direction of the teller we could see locking the door of the small bank office adjacent the ticket office. "It's Shabbat, and everyone is going home now, me too."

"They will reopen," Saint Germain said. "And they will cash the check."

"Young man, I don't know who you are or where you're from, but this is Israel, and banks do not reopen once they are closed, and this one is closed."

"Let me see," he said, taking the check out of her hand, and walking out the door with the agent and me following. He intercepted the banker, who had just turned off the lights, locked the door, and was turning to leave.

"Would you be so kind as to cash this check for this gentleman?" the Master asked.

"Why, of course," the banker said, without a moment's hesitation, as the travel agent blanched. "I'd be happy to cash it." He reopened the door and turned on the lights. Without looking at my passport, as was normally required, he handed me a twenty dollar bill, then turned off the lights, relocked the bank door, and with a nod said, "Shabbat Shalom," and walked toward the lobby.

The agent was pale, but for some reason was still determined not to issue me a new ticket. With the twenty dollar bill and my ticket and passport in her hand, the agent sat down again at her desk and opened the drawer.

"Ahhh," she said, triumphantly. "I don't have any change. I'm so sorry; you'll have to all go home now. Come back Monday."

Not to be deterred from the sure, certain victory which it was Saint Germain's prerogative to ordain, he said politely but firmly, "There is sufficient change in the petty cash box in your desk drawer."

Again the agent blanched, appalled that he knew the contents of her desk, and sighed in final resignation. She stamped my new ticket, pulled out the eight dollars change, and handed it to me along with my passport. As the young man and I left the office, I looked back at the woman sitting at her desk, holding her head in her hands. In the Master Saint Germain, she had met her match.

The Master and I walked together toward the hotel lobby. I was dying to converse with him at greater length, to ask him many questions, though I knew to do so would be a breach of the decorum his appearance in this dimension demanded and would preclude any contact with him of this sort in the future. I knew that I had to continue acting my part in this drama, knowing full well who he was and pretending to be just two tourists talking to each other. I wanted to keep the conversation going as long as I could without violating inner law, hoping for just one more moment with him, perhaps a word of advice, a word of acknowledgment. But he maintained his *persona incognita,* not giving in to my human desire any more than he had to the agent at the ticket office. When we came to the center of the lobby, he turned and faced me, and I roused the courage to ask him a question I thought permissible, "Where are *you* going now?"

"Up," he said, pointing toward the high ceiling of the lobby, as well as the heavens above, the faint smile on his face confirming the double meaning he intended.

"Up?" I repeated, startled at his use of the double *entendre,* hoping he would elaborate.

"Yes, up," he said with amusement. He nodded farewell, indicating that his mission in my dimension was over, then turned abruptly and walked toward the elevator. Even though I knew that his nod was a dismissal, a sign that I should not try to prolong the contact, I could barely restrain my impulse to rush after him. I wanted to join him in the elevator and ask the multitude of questions that were now coming to mind, such as: *What should I do next, and what is the bigger plan for my life?* I yearned to watch him dematerialize before my eyes, as he had done in Muir Woods, but stood still until after the elevator doors closed, and then I turned and left the hotel. Walking down the driveway, I realized that I had forgotten to thank the Master for his help, although I'm sure he knew my heart was overwhelmed with gratitude.

Placing the new ticket to Athens in my pocket, I thanked him silently for all the assistance he and the other Masters had been giving throughout the journey. Pearl had frequently said, "Gratitude, more than anything else, opens the door to the Masters' assistance." As I walked back to the hotel, barely feeling the ground beneath my feet, I laughed at the masterful yet humorous way Saint Germain had responded to my request for assistance. I would need to remember the joy of that encounter during the upcoming ordeal in Athens.

Down and Out in Athens

In the city named after Athena (a Master known in the Golden Age of Greece as the Goddess of Wisdom), I found a youth hostel with a view of the Acropolis, the sacred hill overlooking the city. The Parthenon—a temple emanating such purity and harmony that the sprawling, polluted city at its base showed by contrast the current degeneration of civilization. The measure of the advancement of a civilization, the Masters say, is not their scientific achievements or material comforts, but the closeness of its people to their God Source. In its preoccupation with the acquisition of ever more material things, modern civilization has lost that closeness.

The ancient Greeks were a people who understood the mathematics of creation and saw how all life is an expression of a divine geometry whose proportions are manifest everywhere. When consciously embodied in art and architecture, these divine symmetries reinforce and support the natural order of life; when ignored or perverted, life degenerates into disharmony and chaos.

Living among buildings of harmonious design, whose proportions are derived from the universal order, one can't help but feel supported and spiritually elevated. During my trials in Athens, whenever I would feel overwhelmed I would go where I could see the Acropolis, and immediately my fears would evaporate before the symmetry and splendor of that architecture, bringing me back into harmony with the symmetry of creation.[50]

After paying for a bunk at the Youth Hostel for the remaining ten days I had to wait before I could return home, I found myself completely broke, save for some loose change rattling around in the back of my suitcase. Although I didn't know why the Masters had sent me to Athens, I had faith that I was in the right place and that I had exactly the amount of money I needed, whatever their purpose. I trusted that there was a plan for my life and that God was present at every moment—that all creation exists and has its sustenance in the Mind of God.

---

50 The Parthenon (temple to Athena), as well as the human body, contains many instances of the Golden Section (Golden Mean), the ratio that reduces to *Phi*, one side of a rectangle being .618 times the length of the other side. These proportions that embody the basic structure of creation are intuitively regarded as beautiful. This needs to be distinguished from *Pi*, the ratio of a circle's circumference to its diameter.

I also knew that I was not allowed to tell anyone that I had no money to buy food. Begging did not fit the nobility of the agreement I had made with Saint Germain when I had asked to become his student and for him to clear my human *karma*. He knew my situation and could alter it at any time. Of all conditions, the material ones are the easiest for the Masters to change. It is our emotional and mental conditions that are more challenging—those, the Masters help us transmute over lifetimes. Mere money, the Masters could materialize in the twinkling of an eye, although now it appeared they chose not to do so, in order to let me experience being without—perhaps simply as a test of faith.

After not eating for a few days, I began to feel weak. *Perhaps it's time to leave the Earth—the very reason the Masters brought me here, to complete the Ascension? What better place to leave my body than the mount of the Acropolis? I'll climb up above the city and lie down on the altar of the Parthenon, offering my body to the Gods, and merge finally with my Higher Self.*

I set out to climb the Acropolis, moving slowly to conserve energy. On my way I came to a huge well-maintained park, with lush flowers and beautiful trees. Passing around a hedge, I spied an orange grove whose trees were pregnant with lush fruit. My mouth watered in anticipation of the taste of a fresh orange. I had been guided here, I was sure, in answer to my prayers for sustenance.

I climbed the low fence and picked up as many of the fragrant oranges from the ground as I could carry in my shirt, and careful that no one would see me, hopped back over the fence. Sitting on a bench, I cut into the first orange with the blade of my Swiss Army knife and peeled back the soft skin, revealing the succulent sections of the fruit. I offered a prayer of thanks to the Masters for their providence, but my gratitude was short-lived, as my mouth filled with bitterness. These were ornamental oranges that were not edible, and I spit out the pulp in the dust. In disgust, I threw the remaining oranges back across the fence.

Perhaps the sign I had ignored, "Do not cross fence," *was there for a reason?* I thought of the time Saint Germain, in the guise of a Highway Patrolman, had issued me a traffic ticket, and I remembered that the Masters expect their students to adhere to the currently prevailing laws whenever possible. In the absence of direct, unmistakable guidance to the contrary, their students are expected to obey the laws of the human plane before trying to master those of a higher plane.

Confronting my hunger, I remembered the aphorism, *A wise man, when forced to go without food, will fast.* I had gone weeks without eating in India because of the spicy food, so surely ten days fasting now would do no harm. I had friends who had fasted four times that long to purify the body, and they said that the initial weakness came from the release of toxins, a condition which cleared as the fast progressed.

Feeling much better, now that I had come to a decision, I stood up and continued my walk. But after a few blocks I began to feel dizzy and realized I didn't have the energy to walk miles and then climb the steep hill of the Acropolis, so I decided to go back to the hostel. *It might be better to die there, in my sleep, rather than cause a drama at a tourist landmark,* I rationalized.

But I did not die. Instead, I spent my days in Athens sitting on the bed, meditating and praying. The only food I had was a handful of peanuts offered by the man in the next bunk. Little did he realize how hungry I was and what a feast he had provided. I knew that if I had told him my plight, he would have offered at least enough money for a bowl of soup in the cafeteria, or loaned money which I would have repaid when I returned home. But I knew I was to remain silent. The Masters could arrange for me to eat by inspiring my neighbor to treat me to a meal, rather than a bag of peanuts. Or they could precipitate money directly in my hands or wallet, so I could buy whatever I needed. My part in this movie was to trust the director and give my best performance, though I did not have a copy of the script or know the drama's outcome.

Knowing how easy it was for the Masters to precipitate things,[51] I

---

51 I had seen many instances of precipitation. For example, Sai Baba created objects out of the air only inches from my face, where I could see them materialize. One time he materialized a pint of *amrita* (nectar) for me while I was over a hundred miles distant from him. It took several minutes for the empty can in my hand to fill from the invisible source with the indescribably sweet-smelling, cloudy-looking *amrita.* See: Samuel Sandweiss, *The Holy Man and the Psychiatrist* (Birthday Publishing Co., 1975). I had also frequently slipped on my finger the ring in which was set the huge, flawless amethyst that Saint Germain had precipitated for Pearl. Theosophical literature abounds with the description of the materialization of objects by adepts. *The Mahatma Letters to A.P. Sinnett* is a collection of letters that were precipitated by the Masters, containing advice and instruction to various Theosophists.

prayed every night before I went to bed for them to precipitate money in my wallet. Yet, every morning on arising I would go through my wallet and look for money that might have appeared overnight, and each morning my wallet was empty. I even looked in the wallet's hidden recesses, but there was never anything there.

Still, I did not give up hope. I had run out of gas once in my old Dodge van, and when I had prayed for help, the engine had kept running during the seven mile drive back to town, quitting only as I coasted up to the gas pump. So, I continued to expect a miracle, knowing that just because it had not yet happened, this did not mean it would not happen the next moment, or the next morning on arising.

I never lost hope, nor did I lose faith in the Masters, knowing that everything they did was for a reason. I remembered that Jesus said there was a destiny guiding even a sparrow: *"Yet not one of them falls to the ground apart from the will of the Father."*

Surely, the Masters I had met in physical form on this journey—Saint Germain, Kuthumi, and El Morya—all of whom were also "one with the Father," knew where I was and could help me at any moment. For some reason known only to them, it seemed they intended for me to experience this present deprivation. *What is a little hunger before the banquet of the Spirit to be attained through self-mastery?*

Jesus frequently came to mind, especially the scene in the story where he asked in the Garden of Gethsemane, having seen the vision of his coming arrest, scourging, and crucifixion, *"My father, if it is possible, let this cup pass away from me; nevertheless, not as I will, but as thou wilt."* I was beginning to feel the same desire to escape my ordeal, for I could not see what benefit my hunger was to anyone. Surely the Masters could see my dedication, that if they asked me to, I would fast to the end.

As my friends had said, I found that fasting became easier with time, and after the initial dizziness subsided and my stomach became used to its emptiness, I felt a lightness of being. The real challenge was in transcending the feeling that I was being punished for some wrong I had committed, some *karma* I had created long ago in a past life, that I could no longer remember. It finally dawned on me, *I am not a victim. I am here by choice.*

For an excellent account of this saga, see: *Masters and Men: The Human Story in the Mahatma Letters,* by Virginia Hanson (Quest Books, 1980).

It is only because the Masters love me and feel that I am strong enough, that they are allowing me to confront these feelings of limitation, to raise me to a new level of freedom and Mastery.

THE MAGIC WALLET

On my last day in Athens, my 21st since departing from Calgary, I walked shakily to the bus and placed the last Greek coin I had been saving into the coin box and relaxed in my seat for the ride to the airport, comforted by the knowledge that in a few hours I would be on the plane back to Canada, enjoying a warm meal.

It was dark when the plane landed, and I used my remaining 35 Canadian cents to pay for the bus downtown. My plan was to spend the night on a bench at the bus terminal, a frequent refuge of the homeless. But abruptly, an inner voice commanded: *Go to the Palliser Hotel!*

That's impossible; since I didn't have a credit card, the last time I stayed there I had to pay cash on checking in. There is no way I can go there without money and get a room. Yet I kept hearing *Palliser* over and over, so I asked the bus driver to let me off at that elegant, five star hotel instead of the bus station.

Summoning courage, I walked into the hotel lobby. Walking toward the front desk I said,

Saint Germain, please go before me and arrange everything perfectly, according to the Divine Plan.

The clerk greeted me and without asking for any identification pushed the hotel register toward me. I visualized the perfect room available as I signed my name, mentioning to the clerk that I wanted a quiet room with a bathtub, as I wanted a long soak to help recuperate from traveling.

"Of course, sir," he said, barely looking up, and handing me the key to a room. I waited for him to ask me to pay, but he only said, "Was there something else you needed sir?"

"No, nothing else," I said, astounded that he had neither asked me to pay nor show any identification. Picking up my suitcase and heading for the elevator, I was sure that at any moment I would hear him shout for me to come back and pay. But that shout never came, I boarded the elevator, went straight to my room, and fell asleep as soon as my head hit the pillow.

In the morning, as soon as I woke I got dressed and went down to the hotel dining room, where I ordered a huge breakfast, knowing I could charge it to the room. After a nourishing as well as delicious breakfast, I added a generous tip to the bill, signed it with my room number, and walked out, hoping no one would call me back to pay cash.

Once on the street, I looked for a bank where I could arrange to have some money wired. I was hoping that one of my tenants had deposited the rent that was due, and there would be money in the account. The first bank I came to as I turned the corner from the hotel turned out to be an associate of my home bank. I asked the manager to wire the $350 I hoped was there, but he said that, in any case, it would take at least two days to arrive. I was sure that by then I would be evicted from the hotel, once it was discovered I had checked in without paying.

I went back to the hotel to await further word about the transfer of funds. Entering the lobby, I felt apprehensive, wondering if they had discovered their administrative slip up, and would accost me as I entered. Trying to look affluent, I nodded magnanimously, "Good morning," to the desk clerk, who smiled back, "Good morning, sir," as I walked casually past him to the elevator, without incident.

Back in my room, I meditated on Divine Abundance and affirmed,

I AM the Wealth of God in action, now manifest.

And I asked Saint Germain to take complete command of my entire financial situation. I visualized myself made of golden light enveloped by a green aura—a combination of colors that magnetizes wealth—and ended my meditation by visualizing a rain of gold coins pouring down around me in a pile on the floor. I scooped up these coins in my mind's eye and took one of them down to the front desk and offered to pay my bill, enjoying the surprise on the clerk's face.

Still feeling abundant at the visualization of all the gold coins I had now stashed in my suitcase, I went downstairs for a delicious lunch, that I again charged to my room. At the thought of my gold, I penciled in a large tip, then went for a walk around the block. When I returned to the room, the red light on the telephone was flashing, and I realized with dread that I had a message—*probably a request to come down to the lobby immediately and pay the bill.* I feared an unpleasant scene when I confessed I didn't have any money or a credit card, and knew I'd be thrown out; but when I returned the call, the voice on the phone was cheerful:

"Sir, your bank phoned to say that your funds have arrived, and that you should stop by at your earliest convenience." For the first time, those tenants had paid the rent on time; the funds had arrived, not in two days as the manager had said, but in two hours.

"Why, thank you," I replied nonchalantly, as though his news was of little consequence, then hung up and went downstairs. In the lobby I beamed once more at the desk clerk, my expressions of abundance now genuine, and eagerly walked around the corner to the bank. The manager handed me the draft for the amount I had requested and instructed me to go to the teller's window to get it cashed. While the teller was counting out the Canadian dollars, I opened my wallet and was transfixed with amazement.

Where before my wallet had been an empty cavity, there was now a new crisp Fifty Drachma Note. In Athens I had checked first thing every morning to see if money had been precipitated by the Masters overnight, as I had requested—but it had never happened. Now, when I no longer needed it, here was the money I had asked for, blatantly present in the previously empty bill compartment.

"Is something wrong?" the teller asked, noting my confusion.

"Why no," I stammered. "It's just that there's a Fifty Drachma note in my wallet. I just came from Greece yesterday, and I didn't know I had any Greek money."

She asked to see the bill and admired Athena, patroness of Athens, whose portrait was engraved on the front of the note. As Athena was reported to be the Ascended Master Nada, Saint Germain's Twin Ray, this note was practically his calling card. Certainly, it was a manifestation of grace from both of them, a confirmation that even though they had let me go hungry, I had not escaped their attention.

The teller asked if I would sell the note to her. As it was only worth a few dollars, I agreed, and she handed me some bills from her wallet, along with the money from the wire.

Looking back, I wish that I had kept that precipitated Fifty Drachma note, as a reminder of how easily the Masters can provide everything we need—if it is something we truly require. I had not truly needed money in Athens, for I saw now that I had been a willing participant in this trial, a voluntary actor in the movie of which the Masters are the director. The itinerary for this journey had been planned by the Masters to the last detail, a lesson in adeptship which I could only have learned by the surrender of attachment to all preconceived ideas.

Apprentice to the Masters

With my new abundance, I was able to pay my hotel bill and the parking fee to reclaim my car. Once on the road back to California, I had time to review my experiences and felt grateful that I had been found worthy of these further trials that I knew were part of my apprenticeship to the Masters. Arduous though these adventures were, I knew they were part of the process by which my karma was being dissolved and my ignorance dispelled—so that I might be of service to others. I yearned for these tests to be finished, so my greater service, whatever that might be, could begin.

Chapter 27

Sued

To my great dismay, after returning home from my travels, there was a knock at my door Sunday morning and I was handed an official-looking paper that said, "You are being sued." I had hired one of my tenant's boyfriends to fix the wood stairs going up to her apartment on the second floor of a duplex I owned downtown. I had purchased all the materials he would need for the job: lumber, nails, bolts, and paint and left them at the site, expecting that he would soon get to work and that the job would be done when I returned home over a month later. However, being a lazy fellow who didn't like to work, he had put off the repairs, and one day, on his way to visit his girlfriend, had fallen through the steps he was supposed to have fixed, and sprained his wrist. Rather than accept responsibility for his own negligence, he assumed that since I seemed wealthy, he could sue me and insure his financial security for the next year. Rather than settle for payment of his doctor bill, he insisted on going to trial to claim $25,000 for his pain and suffering. But he did not know that the Masters would come to my defense and that the Light of God would prevail. In preparation for the trial, I decreed,

I AM Divine Justice come forth! Beloved I AM Presence, and Great Host of Ascended Masters, come forth now and bring about the Perfect, Divine Plan for this trial! Please see to it that I AM invincibly protected at all times, in all ways, forever.

The trial went as expected during the morning, each side presenting their view of the basic story. At first the jury seemed to be on his side, for the law stated that it was the property owner's duty to see that the building was maintained in a safe condition, and that I was negligent in not doing so, regardless of having hired him to make the needed repairs. It was my responsibility to have hired someone else.

I continued to call on the Masters and visualized the Goddess of Justice as the presiding judge. In addition, I visualized the plaintiff's attorney as being Saint Germain, who was using this situation for my education and purification, rather than as some evil being. In this way, I eventually

Apprentice to the Masters

managed to transform what I had first seen as a negative experience into a positive one—so that my ignorance would be transformed into wisdom.

Gradually my attorney, whom I also visualized as Saint Germain, cross-examined the plaintiff, and it came out that he was in the country illegally and was living off his girlfriend.

The turning point came in the afternoon. The court recessed for lunch, and I ate by myself at Nature's Kitchen, a friendly natural food café in Yreka. Although my insurance company would cover any losses, I felt a bit queasy, because the plaintiff's attorney, a former business acquaintance I used to have lunch with, had accused me of lying. He had portrayed me to the jury as a greedy slumlord who neglected the welfare of his tenants, interested in making money at the expense of others. I could hardly believe that he would take this case against me and that he would lie—for I had not yet understood that to him, and most attorneys, the law is only a game played for profit. It is only the witnesses who are under oath, not the attorneys, who can distort the situation to their heart's content, and for which prevarications they extract exorbitant fees.

Returning to the courthouse, I found the door locked. The janitor, however, was nearby, and as he recognized me as one of the parties in the case, gladly opened the door and let me in, before disappearing to clean offices down the hall. Since I knew the courtroom upstairs was locked, I waited in the foyer, examining the gold nuggets on display in the cases there. Shortly, there was a forceful knock on the door, and I saw it was the bailiff, returning with the jury.

I went to the door and opened the courthouse for them, and as one of the jurors looked at me with amusement, I heard her whisper to the juror beside her, "I think *they're* trying to tell us something." To them it appeared I was guarding not only the courthouse, but the county's gold as well—a recommendation of trust in my favor.

As the court reconvened, the matter quickly came to a head, and the jury soon retired to reach a decision. Almost immediately they returned, and to my great relief, they decided unanimously that I was not liable—that I owed nothing. And the plaintiff's attorney, who was working on a contingency basis, received nothing.

After the trial, I walked back to Nature's Kitchen to unwind and drink an organic ice cream soda. The daughter of one of the jurors was at an adjoining table and, recognizing me, said, "My mom said it boiled down to the fact that the jury believed you and didn't believe him. It was obvious he was a scoundrel; since he was living off his girlfriend, they saw he was trying to live off you as well. Basically, the jury felt that God was with you."

As I drove back to Mount Shasta, I gave thanks to the Masters and to my own God Self, that I was able to transform this challenge into an experience of growth and Mastery.

Chapter 28

The Last Leaky Pipe

Life as a landlord was becoming increasingly wearisome and time-consuming. Despite the excitement of applying the I AM Presence to work small miracles, I longed to be free of having to fix leaky pipes and burned-out hot water heaters. I dreamed of the freedom to be of greater service to the Masters, and wondered what I needed to do to complete this business phase of my apprenticeship.

Driving home one Friday afternoon from visiting a tenant who hadn't paid the rent in several months, a role in which it was impossible not to appear the villain, I pulled the car to the side of the road under the quiet shade of a tree on the banks of the Sacramento River. I'd had enough. Overwhelmed by the challenges I had faced during the week—collecting rent from tenants on welfare who could barely feed their children, firing friends I'd hired who couldn't do the work as promised, and crawling under houses to fix leaking pipes—I pleaded to Saint Germain, *When can I get out of the landlord business?*

When you have learned the lessons! I heard his immediate reply.

What lessons?

Number one, you must learn to say "No." Number two, you must keep your word in even the smallest things. And number three, you must prove you are responsible, financially and otherwise.

All right, I've got it, I replied, recalling previous occasions during which I had failed these challenges repeatedly during the past year and a half. Just months prior, in the lobby of the Palliser Hotel in Calgary, I thought I had passed the first test when I had said *No* to what appeared to be a beggar asking for money. But my old habit of trying to be kind to everyone had reasserted itself, and I had again, out of pity, taken in tenants who could not pay the rent.

Okay, test me now! I fired back to Saint Germain, confident that now knowing exactly what I had to do, I would prove I had learned these deceptively simple lessons. The desire to be free of the onerous tasks of being a landlord motivated me to succeed where before I had failed.

Immediately the tests began—demonstrating once again that I had not just been hearing my mind, that it was indeed the Master who had responded to my call. I arrived home to find someone waiting for me who wanted to rent a house, but didn't have the required last month's rent and security deposit. I had learned the hard way that these tenants never worked out, that I was not doing them a favor by allowing them to live beyond the limits of their own responsibility. This time, without any bad feeling, I simply said "No." Years later, I read about Trungpa Rinpoche's "Big No." The Tibetan Lama wrote that there is a time in everyone's life when "No" must be invoked as a boundary to put their present situation in perspective and give definition to life.

Shocked at the simple truth of my reply, the would-be tenant realized there was nothing more to say, and walked away without malice or argument. Startled myself at the power released by confronting the truth of the situation with that simple "No," I felt relieved that I had let the responsibility of finding a place to live rest with him, where it belonged, rather than take it on as my own burden; however, I prayed that he would find the right place within his means—and heard later that he had. I felt relieved, as I visualized one of the three items on Saint Germain's examination list being checked off.

The next test came a few days later. I told a new tenant I would have a key made, but after picking it up from the locksmith, I forgot to deliver it and didn't remember until I returned home. I was tired, and it would have been easy to let the matter slide and bring it the next day. But mindful now of the need to keep my word in even the smallest details, I drove the nine miles back to Dunsmuir and put the key in the tenant's mailbox. As I did so, I visualized item number two of the final exam checked off the list.

Keeping my promise in delivering that key was more important than I had realized, as my new tenant had been expecting friends to arrive that night while he was working the night shift at the mill, and he had told them the key would be in the mailbox. If I hadn't kept my word on that seemingly insignificant detail, his friends would have been locked out, with no place to sleep. I remembered then how many times I had been annoyed when people said they were going to do something for me but forgot—the feeling of being neglected.

Passing the last item on Saint Germain's exam was a lot more difficult than the first two. I didn't have a clear idea what it meant to be financially responsible, let alone how to prove I had attained that state of adeptship. But the lesson and the test for this challenge were combined into one. And once again I was faced with the need to follow inner guidance, despite the mind wanting to assert its dominion.

It was tax time. Here was an opportunity, I thought, to prove I was responsible, follow the rules, and hire an accountant to prepare the required forms. The regulations quoted on the instructions for the forms, I discovered, often contradicted the actual statutes enacted into law, and were so contradictory and confusing that I was often left in doubt as to what was required. *Who could read, let alone understand, all eleven thousand pages of the tax code?* I asked a friend, who was also my attorney, if he could recommend someone to prepare my tax forms, thinking that anyone he recommended would have my interests at heart.

"Not to worry," my Jewish friend said, assuring me that his accountant friend from San Francisco would be in town soon and could prepare the necessary forms. This sounded good, and I went away feeling reassured that I'd done the right thing. But as it approached April 15th and the promised accountant did not arrive, I began to get nervous, feeling in the pit of my stomach that something was wrong. But my friend kept reassuring me, "Not to worry, there's plenty of time, and you can always file for an extension."

At long last the promised accountant arrived, and I piled my boxes of bills, receipts, and canceled checks into my car and started for Dunsmuir to turn everything over to him. But rather than feeling better, my anxiety worsened the closer I came to the scheduled appointment. *This is not right!* I heard, shouting in my head over and over as I drove.

I have an appointment; it's too late to back out now, I thought, forgetting that for the Presence it's never too late. Since he was a busy professional who had scheduled a slot for me, I thought it would be dishonorable both to myself and my friend if I didn't keep this appointment, made so far in advance. So I dismissed the voice I was hearing as the voice of doubt, my own mind stressed by the burden of assembling all the financial data the accountant had requested. Torn between trusting the inner voice that was telling me to turn around, and my mind telling me to keep going, I felt paralyzed by inertia and thus kept going.

Although I kept hearing *This is not right,* I continued on downhill, having made up my mind to keep my commitment. *After all, wasn't I just tested to see if I would keep my word?*

I was so concerned with *doing the right thing,* as my mind perceived *right* to be, that I did not see the obvious staring me in the face. If I had followed my guidance and turned around, I would have found the other honorable option, the most obvious one, which was to phone and cancel the appointment. Mistakenly, I thought the accountant was depending on me to show up, when in fact he was overloaded and had only agreed to see me as a favor to my friend. Canceling the appointment would have been doing him a favor—the exact opposite of what my mind was telling me! *Why didn't I listen to my heart?* I had let my fear of transgressing my programming get in the way.

Arriving in Dunsmuir, filled with apprehension, which should have been a clue that I was following the wrong course of action, I met with the accountant and loaded the boxes of tax documents into the trunk of his car for his return to San Francisco. He was going back to the Bay Area that night, where he was swamped with work to complete by the April 15th deadline. "I'll be in touch," he assured me, though I felt uneasy that he avoided looking me in the eye.

At least it was out of my hands now, I thought, and began to feel better. But April 15th came and went, and still I had not heard from the accountant or received the completed returns. Nor did he return my calls. Finally, I heard through my attorney that an extension had been filed. *We still have plenty of time,* he assured me. But the accountant still did not return my phone calls. I was devastated when I heard a few weeks later that he had gone to the Caribbean on vacation.

A few days before the new August filing deadline, the wayward accountant returned from vacation and called to say he was finally preparing my returns. He wanted to know the amount of the "capital gains" on the stock I had sold to buy my rental properties.

"Capital gains?" I said anxiously, remembering that term from childhood as something that had upset my mother at tax time, but which I had never understood. I paid it little attention back then, being more interested in designing space ships in which I hoped I would one day escape Earth. After I grew up and left home, a financial firm handled the family's finances while I traveled the world seeking God, rather than immerse myself in learning business and mastering the complexities of tax codes.

Capital gains, I now learned, was the amount of appreciation in the value of stock my aunt and uncle had purchased in the 1920s and gifted to me. It had appreciated in value and split many times over the years, and now a huge tax was due. Not being prepared for this, I had not saved any money to pay this tax, and my accountant now claimed I owed the

The Last Leaky Pipe

IRS $60,000 on these gains. As I did not have the money, paying this was out of the question. Soon, I received a threatening letter from the local IRS office in Yreka, telling me to report in three days and "bring all your records and an Extension Request filled out in quadruplicate."

For the next few days I hardly slept, spending every minute filling out pages of complex forms I didn't understand, and calling to the Masters to *Take complete command of this situation!* Feeling more dead than alive, I dropped the four copies of the seventy-five-page forms on the IRS agent's desk three days later, just as the second hand of the clock on his cinder block wall crossed the deadline of noon.

"Where's the check?" he said, looking up at me.

"Check?" I questioned, bewildered.

"Yes, the check. Just because you're submitting a request to extend the filing deadline doesn't mean you don't have to pay the taxes that are due!"

"Oh," I gulped, "I didn't know that."

"Your accountant didn't tell you that? What kind of accountant do you have, anyway? Why, I have a good mind to go down to Dunsmuir, slap a lien on all your houses, and auction them off for twenty-five cents on the dollar," the IRS agent leered at me. When he saw my face turn white and sweat break out on my forehead, he knew he had achieved the desired effect, and then pretended to relent. "Well, I suppose I *could* give you a couple of weeks to come up with the money,"

"Thank you, I would be very grateful for that," I muttered, wondering how I was going to accomplish the miracle of raising that amount of money in so short a time. As I moved toward the door to leave, he shouted after me, "Have a cashier's check for $60,000 on my desk two weeks from today, or else!"

I went home, took a long, hot shower and succumbed to the first night's sleep I had allowed myself in days. When I awoke hours later, I stared at the picture of Saint Germain hanging on the wall.

Saint Germain, I said, addressing him as though he were standing before me, *You got me into this business, and I know you can get me out of it. I know that I went against your guidance with the accountant—I should have hired someone local who would have finished the return on time. I will never go against your guidance again, no matter how embarrassing the consequences—but I don't see what good will come of letting the IRS seize my property. Is that really what you want? I know that everything I have comes from you, so please help me now.*

I let go of all attachment to the outcome of this battle with the IRS, for I knew that Saint Germain had heard me, as he hears and responds in the appropriate manner whenever his name is mentioned, and that all was in his hands. There was no point in repeating the prayer again. If the Masters wanted me to have money I would, if not I wouldn't. It was that simple. I was ready to wash dishes at the Jerry's Diner by the freeway, where many of my friends had once worked, for I didn't regard one type of work as being better than another—all work was God's.

I began to see that this was not so much a battle with the IRS as a challenge to cut through the illusion that this agency, or any external appearance of force, had any power over me other than what I gave it. In the movie of my life, this was one of the scenes in which I had agreed to act, and as the movie's central character, I had the power to determine how the scene would play out. There was no escape, for the only way out was to continue through. There was no turning back. Only by cutting through the illusion that I was fighting an opponent outside myself, accepting the unity of all phenomena—where the IRS and I were both aspects of the same naked, cutting blade of awareness—would I be free of fear and hesitation that anything outside myself could affect me. As I realized that this was one more objective teaching, I meditated on the IRS agent as a manifestation of Saint Germain, and saw that the entire movie was his production—to teach me to go beyond the limits of duality. And I knew that the entire situation would be resolved perfectly—for I had accepted that God alone was the only doer, the only conscious intelligence in my life and universe.

Three days later, while sitting at my desk, there was a knock at the door. It was Bud Wheeler, a local real estate agent, and when I opened the door, he came into my office, his eyes glistening as usual, as though focused on the check he was sure you were going to write him. Barely able to contain his excitement, he spit out, "I've sold your house!"

"What do you mean, you've sold my house? It's not on the market."

"Well, I sold it anyway. I was driving a doctor around town who was looking for a place to build his office, and when he saw the lot in front of your house he said, 'That's the place.'" He threw a sales agreement on my desk and placed a pen beside it, impatient for me to sign. Glancing at the bottom line, I saw the offer: After paying off the loan and Bud's commission, I would have $60,000—the exact amount I needed to pay the IRS!

Shocked at how quickly Saint Germain had answered my call for help, I signed the agreement, though I wished I could have held on to the property, which was adjacent to the Bank of America and would eventually have netted me a fortune. Selling it now, I was just breaking even.

Where can you get a business education like this, and at such a bargain price? I thought, looking at the positive side of the situation. As Bud left the office with the signed contract, I felt grateful that the Master had rescued me from the consequences of disobeying his guidance.

When I placed the cashier's check on the IRS agent's desk, he was so surprised that he shook my hand and patted me on the back. On my way out of his office, I felt his basic goodness for the first time. *So, even this bastard has a human side.* I wondered what events in his life had turned him into such a vicious, petty tyrant.

"Next time, you might want to hire a better accountant!" he said with a parting smile, which made me realize that I had truly cut through to the heart of this situation—that by seeing this agent as my guru, and holding that focus, I had created the ground on which our humanity could be liberated.

As I started driving south, back to Mount Shasta, I felt the presence of Saint Germain and heard him say, *"You have passed the third test, my boy! Congratulations! Now, you may do as you requested, sell your properties and get out of the landlord business. No more fixing leaky faucets!"*

A sigh of relief escaped from me, and I was full of gratitude for the freedom I had just been granted. I now felt compassion for all those people who had been my landlords over the years, regretting my anger toward them for the actions I had not understood, nor could have understood until I had stood in their shoes.

It would take years to sell my properties, real estate agents told me, as the buildings did not have full basements and would not qualify for loans. But thanks again to Saint Germain, within two months they were all sold. Some I sold to the current tenants, taking back notes that would help finance my sparse existence for years to come; others I sold to local speculators. Translating a Yiddish expression that described the trials I had gone through, my Jewish attorney said, "You fell into an outhouse, but came out smelling like a rose!" He insisted it was luck, but I knew otherwise—luck had nothing to do with it. Without the Masters, I could have achieved nothing.

Apprentice to the Masters

I could not have learned these lessons meditating in a cave, but only in the struggle of daily life Pearl called *objective teaching*. There is a time to meditate in a cave, but the path to mastery of the world is only achieved in the world, where the actions of others constantly confront you with the aspects of yourself which you have not yet seen or fully resolved. Only by facing these issues does one truly transform oneself and become a Master. One needs to learn not only to transcend, but to transform the Earth plane. So much of modern spirituality leads to "spiritual bypassing," where those who have not yet found the solid ground of basic sanity and compassion for others try to avoid their unfinished emotional lessons by escaping to a more etheric plane, or by embracing organized spiritual dogma.[52]

This path requires one to be a warrior,[53] not to conquer others, but to subdue one's own delusions. Whether a landlord or tenant, boss or employee, husband or wife, parent or child, the enemy is always ignorance—with victory going to the one who wields the *sword of discriminating intelligence* to cut through the illusory nature of existence and embrace the basic goodness of the heart—which is the lesson at the core of life.

---

52 For more on "spiritual bypassing," including the origin of the term, see: John Welwood, *Toward a Psychology of Awakening* (Shambhala, 2002).
53 Chögyam Trungpa, *Shambhala: The Sacred Path of the Warrior* (Shambhala, 2007).

Chapter 29

Teleported in San Francisco

During those years of apprenticeship with the Masters, I hardly knew where I was going to be sent from one moment to the next. Without warning, I would receive guidance to travel that conflicted with plans I had already made, wreaking havoc with commitments. I lost some friends that way, and after a while, declined all invitations, knowing that I might have to back out later. For a while I made it a practice not to make plans at all—to make my sole commitment to be totally aware in the moment—so as to be available to the Presence and the Masters.

However, once I became more sensitive to the impulse in my heart that I recognized as confirmation from the Presence, I began to again accept invitations. I learned that although breaking a commitment went against my basic nature, it was perfectly acceptable to change appointments and plans, for change was an intrinsic fact of human existence that almost everyone accepted—*impermanence* was something everyone would need to accept sooner or later.

It was during this time of hesitating to make commitments that I received an engraved invitation to my distant cousin's wedding in San Francisco, which I felt I could not refuse. He had the same name as I, and we had traveled together around Europe as teenagers sharing many adventures. He was soft-spoken, generous, and had a compassionate heart, and I wanted to be there for him at this special moment in his life. The service was to be held at a synagogue near Golden Gate Park, with a reception following at the Fairmont Hotel on Nob Hill. In the absence of any direct guidance to the contrary, I risked saying that I would attend, though I dreaded the thought that unexpected guidance might force me to cancel at the last minute. I had missed gatherings with relatives before, due to last minute guidance, and I'm sure they thought of me as undependable, to say the least.

I drove to San Francisco the night before and stayed at his mother's home. Marian, to whom I was related on my mother's side, had always believed in me, even when my own mother had thought I was a failure. She had put me up when I returned from India, sick and needing a place to stay, and I felt a loyalty to her. As an only child, raised by a single mother, I had never experienced family, except through Marian including me in hers. Through her maternal generosity, I had come to understand what family meant. Now Marian was buzzing with joy over the marriage of her eldest son to a beautiful Jewish girl of whom she was fond, and who she knew would make her son a skillful and loving wife.

In the morning, I put on the navy suit with silver pinstripes, silk tie, and unworn, handmade Italian shoes my mother had bought for me years before. Peter went to the synagogue in a separate car and I drove Marian, accepting the responsibility of being her escort. When I couldn't find a parking place, I dropped her off at the synagogue and agreed to rejoin her after I parked. She would wait for me in the front row reserved for family.

Circling the block a couple of times, I finally found an empty parking place and rushed back toward the synagogue. But halfway back, I began to feel an agitation in my heart and a churning in my gut—the feeling that I was going the wrong way. *How could I be going the wrong way, when I know I'm going to the wedding?*

Once before, when Marian had invited me to San Francisco for a Thanksgiving dinner that included not only family but friends to whom she wanted to introduce me, at a fork in the road I had been guided to turn east, which took me on a mission across the country to New York. When I had phoned her from Winnemucca, Nevada, to tell her I wasn't coming, I had felt the disdain in her voice. Now my mind raced, and I thought, *not again—she'll never forgive me. I can't miss the wedding. I'm her escort, and she's sitting in the front row, waiting for me!*

I stopped to double check my guidance. Standing in the middle of the sidewalk, I stilled my mind by focusing on my breath. In that stillness, I felt a pull in the opposite direction. When I tried to go against that pull, I broke out in a sweat and felt nauseous—as though something dire would happen if I disobeyed. Yet, I forced myself to continue. *I have to at least return the car keys to Marian and tell her where I've parked, or she'll be stranded.*

When I entered the synagogue, I saw the bride, radiantly beautiful in her magnificent gown, standing arm in arm with her father, waiting only for my return to walk up the aisle. Trembling with embarrassment, I walked up to her father and placed the keys in his hand. He responded with an annoyed look that said, *Don't you see, we're waiting for you to begin? This is my daughter's wedding, don't mess it up!*

"Give these to Marian," I said, unable to think of anything else. "Tell her something has come up. I think I forgot to lock the car and I'm going back to check. Go ahead without me, because I may be late."

"Late? We're starting now!"

"Go ahead—I'll see you at the reception," I said, quickly turning and walking out before the startled father could respond, or Marian could signal me from the front row to join her.

Cool air caressed my face as I reached the street, and I knew, inexplicably, that I had done the right thing, *but for what purpose? Maybe I really did leave the car unlocked, or in a no parking zone? I would feel humiliated if the car she had entrusted to my care were towed away.* Returning to the car, I found it locked, waiting securely in a valid parking place. *Maybe I can run back to the synagogue and still make it in time to witness the marriage?* Yet, I stood frozen on the sidewalk, people walking past oblivious of my plight. *Where should I go?* I wanted to ask someone, but there was no one to ask, only my own God Presence. I tried to calm myself and turned my attention inward.

Beloved I AM Presence, come forth! Thy will, not my will, be done. I AM going where I AM meant to go, doing what I AM meant to do.

Then I called to the Master,

Saint Germain, please help me. Take command here and guide me where you want me to go.

Walking down the sidewalk, I continued to say to myself,

I AM going where I am meant to go and doing what I AM meant to do. I AM the presence of Saint Germain in action.

Coming again to the corner where I would turn left to go to the wedding, I stopped. *Should I go back?* An uneasy apprehension gripped my stomach. I could see everyone sitting in the synagogue, wondering where I was. Marian was probably thinking, *He's done it again, left me in the lurch, embarrassing me in front of everyone.*

I knew I needed to act immediately before I caved in to the ordinary mind's fear and doubt, so I turned and walked down the street away from the synagogue. I felt better, a sign that I was doing the right thing, and picked up my pace—buoyed up by the inner certainty that I was going the right way, though I had no idea where that way would lead or what would be expected of me.

I felt that I was on a mission for some unrevealed purpose, toward an action which only I could carry out. I felt a freedom from human constraint, a euphoria flooding through me as though accelerating into another dimension, where nothing human mattered anymore. A wave of bliss swept over me as it used to when, as a child, I would go into a state of spontaneous, timeless awareness where I would not be conscious of my body for minutes at a time. Something strange was happening, a warm breeze was blowing over me, and I no longer heard tires rolling on pavement, no horns of taxis, no voices calling to friends in the distance, not even the sound of shoes pacing down the sidewalk. The world had disappeared.

Then, in a rush, everything came back. A horn honked, and I found myself on a corner facing a crosswalk, but not the corner where I had been. I didn't know where I was—the scene was completely unfamiliar. I stood there, disoriented, looking into the faces of the crowd on the opposite corner. Then I saw a familiar face, someone I'd met in Pearl's living room months before: Joseph, a former hippie, now a doctor, who had maintained his interest in spiritual things and been attracted to Mount Shasta by the legends of the Masters.

"Peter, thank God!" he shouted, rushing across the street to greet me. "I can't believe it's you! I was just praying to Saint Germain for help," his words cascaded breathlessly. "My wife just left me. I was going back to my apartment to kill myself. But Saint Germain heard my prayer and sent you. Please, come with me," he begged, tears in his eyes.

"Of course," I said, realizing now why I had been pulled to leave the wedding without explanation, "But where are we?"

I scanned the surrounding buildings and street signs, looking for a familiar landmark, for I was no longer where I had been a moment before. Everything was different. During the moment of timelessness I had shifted in space and now was in a different location.

"Well, we're about eight blocks from my apartment," Joseph said, oblivious that Saint Germain had lifted me from the sidewalk near the synagogue and set me down on a street corner a ten-minute walk from where I had been. All Joseph knew was that he had called to Saint Germain for help, and a moment later I had been standing in front of him. As we walked, I listened to Joseph's tale of his wife's departure, still trying to get over the shock of my sudden shift through space, yet filled with gratitude to Saint Germain for using me for this mission. *Surely it's more important to save a life than to attend a wedding, regardless of my family's opinion?*

At his apartment, Joseph made some green tea and poured us each a cup. He talked of his confusion since his wife's departure. The only solution to his pain, he felt, was to end his life. Since I had felt the same loss with Elizabeth, I was better able to understand his feelings, help him overcome his own sorrow, and discover the love within—of which his wife had been but a reflection. As I guided him inward in meditation to feel that love, as Pearl had done for me, he began to relax and surrender to the love of that Inner Presence.

As my words led him inward, Joseph became calmer and stopped thinking about the sad movie in which he had cast himself as the victim. I taught him *Vipassana* to still his mind through observing the rise and fall of the breath, which would help him observe his feelings from outside his ordinary mind, where they would then dissolve into emptiness. I asked him to phone me if he got stuck or needed to talk.

Before I left, I called on Saint Germain to blaze the Violet Flame up, in, around, and through Joseph to dissolve his sorrow, and felt the immediate response as that all-consuming energy poured through us, filling the room with the light of living grace. I was grateful that, despite my remorse over leaving the wedding, I had obeyed my feelings and saved this friend's life—even though it probably took the family many years to forgive me. The path of Mastery is not to ask why, but to follow the inner guidance impeccably.

Chapter 30

Million Dollar Affirmation

Freed from the burden of being a landlord, I began to look for other ways to support myself. I had a meager income from the promissory notes I had taken back from my property sales and was able to survive only because a friend who was a doctor rented me a dilapidated room upstairs in the Victorian house he had remodeled as an office. The rent was low, as the place was so run-down he knew he couldn't rent it to anyone else. I no longer adhered to the belief acquired in India that spirituality depended on the renunciation of material things. I saw that it was the *attachment* one needed to renounce, not the things themselves, and I began to think how I could increase my income.

Over the years I had begun to notice that business cycles corresponded with certain planetary phenomena, and that by calculating these cycles I could predict the fluctuations of the stock market with a fair degree of accuracy. I sharpened my predictive ability in hopes of being able to somehow parlay this knowledge into a positive cash flow.[54]

Sitting in my dimly lit room, I thought, *If only I had an investor with sufficient capital, I could use the leverage of options and futures contracts to make a vast fortune.*

Having previously learned not to misuse my ability to manifest, I now wondered, *Are the Masters testing me again to see if I will misuse my magnetic ability to create, or are they finally providing me with a way to achieve material abundance, so I can be of greater service to them?* After praying and

---

54 See: Lt. Commander (ret.) David Williams, *Financial Astrology* (American Federation of Astrologers, 1984). This engineer for the power company, Consolidated Edison Co. in New York, noticed the correlation of power blackouts with planetary phenomena, then expanded his studies to agricultural and business cycles, and eventually to using planetary aspects to predict turns in the stock market. See also: Richard Tarnas, *Cosmos and Psyche: Intimations of a New World View* (Plume, 2007), for an understanding of how events and relationships have their correspondence in planetary transits in the evolution of the Western psyche.

not getting decisive guidance, I went ahead and decreed to magnetize the money, connections, and resources I needed to put my plan into action.

Less than a week later, my decree began to bear fruit. I ran into a wealthy man named Bernie, who was visiting Mount Shasta with his wife, who had come to see Pearl. I had met him briefly several months before and had been somewhat annoyed by his obsessive chatter about money and the acquisition of things. He was a New Yorker, like me, but hadn't been able to leave New York behind when he moved West, despite living in a pastoral orchard in the rolling hills near Ashland, Oregon. With Bernie, everything was money, and how to get more of it—that was his whole world.

Since he'd had his fill of hearing about Pearl and the Ascended Masters from his wife, I began to talk to him of my investigations into cycles and how everything is interdependent, even such seemingly unrelated things as economic cycles and the heavenly bodies. I told him how I had discovered that the fluctuations of the stock market and other commodities could be predicted with the proper understanding of astrology, never suspecting that such esoteric talk would interest him.

"You can do this?" he said, leaning forward, staring me in the eye.

"Yes, I can," I replied. "I did it before, when I published my predictions in a financial newsletter on Wall Street, and I can do it again. It all goes according to a mathematical formula, and while it is only accurate 67% of the time, with good money management, that's all the edge you need."

"Wow, sixty-seven percent is great," he responded, a glint in his eye.

"I didn't think you would be interested in astrology," I said, surprised.

"Look, when it comes to money, I'm interested in anything that works!"

"Well, this works, and in fact, I'm working on a way to boost the accuracy to seventy-five percent."

"Look, I own a seat on the New York Stock Exchange and have a trader working it for me." Then, leaning forward, he said, "How about I give you some money to invest?"

"Well, yes, I could," I said, feeling lightheaded at this proposal that was obviously in response to my decree. It seemed that by invoking the magnetic aspect of awareness, my fortunes were suddenly changing, but was it in accord with the Higher Plan?

"How about we start with something small, say a million dollars, and see how you do. Then we can work up to the big time. I invest money for insurance companies. They're always looking for things to do with all the cash they have. If you are successful at this, there is no limit to the amount of money you can make. You'll become wealthy beyond your wildest dreams!"

"Great!" I said, barely able to contain my enthusiasm, "When do we start?"

"Well, first of all, you will have to move to New York. I'll phone my trader and tell him you're coming. You'll have to work with him on the floor of the Exchange on Wall Street. He'll be your partner. I'll also introduce you to my accountant and tax man. We'll meet with the lawyers and draw up an agreement, then we'll be in business!"

His wife, returning from seeing Pearl, suddenly interrupted us with a knock on the door. "I'm famished," she said.

"Say, let's take you to lunch," Bernie volunteered.

We met with another couple at Bellissimo, a fancy vegetarian restaurant in town, and ordered a delicious meal. But as the meal progressed and Bernie dominated the conversation with money talk, everyone became bored and I began to feel uneasy.

Realizing that I could hardly wait for the meal to end so I could get away from Bernie, I began to dread having him as a partner. *Do I really want to leave the Paradise of Mount Shasta and move to New York City? And what about my work with Pearl?* Although I felt that I had the essence of Pearl's teachings and knew the Masters would be with me wherever I went, the idea of working on the floor of the New York Stock Exchange, where traders shouted orders at each other at the top of their lungs, was something I began to anticipate with dread. I sent out a quick prayer for guidance, then realized that my reaction to Bernie was my guidance.

At the end of the meal, as we were walking to his car, I said, "Bernie, I want to thank you for your generous offer, but I'm not going to be able to take you up on it."

"What?" he said, astounded.

"I'm just not ready to move from Mount Shasta."

"Well," he said, softening, "I can understand that. Money isn't everything, is it?"

I was surprised by his comment, because money had been the subject of his every sentence since we met that morning.

"That's why I left New York and moved to Oregon," he continued. "Clearly, there is something here in Mount Shasta that money can't buy."

Even this ardent materialist sensed the spirit here, perhaps more than I realized. Could it be that he, too, was a student of the Masters, one who had been sent to test me? Regardless, I was relieved that he understood my refusal to go to New York and had let me off the hook so easily, as I felt that I had been close to selling my soul. Nonetheless, I went back to my dimly lit room in anguish over the million dollar offer I had just rejected.

I remembered what Jesus had said, *A wise man sold all he had to obtain the Pearl of Great Price*—the consciousness of the inner Christ which, after great suffering, I had found. There was no way I was going to relinquish this Pearl for all the things of the world. I knew that, no matter what, I would have enough money for whatever the Masters wanted me to do. Though he had seemed in perfect health, a year later Bernie's body was found floating in his swimming pool, apparently due to a brain tumor. With all his money, he had not been able to prolong his life by a single day. *When the time is up, the story is over.*

Not every effort results in tangible results. Even though my book, *"I AM" the Open Door*, contains precise instructions on the use of affirmations to produce change, there are times when the results are not visible. During those times, the needed change is usually an inward shift of awareness. We need to not judge our efforts in terms of what we can manifest on the material plane, for what we consider a failure often leads to an evolutionary advance, while "success" in creating what we want might lead us to a spiritual dead end. When seen from the Ascended Master Octave, the relative value of success and failure is often reversed. Thus, the attachment of the ego to any particular outcome must be surrendered until the dream and the dreamer become one.

In the East the emphasis has been placed for ages on non-attachment, renunciation, and surrender of the ego, in the West on individuation and creative involvement in the world. Both are necessary aspects of Mastery, which must be developed in harmony. Neither one is more real than the other. As Buddha said in the "Heart Sutra," *Form is emptiness; emptiness is form.*

Chapter 31

You Are Ready

I frequently saw Pearl in the mornings, when we would meditate together and tune in to the Masters for guidance. To my surprise, one morning Pearl leaned forward, took my hands in hers, looked me in the eye, and said, "You are ready."

"Ready for what?"

"Ready to teach. What do you think the Masters have been preparing you for? It is time for you to begin teaching this Great Law."

"What?" I asked, shocked. "I don't feel ready."

"You will never feel ready. Even Buddha and Lao Tzu did not want to teach."[55]

I remembered that when I returned from India in 1971, still wearing my flowing white clothes, bead *mala* in my hand, walking down Telegraph Avenue in Berkeley chanting Sanskrit mantras, people would come up to me and beg me to teach them something. But their attention had been embarrassing, for I knew that I had only found the first step, and I had no idea where to go from there. I wanted only to pursue my path in seclusion. And the further I progressed on that path, the more I felt that it had no end, that enlightenment was relative—awareness continually unfolding. Yet many of those returning from India welcomed followers, feeding them on the insipid, non-dualist gruel that answered every question with the same answer, "If you knew who you truly were, you wouldn't see that as a problem." But they never taught the methods that would help find that

---

[55] There is the story about the Buddha that after attaining enlightenment, the awakened one hesitated to teach, as he felt that most people would either not be interested in or not understand what he had to say; however, when the Gods Brahma and Indra begged him to share his wisdom with others, he relented. Also, there is a similar story about Lao Tzu (literally, old master) who was supposedly leaving the area where he had lived in order to go into seclusion in the mountains, but the gatekeeper stopped him and begged him to commit his wisdom to paper, resulting in the *Tao Te Ching*. The famous first line is, "The Tao (way) that can be written is not the true Tao."

Apprentice to the Masters

Self—instead keeping their followers in a state of wishful hoping for that someday-to-be-achieved realization. And many of those teachers became trapped in that narcissistic delusion of their own supposed enlightenment, mesmerizing their followers as well as themselves with their supposedly advanced state of realization—not realizing that self-realization is only the first step, to be followed by the development of skillful means, enabling one to enter into that very *maya* as a Master to help those very others they see as an illusion. Even when one knows "who one is," problems do not magically disappear, but sometimes require wisdom and insight. Certainly the number of supposedly enlightened teachers that have made fools of themselves should be proof of that.

Eventually one gets beyond preoccupation with one's own story, one's own enlightenment, and gets busy helping others to the extent one is able—even if just through prayer or having an open heart. Sai Baba and Ammachi[56] are perfect examples of enlightened beings who are busy employing the skillful means of their realization in service to humanity—not only giving spiritual teachings, but helping individuals with their day-to-day problems, building schools and hospitals, and doing everything within their power to alleviate human suffering.[57]

There are many paths to enlightenment, including the path of no-path, but there are few teachings on what to do after enlightenment—how to harness that universal awareness to become a creative force in the universe—which is the purpose of the I AM Teachings.

Even though the Masters had raised me into a partially Ascended state in the Atomic Accelerator, I had returned to the human self to integrate that higher consciousness with daily awareness—a process that, through daily meditation and self-observation, was still ongoing. I still felt like just

---

56 Ammachi, also known as Mata Amritanandamayi, or simply "Amma" (mother), is known as "the hugging saint" because of the millions of people she has embraced and showered with her unconditional love. See: www.amma.org.

57 The pursuit of enlightenment for oneself is more the focus of Hinayana (lesser vehicle) Buddhism, while seeking enlightenment for the benefit of all beings is the focus of Mahayana (greater vehicle) Buddhism—even though many of the techniques employed are the same. It is the intent to benefit others and the dedication to liberation for all that makes the difference.

an ordinary person with a blank mind, devoid of bliss and illumination. *How can I teach until that process of integration is complete?*

"Do you think that I am a perfected being?" Pearl asked, hearing my thoughts. "Do you think that if the Masters waited for a perfect vehicle they would ever find anyone suitable to give their message? No, you are ready. You know this great Law, and it's time for you to share it with others."

"But I'm a hermit," I protested. "I just want to be alone to meditate, work on myself, and do work for others from the inner planes."

"Don't you think I felt the same way before you flower children began knocking on my door?" came her response. "Don't you think I would like to have some time to myself? I'm up all hours of the night doing inner work, then I begin seeing people at seven in the morning, continuing until eleven at night. Somewhere in there, I cook a couple of meals for my husband, go shopping, do laundry, clean house, and pay the bills. You think Jerry wouldn't like to come home after work, relax, and watch TV, instead of going into the back room and answering the phone for me while I work with people? You think again. I have been teaching all these years, and now I am asking for some help from you."

Realizing how selfish I had been, preoccupied with my own spiritual growth, never dreaming that Pearl might need help, I relented. "Well, okay, but how is that going to happen?"

"Don't you worry about that," Pearl said, "Just leave it to me. You're going to be busy soon—very busy."

Assuming that Pearl would not have asked me to help her without the Masters' direction, and that her request was the equivalent of a Master telling me what to do, I went home to straighten up my place in case someone showed up—which I thought extremely unlikely. Although, when Pearl went to work on something, there was no telling what miracle she might perform.

Sure enough, the next day there was a knock at my door, and when I opened it, there was a group of people standing outside, who wanted to come into my apartment and talk to me.

"Pearl told us to come see you," a girl in an Indian print dress said sweetly.

I led them in, unsure what to do, and then the half dozen people took seats, some in chairs, some on the floor. As they sat there quietly looking at me, as if for a show to begin, I felt like a performer standing before an expectant audience. *What do I do now?* I wondered.

Just make small talk, I heard Saint Germain say, just as he had told me in the airline ticket office in Tel Aviv.

"So, what brings you people to Mount Shasta?" I asked. Going around the circle, they began answering my question one after another. As they spoke, I inwardly invoked the Masters, and soon felt their unmistakable energy descend into the room.

"Do you feel that?" I asked, finally calling attention to the Masters' presence. "If you turn your attention within, to the center of your being, and say silently to yourself, 'I AM the Living Light, I AM the Sun of God,' you will feel the Living Light in your heart begin to intensify, and the more you focus on that light, the brighter it will become."

As they did what I suggested, each of them became aware of that inner flame that was the Source, and the mundane consciousness of the group dissolved into transcendent awareness.

"Now, whatever you say with I AM becomes a seed that will grow in your life. The more you focus your acceptance and attention upon that seed and water it with your attention, the more real it will become." As I spoke, the energy intensified in the room. An hour later they left in silence, without saying a word.

Months later, I heard from a friend who had spoken to one of that group, and he said that person had told him, "I've always been an atheist, but if ever I felt God, it was that day in Peter's living room." And I knew then that Pearl had been right, that I did have something to teach, but I still wondered, *Is this the way to teach it?*

Throughout that summer many more came, wanting to hear about the Masters, feel their energy, and experience the reality of the I AM. And as the Masters poured out their grace, most experienced some form of spiritual opening and awareness of the Higher Self. Not only were they benefiting, but I, too, was so raised by the Masters' energy that by the end of the day I often didn't need to eat—like Pearl, who for the last several years of her life needed no physical nourishment—thriving only on light.

However, my new work had an unimagined effect on my life, for by the end of the summer, some of my friends had become distant. "Since when did *you* become a guru?" one asked. They, too, had spent many hours in Pearl's living room, and they wondered, *Why is Peter special? Why don't people come to see me?* They didn't know that Pearl had set me up, that what I was doing was not for my own gratification, but was a difficult assignment I was trying to carry out at her request.

Nonetheless, I began to feel shut off, that my life was becoming narrower in terms of what I could do. At least Pearl had a husband she could talk to at the end of the day, while I felt alone on my pedestal. I could not go anywhere without people watching me and wondering what I was doing. Even in restaurants, they would look to see what I was eating. Everything I said or did was scrutinized for possible contradictions, as though they were waiting for me to slip up, so they could say, "He's not living up to the teachings."

Although those who came benefited, I found that being known as a spiritual teacher made me feel trapped, like a caged circus animal waiting to be led on stage to perform the act for which it had been trained. People looked at my behavior as if to evaluate my spiritual realization, as if obedience to rules was a sign of evolution. I wanted to be free of their eyes constantly watching, to live in the moment, free of jealousy, judgment, and expectation.

Is this selfish? Am I being rebellious? If the Masters want me to teach, I will continue, but I began to wonder if that was their will or Pearl's. *Is she as infallible as I think?* For the first time, I began to doubt my teacher. Although she offered praise, saying how much I was helping people and relieving her of a portion of her burden, I felt suffocated and I wanted to get out of town, where I could be myself again.

Having learned the importance of trusting that feeling, even though it contradicted my mental framework—in this case what my teacher was telling me to do—one day the desire to escape became so strong that the feeling won out and I canceled all my appointments. I pulled down the window shades, quickly packed a bag, which I threw into the back of my car, and then hit the open road.

As I drove, savoring my freedom, I realized that my time as Pearl's student was drawing to a close. My apprenticeship was ending, and I knew that I needed to trust my own guidance above the directions of anyone else, even if that meant the ultimate test—disobeying my teacher.

I was not to repeat Pearl's work. The Masters had other work for me, about which they had not told Pearl, and I was soon to travel as their agent, not only on inner planes but in the outer world as well.[58]

---

58 On this trip I went to visit my old friend, master astrologer William Lonsdale (now Ellias), who used to live in Mount Shasta. When he

looked at my chart, he said, "With what's happening with your Mercury this summer, there is no way you are going to stay home." I had always avoided Astrology, as many practitioners focused so much on negative, deterministic interpretations, but through William I saw that it could be used to help people understand themselves, put them in touch with their unique gifts, and empower them to act with greater wisdom. One should not avoid Astrology any more than one should ignore the weather report because one might learn of an impending storm. I was later to study Astrology in depth, and I found that with this tool I could help many people.

Part V:

Direct Engagement

CHAPTER 32

Saint Germain on the Battlefield

Jesus said, *"I come not to bring peace, but a sword,"* which is often interpreted to refer to the symbolic sword of truth, but I began to see that this sword can also manifest on the physical plane as confrontation—the struggle through which ignorance is brought to the surface to be consumed. I began to realize, much to my surprise, that although the Masters seek to bring about peace, they do not attempt to establish outer peace at any price—at the expense of truth—and that they often use conflict to bring about that revelation of the truth which leads to greater harmony.

As fallible mortals, conditioned by our upbringing and the distortions of the news media, I saw it was frequently impossible to know the truth behind political turmoil. Nonetheless, we are frequently pushed to take sides, for abstaining from action to preserve the *status quo* does not lead to resolution or freedom from delusion. Situations whose antecedents are unconscious, buried in the obscure karmic dregs of past ages, are resolved only by being brought to the surface through some form of action, where the hidden forces can at least be seen.

I fantasized that all conflicts could be resolved if the parties would sit down together in mediation and invoke the Masters. However, until everyone is enlightened, there would always be different interpretations of what the "guidance" was. The reality was that the Masters could only intercede in human affairs to a certain point, until everyone was able to drop their "view point," their human opinion of right and wrong; so in the outer world push often comes to shove. And the Masters, concerned more with the ultimate awakening of humanity rather than a temporary peace, take sides in those struggles and render assistance on the inner and outer planes to bring about the highest Divine Plan.[59]

---

59 There are references to the intervention of the "Gods" and Masters in human conflict going back in history thousands of years. The *Ramayana* of ancient India tells how the *avatar*, Rama, slew various demonic beings and participated in battle against the army of Ravana. The *Mahabharata* refers to the battle of Kurukshetra, in which the later

Now, I was shocked to find myself placed by Saint Germain on one of those sides. This was a complete turnaround for me, as at one time in my life I had tried to apply the teachings of Jesus literally. When I had tried to prevent a man from taking something of mine and he had struck me in the face, I had stood my ground and *turned the other cheek,* as Jesus taught. Now I found myself holding that sword that Jesus brought in my own hand, the same that was Manjushri's sword of discriminating intelligence and Archangel Michael's Sword of Blue Flame—the same sword which on occasion manifested as confrontation and even war.

Despite my reluctance, I found myself becoming a warrior. I was pushed by Saint Germain, much as Krishna pushed Arjuna in the Vedic classic, the *Bhagavad Gita* (Sanskrit: Song of God) to engage in combat. In that classic of ancient India, Arjuna looks out on the battlefield and sees in the opposing army many of his former friends, teachers, and relatives, and shrinks from the impending conflict. Lord Krishna, the *Avatar* of that age, seeing Arjuna's reluctance to fight, appears beside him in his chariot and informs him of his sacred duty to engage in the conflict—that he, Krishna, Lord of the Universe, knows each soul's karmic lessons, what they need to learn in this lifetime, and has already decided who will live or die. If Arjuna withdraws from the conflict, both sides will remain in ignorance, and their spiritual evolution will cease.

Arjuna was told to act, but without attachment—to carry out his duty, knowing that it was God, the I AM, that was the doer, not the human self. Not acting from human desire was the key—the path to liberation, for when acting out of emotion, a karmic residue is created, like the mark left when drawing a line in the sand, impelling one into birth after birth to resolve. When an enlightened person acts, there is no attachment; like a finger drawn through water, it leaves no mark—and there is no karma, only freedom.

---

divine incarnation, Krishna, participated as Arjuna's charioteer. Alice Bailey is reported to have said that the Master Djwhal Khul informed her that the Masters had supported the Allies in the Second World War. My mention here of the Masters' defense of Israel is not meant to endorse all of Israel's actions; however, that country was formed under international law by the United Nations, and its existence is part of the Masters' plan. Of course, the same light of God exists in the heart of all people of every nation, regardless of the perfidy of their governments.

The Ascended Masters, like Lord Krishna, did not abstain from activity in the world, nor did they avoid confronting violence—for they were not concerned with abstract spirituality divorced from life, but were guiding humanity on the path of self-knowledge, which could only be attained through direct engagement and involvement in the world of strife.

I began to have inner experiences with Saint Germain, who, like Krishna guiding Arjuna, directed me into political and military confrontations as his emissary. These were not situations where I had an emotional attachment based on a predetermined view of right or wrong, but where I suddenly found myself an actor in a movie, guided by a director whose prompting I could only feel within. I found myself guided to act contrary to the "politically correct" opinion of those who were apparently well informed—who thought they knew the correct outcome for every world situation. I thought many times of how Pearl often repeated the words of Godfre Ray King, "Never underestimate the arrogance and ignorance of the human intellect."

My first conscious action in a global confrontation took place when Israel was attacked simultaneously by both Syria and Egypt on Yom Kippur and was struggling for survival. One night, while my body was asleep, I suddenly found myself in a more subtle body, wearing an Israeli military uniform. I was commanding a tank battalion and had been given orders to advance and engage the enemy under cover of night. But as we advanced, I began to have a sinking feeling that we were driving into a trap, and I recognized that feeling as a warning coming from the Higher Self. Despite the darkness, I noticed a ridge of sand dunes on our right that blended in with the rest of the barren landscape.

What lies beyond those dunes? I wondered.

I gave the command to halt the advance, and our tank stopped. I threw open the hatch, and the wind blew sand in my face. Spitting out the grime, I held the night vision binoculars to my eyes, but could see nothing. This ridge looked like all the others. I sent out a mental SOS to the Master Saint Germain. My orders were to advance toward the enemy's capital, but my inner senses were drawing me toward that ridge. As I was contemplating what to do, a jeep pulled up beside my tank and a high-ranking officer addressed me.

"What's the problem, soldier?" he asked, in a voice that commanded instant respect.

"Sir!" I exclaimed, snapping my hand to my forehead in a salute. "I think there may be enemy tanks over that ridge."

While I explained my caution about being outflanked, I realized I didn't know this officer. Although he seemed familiar, I couldn't quite place him. The ribbons on his chest gleamed iridescently in the dark and his uniform was immaculate, as though he had just left the parade ground—not like someone who had just driven twenty miles through the blowing sands of a war zone. *What is he doing out here in an unarmored vehicle?*

"You're in command; follow your hunch," he said, and before I could ask his name and under whose command he served, his tires spun up a plume of sand, and he drove off into the night.

Follow my hunch? What kind of an order is that? I made a mental note to ask Central Command when I returned, if I returned.

My hesitation was now gone, however, and I gave the order to turn right. Mounting the ridge, I looked through my binoculars again. Just as I anticipated, dozens of enemy tanks were grouped on the plain below, waiting to close in on our flank once we passed below them. To avoid being detected, they had pulled far back into the desert, so far that we were out of the range of their guns. In addition, I realized that they had advanced so far into Israel they were no longer under the protective umbrella of Egyptian missiles. Knowing that our newly-designed cannon could reach them, I gave the command to target and fire. The sky lit up like giant flashbulbs going off, deafening explosions puncturing the stillness. Within a short time, most of the enemy tanks were decimated, the remainder in retreat, with only little damage to us. Thanks to that mysterious officer, who had appeared out of nowhere, like Arjuna in his chariot, I had been able to save our unit and defend the Israelis against those who were trying to drive them into the sea.

After our victory and the war was over, I found myself sitting in a café in Malta, overlooking the Mediterranean. The blueness of the water beneath the bright sun dazzled my senses, imbuing me with energy and gratitude—I was still alive!

Sipping a glass of sparkling mineral water with a twist of lemon, I read in the newspaper about the signing of a peace accord. As we had destroyed most of the enemy tanks and air force, I knew that our victory would bring a cessation of warfare in the area for years to come. Then I recalled that I'd never heard back from Central Command about the officer who had appeared that night in the desert and told me to follow my hunch. I couldn't get the thought of him out of my mind, but after repeated inquiries, I had been told to drop my investigation. My answer to his identity was to come more directly.

While continuing to read, I felt an electrifying current pass through my body, one strangely familiar. Looking up, the officer I had just been thinking about was standing before me, the same iridescent ribbons decorating his chest. I rose immediately and saluted. He returned my salute, then broke into a smile and offered me his hand. As I looked into his violet eyes, I realized that it was none other than my beloved Master, Saint Germain. Despite his appearance as a high-ranking Israeli officer, his cheerfulness put me at ease.

"Congratulations on your victory, my boy," he said, affectionately. "I put you in command because I knew I could count on you to obey your Higher Self. Your intuition and leadership helped bring victory, and the negotiations now being concluded will bring relative peace to this long-troubled area for years to come."

He smiled, his penetrating eyes looking into mine, seeming to enjoy my surprise at the military uniforms we were both wearing. I was not used to associating the military with anything spiritual, let alone with an Ascended Master. Then he bowed with the elegance for which he was famous in the courts of Europe a century before—and dissolved before my eyes into empty space.

Chapter 33

One with God Is a Majority

"I'm only one person, what can I possibly do to benefit the world?" many people used to ask Pearl.

She would smile, point to her heart, and say, "One with God is a majority! God knows all things and can do all things, and when you are in touch with your God Source, you are in touch with that Almighty Power. There is nothing that Presence cannot accomplish. Try it, and find out for yourself!"

Pearl taught how to invoke that God Power consciously to bring about changes in one's outer self and in the world. Since in our normally deluded state, where we rely on intellect and the limited data of the five senses on which it bases its opinions, we have little understanding of the Masters' Plan for world affairs, she said that the safest course of action was to call for the Masters' intercession without holding any definite view about what form that intercession should take. The only action needed was to call the Masters into action and visualize them above the place or situation where they were required, beaming rays of light down into it—and since our consciousness is one with the Masters, they would empower that visualization by the power of their own attention.

I had the opportunity to apply that suggestion while watching the news on television one evening. Seeing that the hostility between Israel and Egypt was again heating up, rather than sit back and be a passive observer, I invoked the Master Saint Germain to intercede.

Standing in front of the television set, I decreed,

In the name of the Love, Wisdom, and Power that I AM, I call on Saint Germain to take complete command of the situation in the Middle East, right now!

I repeated the invocation three times, and as I spoke, I visualized the luminous presence of Saint Germain above Israel, Lebanon, Syria, Jordan, and Egypt, sending rays of light down into the capitals of these countries. I also visualized great waves of shimmering, violet light radiating out from Israel to all the surrounding countries. Then I let go of this picture in my mind and went to bed.

The next morning I went into town, picked up my mail, and took care of a few other errands. When I returned home, I was hungry and decided to have something to eat. I went into the kitchen to make a sandwich and turned on the radio to hear what was going on in the outer world. To my surprise, I heard the reporter say, "The Prince of Romania has announced today that he is taking complete command of the situation in the Middle East."

I could hardly believe what I had heard. "The Prince of Romania" referred to Count Rakoczy of Romania, a name Saint Germain had used in the 1800s, referring to a *persona* he had created to move among certain circles of the European nobility.

Eager to hear more, I left the radio on for the remainder of my lunch and kept tuning in throughout the day to catch the hourly news broadcasts, but heard no more. That night, when I came home in time for the six o'clock news, I was excited to hear more about the Prince of Romania and his intercession in the Middle East, but his name was never mentioned again.

Did the commentator actually speak the words, "Prince of Romania," or had Saint Germain spoken the words directly to my mind, creating the illusion that they had come from the radio? Either way, he showed me that he had responded to my request, and I felt that he wanted me to pay closer attention to events in the world—and do inner work to invoke the intercession of the Masters wherever my attention was drawn.

Chapter 34

Saint Germain in Madrid

Soon I was to serve the Masters again, not on the inner planes this time, but in my physical form in the sphere of international politics. As was usual before I was called on a mission, I had premonitions of my future travel weeks before departure. My thoughts began to turn toward Europe, especially Spain, and as time passed, my desire to go there increased. Then one night I dreamed of a map of Europe. London was highlighted and from it a line was drawn in a triangle connecting Paris, Zurich, and Madrid. I awoke feeling that these were cities I was meant to visit on the upcoming trip. Since I had traveled extensively in Europe in my youth, and no longer felt inclined to be a *bon vivant* traveling the Continent, I was sure that this pull to travel there was guidance. In response to my request for clarification of the Masters' plan, where and why they wanted me to travel, I heard only silence.

If I knew the plan, my mind would begin to question and embellish, so it seemed I would have to rely, as usual, on *what I felt within*. I knew that as I embarked on this adventure the plan would unfold moment by moment, and success would depend on how well I could get personal desires and preconceptions out of the way, tune in to my Higher Self, and execute impeccably its promptings.

Having passed the previous financial tests in real estate, I now had enough money to travel without fear of being stranded in some foreign land, so I purchased a plane ticket. I would fly from San Francisco to London, and then take the Orient Express across the Channel to Paris. I'd last been to Europe in the '60s as an adventure-seeking poet, sleeping under bridges and in artists' lofts. Now I would stay at the Clarendon, one of London's better hotels.

After I landed, took a taxi to the hotel, and checked in, I was excited to go out on the town and visit some of the pubs that had been my old haunts, and to see if any of my old poet or musician friends were still around; but despite my wish, I was unable to leave the hotel. I went down to the lobby and walked as far as the front door, but felt stopped as though by an invisible wall. Returning to my room, I realized that for a *Bodhisattva*, there is no time off. Since that day in Muir Woods when I had been taken

Apprentice to the Masters

out of my body and seen the suffering of humanity—and chosen to return to Earth to work with Saint Germain—my time had no longer been my own. Now I sat down in my room and turned my attention inward. I reminded myself that I was not here on a whim, but on a mission for the Ascended Masters.

Entering the inner stillness, I visualized London and the British Isles enfolded in light. As I did so, a serenity descended and the walls of the room seemed to disappear. I became a crystal, through which a thousand beams of light were flowing out to sentient beings. The light of the I AM Presence was streaming down into the top of my head, descending into my chest and out through my heart like a sun radiating into space. I called for the Masters to amplify that light and to raise the British people into the consciousness, activity, and dominion of the I AM God Presence forever. As my inner sight was opened, I saw the Masters going forth to implement that visualization—projecting myriad rays downward into every person.

After I returned to more normal awareness, I realized that I had been prevented from leaving the hotel to do this very work. Invoking and transmitting that light was the reason I was there, and I was grateful that instead of indulging personal whims and reawakening old desires, I had been obedient to my God Self.

I took a taxi to the train station the next morning and boarded the famous Orient Express—often the setting for novels and films of international intrigue—whose final destination was Istanbul. Although I kept my eye out for the Masters, I didn't see any noteworthy characters on board. However, I sensed their etheric presence, and as the train sped through the countryside, I felt them pouring light through me, using me again like a crystal to focus that energy and transmit blessings to the people and countryside through which we passed.

Late in the afternoon I arrived in Paris and stayed with my cousin, who gave me her attic room for the night to be a solitary retreat. As in London, rather than go out and visit my old haunts in the Latin Quarter, I spent most of the night in meditation—pouring the Violet Consuming Flame out to the city, invoking the Masters to sustain that purifying quality of light and extend unlimited blessings to the people of France. I saw that beyond the shadow of a doubt, *even the prayer of one person, if aligned with the I AM God Presence, can change the course of history.*

The fragrance of freshly baking baguettes of bread mingled with the scent of brewing coffee from the omnipresent cafés was filling the streets with that seductive aroma that could only be Paris. Yet I was no longer so attached to the allure of the five senses, nor even the mental stimulation of *Les Deux Magots*,[60] the café where Camus, Hemingway, Picasso, and other seminal thinkers and artists had converged, and where in my childhood I had seen Jean-Paul Sartre and Simone de Beauvoir conversing over espresso. Now the thought of that café, where such intellectual speculation took place, devoid of the inner stillness where truth could be perceived directly, reminded me of the proverbial blind man looking in a dark room for a black cat which was not there.

Without hesitation, I again boarded the Orient Express for Zurich. Though I had friends there, I stayed at a hotel on the *Bahnhofstrasse* in the heart of the city, to spend another night in meditation. I knew that if I stayed with those friends, they would have thrown a party, which would have prevented the inner work for which the Masters had sent me here. Again, I thought of the motto of the Great White Brotherhood: *To Know, to Dare, to Do, and to Be Silent.*

From Zurich, I flew to Madrid. While in flight, I kept thinking of the Ritz Hotel, one of the grand hotels of Europe, located in the heart of Madrid. The Ritz was one of Ernest Hemingway's haunts, where he had stayed as a war correspondent after the First World War, rubbing shoulders with bullfighters and poets and courting beautiful women. My mother and stepfather had dreamed of staying at the Ritz on their tour of Europe, but they couldn't get a reservation at any price a year in advance. The nobility and political elite of Europe stayed at the Ritz, and the place was perpetually booked.

Arriving at the Madrid airport, I had the almost overwhelming desire to flag down a taxi and say, "Take me to the Ritz," but I didn't want to take a chance on there not being a room—forgetting that the Masters, under whose guidance and protection I was traveling, never left anything to chance—so my doubt led to the hotel booking counter instead. Even

---

60 *Magots* does not refer to the English word "maggots," as I had thought as a child, but to the two porcelain statues of Chinese traders mounted inside, rumor has it, or possibly to Confucian wise men. Like many of the intellectual conversations which occurred in this *café aux intellectuels* (as it prided itself on being called), definitions of words are the subject of many idle hours of dispute and the basis of most Western philosophy.

if I were able to get a room at the Ritz, I reasoned that it would probably be too expensive. So, I played it safe and booked a room at a cheap hotel.

As I arrived at the hotel, something felt wrong, and I began to doubt the wisdom of my actions. The room was noisy, and when I asked to change it I was shown to a dark, dingy room facing a back alley lined with garbage cans. Again, I felt that I did not belong here, that it was not where the Masters wanted me to stay, and that I had allowed my mind to interfere with guidance. Sitting on the bed and trying to still my mind, which was whirling in a chaos of conflicting thoughts and feelings, I kept hearing, "The Ritz, the Ritz, go to the Ritz Hotel."

Suffocating in this room, where I couldn't open a window without smelling garbage, I called on Saint Germain. I was so conflicted that I doubted the source of the words he was shouting in my head. *How humiliating to go to the front desk again, after putting them to the trouble of changing my room, and telling them I didn't want to stay here after all.* I broke into a sweat at the thought. Yet, that was exactly what I had to do. *Why didn't I follow my guidance in the first place? If I had, I would be spared this humiliation.* I sat on the edge of the bed and by observing my breath was finally able to slow down my whirling mind. Then I affirmed,

I AM the presence of Saint Germain.

Suddenly, I felt pulled to go out of the room and into the hall. Grabbing my still-unpacked suitcase, I descended to the lobby, approached the desk, and overcoming my embarrassment, told the clerk I had to leave. His face florid with contempt, he said a refund was out of the question. I shrugged, accepting the loss as the consequence of my disobedience, pushed open the door, and walked out into the street, where immediately I felt better. I knew where I had to go.

The fresh air filled my lungs as I walked downhill to the plaza, calling constantly to the Master, affirming,

I AM the commanding, governing presence of the Ascended Master Saint Germain, going before me to the Ritz and bringing about the perfect Divine Plan there.

My human mind could not conceive how they could have a vacancy, or how I would be able to afford a room if they did, but I knew that I was being pulled there by an inner force beyond reason. I crossed the Paseo del Prado, passed through a small, green park, and there before me stood the Hotel Ritz in its impressive splendor. I walked up the white steps and was greeted with a salute by the doorman, who opened the portal into the spacious lobby. It felt good inside. A string quartet was playing Mozart's *Eine Kleine Nachtmusic,* the music which reminded me of a past age where in beautiful chateaux I had danced the *quadrille* with noble ladies, even then working as an emissary of Saint Germain.

Gliding across the thick, red carpet as if in a dream, I arrived at the reception desk. The phone rang and the clerk answered. When he hung up he gave me his full attention, and asked how he could be of service. I mustered some courage and asked for a room.

"That phone call was a cancellation. We have just this one room, and since you are here now, you can have it for twenty-five dollars."

Shocked not only that a room had just become available, but also at the price I would have paid for the cheapest motel room at home, I could only nod in acceptance. After registering, I was escorted upstairs to a room suited for royalty. The doorknobs were gold-plated and a crystal chandelier hung over the bed. The bathroom was white marble, containing a huge claw-foot bathtub with gilded faucets.

After settling in to my regal quarters, I went down to the lobby, where a doorman opened the doors into a living room lavishly appointed with artistically-covered sofas and overstuffed chairs. Another doorman opened a door into the dining room, where a violinist moved among the tables serenading the guests. The *maitre d'* showed me to a table, pulled out a chair, and pushed it in as I sat down. I was immediately surrounded by waiters. One brought a crystal goblet of water, another placed a linen napkin on my lap, another offered a silver tray of bread accompanied by a dish of iced butter balls before me and handed me a menu. I felt welcomed by the Masters. They seemed to have forgiven my disobedience in going to the previous hotel, and I felt their personal greeting.

When my waiter came I felt embarrassed, after perusing all the elegant entrees, to ask for only soup and salad, but the waiter bowed and said, "Of course, sir, I will bring the *Chef du soupe* and the *Chef du salade.* One after the other, the two chefs arrived at my table, bowed, and inquired as to my pleasure, promising to bring whatever was in their power to produce.

As I buttered a warm, freshly-baked roll, I watched the violinist serenade a beautiful woman at a nearby table. She was exquisitely attired in a red, *décolleté* dress reminiscent of a previous, more elegant age. I smiled at her, and when she returned my attention, I thought of requesting the waiter to deliver a note, asking her to join me for dinner.

But suddenly the thought vanished like a bubble pricked by a pin. *Romance is not why I am here.* Even though I was free of the observant eyes of the people where I lived and with whom I walked the same path, I was not free of the all-seeing eyes of the Masters and my commitment to celibacy. I knew I could not serve two masters at the same time, one raising my energy into the expanded consciousness of higher planes, the other pulling it down into the domain of the five senses. At this point in my evolution I needed to be one-pointed in focus. Even though there is only one Divine Energy that circulates through all the centers of the body—whether used for procreation or for conscious self-awareness—I knew that to achieve mastery I needed to keep my attention focused on the higher centers at this time.

Realizing this was another test—one that had come when least expected—I dissolved the fantasy of a liaison with this mysterious woman and returned my attention to my own center. Here, within my own mind and body, was where the male and female polarities needed to be united in what was known alchemically as the *Marriage Made in Heaven,* an inner union manifesting a bliss beyond anything attainable on the physical plane.

I used the Violet Consuming Flame to dissolve and consume all random thoughts, anything less than the purity of intent I felt the Masters required of me for this mission. Then I returned to my room and entered deep meditation. That night I dreamed of the Master Saint Germain, but on awakening the next morning I could not remember what he had said—although I had a premonition that today was going to be an unusual day in which I would carry out an important work for the Masters. Having no idea what I was supposed to do, I dressed and went down to the hotel dining room for breakfast. I was hungry after the incessant travels of the past few days, and the chef, as if anticipating my appetite, prepared a superb omelet.

Leaving the dining room after this late breakfast, I entered into the salon, where I noticed a quiet intensity permeating the hotel—a sense of expectancy in the air like electricity before a storm. The sofas were being moved to the back of the room, leaving only a single Victorian wingback chair in the center of the room on which, like a throne, I planted myself to watch what was going on. Though wide awake, I began to feel a certain surrealism to the scene I saw unfolding.

A wave of men in dark suits, wearing sunglasses and microphones in their ears, swept into the room, obviously agents of some sort of Secret Service. They scanned all the furniture with electronic probes, except the chair in which I was sitting in the middle of the room. I stayed seated, fascinated at this scene arising like an apparition before me and in which I was becoming an actor. Soon the double doors from the lobby on my right flew open, and a crew of uniformed men began unrolling a red carpet. They rolled it past my feet to the magnificent double doors on my left, which was the entrance to the grand salon.

Since the hotel had been emptied by the security force, I sat there alone in the stillness. Then I felt a reassuring radiation that I knew could only come from the Ascended Masters. Subtle at first, it increased in intensity. Feeling my consciousness merge into this expanded field of awareness, I felt the flame in the center of my being grow strong, and I visualized this light going forth through the city, the country, and all of Europe, raising everyone into the conscious awareness of their Source.

As my inner sight opened from this increased radiation, I saw that a meeting was being hosted on the inner planes by the Great Brotherhood of Masters, attended by the leaders of Europe and their representatives. This convocation was important for the peace and economic well-being of Europe, and focused on fostering the plan for the European Union. It was being held at a crucial time for Spain, shortly before the death of the right-wing dictator, Generalissimo Franco, after which the crown prince, Juan Carlos, would restore a parliamentary democracy.

The leader of this inner plane meeting was none other than the Master Saint Germain, a figure elegantly attired in the indigo cape he had so often worn in the courts of Europe two centuries before. His gold, jewel-encrusted, Maltese cross sparkled on his chest, and at his side hung a magnificent, diamond-studded, ceremonial sword. Many other Masters were there, and I was surprised to see that a number of well-known world leaders were also present in their higher bodies, secret members of the association of light known in the outer world as the Great White Brotherhood.[61] Many

---

61 "Great White Brotherhood" is a misnomer, as its members are female as well as male, and of many different races, white pertaining only to the color of their robes and the light they emanate. "Order of Light" might be a more appropriate term.

were members, unknown even to themselves, knowledge of which was not necessary for their daily work. Although I recognized some of the leaders from newspapers and television, I realized now that many were spiritually advanced far beyond what one could learn about them in the media.

Thunderous applause and cheering, followed by a barrage of flashbulbs that lit up the room, suddenly erupted from the salon to my left, snapping me out of my meditative reverie. The doors suddenly flung open, revealing a room filled with statesmen, business leaders, photographers, and reporters, and I realized that the meeting I had seen in meditation was also taking place on the physical plane in that very room. *But was Saint Germain present here as well?*

From the throng emerged two men in military uniforms, heading toward me down the red carpet. I immediately recognized the cavalier Prince Juan Carlos, who was to be the next King of Spain, a sash of ribbons and medals hanging from shoulder to hip and a broad smile on his face. With his dark eyes gleaming, the other military figure was even more striking. I had not yet identified him, but both were headed toward my chair.

I wondered again, *Am I invisible? How can I be in the center of a world political event without anyone seeing me?* I felt a moment of panic as these two eminent statesmen advanced. *Should I leave?* But a force held me in my chair. I reflected that it would be more awkward to rise and leave as they approached than to simply remain seated and act as though I belonged right where I was. So I continued to sit, assuming that my presence was part of the Plan—and invoking the blessings of the Inner Light on all those who passed before me.

Just as the two military men decked in ribbons were about to pass by, the one walking beside Prince Juan Carlos cast a glance at me and winked. As he walked by, I realized that he was the same officer who had appeared out of nowhere and helped me that night in the desert during the Middle East War, and who I later saw at the café in Malta—my beloved friend and mentor, the Ascended Master Saint Germain.

If I had not been riveted to my seat by the spiritual energy, I would have gone up to him. Instead, I remained speechless as the two men walked past me arm in arm, as was the custom in Europe, through the doors to the hotel lobby.

Behind them came a procession of diplomats, some of whom I had just seen while in meditation and others whose faces I recognized from the newspaper as the leaders of the emerging European Union, all of them proceeding past me down the red carpet. As they walked close by, apparently oblivious to my presence, I visualized light going from my heart to theirs, and the great Masters of Wisdom above them guiding and directing them in their work for humanity.

After the last one passed and the room was empty, the spiritual radiation dissipated and I felt released from my chair. I got up and walked into the lobby. The doors of the hotel were open, so I walked out onto the front steps. On either side were dozens of military police standing at attention, rifles in hand, and at the bottom of the steps was a black limousine with a Spanish flag on its hood, surrounded by the dark-suited Secret Service Agents to whom I must have been invisible. Saint Germain and the Prince were ushered into the limousine, and as the phalanx of soldiers parted, an escort of motorcycle police led the limousine away from the hotel.

As the hotel guests were allowed to return, I, too, went back inside, and the hotel began to return to normal. Once inside, I heard Saint Germain say inwardly, *Your work here is finished. Now leave.*

I went to the concierge to ask him to book a flight, but he said with finality, "All flights out of Madrid are booked."

Following my inner guidance and disregarding what the concierge said, I went back to my room and packed my few things. Then I returned to the lobby, checked out, and asked the doorman to get me a taxi to the airport.

At the ticket counter, I asked for a flight to London, where I would meet my connecting flight back to the States, but the clerk said, as predicted by the concierge, "All flights are booked. There are no openings for two weeks."

Knowing that Saint Germain would not have told me to leave if it were not possible to do so, and remembering my recent experience of getting an unexpected room at the Ritz at the last minute, I told the clerk confidently, "I am sure there will be a seat on the next flight. I am going to sit right in that chair over there, so you know where to find me."

She looked at me skeptically and shrugged, "You're wasting your time, but you can wait if you want."

Ten minutes later, she ran up to me, waving her arms. "Sir, sir, there's been a cancellation. Quick, you've got to run," she shouted breathlessly, grabbing my ticket and thrusting the boarding pass into my hand. "It's a miracle. I don't know how you got a seat!"

By the time I reached the plane, all the other passengers had boarded, and I was greeted by a smiling pilot and stewardess who secured the cabin door behind me. Another stewardess approached with a smile and escorted me to my seat, "I hope you don't mind, sir, your seat is in first class. If there's anything I can do to make your flight more enjoyable, please let me know."

Three days later, I was back in Mount Shasta. Even though my visits with Pearl had become infrequent at this point, I occasionally sought her out and shared my adventures with her. Now, I told her about my trip to Europe.

"Was there a man in a military uniform who smiled at you?" she asked, giving me that penetrating look that let me know that she knew more than she was revealing.

"Yes, there was," I said, describing the procession I had witnessed in the Ritz Hotel.

"And who do you suppose that man was?"

"I know, Saint Germain."

"Three days, ago," she continued, "I had a vision where I saw the two of us attending a meeting of world leaders with the Master Saint Germain presiding. This was an important meeting for the future of Europe, and I can tell you that the Master is very pleased with you. Now your real work is beginning."

Then she smiled mischievously. "I have also been shown that you saw the Master twice during your stay."

"Twice?"

"Yes, haven't you guessed?"

"No, I only saw him once, with Prince Juan Carlos."

"He appeared to you before that, as one of your tests, perhaps one of your more challenging ones."

"Really?" I said, still mystified.

"Do you think Saint Germain can only appear as a man? He can appear in any form he desires, even as a woman—and a beautiful one at that."

Then I realized, "Why, he was the woman in the dining room in the red dress!"

Chapter 35

Mission in Grand Central Station

On trips to the East Coast I stayed with my mother and stepfather at their home in the suburbs of New York City. Family visits were often trying, as I always felt my mother's frustration that I had "done nothing" with my life—not achieved the same social and financial status of my peers—and she blamed herself for not having been more demanding of me as a child. She thought my spiritual pursuits were a waste of time and that they kept me from getting ahead in the world, unlike my high school friends who had become doctors, lawyers, and even an astronaut, and she frequently wondered where she had gone wrong in raising me. It took me many years to realize that she had been trying to live her life through me, resentful that I was not doing the things her parents had prevented her from doing, as they were not occupations suitable for "ladies" in those days.

Growing up with the feeling that I was never good enough, I felt a lot of anger—which I repressed, and which later emerged as chronic fatigue syndrome. It was not until mid-life that one day I unexpectedly discovered this anger buried deep within, and it came to the surface in a rush. Although I lived far from her at the time, the anger found vent first toward my mother, then toward the Masters for not having interceded in my life and spared me the suffering. At the moment of epiphany when I saw the pain and understood where it came from, I realized that no one was responsible for that situation other than myself—due to having set up the causes through prior actions in past lives—and instantly most of the fatigue disappeared. I saw that I had chosen this soul to be my mother in this life to learn forgiveness and to mirror traits I needed to dissolve within myself. So much energy had been tied up in repressing that anger, manifesting as depression (which is really self-anger) during much of my life, that when that energy was freed up by taking responsibility for my own life and emotions, I was flooded with boundless energy. But to get to that moment of confronting the *controlling mother within* took a long time.

On one of these trips back East, while eating dinner one evening I felt a sudden, inexplicable urge to take the train into New York City, though

I could think of nothing there I wanted to do on the spur of the moment. By the time dinner was over, the only thought in my mind was to go into the City. Perhaps I was being called to visit Hal Honig, who the previous year had flown out to Mount Shasta to meet Pearl, and to whom I had introduced Sai Baba. He lived on Central Park South, walking distance from Grand Central Station, but I was hesitant to drop in on him without calling ahead, as friends did in Mount Shasta. I decided that since I didn't know if this was really the plan, I'd just get on the train and call him from Grand Central Station once I was in the City, if that still felt right.

When I told my mother what I was doing, she exclaimed, "You're out of your mind to go into the City at this hour without any plans! Why don't you go some other time, when you know what you want to do and you can plan ahead? Do you even know if Hal is home? Why don't you call and make arrangements to meet later in the week?" Her advice was reasonable, but my inexplicable pull to leave was immediate, and I knew that I needed to just go—so I left with a brusque goodbye and walked the mile to the train depot.

As soon as the train pulled away from the station and I was relaxing in my seat, I felt Divine Energy flooding into me and knew that I was on a mission. There was an activity of the Ascended Masters taking place, and I began to do inner work, calling for the Illumining Revealing Presence to show me what was transpiring and what I needed to do. I sensed danger, and that I needed to be on guard. As the train sped onward toward the City, I affirmed within my heart,

I AM the Presence of God in action here, doing what I AM meant to do, in Perfect, Divine Order.

The closer I approached the City, the more certain I was that there was danger ahead, so I invoked Saint Germain, visualizing him above New York, pouring down rays of light into the City. Then I visualized my own Higher Self in action with him, radiating light, and decreed,

I AM the Presence of God, blazing the Violet Consuming Flame up, in, around, and through New York City, dissolving and consuming anything less than perfection.

I knew that these statements, far from being empty words, were actually Words of Power, calling a new reality into being, by the power of consciousness. Through the interrelatedness of all things, my thought affected all thought. This was not simply the power of positive thinking, but the ancient teachings of the Far East given in a modern form. Instead of visualizing the wrathful beings and enlightened *Bodhisattvas* depicted in Tibetan *thangkas* (Tibetan: tapestries of deities), I was invoking the Masters, with whom I was more familiar.[62]

As the train sped toward Manhattan and its destination, Grand Central Station, and knowing the Violet Flame would dissolve any negative force, I imagined the City enveloped in a huge ball of intense violet light as though inside a sphere of amethyst, and called inwardly to the Master Saint Germain, *Please intensify the Violet Flame throughout New York; keep it fully self-sustained and take complete command of this entire situation.*

In response, the energy that had been pouring through me intensified. As we neared the City my inner sight opened, and I saw in the sky above Grand Central Station the radiant presence of my loyal friend, the Ascended Master Saint Germain, pouring down great rays of violet light from the palm of each hand into the station below—the beams of amethyst light converging on one of the lockers that lined the corridors of the station.

As the train pulled into Grand Central, I again called my Higher Self into action, decreeing,

I AM the Commanding, Governing Presence of God going before me, commanding perfect peace and harmony and the Ascended Masters' Divine Plan in all activity.

I AM the presence of the Ascended Masters and Ascended Master Friends, raised up before me, directing and protecting me at all times, and bringing about the perfect, Divine Plan here.

As I stepped from the train, a policeman appeared at the door and said, "We're closing the station; everyone come with me." He escorted us all to the main doors of the station, ushered us out onto Forty-Second Street, and then placed a barricade across the door so no one could return or enter.

---

62 Most lamas would be the first to admit that which particular deity is invoked is not as important as the intent one keeps in mind, the intent being the operative consciousness and force.

Apprentice to the Masters

Finding refuge in a Horn & Hardardt coffee shop across the street, I continued to decree and visualize the Violet Consuming Flame blazing through Grand Central Station, through Manhattan, and throughout all the other boroughs of New York City.

A half-hour later, I watched through the window as a policeman removed the barricades so people could again enter the station. I left the coffee shop and went outside. The air was thick with the familiar smell of exhaust, roasting bagels, and chestnuts of street vendors. I coughed as I walked to the payphone on the corner, thinking how different this air was from the pure, mountain air to which I was accustomed. I dialed, and Hal answered.

"No, this is not a good time to come over...I have friends here. Anyway, this is New York, not Mount Shasta, and people don't just 'drop by,'" Hal admonished, reminding me of the advice my mother had given. Then I realized that the thought of visiting him earlier in the evening was simply the form the guidance had taken to get me out of the house, on the train, and headed in the right direction. As often happens, the mind had framed the guidance in a context it could recognize and on which it could immediately act. I had known, correctly, that I was to go into the City immediately, to which the mind had tacked on the supposed reason. Only as the journey unfolded had the next part of the guidance emerged—not as a voice, but a feeling.

Now in the City, seeing that my thought to visit one of Pearl's students was incorrect, I thought of going downtown to my old neighborhood in Greenwich Village where I used to read poetry in bars, or visiting Cafe Wha? where as a kid I'd seen Dylan, only a few years older than me, belting out Woody Guthrie songs over the din. But that was like a past life,[63] and it was getting late. I felt that my work for the night was

---

63 The obsession many have with past lives and what important historical personage one was, is one of the greatest traps on the spiritual path. To dwell on those phenomena only boosts the ego's hold over the door to higher consciousness. If you are really supposed to know who you were, it will be revealed inwardly, not by a psychic who gains a livelihood by boosting people's egos; and the purpose will be to teach, not to enhance one's feeling of self-importance. If, in fact, one could see all one's past lives, the experience would be terrifying, as they were not all beneficent; otherwise one would most likely not be here, still struggling with the

done—no point revisiting a place simply for memories. They were not real anyway, at least no more real than I wanted to make them, and I had already crossed the threshold of a new world.

Crossing the wet, black street, which was iridescent from the oil leaks of countless passing cars, I walked over a plume of steam hissing up through a manhole cover—coming from what subterranean fires I knew not—and pushed once more through the revolving doors of Grand Central Terminal, one of the great hubs of the universe. A form loomed out of the darkness, appearing to be a policeman, and he greeted me, twirling his baton.

"What happened?" I asked.

"There was a bomb in one of the lockers, all set to go off, but for some reason it didn't detonate. It's a miracle no one was hurt."

He then stepped back and bowed slightly to let me pass, "It's a miracle," he repeated as I walked by. I had not taken more than two steps into the station when it crossed my mind that he was Saint Germain. I whirled around, but no one was there. Perhaps he had stepped outside? In any case, I knew that Saint Germain had been present that evening in one form or another.

As I rode the train back home, I felt grateful for having been called to be a part of his activity in averting a catastrophe in the City that night. I saw clearly that my calls had been necessary, since the Masters can rarely intervene in humanly-created conditions unless invited. That night I had been sent to make the request that invoked the Masters into action.

When I returned home, not more than three hours since I had left, I was reproached by my mother, "Well, that was a wasted trip! I guess now you'll know better, and phone ahead next time before you decide to visit someone."

I said nothing about my covert role in the night's events, remembering the motto of the Great White Brotherhood: *To Know, to Dare, to Do, and*

---

effects of past karma. I was told by three women, in one year alone, that it had been revealed to them they were Mary Magdalene. Mental wards are filled with men who think they were Jesus or some other famous personage. Ram Dass told me that his brother was in a mental ward, claiming to be Jesus. Ram Dass told him that he should claim to be *a* Christ (as he did), not *the* Christ. The important thing is to embody the Christ consciousness or Mary consciousness now. For practical purposes, the past and future are irrelevant, for enlightenment takes place only in the present.

to Be Silent. Anyway, I knew that my mother would not have understood what I had accomplished, no matter what I told her, so there was no point in arguing and creating bad feelings. Instead, I walked upstairs and went to bed.

The next morning, I rose early and again felt the inexplicable pull into Manhattan. Retracing my steps of the night before, I boarded the train and soon found myself again walking through the terminal which I had just played a key role in protecting, now operating at its normal level of friendly chaos. Pushing my way through the crowds, I took the subway downtown to visit Weiser's Metaphysical Bookshop, one of the largest occult bookstores in the world, where, when I had lived in the City in the '60s, I had found the *Gospel of Sri Ramakrishna,* the classic on *Raja Yoga*[64] by M. that had started me on the spiritual path.

This time the trip was uneventful, though to my surprise, the air was as clear as Mount Shasta's and the sky was a faultless blue. People inhaled deeply, as though breathing for the first time. A man leaned against a building, head tilted skyward, drinking in the sun's rays, a rare scene in a place where everyone was usually in a hurry. For the first time I could remember, New Yorkers seemed relaxed and happy—as though overnight the City had become transformed into Buddha's Pure Land—a Paradise one can inhabit through the purification of thought.[65]

"It's the most beautiful day I can remember," I overheard a man saying. And as I walked along, the sun pouring down, I too felt a fullness in my heart—knowing that in some way I had played a part in the City's transformation.

---

64   *Raja* or "royal" yoga is concerned with the cultivation of higher consciousness, while the purification and discipline of the body taught in *Hatha yoga* is the usual first step.

65   The Pure Land is a blissful Paradise ruled by Amithaba, Buddha of Infinite Light, where beings exist free of all mental defilements and obstacles, and receive spiritual teachings directly from the Buddha. One can attain that consciousness *now* by visualizing that one's present world *already is* the Pure Land: See the earth upon which you walk as made of lapis lazuli, the leaves of the trees as made of rainbow light, the flowers filled with exquisite jewels, and you, yourself, are a manifestation of the Lord of Infinite Light, and everyone you encounter is a fully enlightened Buddha—for what your attention is upon, you become.

Part VI:

Through the Open Door

Chapter 36

Partings

Since the day Saint Germain appeared in Muir Woods and sent me to Mount Shasta to study under Pearl and become his apprentice, I had taken for granted that Pearl would continue to be my teacher. We had worked together for years with love and mutual respect, frequently able to communicate telepathically, and the thought of any rift between us was inconceivable. She was the spiritual mother I had never had, who accepted me as I was, unconcerned with my status in the world.[66]

As the ancient Indian *Vedas* say, no relationship is as close as that between guru and disciple, for the guru is a manifestation of God, an image of one's own Higher Self. *Guru* means one who leads one from darkness to light, and that was the role Pearl had played for me. Between guru and disciple there is the deepest devotion, even beyond that between parent and child, for this commitment is one that transcends lifetimes and ends only with the realization of God. Although Saint Germain was the guru to whom I had become an apprentice, Pearl was the guru to whom he had directed me for training.[67]

Pearl and I both knew we were part of Saint Germain's spiritual family

---

[66] When the Tibetans came to the West they were appalled by the lack of self-worth people felt, no doubt partially due to the lack of nurturing in childhood. That is why the greatest gift one can give another person is simply to see their innate goodness, the God within that they truly are. And the greatest thing one can do for oneself is to feel and dwell on that same basic goodness within, that is one's basic nature, an expression of the I AM THAT I AM.

[67] One's own I AM Presence is the ultimate guru, of whom all other gurus are an externalization. On that ultimate level, the guru and God are one. However, until one is able to contact and receive instructions directly from that Source, other individuals manifesting varying degrees of enlightenment are invaluable guides. A true guru does not desire disciples and will, in fact, either send you away or cause you to become disillusioned with them at the point when you are ready to move on to a greater degree of self-realization.

and that we had been working together in his service for lifetimes. Over the years I had become her assistant and protégé, the one she was training to continue her work, so I little suspected that our bond was about to be shaken, and from a most unexpected source.

It all began when Pearl's friend and self-appointed guardian, an elderly woman by the name of Sunny, found a manuscript while cleaning Pearl's attic. It contained discourses the Masters had given through Pearl and her Twin Ray, Bob, to a small group of I AM students many years earlier, after Godfre Ray King's ascension, but which had never been published. Sunny was, like Pearl, a former student of Godfre Ray King, and later had worked for Mark and Elizabeth Prophet (who started the Summit Lighthouse) and Geraldine Innocenti (who started the Bridge to Freedom)—groups that attempted to carry on the work of the "I AM" Activity. However, she had little skill in getting along with others, and was used to giving orders and having them obeyed—a quality that leads to the downfall of many groups.[68]

"Pearl, you've got to publish these discourses," Sunny ordered one day, in her well-meaning yet militant style. "They need to be out there helping people."

Since Pearl had not received direct guidance about what to do with the manuscript, she complied with Sunny and turned the discourses over to a group of students for editing under Sunny's direction. Sunny's aloofness soon alienated many of them, and she complained bitterly to Pearl about the shortcomings of today's youth.

Frustrated with the impasse, Pearl placed the partially edited manuscript in my lap one morning as I was sitting in her living room and said, "It's yours. I've had enough of this bickering. Do what you want with it. Publish it or burn it. At this point, I don't care. I just don't want to hear another thing about it."

I felt honored to be entrusted with publishing the words of the Masters

---

68 John Welwood, *Toward a Psychology of Awakening*. This is another instance of what John Welwood calls "spiritual bypassing," so prevalent among spiritual seekers. Many ascetics who renounce the world do so as a means of not having to look deeply into their own natures and transmute the unregenerated ignorance still lurking there, perhaps hiding behind an authoritarian role—which will ultimately have to be dealt with later, in this or a future lifetime.

Partings

and gladly accepted the assignment. Christmas was fast approaching, and as I was planning to visit my family in New York, I told Pearl that I was sure I could find a publisher back East. I promised to respect her wishes and not bother her again until the job was done and I placed the finished book in her hands.

Taking the manuscript with me to New York for the holidays, I finished the final edit myself. As no one speaks in complete sentences—the Masters included—editing consisted of deciding how to punctuate sentences that went on for pages, and what words should be capitalized for added emphasis. On my first reading of the books of *The Saint Germain Series*, I had been annoyed by what seemed at the time to be the excessive use of capitals, but now the Masters showed me that the capital letters could act as Cups of Light that transmitted energy, and I prayed to know which letters to emphasize.[69]

I found a publisher auspiciously located over an old amethyst mine. Hal Honig in New York had agreed to pay for the publication, and I cheerfully turned the manuscript over to the publisher and headed back to my parents' home in New York for Christmas. Feeling confident that I had done an excellent job of the entrusted mission, I sent Pearl a copy of the final manuscript and told her that the mission had been accomplished. I told her the name of the publisher and said that soon she would have the first copy in her hands.

My feeling of accomplishment was short-lived, however, when a few days later the publisher phoned with shocking news. He had received a call from Sunny telling him that I was not authorized to publish Pearl's book, that I had "absconded" with the manuscript and altered the text. She was the editor in charge that made all the decisions, she claimed, and if he proceeded with printing, she would sue. He said that under that threat, unless he received written authorization from Pearl, he had no choice but to cease publication.

I was devastated. I had been given a sacred manuscript by my teacher, then accused of its theft. I had spent weeks editing and gone to great

---

69   Nouns and other parts of speech were capitalized in English until about the middle of the eighteenth century, when that practice fell out of fashion (perhaps because of the difficulty in setting type by hand), but nouns are still capitalized in some other languages, notably German.

personal expense traveling to find the right publisher—all for naught. Then I heard from a friend back in Shasta that when Sunny discovered I had the manuscript and was publishing it without her approval, she called me a renegade and spread rumors of my "disobedience."

This will all be cleared up as soon as Pearl tells Sunny the truth, that I was acting at her request, I thought. But that clarification never came. She never told Sunny what she had done, or wrote the publisher to set the record straight. I was left dangling, knowing that my reputation was being trashed, wondering when this confusion would be resolved so that I could return to Mount Shasta, and Pearl and I could resume our spiritual work together. I couldn't believe that this illumined being, who could see and converse with her own I AM Presence and who talked with the Masters daily, still had such a blatant human weakness. I did not realize until many years later that Pearl's actions, which I took as her weakness, may have been at their direction. I came to see that the Masters often use these human situations to bring to the surface unknown weaknesses, so we can see and overcome them. Shakespeare wrote, "by indirections find directions out,"[70] and indeed the Masters use these indirections, that often appear as disasters, to align us with our true direction and higher purpose.

It never occurred to me that Pearl would not notify Sunny that she had asked me to be sole editor, and that she had completely left her out of the communication loop. I have found that despite their much-vaunted spiritual advancement, some of the long-time students of spiritual groups tend to become *prima donnas,* sadly lacking in their ability to work with others. I marveled that a group of friends aligned on the same path could have such a hard time working together. Pearl said that one of Godfre's students had asked Saint Germain the same question: *Why are we having such a hard time agreeing on anything?* The Master's mirthful reply had been, "That, my dear, is why there are so many of you and so few of us (Masters)."

As time elapsed and Pearl failed to confront Sunny or speak up on my behalf, explaining that I had been acting at her request, I began to psychoanalyze what I considered to be Pearl's weaknesses. Dreading Sunny's wrath if she told her she had been replaced as editor, Pearl had

---

70 William Shakespeare, *The Tragedy of Hamlet, Prince of Denmark,* Act 2, Scene 1.

taken the easy way out and sacrificed me instead, since I was not there to defend myself. I found it inconceivable that her actions might have been guidance.

Is Pearl going to sacrifice our relationship because she doesn't have the courage to tell Sunny the truth? Surely, by the time I return home, Pearl will have cleared up this confusion. The book will be in her hands, and I will again be her protégé.[71] But the situation did not improve. In fact, I was told that Pearl was siding with Sunny and echoing her claims about me to the rest of her students. I was devastated. *I have been set up and betrayed by the one to whom I am closest. I am being destroyed by the very one who compelled me to be a teacher.* I decided then and there never to give credence to gossip I heard about others, for there are always many sides to every story, and rued that I was not at home to present my side of the story.[72]

I found some comfort, however, in how similar my situation was to Saint Germain's during his final lifetime as Sir Francis Bacon. He was set up by King James, to whom he gave unswerving service and loyalty, only to be betrayed by him. Later, as an Ascended Master working behind the scenes to avert war and revolution in Europe, Saint Germain was betrayed repeatedly by the king's ministers, who sought to profit from war, as do many military contractors and their minions in government today. They portrayed him as an imposter and charlatan, and the kings he secretly worked for were forced to deny any knowledge of his behind-the-scenes negotiations for peace. Of course, as he was an Ascended Master working in a manifested body, no jail could hold him, and he would simply dematerialize—much to the discredit of the jailer.

I should have been proud that the Masters found me worthy to go through similar trials as Saint Germain's predecessor, Sir Francis Bacon, yet I felt only despair. Unlike Saint Germain, I still had an ego concerned with reputation, and I was in a human body that I was not yet able to

---

71 The book was eventually published as *Step by Step We Climb* (Pearl Publishing of Mount Shasta, revised edition, 1989), the first in a series of three books. The first two are discourses given by the Masters; the last book contains discourses given by Pearl from the raised consciousness of her own Christ Self.

72 It is this very identification with our "story" that keeps us trapped in the cage of ego. Through self-realization, we eventually drop that story and experience the unlimited consciousness of pure being.

Apprentice to the Masters

dematerialize, or I would surely have done so—and rematerialized in the midst of my friends to speak the truth.

I did not share the news of my discredit with my parents. My mother already took a dim view of my life in Mount Shasta and my lack of what she considered a meaningful occupation. Perhaps she was also jealous of Pearl. When she had met her years before, my mother had burst into tears—as did many when they first met Pearl, so charged was her presence with unconditional love. So, I nursed my wounds in silence.

ELIZABETH COMES TO VISIT

It was the week before Christmas, and I sat glumly at my parent's dinner table, keeping the thoughts of the rumors that had been spread about me to myself. When the phone rang, my mother answered—it was Elizabeth, the girl I had been in love with this past year, but had avoided dating out of deference to Pearl and my commitment to the Masters. She was now calling from her parents' home, where she, too, was visiting for Christmas. "Just calling to wish you and your family Merry Christmas," she explained, but before I knew what was happening, my mother, sensing a connection between Elizabeth and me, had reclaimed the phone and invited her to come east to stay with us and celebrate the New Year.

Despite my mother's disapproval of my career choices, I knew she wanted the best for me. With the right woman, she thought, I would be happy and inspired to make more of myself in the world—the conventional misperception that permanent happiness can ever be found in the duality of the world.[73]

---

73 Permanent happiness can never be found in the pursuit of the *Eight Worldly Dharmas,* the desire for pleasure, praise, fame, and gain, while simultaneously trying to avoid pain, blame, disgrace, and loss. We vacillate between these pursuits, identified with our own movies, seeking what makes us feel good while avoiding what makes us feel bad—not realizing that the determining factor is not the circumstances themselves, but all the time within our own minds—how we choose to view ourselves in terms of those circumstances. Some people even go so far as to project their disappointment at things not going their own way, as an external *sinister force,* and do affirmations in a desperate attempt to

Thinking that Elizabeth might be *the one* for me, my mother, like Pearl, was playing an unconscious role in the Masters' plan for my further teaching and testing, and the ongoing purification of the ego.[74] Like the Hindu goddess Kali, who destroys whatever is illusory in the lives of those she loves—that they might attain ultimate happiness—both of these women were instruments of the Masters in my continuing apprenticeship.

Elizabeth arrived the day after Christmas, looking as beautiful as ever, arms full of presents for me and my parents, her dark eyes shining with love. At first everything went well, and I could barely contain my infatuation. We didn't talk about our previous misunderstandings and the wounds they had produced, and before long we began to express the love that was impossible for us not to feel when we were in each other's presence.

It seemed clear: *At last the Masters are joining us together. Would they have allowed her to come here if that were not the plan? But what about my vow of celibacy to the Order of Melchizedek, that I had made sitting in Pearl's garden many years ago? Perhaps we were to have a celibate marriage like Pearl and Jerry, who were brought together to serve humanity, rather than solely for*

---

change the outcome according to their own will, not realizing that they don't always know the best outcome of a situation, and that the source of their pain is within themselves. As Pema Chodron says in *When Things Fall Apart: Heart Advice for Difficult Times* (Shambhala; Boston, 2002), the disappointment and pain generally come from holding too tightly to the illusion of control.

74   Despite frequent reference in spiritual disciplines to the need to "destroy the ego," this is only a manner of speaking that should more accurately be "purify the ego." We accomplish that purification through self-observation, so that it no longer controls us and instead becomes our servant. The ego, rather than being an enemy, then becomes a useful vehicle that we inhabit consciously and that allows us to function in the world—much as our car is our vehicle to get us from point A to point B. Although we are not the car, we nonetheless need to clean and carry out routine maintenance on it so that it serves us well, without any cause for concern. Getting more specific, we could compare the ego to the car's windshield; when it is dirty it can cause all kinds of misperceptions and even an accident, yet when it is clean we don't see it, and we hardly realize it is there. Only when the aggregates of consciousness are dissolved at the time of Ascension (attainment of the *Rainbow Body*), can we truly say the ego dissolves.

human pleasure? But the idea of a celibate relationship quickly faded before the magnetic attraction I felt. Fortunately, I thought, my mother had put her in a room downstairs at the far end of the house, so I was not tempted by her continual proximity.

I didn't tell Elizabeth or my mother about the accusations being made about me. Instead, I pushed all that aside to spend idyllic hours with Elizabeth. Enjoying the Christmas spirit that filled the air, we walked hand in hand through the neighborhood in the fresh snow, admiring the twinkling lights in neighbors' yards and looking into each other's eyes—our hearts open, everything seeming to confirm the rekindling of our relationship.

In stark contrast to the daytime euphoria, however, I had terrible dreams, waking in a sweat. In most of them I was about to be swept away by a massive *tsunami*. I had parked my car on a precipice over the ocean, but could not get the door open, for I realized I had lost my keys. Desperate to escape the tidal wave towering above me, I tried to open the car door, but knew I was about to be swept away.

Perhaps it's only my ego that is going to be destroyed, which happens to some degree in all relationships? But I feared the dream was a warning. Otherwise, why would I feel such terror? What if Elizabeth is one more test? What if the Masters are using her to see if I will choose her or them? But it's Christmas; they wouldn't test me now when my heart is so open, would they? It seems I should be able to have human love as well as serve the Masters.

I felt I was teetering on the edge of a cliff, and I feared that if I were to kiss Elizabeth on the lips I would be swept over the edge. I prayed for clarity and strength to do the right thing. Seeming to be an answer to that prayer, I read that night in *The "I AM" Discourses* a passage that said essentially, *If you have doubts that someone might not belong in your life, call to the Masters to take charge. Call for that person to be removed if they are not meant to be there. Then, when you see the Law beginning to work, and they begin to depart, do not let your sympathy over their suffering draw them back.*

Taking the clue, I invoked the Masters to come forth between Elizabeth and me, and affirmed,

> *If we are not meant to be together, make that crystal-clear, and if we are, dissolve all doubts.*

After falling asleep I dreamed of Elizabeth and saw a future life together. I saw our two children, a boy and a girl, and heard their names.

Partings

Yet because of the disharmony between us, the Masters were no longer in my life. I saw that Elizabeth wanted to pursue a different path than mine, that her desire for a career would take her in a different direction, and that our marriage was doomed to divorce. It was clear that our life together would lead to suffering, not the happiness I anticipated, and my recent dreams of a tsunami were a warning from my Higher Self. I remembered *Zanoni*, the novel by Sir Edward Bulwer-Lytton, transmitted telepathically by Saint Germain—telling of the young Master who, through his love for his student, and against warnings from *his* Master, loses all his powers and his ability to help anyone, even himself. His marriage ended his Mastery.

The next morning I tried to explain that turmoil to Elizabeth, but my clumsy words proved futile. She insisted that what I perceived as guidance from the Masters was only fear of intimacy, a projection of an unhealed part of my psyche, and that my desire to be alone was selfish. The more I tried to explain my conflict between desire for personal happiness and service to the Masters, the more I offended her. Everything I said seemed wrong. Soon she became so enraged that I left the room, rather than endure her wrath. I couldn't imagine spending another day in the house together at the mercy of her venomous words, and I returned to the room only long enough to ask her to leave.

"You invited me here for the holidays," she retorted, "and my parents spent a lot of money on a plane ticket to get me here, and now you're telling me you want to be alone and are asking me to leave—is that it?" she shouted furiously.

I choked back tears, realizing that everything she said was true, though only a portion of the whole story. There was nothing more I could say, even if I had been able to talk, for I knew my rational logic would fail against the logic of her passion. Remaining silent, I left the room. Soon I heard her calling the airline, changing her reservation to leave that afternoon.

I drove her to the airport, tears running down my cheeks. As I was unable to speak, we drove in silence. I wanted to change my mind, to beg her to stay, even for just another day, but I remembered the warning I had just read, "Don't allow your sympathy for someone who is not meant to be in your life draw them back, once they have started to depart." *No, I made my choice, and now I will have to live with the consequences.*

"Are you okay?" she kept asking me, but the love I heard in her voice only made me feel worse. *How can I be sending away the one I love?* It was

New Year's Day, when most of the world was still celebrating the birth of Christ and the start of the new year, while for me, I felt a part of me dying—as in fact it was.

After an almost speechless separation at the airport—there was nothing left to say—I drove home in a daze, then flung myself on my bed, where I laid for three days. *So, you really can die from a broken heart—this was the suffering I saw when, standing beside Saint Germain above the Earth, I looked down and saw the misery below.* He had offered me liberation, and I had turned it down to come back to this small, blue planet floating in space, to assist others. Now I was the one who needed help. Like Zanoni, in Edward Bulwer-Lytton's novel, I had lost my power to help anyone. *What good had coming back to Earth accomplished? Where is Saint Germain now when I need him?*

I felt numb, without the desire to live. I had not eaten for days and was unable to meditate. My mind spun round, dwelling on my sorrows. *Where has all my spiritual work gotten me? I am 33 years old and a failure, as my mother has always believed. I have no career, no money, and just destroyed my one true love. And my teacher, to whom I gave strict obedience, under whose guidance I dedicated myself to the Masters, has betrayed me and destroyed my good name among my friends. And where are the Masters? They, too, have turned their backs on me. My life has been a waste.* But this moment, the darkest of my life, was just before the dawn. Though I was not aware of the Masters, they were very much aware of me, this crucifixion being just the doorway at which all human attachment had to be left behind and through which awaited the resurrection the Masters were soon to grant. I would soon have direct contact with them more glorious than I had ever dreamed, and which would expand my ability to serve to a new level.

THE DWELLER AT THE THRESHOLD

Those three days were the darkest of my life. I felt dazed, sleeping and waking merged, boundaries between past, present, and future dissolved, and I relived past lifetimes. I found myself in my Higher Mental Body at the retreat at the Royal Teton, where, seated in front of a vast screen more lifelike than a modern movie theatre, I was shown ages past where great depravity had prevailed on Earth. People had vast powers, but had not yet experienced the consequences of the misuse of those powers. They indulged their fanciful desires in pursuing all manner of depraved activity—inflicting great suffering not only on each other, but on those developing souls on Earth for whom they had journeyed through space eons before to assist. People were enslaved and used as objects of pleasure, or sacrificed to demonic entities that absorbed the life force from their blood—the origin of the ritual sacrifices of animals which continue in some cultures to this day. These magicians, although possessed of extraordinary power, assumed more and more control over people's lives, demanding to be worshiped as gods in exchange for the protection which their powers enabled them to extend to their followers. People had not yet learned that a real God does not want to be worshiped, for they need nothing, and want only for humanity to find the God Presence within.

I was taken even further back in time to when Divine Souls were sent to Earth and their mission explained. These Twin Flames, who existed as the outer manifestation of the male and female aspects of the God Self, were the embodiments of love made manifest. Although at first all went according to plan, these neophytes, never having experienced resistance to will or existing as separate beings outside each other, became impatient with the slow pace of evolution and decided to alter the plan to make it more in alignment with their own newly-awakened desires. Rather than remain separate from evolving humanity purely in the role of teachers, some were motivated by personal desire and decided to become more intimately involved, believing that by mating with humans they could speed up evolution: *...the sons of God saw the daughters of men that they were fair; and they took them wives of all that they chose* (Genesis 6:2).

My own beloved Twin Flame, whom I knew now as Elizabeth, had watched with horror as I turned my back on her to involve myself with other women. As our connection was eternal, I rationalized there was no harm in loving others, for I had not yet experienced separation or the absence of love. I took her presence for granted, since she was a part of myself, and selfishly thought she would always be there for me. Reliving that moment, seeing the recognition of my abandonment in her eyes, rent my heart. I saw that I was the origin of her present-day mistrust of men and her seeming desire to inflict suffering on me by her dalliance with others. I had created the present karma which now prevented us from being together, reunited as the One we truly were—and were destined one day to become again. I had created a wound that had been injured again and again over the ages, and which some day would need to be healed.

Then I saw the end of that age, when the earth sank beneath the ocean in a series of vast cataclysms in which much of humanity was destroyed. The initiates had gone into the center of the Earth, to continue the evolution of civilization in a place of peace and harmony, allowing those still ensnared in duality to continue their struggle on the surface, incarnating over and over to learn their lessons and finally redeem themselves from the consequences of their ignorance and unrestrained desires.

I saw that in those subsequent ages Elizabeth and I had known each other in many different embodiments, and that in all of them our relationship had been destroyed by her unconscious mistrust. Despite the love we felt on meeting, eventually she would begin to doubt, then to flirt with other men and flaunt her affairs in my face. Not only was she protecting herself from the heartbreak her soul remembered, but she seemed intent on causing me to experience what I had once inflicted on her. Perhaps she was teaching me to appreciate who she was and realize the sanctity of our union—so that in some future age I would be ready to resume that sacred bond, the *marriage made in heaven*—the secret polarity in the heart of God.

When I returned to my body after these visions I would awake crying, knowing how in betraying Elizabeth I had betrayed something sacred, the inner part of myself—the consequence that had come from following my desires. Filled with remorse, I wondered if I could ever redeem myself. Soon I was to face the self-created demon of my own negativity, created by all my negative thoughts, feelings, and actions on Earth, and that would come to me in a most terrifying form—what is known in occult circles as the *dweller at the threshold.*[75] This monster was the wrathful entity with flaming eyes of Tibetan *thangkas,* the self-created demon returning to its creator on whom it depended for sustenance, which all must eventually slay. It was this entity that whispered temptations to the lower self, encouraging

---

75 Sir Edward Bulwer-Lytton, *Zanoni: A Rosicrucian Tale* (Kessinger Publishing, facsimile of 1842 ed., 1942). Available online as a free download. This book shows, in the form of a novel that was transmitted telepathically to the author by Saint Germain, what happens when someone tries to attain spiritual initiation without first eliminating the dweller at the threshold. See also: Elisabeth Haich, *Initiation* (Aurora Press, 2000).

selfish actions, sustaining itself on the emotional *loosh*[76] that it stimulated us to generate.

This was the eerie shadow I had seen as a child. When alone in the house, I would see it out of the corner of my eye, lurking in wait as if wanting something from me. Or it would come in dreams, a demon too terrifying to look upon directly, that would try to suck the life force from me—and I would awaken in a panic, heart pounding. It was also the being I would see come through others' faces when they were angry or fearful, the twisted mouth and glowering eyes of their own demonic creation—the unconscious force that drove people to act out of the passion of the moment, often inflicting harm on those they most loved. This was the force that made people seem to have a split personality, for actually they were possessed by a part of their own consciousness.

This entity could only be dissolved through the conscious use of the light, especially the Violet Consuming Flame and the Sword of Blue Flame—and through self-observation, which dissolved attachments to emotional programming and deprived the entity of the emotional food on which it lived. Otherwise, continuing to dwell in unconsciousness, one had to endure the slow, purifying activity of the fire element which manifested as suffering—the slow, painful path of purification which most of humanity had to endure lifetime after lifetime, until they awakened from their ignorance.

Without warning, one night this monster came to do battle. While my body slept, I was drawn toward a terrible wailing outside the door of my room that pulled me to investigate. Leaving my denser body, I went

---

76   Robert Monroe, *Journeys Out of the Body* (Doubleday, updated 1992). *Loosh* is a modern term for the *astral light*, the energy that permeates the non-physical realm that is filled with the mental and emotional emanations of humanity. Monroe thought at the beginning of his work that because he was in contact with beings "out of the body," that they were privy to advanced information. He did not realize that this realm was filled with deluded, earthbound spirits and thought forms that were willing and able to mislead one into believing that what they espoused was truth; however, he did discover that they pursued humans to live off their energy. These are the beings psychics often commune with, thinking they are in touch with Masters and "Guides."

forth in higher form and opened the door. There, at the head of the stairs, was the demon, towering a full head above me. It had chosen the location where two terrifying things had happened to me as a child, and where I was most vulnerable to fear. I had fallen down these stairs when I was five years old, and though not physically harmed, I had realized then that I would someday die, and for the first time felt the nearness of death. I used to spend many hours at the head of these stairs, looking down their polished oak surface, contemplating the sensuousness of the presence of death I had felt at that moment. Then one day, my attention had been drawn to the inlaid mahogany china cabinet against the wall, reaching almost to the ceiling. In its base was a locked cupboard, but for some reason the key had been left in the lock. Turning the ancient-looking key, I found secreted in an old wooden box a horrifying human skull carved out of ivory, several inches in diameter, hidden there by a long-forgotten uncle who had picked it up on his travel to the Orient—and it held a morbid fascination for me. A snake coiled on top of the skull peered down into an empty eye socket, and I felt that this horrifying object, which drew me to open the cupboard to meditate on it again and again, held some unrevealed wisdom which I had yet to fathom. In some way, like the wandering ascetic I had been in India in past lives, meditating among the burning corpses in the charnel grounds, I was continuing in this life the same meditation on the impermanence of life.

The demon snarled and drew a saber made of red light, similar to Darth Vader's in *Star Wars*,[77] a movie which would not be released for another year. Terrified, I reached to my side and drew a similar saber, emitting blue light. As we engaged in combat, I realized that I was more afraid of this being's energy than I was of his saber, and I felt him trying to drain my life force. I recognized now that this was the being that had haunted my dreams since childhood, which had caused me to be sick and afraid, and had fed on my energy.

Rather than wait, I lunged forward, swinging my weapon, yet felt my energy dissipating. I seemed unable to prevail, my attacks only provoking counter-parries deflecting my blows. As I gave in to fear and lost strength, my opponent gained the very energy I lost, gloating as he grew stronger.

When I realized that this was a being of my own creation that drew

---

[77] Lucasfilm, 1977.

its strength from me, I knew that the only way to survive was to conquer my fear and take back my power. In confirmation of this insight, the look of superiority disappeared from the demon's face, and, for the first time, I beheld concern.

Shifting my weapon to my left hand, I pointed my finger at the assailant, and feeling the God Presence surge within me, said,

In the name of the Christ that I AM, I say to you, you have no power. I created you.... By the Power of God That I AM, I now dissolve you!

The entity snorted, as though mortally wounded, and took a step backward, flailing the red light saber to ward off the blows that I now rained down fearlessly. Fear gone, I confidently moved forward, empowered by my new awareness as Creator of my own world.

"You have no power," I kept affirming, as I advanced. Even though I knew that I was this demon's source and sustaining power, were I to lower my guard or give in to doubt, I knew that I could be harmed—indeed, many people go insane from inexplicable causes or die unexpectedly in their sleep.

As I advanced again, I noticed that the entity had become smaller and was now my own size—though still terrifying—and I felt I was in a battle to the death. All the fencing I had done in college was now standing me in good stead, and I remembered my coach's words, "Victory goes not to the strongest, but to the one who can best observe himself," for in that inner awareness your opponent's weakness is revealed.

Now the being seemed no longer able to attack and could barely hold his saber aloft to protect himself. Seeing the opening, I lunged straight and drove my saber into its chest. With a look of horror, he collapsed on the floor, and I watched, fascinated, as he slowly shrank in size, becoming less and less distinct, until I could see the floor through his transparent form—finally dissolving into a vapor, which dissipated into the air.

With a shock, I sat up in bed, shaking, drenched in sweat from my terrifying ordeal. The weight of the fear of eons past had been lifted, and I felt an inexpressible lightness and sense of relief. I had slain this *dweller at the threshold* that kept human awareness locked in its cage of fear and doubt, lest we discover who we truly are and assume our God Dominion. It was imperative to dispel this entity before I could receive the light the Masters would bestow in the empowerment that was soon to follow.

Chapter 37

A Greater Service

I paced the floor of my upstairs room, looking out the window as I had as a child, at the bare branches of the old maple tree and the chilling January sky. I was unable to rid my mind of Elizabeth, whom I had sent away ten days before, and my heart was as bleak as the landscape. *Where are the Masters, now that I have sacrificed my love for them?* I wondered.

Suddenly, the noble face of Kuthumi Lal Singh appeared clearly in my mind's eye—the Master with the kind, expressive eyes and long, auburn hair I had met on my trip to Israel, and his words startled me: *We have put you through every test we could think of, this last test being the most difficult, and you have passed them all. Our congratulations. Your greater service is now about to begin. Sit and meditate.* Then he was gone.

What greater service? I wondered, as I went to the ancestral oak armchair in the corner of the room to meditate. My mind was still in a whirl. Since Elizabeth had left, I had been trying to sit and focus on my breath to still my thoughts, a practice that had always worked before, but now peace was elusive. I still felt the pain in my heart over our separation.

Why not focus on the pain? it suddenly occurred to me, remembering a Buddhist teaching that said *take the path as the goal.*[78] Focus on what is going on for you at this very instant; identify it and experience it fully with full awareness—for what we refuse to look at is what controls us. Once seen, it disappears.

Though I cannot focus on the light, I can focus on the pain—the ache in my heart. Instead of struggling to avoid it, to fill my mind with bliss, I turned my awareness back on itself, on what I was feeling, and the pain became a life raft on the sea of my conflicting emotions. My mind stabilized.

I had heard from women that during childbirth, unable to focus on anything else, they had concentrated on the pain, and it was that focus that had helped them survive. Now, instead of struggling, I focused on what I was feeling. My pain came rushing in, filled me, and then surprisingly subsided. I felt calm and serene—as the awareness of my

---

78 Chögyam Trungpa, *The Path Is the Goal* (Shambhala, 1995).

essential nature returned.[79]

As I sat, appreciating the first calm moment I had experienced in weeks, a ball of brilliant golden light descended through the ceiling and hovered in front of me. This opalescent orb pulsed with intent, heralding something momentous about to happen. I stared, shocked, not knowing what to do. Then heard a commanding voice,

Write!

Write what?

Write! The voice said again, with increased insistence.

But I have nothing I want to write, I complained.

I said, write!

Not wanting to argue with this presence that seemed so insistent, though I wanted to sit and meditate in the inner stillness that I had just regained, I thought I'd better go to the desk and at least make an effort to write, although I had no idea what.

As I went to the desk, the ball of light followed. No sooner had I picked up the pencil lying beside a yellow legal pad, than I heard the voice say,

In the center of your being is a great light, and you are that light.

What comes next? I asked.

Write down that sentence; then I will give you the second sentence.

As I began to write, the ball of light expanded, and a figure of unimaginable majesty emerged, clothed in a white robe, with a panel of sapphires hanging from his waist to the hem of his garment. It was a being whose radiation I had felt while meditating with Pearl, but never seen—one who had other names, but I knew him by the title of his office, the Great Divine Director, a central figure in the Great White Brotherhood. I

---

[79] Tsultrim Allione, in her excellent book *Feeding Your Demons* (Little, Brown and Company, 2008), talks about the healing that occurs when you face your affliction, your demon, and talk to it as you would to anyone who wants something from you. By understanding it and giving it your love, it is healed, as are you. She points out that the great afflictions of the world are caused in large part by the projection of our own demons onto others. In her book she gives five easy steps for confronting and pacifying that part of ourselves we often seek to avoid. Jesus also gave a similar teaching when he said, *"Love your enemies."* That is easier said than done, but Ms. Allione teaches an easy method.

had only heard rumors of his vast activity. Now he towered above me as I wrote, his radiation setting my nerves on fire, and I felt as though my body were dissolving into light.

I can't take this energy, I protested.

You can, and you will! he replied, with an authority that dissolved opposition.

As I finished recording the first sentence, true to his word, he spoke the next, and then the next, almost too fast for me to scribble down. As I wrote, I felt my awareness pulled upward, human consciousness dissolving, as I was raised into the I AM Presence. One with my God Source, I became conscious of everything in the environment simultaneously.

There was no gravity, no up or down; my awareness extended beyond the roof of the house, surveying the neighborhood with spherical vision that allowed me to see in every direction simultaneously. The sun was shining directly above in an azure sky that had been cloudy only minutes before, squirrels were chasing each other through the maple tree beside the house, and children were riding bicycles down the street. Far below, I saw the slates of the roof, and through the roof I could see my body at the desk, hand scrawling over the yellow pad with lightning speed:

This is the Truth of your being. You shall know This Truth and this truth shall make you Free. This is the Truth Jesus spoke, the truth for all men, that all men can know....

What you are, what you experience at any given moment, is simply the result of what you have allowed your attention to be focused upon....

In the center of your being you have a Divine Director—the Consciousness of the Real You—that will guide and direct you in your choice at every moment, if you will turn your attention to it. And It is a Great Blazing Sun Within You. I thank you.[80]

There was nowhere I could not see, nothing I could not comprehend. Then, without warning, I was back in my body, charged with the superhuman energy of the Great Divine Director, his energy coursing

---

80 The Ascended Masters, with Peter Mt. Shasta, editor, *"I AM" The Open Door* (Pearl Publishing, Mount Shasta, 1978) p.2.

through my nerves, charging every cell of my body with scintillating light.

Unlike the channels who try to get a message, often hearing some aspect of their own mind or a lower level being inhabiting the astral plane, I had not invoked this contact or tried to channel a message.[81] This contact was initiated by the Master himself, who had descended in visible form. This was not a mental or "psychic" process, but the most powerful experience of my life, from the etheric down to the cellular. I saw now why I had needed to slay the *dweller at the threshold* first, which was the repository of all my human fears and doubts, for this powerful energy amplified everything acting in my aura. Had that purification not taken place, the Masters could not have approached so closely, for they would not have wanted to amplify a negative condition that would later have been more difficult to dissipate.

After an hour, my fingers aching from writing faster than I had ever done before, the words stopped as suddenly as they had started. The majestic visitor stepped back, and with devastating compassion said,

---

[81] There is a vast difference between what passes as "channeling" and the genuine transmission that occurs when a Master steps forth and consciously uses an individual to give a message. The Great Ones have better things to do than fulfill the desires of everyone who wants to receive a message from them. For the most part, these desires result in "messages" originating either from the mind of the one seeking to channel—which may nonetheless contain much valid information—or from astral entities masquerading as Masters. The danger here is not only that these entities draw energy from those invoking them, but that individuals never find their own Inner Master and remain dependent forever on others.

The key to determining where a message is coming from is the energy and consciousness that accompanies the transmission. When a Master is present, the conscious energy of the Master is so all-pervasive that one is raised in consciousness. For the most part, the information is already known or the teachings are readily available—for there really are no new teachings. When the energy is flat or negative and the speaker has to rely on dramatic gestures, strange mannerisms, and sheer decibel volume, it is not the working of a Master. "*Then the LORD said unto me, 'The prophets prophesy lies in my name: I sent them not, neither have I commanded them, neither spake unto them: they prophesy unto you a false vision and divination, and a thing of naught, and the deceit of their heart'*" (Jeremiah 14:13-15, King James Bible).

I thank you. Then he dissolved into a ball of light and returned back through the ceiling, and I was alone again.

Why did he say, "Thank you?" It is I who should thank him. I had never experienced such power, and at the same time such humility. It seemed that the greater the being, the more humble. Only in the human and lower astral worlds do beings get puffed up at their own importance.

I didn't believe that any drug-induced experience could surpass the ecstasy I was feeling—for every cell of my body was filled with light, my previously desolate heart now emanating transcendent love. From that moment on, the only thing I wanted to achieve in life was to become what that being was—a living God Presence. No human relationship could again tempt me away from that goal.

The next day Saint Germain also appeared in his body of light, and I transcribed the discourse he gave. Then every day for the next ten days I was visited by various Ascended Masters, and I wrote down the discourses they poured forth, among them Jesus, Mary, Quan Yin, Hillarion, El Serapis Bey[82] and many others well-known to students of the Ascended Masters, each bringing their own characteristic energy and wisdom. Though their energies were different, a feeling of joy accompanied each one, causing my heart to overflow with the grace and love that their presence showered on me. From the abject sorrow I had been feeling, my life had changed one hundred eighty degrees.

I realized that only by making the painful choice to renounce life with Elizabeth, could this door into the Ascended Master Octave have been opened for me. I understood now what Jesus meant when he said,

I come to bring the life more abundant.

---

82   Madame Blavatsky received many materialized letters from El Serapis Bey, Chohan of the Fourth Ray, and known to be a strict disciplinarian, but with a wry sense of humor. One of his most frequent pieces of advice to students was to "Try, and if you're not successful, try again…and my final advice to you is to Try." See: Charles J. Ryan, *H.P. Blavatsky and the Theosophical Movement, A Brief History* (Theosophical University Press, 1937). See online version: www.theosociety.org/pasadena/hpb-tm/hpbtm-5.htm. Here Blavatsky says, *"(The Master) is a Savior…who leads you to finding the Master within yourself"* (Ch. 6).

This awareness of the fullness of God was that abundance. A door had been opened for me to a love greater than I had imagined existed, one not subject to the vicissitudes of human relationships. Since I felt I had gone through a door, I took the title for the discourses I had just been given from the words of Jesus, *I am the open door which no man can shut.* This small volume of instruction on the understanding and application of the I AM Consciousness was published as *"I AM" the Open Door.*[83]

I had become so accustomed to the Masters' daily visits and the uplifting euphoria that accompanied them that I did not realize they would not continue once the book was completed. When the transmission was complete, their visits stopped. Being deprived of their presence was like being cut off from some exotic elixir on which I had become dependent. Only by going deeper than ever before within myself was I able to contact them, a challenge that forced me to delve ever more single-mindedly into that place where *the Masters and I are One.*

---

83 The Ascended Masters, with Peter Mt. Shasta, editor, *"I AM" The Open Door.*

Chapter 38

Face to Face with the Master

Saint Germain had just finished dictating a discourse and disappeared—or so I thought. His electrifying presence had left me euphoric, so energized that I was unable to sit still, and so I paced back and forth in the room that had suddenly become too small. Filled with gratitude, I longed for some way to express my feelings to the Master.

I remembered reading a story about Saint Germain in *The Voice of the "I AM,"* a magazine published by the Saint Germain Foundation, that told how Saint Germain bowed to Jesus whenever he saw him, until one day Jesus said, "My good brother, why do you bow to me when you can do all that I can do?"

"I bow to you as a tribute to the light," Saint Germain said in response.

Now I, too, wanted to express my tribute to the light, so I imagined that Saint Germain stood before me, and leaned forward from my waist and said, "I bow to you, Saint Germain."

His response was instantaneous. A shaft of violet light shot down into the room, in the midst of which stood Saint Germain, clothed in the uniform he wore in the French court—indigo cape, jeweled sword, gold Maltese cross on his chest—the essence of Mastery. He stood before me for a moment, a mirthful smile playing on his handsome face, seeming to enjoy my surprise—then extended one foot and bowed to me with a sweep of his arm, as only someone used to the courts of Europe could, and said with a love and humility that took my breath away, "I bow to you, too, Peter."

Straightening, he smiled again, shot me a penetrating look that pierced me to the core—then rose upward through the tube of violet light through the ceiling. I stood in the middle of the room, electrified, filled with a joy I was barely able to contain. *So, he had been aware of me the whole time without my knowing it, hearing my every thought. How many other times was he present without my knowing?*

His appearing in his etheric body like that was far more exhilarating to experience than when he appeared in an apparently ordinary, human body, for when in the physical world, he had to refrain from doing anything that would attract undue attention. In his more etheric form, however, he could emanate his true essence, which partially raised one into his octave.

Apprentice to the Masters

A week later, as I was preparing to leave New York and return to California, I again felt Saint Germain's uplifting energy, subtle at first, and I thought of the many occasions when I had met him in an ordinary physical form but had not realized until later, sometimes years later, who the stranger of my encounter had been. Now, as the Master's energy increased, I began to see him inwardly, and I was surprised to hear him say that he would be on the plane with me going back to California.

"What form will you take?" I questioned.

I longed to ask if he would be tangibly present in a human form and let me recognize him as he had at the Shakespeare play in Ashland, but I did not want to beg such an indulgence. I was well aware that the Masters discouraged such selfish requests, preferring their students to ask, *How best can I serve the light and help others?* That desire to serve humanity would then draw the Masters to them like a magnet, although often without their awareness, for to appear in a visible form would often present a distraction that would interfere with the work at hand.

"There is something you would like to ask?" Saint Germain interjected, hearing my thoughts.

"Well, I have always wanted to meet you face to face, look you in the eye, and shake your hand with the absolute certainty that it was you," I replied.

"Done."

"Done?" I echoed, astounded.

"In gratitude for your obedience, and the difficult sacrifices you have made in serving us, I will give you your long-cherished wish as my present to you. However, I will be traveling *incognito*. I will not walk onto the plane in my indigo cape and sword, of that you can be sure! So choose a name by which you will recognize me."

Remembering the name of the autobiographical character Hemingway used in many of his short stories, I said, "Use the name Nick Adams."

"Very well, Nick Adams it is," he said with a confirming nod. "I will see you on the plane," he said in parting, then was gone. *I wonder if he was the one who inspired me to use that name, knowing that at some time in the future I, too, would be writing about this incident?*

Busy with packing and making many last minute arrangements, I forgot about the promised rendezvous. Despite my many experiences with the Masters, a part of my mind still remained skeptical that what I had been told on an inner level would actually take place in the outer world. Rushing to get to the airport well ahead of time, I discovered that the flight

I had booked was canceled and that, strangely, I was being put on not just a different plane but a different airline.

At the check-in counter, the clerk asked me if I wanted a smoking or non-smoking seat (as in those days smoking was permitted), and I was surprised when I spoke the words, "Smoking, please." The idea of being closed in a plane for six hours with a crowd of smokers, breathing their stale exhalation, unnerved me, but I seemed unable to retract my request. No words would come forth, but I thought, *I can always change my seat later.*

Once onboard the plane, I found my seat and began stowing my bag in the overhead compartment, when suddenly I felt an electric current go through me. I looked toward the front of the plane. The cabin door had just been shut behind the last passenger, a businessman in a dark suit. For a moment he joked with the stewardess about having made the flight *just in the nick of time,* then turned and came down the aisle.

When the amiable fellow reached me, he stopped and held out his hand, and I realized that he wanted to shake hands. *That's strange, passengers don't shake hands at the beginning of a flight, only at the end after getting to know one another.* But not wanting to seem unfriendly, I extended my hand, which he shook very deliberately.

"Hello, Peter," the businessman said, looking me straight in the eye, "My name is Nick Adams...I believe I have the seat next to yours."

Nick Adams? Now I remembered Saint Germain's promise, the gift he said he would offer—and I realized that I was in the presence of the same beloved Master who had been watching over me throughout this lifetime and whom I had served in many past lives, that this businessman now holding my hand and looking me in the eye was none other than Saint Germain, the ubiquitous Master under whom I was serving. I stood motionless in the aisle, my heart beat wildly.

"Perhaps if you take your seat, I will be able to sit down," he said, bringing me back to the present.

I slid, but mostly fell, into my seat by the window, and the Master traveling under the name Nick Adams slipped into the seat beside me. In the realization that the living, breathing presence of the Ascended Master Saint Germain was sitting beside me, I could barely contain myself. He had given me his word that I would see him on the plane in a form I would recognize and had used the name I requested—keeping his word to the letter.

Now, what should I do? I looked sideways. Here was an ordinary-appearing man wearing a business suit that was indigo with subtle, silver stripes. No one would suspect that he was anything other than an executive or salesman traveling on business. I knew who he was, however, and sensing the opportunity of a lifetime—knowing that Saint Germain would be sitting next to me for the next six hours—I vowed to ask him everything I had always wanted to know about the ultimate nature of reality and, on a mundane level, what I should do to heal the rift with Pearl. And, most important, the question that was always in my heart: *Will Elizabeth and I ever be together in this lifetime?*

Just as I was about to lean over and say, *Look, since I know who you really are, let's talk,* he lit up a cigarette and exhaled a ring of smoke into the air in front of him. It was a perfect circle that, despite the air conditioning, hung in space. Then the "No Smoking" sign lit up, and he extinguished the cigarette in the ashtray in the armrest.

Am I dreaming? A Master would never smoke, would he? Fastening my seat belt, I closed my eyes and tried to come to terms with my doubt. Soon the engines whined as we accelerated down the runway and the plane surged into the sky. Then I recalled he said he would be traveling incognito. *Of course—smoking is part of his disguise, the persona of the traveling businessman.*

After we reached cruising altitude, I again leaned over and was about to ask if we could talk, when I thought better of it. *Better to go along with his role and be subtle. Start out slowly, then later, when things are going smoothly, work the conversation around to what I want to talk about,* I thought, forgetting that Saint Germain knew my every thought, and that he was not only in complete control of our conversation, but of every aspect of our flight. Had the engines stopped, he could have transported us back to California with the power of his awareness—as he had transported me in San Francisco once before.

"Traveling for pleasure?" he asked, breaking the awkward silence.

"Yes," I nodded. "I'm going back home after visiting my mother."

"Oh," he said casually, lighting up another cigarette.

"How about you?" I replied, trying to follow his lead, "Are you traveling for pleasure?"

"No, I'm on business."

"What business is that, if I may ask?"

"Realty."

"Realty?" I echoed, making sure I had heard correctly, *or did he mean "reality?"*

"Yes, are you interested in real estate?" he asked to my surprise, for though I had just gotten out of the landlord business, I was now considering getting a real estate license. Selling property would be a lot less stressful, I thought, and probably more lucrative, than fixing run-down places and renting them out to perpetually needy tenants.

While I was pondering how to answer his question, he gestured to the passing stewardess who was pushing the beverage cart down the aisle, and purchased a glass of red wine. Reaching into his pocket, he pulled out some dollar bills, telling her to keep the change. *Wine? A Master drinking alcohol?* My mind began doubting again. *And where did he get money? Was it legal to precipitate money?* My mind started going wild again as I imagined what would happen if all the Ascended Masters began precipitating money, *Wouldn't the sudden increase in the money supply cause runaway inflation?* As the stewardess placed the glass of red wine on the open tray, my mind flipped back and forth between belief and doubt, and for the sake of my sanity and peace of mind for the rest of the flight, I decided to relate to this man beside me as simply a bored businessman who wanted to talk.

"Yes, real estate," he said again, "…not a bad way to make a living." Then he went on to talk about his experiences in that profession, encouraging me to become an agent.

Though I felt none of the spiritual radiation he emanated when appearing etherically, I began to realize once more that, indeed, this really was the one who had promised he would be on the plane, traveling incognito, and that he would use the name Nick Adams—and here he was. *His disguise is to put me at ease and so he won't attract attention.* Gradually I accepted his persona as a Realtor and continued the conversation he had set in motion.

Soon lunch was served, and when the stewardess asked him what entrée he preferred, he shocked me again by saying, "Steak, and another red wine."

Cigarettes, wine, meat; what kind of a Master is this? I now watched with shock as he devoured his steak with seeming gusto. Of course, he would soon dissolve his body and with it anything he had ingested; nonetheless, I was forced to give up long-held beliefs about right and wrong, my judgments about what behavior was spiritual or not.

Before I realized the passage of time, we landed in San Francisco, and

I reflected sadly that I had not been able to ask any of the questions in my heart. Leaving the plane, I kept a close eye on the Master, for I wanted to see him disappear before my eyes as he had done in Muir Woods many years before. Not letting him out of my sight, I walked closely beside him, which he did not seem to discourage. *Would he grant this wish, too, of allowing me to watch him shift dimensions?*

Arriving at the baggage claim area, we approached the carousels, one of which soon began disgorging luggage.

"Is that our carousel?" he asked, pointing to where luggage from one of the flights had begun disgorging to a waiting crowd.

Peering in the direction he pointed, I saw that it was the luggage of an earlier flight, but when I looked back he was gone. *He gave me the slip. Why had I looked away? Why had I allowed him to divert the conversation to real estate? When would I have such an opportunity to talk to the Master again?* I accused myself of not being more persistent, of not making better use of this once-in-a lifetime opportunity.

Soon, though, I realized that it was only because he knew I would follow his lead and respect the rules he imposed that he had allowed me this experience—for the Masters can only draw close to those whose emotions are calm and minds are stable, who will follow their lead, and who will remain obedient to the inner command of the I AM Presence. Otherwise, the added energy of the Master's presence would further aggravate any imbalance already there.

Perhaps the encounter was not a loss after all, I reflected. Who knows what transmission may have taken place on higher levels? Certainly, he had boosted my self-confidence and prepared me to deal with those back home who were speaking ill of me, and whom I would soon have to face.[84]

---

84 I thought of this incident with Saint Germain many years later, when people claimed that being extremely sensitive or spaced out was a sign of advanced spirituality. Here was a being that had attained the *Rainbow Body*, sitting in a smoke-filled airplane for six hours, making small talk without showing the least sign of discomfort or spaciness. As one enters a higher level of awareness, there is sometimes an initial disorientation, but as one becomes stabilized in that consciousness, the ability to function in ordinary reality returns, for the ordinary is the ground of Mastery.

Chapter 39

The Good Karma Café

After Saint Germain's disappearance at the San Francisco airport, instead of following through on my plans to catch a connecting flight north and return to Mount Shasta, I felt an inexplicable urge to spend the night in San Francisco. I wondered if perhaps there was some guidance the Master had communicated on subtle levels during the flight, of which my ordinary mind was unaware. I phoned my cousin, who, although not happy with my unannounced arrival, had become used to my sporadic comings and goings, and welcomed me to spend the night at her house on Twin Peaks. Although she did not believe in the Masters, through some mysterious influence which she would call "coincidence," she had built her house long before I had ever heard of the Masters, overlooking Saint Germain Avenue. I used to stand on her balcony, from which I could see the entire Bay Area from the Golden Gate Bridge to the Bay Bridge, and gaze down in amazement at the "Saint Germain Avenue" sign below that let me know the Master was working in her life, despite her complete disbelief in anything not based in the logic of physical science.

She was happy to see me, and after we had discussed the family, she showed me to the room she kept for guests on the second floor. Then she said that if I needed to go anywhere I was welcome to use her car, and she placed the keys in my hand. I thanked her for her generosity and told her that I planned to get an early start in the morning to catch the next flight home, and that I probably wouldn't go anywhere.

However, when she told me that my distant cousin Ariella was in town, whom I hadn't seen in years, I decided to give her a call, since I had nothing else to do. She was excited at the idea of meeting, and I agreed to drive over to her place and we would go out for dinner.

I left the house in my cousin's car, winding past Saint Germain Avenue, wending my way carefully down the steep San Francisco hills, according to the instructions I had written on a scrap of paper I clutched in one hand. But as I reached the bottom of Twin Peaks, instead of turning left, as written on the instructions, I felt a pull to go right. *Oh, no, here I go again on another assignment that's going to upset both my cousins this time, and reinforce their impression of me as a total flake....* This was in the days before cell phones, and as it was rush hour and no parking spaces were available, finding a place to phone was out of the question. Since I didn't know the city well, I had started early, and prayed that wherever I was being led, I would still have enough time to arrive for my dinner rendezvous.

Turning here and there, dodging trolley cars and buses, I wended my way through the congested city streets, wondering where I was being led. But as long as I felt that subtle guidance in my heart, I knew that everything would unfold according to the Plan and I would arrive at the destination the Masters intended.

I found myself on Mission Street and thought, *How appropriate;* for I felt I was truly on a mission, *but for what purpose?*[85] Cruising around a corner, I saw a sign that immediately caught my eye. It said, in beautiful letters, "Good Karma Café," and I knew from the excitement in my heart that I had found the intended destination. As if in confirmation, a car pulled away from the curb, leaving a convenient space, so I parked and went in.

It was one of those hippie hangouts unique to San Francisco in the '70s, Jefferson Airplane's "Somebody to Love" floating in the charged atmosphere. Standing just inside and seeing that the place was packed, with no place to sit, I wondered, *What am I doing here?* I was supposed to be on my way to meet my cousin. *I must have gotten the guidance wrong.* I decided to use the rest room and leave, realizing as I wended my way to the back of café that I could still make it to Ariella's on time. I made a silent call to my Higher Self, knowing the power of words to invoke consciousness into the physical reality:

> *I AM the Commanding, Governing Presence, bringing about the Perfect, Divine Plan here, for I AM the Presence of God in Action.*

As I emerged from the rest room, my attention was immediately drawn to one table, and as I approached, I saw that lying on its black surface was the unmistakable green book with the gold embossed title, *Unveiled Mysteries*. At that table a young man sat alone, intently staring at the book, as if trying to plumb its mysteries without opening its cover. The only free chair around was at his table, and I thought of asking him if I could sit

---

85 Despite having a cell phone with a global positioning system, you still need to look within your heart to know where to go.

down, though intruding on someone's privacy went against my nature.

"That's a good book," I said, pausing as I neared his table.

"Do you know anything about it?"

"Why, yes, I do," I said.

"Why don't you have a seat," he said, beckoning to the free chair, and I realized then that he was the one I had been sent to meet

"What do you know about this book?" asked the young man, who introduced himself as James. "Today is my twenty-first birthday, and my aunt, who is director of the "I AM" Sanctuary in Santa Fe, just sent it to me as a present. I can't tell what to make of it, if it's true or not."

"That book has been the center of my life for the past few years," I said, and began to tell him of my adventures with Saint Germain, the most recent one having been on the airplane only hours before, and he sat there, eyes open wide as I talked.

As I came to the end of an account of one of my contacts with the Master, he exclaimed, "That's the most amazing thing I've ever heard. And what is more amazing is that I had just said to myself, 'Saint Germain, if you are real and this book is true, send someone in here right now to tell me about it,' and then you came in and started talking to me. That's the first time in my life a prayer has been answered."

Concerned about my cousin who was expecting me, I excused myself and used the café phone. Ariella said that a girlfriend had come over and they had fixed themselves something to eat, and that it was fine with her if we waited until some other time to reconnect. I was grateful that there were other people who also knew how to surf the unexpected waves of life without falling into the ocean of rejection, blame, and anger that I had become accustomed to in childhood.

I went back to the table and talked with James for another half hour, telling him about the individualized God Presence and how easy it is to call into action in every aspect of our lives. He sat there, grateful for this birthday message I had obviously been sent by Saint Germain to deliver. Finally, as the energy of our meeting waned, I said goodbye and walked outside into the cool San Francisco night, reflecting on how perfectly life unfolds when we follow the inner promptings of our heart. Despite initial appearances, in service to the God Presence, the fruit of all actions is sweet.

On my return to Mount Shasta, I found that news of the discourses the Masters had dictated to me had begun to circulate, and to the previous charge of absconding with Pearl's manuscript, I was now further accused of plagiarizing Pearl's words and passing them off as my own. My friends were caught in a bind—I was their trusted friend of many years, but Pearl was their teacher who had connected them with the Masters and their own Inner Light. *Who should they believe?*

It took me many years to see that this quandary was one faced by many students on the spiritual path, one that arises eventually in every group and organization—an inevitable falling out, showing everyone when it is time to move on, to break free of their dependency and apply the teachings. One has to attain one's own strength of character, wisdom, and mastery, rather than relying forever on another.[86]

Feeling that I needed to escape this hornet's nest of gossip and recrimination, I left town and moved in with friends who had just moved up from Big Sur and were not a part of Pearl's group. They kindly rented me a room in their home on a back street in Weed, the town where I had spent my first night after meeting Saint Germain in Muir Woods. They, too, had suffered from belonging to groups in the past, and their discriminating, self-reliant intelligence was a refreshing change. They gave me the nurturing support I needed to help make this transition from herd consciousness to once again being an individual, free agent.

I kept to myself, hearing now and then through the grapevine that Pearl was offering me as an example of someone who had fallen off the path and, like Krishnamurti, rejected the Masters. This was ironic, because that was exactly what Godfre Ray King's wife, Lotus, had done to Pearl when she and her Twin Flame, Bob, had presented her with the book Saint Germain had dictated to them. Lotus had refused to read the book or to acknowledge that the Masters would come to anyone but her, which had led Pearl and Bob to withdraw from the Saint Germain Foundation. *Now Pearl is doing to me exactly what was done to her*, I thought, marveling at how it seemed she was projecting on me this unhealed wound; I had become the projection of her own long avoided demon.[87]

I wondered why this sacred relationship with my teacher had become

---

86 Krishnamurti made a similar break from his teacher and mentor, Annie Besant, as well as the Theosophical Society that had supported him, when he refused to play the role of Messiah for which he had been groomed.

87 Tsultrim Allione, *Feeding Your Demons*.

so confused, and I asked for illumination. Then one day I wandered into *The Golden Bough Bookstore* in Mount Shasta and affirmed,

I AM the Illumining, Revealing Presence, showing me what I need here.

I AM being guided and directed from within to the perfect book that will show me what I need to know.

Following my heart, I was led to a series of books with plain, dark blue covers, the works of the occult writer Alice A. Bailey, and as I ran my fingers along them, they stopped at a particular volume. Flipping it open, I saw exactly the message I needed. To paraphrase:

…every student must someday be rejected by their teacher, and every teacher must one day feel betrayed by their pupil, so that each may evolve beyond the limitations of the teacher/student paradigm. This apparent betrayal should not be seen from the human perspective, but as an initiation on the path of spiritual evolution.

I realized I needed to stop blaming Pearl, and accept our falling out as an inevitable step on the spiritual path. Now I would have greater freedom to act, without feeling that my teacher was looking over my shoulder all the time. I now had the time to distribute my new book, and almost immediately it became a hit. The controversy surrounding it turned out to be excellent advertising. Everyone wanted a copy, and I began to get requests from bookstores around the country, as well as letters from people whose lives it had changed. Many said they could feel the radiation of the Masters emanating from its pages. Letters poured in from various groups, requesting me to come and talk.

A woman named Tahira told me that when she received the book in the mail, she flipped it open and asked Saint Germain to show her if he was real and the book contained truth, and then left it lying on the table to go to the bank. When she returned an hour later, although she lived alone, the book was gone. Several months later, after moving into her new apartment, the book dropped out of the air—giving her the confirmation she had requested.

Chapter 40

The Indigo Volvo

Eventually, following the suggestion that Saint Germain had made during his appearance on the plane as a Realtor, I obtained a real estate license and went to work for a local broker. It didn't prove to be the road to easy riches I had imagined. People phoned at all hours, sometimes after I had gone to sleep, with no intention of buying, just out of curiosity. Weekends were spent driving people around the countryside, some who just wanted a pleasant way to pass the day. And people who had read my book began wandering into the office, wanting to hear about my experiences with the Ascended Masters, much to the annoyance of my associates.

After a year of working in the real estate office and not making much money, I began wondering why Saint Germain had guided me into that field; *Perhaps simply for the life experience? Through understanding the tests and challenges others went through, I would be better able to help them.*

Gradually, I began looking for other ways to support myself. *If I'm not going to get rich in real estate, I might as well do what I enjoy.* It didn't seem that the world needed another real estate agent. Since the reason I was on the Earth was that I had made the choice to remain and help others, I sought an occupation that would bring benefit—and I trusted that in helping others I would be taken care of myself.

I had a love for natural healing and had acquired knowledge of herbs on my farm in upstate New York after my return from India. I had also studied Homeopathy with a doctor in New York City. Its mysterious healing power had helped me tremendously, and I had continued to study this amazing form of healing, which worked on so many levels, from physical to spiritual.

One of my clients had paid for me to attend a Homeopathy workshop in Albuquerque with an eminent doctor from India. However, on my way home, the old Rambler station wagon I'd had for only a few months shot a rod through the cylinder wall. It had begun making strange noises on my way to Albuquerque, and on the way back began burning a quart of oil every fifty miles. Praying that it would get me home before its demise, I was driving uphill through the canyon twenty miles south of

Mount Shasta when a cloud of steam blew up from the hood and the engine died. I coasted onto the shoulder, putting out an emergency call to Saint Germain. Then I got out, lifted up the hood, and stuck out my thumb. I did not have long to wait for my prayer to be answered, as the first car to come along stopped. I climbed into the front seat and was shocked to see a woman behind the wheel.

"Women don't usually pick up men stranded by the side of the road," I said, thanking her.

"No, I don't usually, but I felt your peaceful energy and knew it was okay to give you a ride."

Is this Saint Germain in disguise, or is she simply a kind human whose Higher Self has responded to my prayer? I looked at her, grateful for her compassion and sensitivity to guidance, still wondering if she was really who she appeared to be, or a Master in disguise. Regardless, she was still a manifestation of God, and I reminded myself that one of the highest of the Buddhist teachings, that of the Pure Land, is to view everyone as a divine being, every thing as composed of rainbow light, every location as Paradise, and every incident as a manifestation of the guru's grace.

After this angelic being dropped me off in Dunsmuir, the nearest town, I called a tow truck, and they agreed to dispose of the Rambler if I would sign the title over to them. The value of the parts, they said, would equal the cost of the towing charge.

I had bought the car for five hundred dollars from an artist friend, who was also a student of Pearl. Even though I knew he didn't have the money to do regular maintenance, I had felt it was Saint Germain's wish. *But why did he guide me to buy such a junker? Perhaps it was to help this fellow, who barely survived from one commission to the next, my needs for transportation being secondary?* The Masters often have reasons that exceed the scope of our present understanding. Once we ask for their guidance, we can only follow where it leads, no matter how unusual the request. I thought I had followed that guidance, and it had left me stranded by the side of the road. *Was I mistaken, or was there some higher purpose in this seeming catastrophe?*

In any case, I now needed a new car. I would not have long to wait to see that behind this event the Master had a plan—one that would increase my faith in his understanding of what I needed on every level.

As I had spent my meager savings during the trip to Albuquerque, I wondered how I was going to make house calls to visit people who needed healing. I used to walk to people's homes, but that was when I lived in

The Indigo Volvo

town. Now I lived in a cabin on the side of the Mountain, so I prayed to Saint Germain, *If you want me to continue my healing work, I'm going to need a car. I'm sure you had reasons for wanting me to buy that Rambler, but this time I'd really appreciate a good car, and soon—like in the next few days.*

I didn't tell anyone about my prayer, nor did I look in the paper for another used car, because even if I had found one I liked, my bank account was empty. I made no outward effort, since there was nothing I could do anyway. I just trusted that my prayer would be answered in Perfect Divine Order.

Two days later, a stranger pulled into the driveway. I went out to see who he was, and he introduced himself as David.

"You are Peter Mt. Shasta, aren't you?"

"Yes, why?"

"Well, my wife and I have a present for you. It's a long story, but I need you to come with me and pick it up."

"A present?" I asked, a bit perplexed, since I'd never met the man before.

"Yes," he replied.

"You want to give me a present, but couldn't bring it with you?" I asked skeptically.

"No, you need to come to my house in town and pick it up."

This is strange, I thought suspiciously. A few friends had given me "presents" with strings attached, that they later wanted returned, and people were frequently trying to involve me in schemes that promised something for "free," which I later found were fraudulent or involved a hidden agenda. So, hearing this offer from a stranger, I was wary.

I didn't feel any warning energy, though, so I thought, *What the heck; I'll go along for the ride and see what happens,* and I got in David's car.

"I can tell you doubt my motives," David said intuitively, as we drove down the road. "You are well-known in this town, and I'm sure that many people are trying to involve you in various schemes."

You got that right, I thought.

"Well, I would like you to put those thoughts aside and reprogram your mind to receive abundance. I want you to know that I am giving you something without motive, without attachment or expectation of anything in return. Can you accept that?"

"Yes, I think so," I said, feeling the sincerity in his voice.

We arrived at David's spacious home, where he introduced his beautiful wife Thea to me. Then, motioning toward the far side of the living room, he said, "There it is."

I looked in the direction he was pointing and saw a quartz crystal the size of a coffee table. "Wow, thanks," I said half-heartedly, as I did not feel the same excitement over crystals as those who worshiped them as the source of power rather than their own God Presence. But I was aware that a crystal this size was valuable and wondered what it was worth. *Do I dare sell a present? I could certainly use the money.*

"No, not the crystal," David said. "Your present is on the crystal!"

Moving closer, I saw a worn slip of paper lying on the top of the huge translucent gem. In the dim light, I could barely make out what it said, but getting down on my hands and knees, I saw it was an official document. Finally, I was able to read in the dim light: *State of California Vehicle Registration.*

"Vehicle Registration?" I stammered.

"We are giving you our Volvo," David said. "It's the car I was driving before Thea and I got married. Since I have a new car and my wife has her own, we really don't need a third car. We had it completely overhauled and put an ad in the paper, but didn't get a single phone call. We figured it must be meant for someone in particular. So we prayed to the Masters about what to do.

"We were sitting in our hot tub last night, watching the sun set behind the mountains, and Saint Germain appeared in front of us. He said, 'Give the car to Peter Mt. Shasta,' and then disappeared. We both have read your book, *'I AM' the Open Door,* and know that you are helping others, so we wanted to help you, but we didn't know if you needed a car."

"I do, in fact I have been praying to Saint Germain for one."

"Well, the Volvo is yours." He pulled out a pen and signed the transfer document. "Let's go outside, and I'll show it to you."

In the driveway was parked an indigo Volvo that was obviously well cared for, with shiny new tires. I was speechless. My prayer had been answered, and in a way no less remarkable than I would have expected from Saint Germain, the Master to whom I had apprenticed myself, and who was playing such a central role in my life.

I accepted the present with gratitude, not only to the Master, but to these generous friends of Saint Germain, because they had followed his guidance so graciously, without question or attachment.

Gratitude is the open door through which all blessings flow, the

Masters say, even gratitude for adversity—which is one of the greatest teachers. Had the Rambler not broken down, I would not have been given this gift of a better vehicle, nor received such overwhelming proof of the Master's omniscience, compassion, and generosity. Every time I opened the door of the Volvo and felt the solidity of the steering wheel in my hands, a wave of gratitude flowed through me. I was reminded that the Masters knew my needs far in advance, and how they seemed to use every aspect of life for teaching.

Chapter 41

Gold Venture

I practiced healing for many years, using herbs and homeopathic remedies as sacraments that invoked healing on whatever level it was required. Since all phenomena are interdependent, I also used Astrology to show how the heavens are a mirror of life and health, and indicative of where the stress originated and how it might be alleviated. All levels of life are aspects of one's consciousness, so often just giving a client an insight was enough to catalyze healing—other times an herb, remedy, or touch was effective. However, since all healing ultimately comes from God, I would pray inwardly to be an instrument of healing even before a client arrived in my office, and again after they left. Often I would awaken during the night and continue visualizations, affirmations, and mantras to direct healing where it was needed.

How to make a living doing this was the problem. Neither I nor the person seeking healing wanted the emotionally complex issues connected with money to stand in the way of healing; however, one of the laws of healing is to feel gratitude, and to honor the healer as the vehicle through which God's grace flows—whatever form that might take. So, rather than charge a fee, I frequently accepted donations, but found I could barely survive on what people offered—despite the often profound healings. People wanted to feel they were healed directly by God—who did not need money—forgetting that God's intermediaries were on the physical plane, and to survive they did need money. Just accepting that we are on the Earth and that the healer has a right to make a living was a hurdle for some, which when understood, often preceded their healing. I saw that much ill health was caused by the misperception that being spiritual meant cutting off the connection with the Earth, denying the body the food and other comforts it is craving. Even a greater obstacle to health was the condemnation, envy, and judgment of others, that worked like an infection in people's lives.

Did I need to change careers again in order to survive? El Morya, the Master in the turban I had seen on the flight to Israel, was reported to have once said, *The best way to become a Master is to master everything.* The frequent changes in career I was guided through seemed to lend that some credence, although I knew it is not so much the world, but ourselves, we must master. When we have mastered ourselves, nothing is an obstacle.

Now that I had broken with Pearl, I no longer needed to spend long hours in her living room listening to her tell newcomers the stories of her experiences with the Masters I had already heard many times, nor did I need to spend time teaching them the basics of the path, as she often asked. In this free time I could now meditate on and immerse myself in the inner world—and commune with the Masters. As I became more aware of my oneness with them, the limitations of the physical world began to drop away. I began to see how the Masters wield specific energies for the benefit of humanity—and gradually I became more involved in their work.

I was more able to come and go from the Ascended Master retreats, traveling in my Higher Mental Body,[88] which operates between the physical body and the I AM Presence. In this octave I was astonished to see how the Masters participate in and direct much of daily life, and how often individuals who impact the mass consciousness, often without their awareness, are trained by the Masters in their retreats. Many influential figures, world leaders in all fields—politicians, financiers, scientists, artists, and entertainers—are taken by the Masters, often in their sleep or, if during the day, in one of their higher bodies, to these inner locations where they receive instruction. Later they may remember their visit only as a dream, or act on an "intuition" based on the guidance they received—and are surprised how certain events seem to fall into place as though *meant to be,* not realizing that all outer phenomena take place first on inner levels. It is experienced as *déjà vu* because it has *already* happened.

On one of these occasions, I was taken to an Ascended Master retreat located inside a mountain near Burbank, California, where a film project was being developed. The retreat resembled a luxury hotel with all the amenities, yet retained a utilitarian simplicity that supported the focus required to develop creative projects and bring them to fruition.

---

88 The various bodies can be equated with the Sanskrit terms *Dharmakaya, Sambhogakaya* and *Nirmanakaya,* representing the I AM Presence, the Higher Mental Body, and the human self. Frequently in Tibetan *thangkas,* one will find Amithaba Buddha at the top, Chenrizig in the middle, and Guru Rinpoche or some other being manifesting on the physical plane, all representing the Buddha nature as it expresses through the three *kayas* (bodies).

The Master in charge introduced the scriptwriter, who did not realize that the origin of his story was an inspiration he had received from this Master. While refreshing drinks were served, the producer, director, and lead actors, as well as the investors who would put up the money, were all introduced and shown what involvement was expected of them in this project. This was a preliminary meeting that would later be mirrored in the outer world as meetings in agents' offices and at a major film studio, but was occurring now on inner planes that circumvented the greed and clash of egos that would accompany a deal of this magnitude made without the oversight of the Masters. Even with the Masters' assistance, there would still be the inevitable creative conflict, as, for a film to be made, hundreds of individuals need to come together and work as one being, toward a common goal—production of a film.

Though the film being produced was going to be presented as science fiction, it was based on an actual contact that had taken place between our government and beings from another world, an event the government had suppressed—the truth of which the Masters now wanted to be made public. Although presented as entertainment, the film was intended to prepare humanity for the return of our ancestors, who, although assisting us covertly, are awaiting the moment to make their tangible presence known—an event which will most likely occur in the near future, at a pivotal moment in the transformation of life on Earth.

Also present, to my surprise, was Semjasse, the beautiful female voyager from the Pleiades, who had first visited me when I arrived in Mount Shasta, and with whom I later had a rendezvous at Lake Louise. At Saint Germain's request, she had educated me on the Pleiadian mission to Earth and how I was to interface with them in that mission—although access to the detailed memory of those meetings would not be allowed until a future time, when the knowledge would be required. However, now she was wearing a stylish pant suit, in which she fit in with the other Hollywood celebrities and power brokers.

The Master, who had accompanied me, and I seemed invisible to the others, or perhaps they were so focused on the project they simply paid us no heed, but as I observed the meeting, I felt strongly the importance of this film. I had the desire to be of whatever assistance I could in any future film projects that would awaken humanity to knowledge of higher worlds and their own divine origin.

Little did I suspect then how soon, and in what an unusual manner,

Apprentice to the Masters

I would become involved in the film business—and how dangerous that work would be when I encountered demonic forces opposed to humanity gaining that knowledge.

A gentle breeze blew against my cheek, and I realized that I was on a tropical island in the South Pacific. An Asian woman was smiling at me, and in her eyes was a hint of future intimacy. On awakening, I realized that I'd seen this woman in dreams several nights in succession. As I contemplated this vision, the memory of Elizabeth and my vow of celibacy faded. *Was this beauty someone I was destined to be with, or was she another test? Would I be dreaming of her so frequently if I were not going to meet her soon?*

While reliving the dream of this woman in my mind, I received a phone call from Jason, a friend in Hawaii who knew me through reading my book *"I AM" the Open Door*, which had been given to him by a mutual friend. Jason had made a fortune in real estate while a young man and had retired to the Big Island with his wife Dechen, to lead the good life. On the beach one day, perhaps while waiting for the ultimate wave to surf, Jason began reading *The Magic Presence*,[89] which tells of Godfre Ray King's exploits with Saint Germain. Jason had come to believe that the material world, which he had mastered to the degree of having been able to retire early, was a dead end if one did not use that leisure to pursue Spirit and help others. He was soon to come to the realization that, as the Tibetans say, *Samsara and nirvana are one (illusion and reality)—you cannot understand one without the other.*

Reading on the beach how the Masters had assisted Godfre and his colleagues to prosper in gold mining, he saw that the pursuit of spirit and the material world were not necessarily at odds, that they could both be carried out simultaneously. If the Masters had helped Godfre find gold, maybe they would also help him develop the gold claims owned by his father-in-law, which were lying undeveloped, and whose wealth would prosper many deserving souls.

Feeling divinely inspired, Jason decided to develop this potential wealth for funding humanitarian projects. He didn't need more money himself, as he had made enough to live on indefinitely, but as a compassionate

---

89　Godfre Ray King, *The Magic Presence* (Saint Germain Press, 1989).

being, he wanted to benefit those whom he loved and in whose projects he believed. To further the development of these gold mines, he formed a joint venture, selling royalty shares to those he wanted to prosper. When people heard of his project, which he had dedicated to the Masters, hundreds of people who shared his vision bought shares, and many volunteered to help him in this project without any thought of pay.

Now he was calling from Hawaii to say that after reading my book, he wanted to give me a royalty share. As I didn't have the five thousand dollars that a share cost, I was grateful to be included in the project, already thinking how I was going to spend the vast sums he predicted would soon be pouring into our bank accounts. Talking to him over the phone, I found his excitement infectious and soon began making plans to go to Hawaii to help with the project. Although I would volunteer my time, I hoped that at least my living expenses would be covered. *Perhaps he had a bungalow overlooking the beach where I could stay? In that tropical paradise I would not need much money, and anyway, in a few months I would be wealthy.*

With a casual *"Mahalo"*,[90] Jason said to come out to the Islands. It was all set; I was to fly out in a week. We would have brunch Saturday morning and discuss what part I would play in this unfolding adventure. Little did I dream what an adventure it would be, that going to Hawaii was only the first step in a journey that would lead, not to a physical mine, but to gold of a completely different sort—one that would require courage and training from the Masters to refine.

After landing in Hilo, I took a taxi to the motel where I would spend my first night. As I walked to my room, I saw the billowing waves of the ocean through the palms and heard their thunderous crash on the shore. Since it was early in the day and I was not going to see Jason until the following morning, I had the whole day to relax from the trip. I changed into my bathing trunks to go for a swim, but on coming downstairs I was told at the front desk that the coast on this part of the Island was too rocky for swimming. Eager to cool off, I headed for the pool.

I opened the pool gate and found the place almost deserted, only a single woman lying on a chaise lounge at the opposite end. The noise of the gate closing startled her, and she sat up. Her long, black hair fell about her shoulders, and as she looked toward me I saw that she was Asian, eyes

---

90 Hawaiian: "Thank you." Literally, "May the breath of God be in you."

reminiscent of the woman I'd been seeing lately in my dreams. *Could it really be her? Is this why I've been brought here?*

Without another thought, I plunged into the pool and swam to the other end. Pulling myself out of the water, I sat dripping beside her. I turned to look directly at her, and saw looking back at me the same eyes from my dreams, the same intimate smile, and I could not withdraw my gaze. She seemed to welcome my directness, and returned my gaze. *Does she recognize me, too?*

This was truly the woman I had been dreaming about—sitting here before me in the flesh. Yet as we sat there smiling, our hearts seeming to beat in unison, I could think of nothing to say. For a moment my mind went blank. Though I wanted to bury my face in her long, dark hair and inhale the fragrance of the plumerias which seemed to be emanating from her, I was speechless. Suddenly, a pang of caution turned my attention inward. *Where is this heading, and is that truly what I want? Is this for our highest good, and the Masters' Plan?*

I called to Saint Germain, yet even before hearing a reply, I knew with the same pang of remorse as when I'd parted from Elizabeth that this was a further test on my path of apprenticeship. This woman, the seeming embodiment of every feminine grace, was the reflection of all that I lacked within myself, and therefore desired. Yet I knew if I allowed inertia to take its course and tried to fulfill that longing in the pursuit of temporary fulfillment, I would fall from the grace of the Masters and lose sight of my lifetime goal.

I had made my decision. I stood up, and without having said a word, plunged again into the pool and swam back to the opposite side, where I had entered. Without looking back, I picked up my towel and walked back up the stairs to my room.

Did I just turn my back on the woman of my dreams? Is this the one I'm destined to be with, who would bring the happiness the Masters have brought me here to meet? Should I rush back downstairs? I pushed aside the curtains and looked down on the pool, but she was gone—the whole pool area was completely empty. I wondered if she was even a real woman? I remembered how once before Saint Germain had tested me by taking on the form of a woman at the Ritz Hotel in Madrid. If this woman I had just met was really meant to be in my life, the Masters would bring it about one way or another, and I would meet her again. When something is destined, it cannot be avoided. Once more I was torn between indulging my lower self, which led to the bondage of the five senses, or disciplining my attention and following my Higher Self to liberation. Sometimes it is not clear which self was which, for relationship is also a part of Mastery, but in this case I knew that I had made the right decision.

When I phoned Jason to tell him I had arrived and to confirm our meeting the next day, to my dismay his wife said he had just left for Los Angeles. An investor was flying in from Europe, and Jason had needed to travel immediately to meet him.

"Can you stay for a week until he returns?" Dechen asked, not mentioning the beach house I had fantasized or any place else I could stay. And since I couldn't afford to stay in the motel much longer, I sensed that the door here had suddenly closed.

"No, I can't wait that long. I'll go to LA and meet him there." I felt that once he and I connected in person, everything would fall into place.

It seemed I'd wasted time and money. I had spent almost everything I had on the plane ticket and the motel, anticipating that when I began working on the gold mining project, all expenses would be covered. Disillusioned, I picked up the phone to reserve a seat on the next flight to LA, departing in the morning. *Did the Masters bring me to Hilo only to test my vows, the commitment to the Order of Melchizedek?* The next morning, as the plane ascended from the runway and climbed high into the sky, I realized that the name Hilo contained my answer: *hi—low*. There had been a choice between two paths, one high and one low, and I had chosen the higher.

I did not realize that the trial between the conflicting forces within myself was only the beginning of an adventure that would take me into the midst of a struggle between outer forces that infused the world. Up until then, I had viewed evil as merely the absence of good, darkness as the absence of light, rather than objective forces. Now I would go head to head with forces of evil, a dark brotherhood which I thought only existed in occult novels, and which sought to control humanity.

Chapter 42

The Battle for Hollywood

In Los Angeles I stayed with a friend, who offered to put me up for a few nights until I could connect with Jason. But he became tied up with other investors seeking to participate in the gold project, and our meeting was postponed yet again. After days of further delays, and feeling I was overstaying my friend's hospitality, I began to wonder, *Is there some other reason I am in LA other than to meet with Jason?* In meditation, I invoked God:

> *Beloved I AM Presence, Great Host of Ascended Masters, come forth! Take complete command here, and show me beyond the shadow of a doubt what I should do!*

Immersed in the sea of awareness, where ego dissolves and self merges with Source, I was free of fear, doubt, and uncertainty, reborn into a consciousness without reference points—one of luminous, pure being. Refreshed by this immersion in Source, I later returned to the world of duality to observe an idea arise like a bubble in the still pool of my awareness. In that bubble I saw written "Rebecca," a friend from Mount Shasta I hadn't seen in many years, and I knew that I should phone her. I had heard she was in Los Angeles and that she was no longer the hippie who had camped in a teepee on the Mountain, but was now a "head hunter" and deal maker in the movie business. She lived in Grenada Hills in the San Fernando Valley with her boyfriend, freelance artist Thomas Lake, who worked in the movie business, and her twelve-year-old son, Arthur.

I followed through on the vision and phoned her. She was happy to hear from me and offered an invitation to come out that afternoon. Her spacious home in the hills amid horse stables was more rural than my apartment in Mount Shasta. Walking around the neighborhood, she and Thomas led me on a path into the Santa Susanna Mountains. We walked uphill until we came to a lookout where we could see the entire San Fernando Valley spread out beneath us.

Later, over dinner, we began talking about the movie business and the power of film to expand the consciousness of humanity. Since *Star Wars* had raised the bar by revealing universal truths through characters such as Yoda and Obi-Wan Kenobi, it seemed that by presenting advanced concepts as entertainment, anything was increasingly possible. As dinner progressed and I told of meeting Saint Germain in Muir Woods and other experiences with the Ascended Masters, Thomas became excited and said, "We've got to make a movie of this!" He wanted to start writing immediately and asked me to move in and share their house so we could work together. He had always dreamed of starting his own studio, and saw our collaboration as a move in that direction. Wondering if this was going to be a new career at which I could make a living, I silently invoked the God Presence:

I AM the Illumining, Revealing Presence of God, showing me the Divine Plan. Take complete command, and reveal to everyone here the part they are to play.

Gradually, a scintillating radiation began to fill the room, which I could feel raising my vibratory rate. Rebecca, who had also studied with Pearl, finally blurted out, "Good Lord, don't you guys feel that? Is there any doubt in your mind that this is the plan, that the Masters want you and Thomas to work together?" I was glad she had been the one to identify the energy and had interpreted it as an invitation. Her words certainly seemed to be the answer to my call.

I now knew that working with these Ascended Master Friends was the next step on my circuitous path. It was clear from my frequent visits to the etheric retreats, especially the one in Burbank where I had seen the film deal put together, that the Masters wanted certain truths, especially that of the individualized God Presence, to be made known through feature films. Excited, I began thinking of the films Thomas and I would produce for the Masters.

Their two-story house had an unused room which I was given, and Rebecca told me not to worry about money, as they would furnish me with everything I needed. She asked only that I drive her son to his Montessori school in the Valley every day and pick him up again in the afternoon—engaging me as a live-in chauffeur/screenwriter. I was better off than many of those who came to Hollywood to promote themselves, who had to wait on tables, park cars, or prostitute their talents in other ways before they could interest anyone, if ever, in what they were promoting. Over the course of my stay, the chauffeuring job morphed into being a private messenger for her as well, and I would make deliveries to various high-powered film executives. Since I was told to put the documents in the hands of only the specific addressee, not a secretary or subordinate, I often found myself face to face with some well-known Hollywood producers. To my surprise, they were often interested in me and who I was, and when they heard I was from Mount Shasta, they wanted to hear about the Masters and UFOs rumored to use the mountain as a base.

I moved in the next morning, and as soon as I had unpacked my few belongings, Thomas and I went outside and sat by the pool to discuss our first film. Under the eternally blue sky of southern California, we looked out over the San Fernando Valley—a place reminiscent of Steven Spielberg's film, where E.T. had landed and stumbled downhill into a suburban home like this.

Little did I realize that a real extra-terrestrial would visit soon, and that I would need his protection in a real-life battle being waged among the Masters and a certain extra-terrestrial race striving for control of the Earth. Sitting on the green, immaculately-trimmed lawn, embraced by the balmy air, it was hard to imagine that the whole world was not as tranquil as this southern California paradise. However, this place would not remain peaceful for long, once our project to enlighten humanity came to the attention of those powerful aliens seeking to further enslave the Earth's population. My trust in the basic goodness of all beings was soon to be challenged.

Our writing went spectacularly at first, and I enjoyed the excitement of writing a story that I felt certain was going to be made into a movie, especially one that would raise all who saw it into a higher consciousness. At the end of a day of writing, and excited about my new career as a screenwriter, I would doze off to sleep at night in my new home, thinking about our forthcoming films. This new mission from the Masters, of making their teachings readily acceptable, which had dropped into my lap out of the blue, seemed to be unfolding perfectly. However, my confidence was short-lived. A few nights later, I woke to the certainty that I was not alone. I felt a malevolent presence in the room, and the crack of a whip snapped me upright in bed, staring into the shadows. As my eyes adjusted to the darkness, I saw that by the door stood a figure in black armor and helmet, holding a whip in his hand. He cracked the whip again, flicking the space above my head, amid peels of defiant laughter.

In a chilling voice, he said, "I know of your plans, and I am here to stop you...none of the work you and Thomas do will succeed."

"That is what you think," I replied, then shouted at this being that exuded pure malevolence, "The Light of God Never Fails!"

But he only laughed arrogantly, "Your words don't frighten me. None of your scripts will succeed, because I will stop them."

"I challenge you in the name of the Christ, be gone!" I fired back, but he laughed again, then vanished into the darkness, and I fell back into an anxious sleep.

I awoke in the morning with my head still in the dark cloud of the night's visitation, but didn't tell Thomas and Rebecca. *After all, maybe it was just an astral being, some disembodied soul trying to scare me, and nothing will come of it.* I was confident that the Light would triumph over this specter of the night, whatever illusory thing it might be, and I didn't want to introduce any doubts into the minds of my new associates. I used the Violet Consuming Flame to dissolve my fears, and banished the memory of the event.

During breakfast, Rebecca invited me to go with her and Thomas that evening to see a well-known psychic by the name of Grey, who channeled a being from another world by the name of Ashbar. Knowing the Masters' warnings about staying away from channeling and psychic phenomena, I didn't want to go, and that feeling only intensified when I heard the entity's name. I had a bad feeling about him, but Rebecca and Thomas had been going to these channelings for months and were so enamored of him that I felt to say no would disrupt our harmonious association.

They visited many psychics, I was soon to learn, spending a major portion of their budget on finding out when various projects were supposed to succeed. Despite the fact that many of these channeled entities called themselves "Saint Germain," none of them agreed, and little of the information proved accurate. Yet Rebecca and Thomas' ardor for ever-new psychic input seemed never-ending.

The longer I stayed in Los Angeles, the more I saw how these psychics fed off human vanity, telling people how special they were, what famous personages they had been in past lives, or how famous, happy, and rich they would soon become. If things didn't work out as they'd promised, the psychic would channel that the situation had changed, and that they should come back for frequent updates. This way people never developed their own inner guidance or took responsibility for their own decisions—which precluded any growth. Although mirroring the spiritual world, the psychic domain is only a seductive reflection, full of human thoughts, emotions, and disembodied entities, and devoid of true light.[91]

Few realize that we dwell in a pool of psychic energy in which disembodied spirits—people who have died—as well as humanly created thought forms, seek to live off our life force. They accomplish this by attaching themselves to people who open themselves up to psychics and the energy they channel. Or they try to provoke us to strong emotion, such as fear, anger, and lust—generating *loosh,* the psychic force on which they sustain themselves.[92]

I was fortunate during the days of darkness ahead, that I had developed the facility to dissolve this *loosh* with the Violet Consuming Flame, a transmuting activity which can be invoked at any moment. However, the energy I would soon confront did not reside on the astral plane, but came from another world. I had always thought that Earth must be the least developed planet, that residents of other worlds must be more highly evolved. I never realized that there were beings from other worlds visiting the Earth who, although more technologically advanced, had the aim of enslaving humanity and colonizing it for their own purposes.

With a sense of foreboding, I accepted Rebecca and Thomas' invitation to attend the channeling that evening. When we entered Grey's house in West Los Angeles I felt a tense knot in my solar plexus, and a wave of nausea swept over me. I kept looking toward the door, trying to think of some way I could excuse myself, but felt compelled to stay, in order to discover what sway this channel had over my friends. The longer I stayed, though, the more I felt a psychic force begin to envelop the group and try to bring it under its control, and I asked myself, *Why did I let Thomas and Rebecca bring me here?* The line from the poem by Alexander Pope ran through my head, *Fools rush in where angels fear to tread,* and I had certainly rushed into this den of darkness. Now that I was stuck, I asked for protection and visualized myself surrounded by a ball of light.

Sitting on cushions on the floor before the channeling began, we watched as Grey sat motionless in the chair at the front of the room.

---

[91] *"Tell me, my friend, do you know of two (psychics) that agree? And why, since truth is one, and that putting entirely the question of discrepancies in details aside—we do not find them agreeing even upon the most vital problems."* Master Kuthumi Lal Singh, *The Mahatma Letters,* 2nd ed., Letter 48.

[92] Robert Monroe, *Journeys Out of the Body.*

Suddenly he stiffened, as Ashbar seemingly entered his body and Grey appeared to go unconscious.

"Good evening to you all, in the name of all that is...." began the Entity, in a deep voice that made me shiver. To my surprise, despite the energy of evil that filled the room, a discourse of great intelligence and wit followed. Had it not been for the entity's brilliant insight into human nature, the feeling of revulsion in my solar plexus was shouting only one message: *Run!* But since I could not leave without upsetting my friends and the rest of the group, I remained a captive.

Ashbar claimed to come from another star system in a different space/time continuum than ours and to be living on a large star cruiser from which he visited the Earth, a sort of orbiting broadcast station. I saw that what was so seductive was the intimate knowledge he had of the minds and lives of those in attendance. He had the ability to speak to people about details of their lives, private things of which even friends were not aware. This caused them to mistakenly believe *If someone knows me this well, they must not only be enlightened, but also benevolent.*

Although much that he said was common sense, some of his statements were deceptive, and I thought, *You can catch more flies with honey than vinegar.* Only by speaking words of wisdom can the elect be caught, the brilliant ones who, despite their vast intellects, miss seeing the forest for the trees. They miss the obvious, because they are out of touch with their hearts. I knew I was in the presence of a master deceiver, sowing trust in the minds of his followers so he could later harvest their souls. Here was an otherworldly Jim Jones, the cult leader who doled out the cyanide-laced Kool-Aid to his unquestioning followers. *How sad,* I thought. *People want to believe in someone so badly because they do not believe in themselves—they do not yet know of their own individualized God Presence that is with them always, ready to pour out whatever they need.*

During the question and answer session that followed the channeling, someone asked Grey, "If you're so enlightened, how come your energy is like Darth Vader (the villain from *Star Wars*)?" But this master deceiver gave the elusive answer, "All is in the mind of the beholder. You could only perceive in me an aspect of yourself." *Truth again, but used to dissemble.* He had diverted the attention away from the obvious.

After returning home, Rebecca and Thomas asked me for my impression. I told them, hesitatingly, that I didn't trust him, that despite his brilliance, I didn't like his energy. When I mentioned the person who had said he felt like Darth Vader, Rebecca said that his demonic sounding voice was caused by the stress on the human vocal cords of a higher being, and that I would get used to it.

That's called "possession," I wanted to say, but kept quiet. There was no distortion of Pearl's voice, or of Godfre Ray King's voice, when they spoke, despite the cosmic beings who worked through them. Nor were they taken over by anyone other than the God Self. And when the Masters had appeared to me and dictated the discourses for *"I AM" the Open Door*, the energy had been euphoric and benevolent. An exquisite radiation had filled the room, that anyone present would have felt.

Soon Thomas and I were so engrossed in a script that I didn't give much more thought to Ashbar. We began working on our plan to bring the Ascended Master teachings into film with a fascinating trilogy about Saint Germain's most recent embodiments.

The first film in the series would chronicle Saint Germain's earlier life as Sir Francis Bacon, son of Queen Elizabeth I and the Earl of Leicester by a secret marriage in the Tower, and rightful heir to the throne of England. When he could no longer advance the cause of the Light in England, he feigned death, staged a mock funeral which he himself attended, and disappeared to the Continent, where he headed several occult groups. Eventually, he disappeared to the Himalayas, where he completed his Ascension.

Doing historical research at the University of California, I discovered that there was indeed a hidden code in the Shakespeare plays that revealed their true authorship, as well as the secret of Francis Bacon's birth to the "Virgin Queen," Elizabeth. I discovered that "Shakespeare" was a reference to Athena, the Greek goddess of truth, who shook her spear of wisdom at ignorance. It was also the name of a stable boy at the Globe Theater, who was paid for the use of his name.[93]

The next two films in the series would focus on Saint Germain's later appearances, the first as an Ascended being in Europe prior to the French Revolution, who appeared as several different personages, depending on

---

[93] Marie Bauer, *Foundations Unearthed* (Veritas Press, 1948) p.3: "William Shakespeare, the Stratford man, most definitely could not have written them (the plays), because it has been proved time and again, beyond the shadow of a doubt, that William Shakespeare could not read or write."

the needs of the occasion. He worked to reform the nobility and awaken them to the needs of the people, warning of the impending anarchy and Reign of Terror.

The last film would tell of the Master's secret work in founding the United States, a country whose destiny he helped shape.[94, 95] He had the vision of America as a land free from the control of the international bankers who ruled the Old World from behind the scenes.[96] The series would end showing his current role in international affairs, also as mentor of the New Age, a time when many individuals will realize their God Dominion.

Because of his previous work in the film industry, Thomas had contacts in Hollywood, and we soon had interest in our work from several producers. An occult group involved with delving into the mysteries of Francis Bacon came forward and expressed their willingness to be of assistance—as they too wanted to see the Masters' Plan for humanity made known. Throughout the series of films, we revealed how the Masters' plans had been subverted by the international financiers,[97] who were working behind the scenes to subjugate humanity.[98, 99] We hoped that by making

---

94 Manly P. Hall, *The Secret Destiny of America* (Philosophical Research Society, 2000).
95 David Allen Rivera; ir.nmu.org.ua/bitstream/handle/123456789/118455/60185df6d39672b90c4762609b00492e.pdf.
96 G. Edward Griffin, *The Creature from Jekyll Island: A Second Look at the Federal Reserve* (Amer Media, 2002). Also: James J. Puplava interview with G. Edward Griffin, October 28, 2006, at www.financialsense.com/Experts/2006Griffin.html: *"The Federal Reserve Act was not drafted in the halls of Congress, it was drafted in secret on this private island off the coast of Georgia which was completely owned in those days – it was a private club actually called the Jekyll Island club – by a small group of billionaires from New York...."*
97 John Perkins, *Confessions of an Economic Hitman* (Berrett-Koehler, 2004). How the International Monetary Fund and World Bank take over third world countries through making loans they know can never be repaid.
98 Webster G. Tarpley, "Part 7, British Financial Warfare: 1929; 1931-33, How the City of London Created the Great Depression," excerpted from *Against Oligarchy: Essays and Speeches 1970-1996*, downloaded from tarpley.net/online-books/against-oligarchy/british-financial-warfare.
99 Matt Taibbi, "The Bailout, How Goldman Sachs Runs Washington,"

the truth known, these secret forces seeking to control the world would be overthrown and individual freedom once again flourish. The occult group's members were afraid, however, that these very banking families that had worked to gain control of America, and who owned the media, would do anything to prevent our films from being produced, possibly closing them down as well.

Before long we had written a synopsis for our first film, known in the movie business as a "treatment," which I named *The William Shakespeare Conspiracy*. In it, we told how Francis Bacon's secret plan for the New World, his memoirs, as well as the manuscripts of the Shakespearean plays and the original King James Bible—which he edited and which to this day has never been found—were all brought to colonial Williamsburg and hidden in a vault buried beneath Bruton Church. That vault was found in 1938 by Marie Bauer Hall, an occultist who deciphered the code of the plays and realized that the Bruton Church that was restored was not the original one where the treasure was buried.[100] But her excavation at the site was halted, and it is theorized that during the night the copper containers that held these manuscripts were likely removed. In this repository were original manuscripts detailing the true history of England and the hidden financial forces at work behind the crown—secrets which, if revealed, would threaten the current version of history and the centuries-old control certain families and secret societies have on world power.

Such efforts to control humanity, I was soon to learn, did not originate on Earth, but were the work of certain beings from other planetary systems who wanted to enslave humanity for their own purposes. To achieve these ends, they took birth as humans, often oblivious of their origins until awakened to their purpose later in life. They worked as well on the invisible planes as a sort of Dark Brotherhood, influencing various people in positions of power for their own ends. These forces would use whatever means were at their disposal to prevent their plans from being revealed or interfered with. As this dark order was obviously already aware of our efforts to bring higher consciousness into the film business, they struck just as Thomas and I were preparing to pitch *The William Shakespeare Conspiracy* to an agent who had connections at a major studio.

Rolling Stone, July 2009. How the same forces today are actively working to control the government and the money supply.

100 Marie Bauer, *Foundations Unearthed,* p.3.

Attacked

It was Halloween, when astral entities that feed on human fear and anger become empowered by the attention on demonic thought forms created by marketing and the media. It seemed as if whole neighborhoods were transformed into hell realms, populated by roving demons. Our neighborhood in the Valley was somewhat spared due to its remoteness, so with no ghoulish "trick-or-treaters" expected to knock on our door, we went to bed early.

Sometime during the night, I was awakened by an evil presence in the room. Sitting up, wide awake, I was terrified to see the man in black armor who had so defiantly threatened to stop my work, but this time he held a long spear in one hand. Not alone this time, legions of warriors stood behind him. On either side of him crouched huge, red-eyed dogs, their fangs dripping, barely able to restrain themselves from rushing toward me.

As I lunged to turn on the light, I felt a searing pain, and realized he had thrust his spear into my left hip. As the light came on and I whirled around, he withdrew his lance and retreated a few steps.

"Mighty I AM Presence, great host of Ascended Masters, come forth!" I called out. "Jesus, Saint Germain, Archangel Michael, come forth and take command here!" I pleaded for help, but to my shock and dismay there was no response. I was alone with these demons, and I realized, *No one is coming to my rescue—I am going to have to save myself.*

The being in black threw his head back and laughed as he had before, "Words…you think I am afraid of words?"

His voice was familiar. *Where have I recently heard that deep, controlling voice?* Suddenly, the truth struck me in the solar plexus: *Ashbar, my partners' psychic mentor! Their own teacher was working against them, against our efforts together for the Masters.*

"I told you, your scripts will come to naught. I will block your work with Thomas, and there is nothing you can do to stop me!" he threatened, taking a few steps closer, as he raised his lance and prepared to jab me again. Although I saw no blood on the sheets, I was sure I was bleeding heavily, for his first thrust must have penetrated to the bone. The pain was so sharp I was unable to stand, and fearing that his next strike would hit a more vital organ, I wondered, *How am I going to defend myself?*

Dismayed that no Master had responded to my call for help, I felt abandoned by those I had sworn to serve and who had always protected me. Alone in my fear, I turned my attention within and felt my heart pounding. *My fate is in my own hands!* I realized. Yet, fighting seemed out of the question. Unable to rise, I watched the monstrous, red-eyed dogs glowering and growling as they inched closer, realizing they would soon be upon me—and Ashbar's legions raised their lances and advanced.

Fully realizing now that no Master was coming to intervene, and that I was unable to stand to protect myself, my attention dove to the center of my being and immersed itself in the wellspring of my own Divinity. There, suddenly charged with energy, and emboldened by my own God Nature, I called forth that Infinite Power before which no evil can endure:

Divine Love, come forth!

And from the central sun of my own being shot a fiery ray of light, piercing Ashbar's heart, enfolding him in its all-embracing presence. Stunned by my unexpected response, he took a step backward.

Continuing to go deeper into my heart, I tapped into a reservoir of love that I didn't know I possessed, and I called that essence forth to bless Ashbar and his hoard, watching that light engulf every being in the room.

As the love penetrated their hearts, I saw my adversaries continue to retreat. Seeing the Power of Love, this newly-discovered, ultimate weapon, I turned my attention deeper yet, and sent out another golden ball of this miraculous substance—and this wave of energy caused the demon to cringe, and his entire entourage to retreat. Even the red-eyed dogs cringed backward, whimpering. Continuing to emanate more of this energy and consciousness, which is the power that holds together every atom in creation, I watched these demonic beings retreat like shadows before the approaching dawn.

Trembling with exhaustion, I lay on my bed astonished, not only that the Masters had not responded to my call, but that I had been able to protect myself. *Who would think that love would prove the most powerful weapon of all?* Although I knew that the Masters were always watching and that nothing transpires without their awareness, it seemed that they wanted me to learn that *all I need is within me—that same force they wield, I wield also.* Had I not had the need to invoke it, that power would have remained dormant. Mastery is not achieved by relying on the Masters, but in applying Mastery.[101]

Now that Ashbar and his hordes had withdrawn and would hopefully leave me alone for the rest of the night, I pulled back the sheet to examine my wound. Expecting to find a pool of blood, I was surprised to find that my body was unmarked, though drenched in perspiration. Exhausted by my struggle, I fell back asleep.

In the morning I awoke to a piercing pain where Ashbar's spear had struck my left hip, a reminder that my attack during the night had not been a dream, but very real. When I hobbled downstairs to have breakfast with Thomas and Rebecca, and they asked why I was walking so strangely, I told them of my assault during the night—and that the attacker had been none other than their guru, Ashbar.

"Impossible!" Rebecca exploded. "Ashbar is a being of more love and wisdom than you can possibly comprehend. He would be incapable of harming anyone. You must have just had a bad dream," she fired, storming out of the room red-faced. Thomas, however, was more open and wanted to hear my story again, asking why I hadn't called out for help. I explained that I had felt that by calling for help I would have been invoking fear, and that they would have used that sign of weakness to attack. The love had thrown them completely off guard.

Thomas questioned me further, and I told him about the first time Ashbar had visited me the night had I moved in, but which I had kept to myself. Just as I was telling him about Ashbar's threat to stop our work, the phone rang. It was the agent who had been interested in *The William Shakespeare Conspiracy,* and who we were to meet that afternoon, now canceling our appointment. He said he had bounced the idea off some people he knew at various studios, and no one wanted to risk the wrath of the shareholders by challenging the accepted view of history supported by the establishment. The big money families wrote history for their own ends, the control of humanity, and they were all afraid of the consequences of such a revelation. They owned the school textbook publishing companies that hid the secret role of their families in engineering a one

---

101 Which is perhaps the realization Krishnamurti hoped to convey by his dramatic break from the Theosophists, and his later teachings on the need to discover the true Self, which he said could only be found through self-observation.

world government under their control. Thomas looked at me in shock, the synchronicity of the phone call giving some credence to my statement that Ashbar was indeed working against us.

"Please don't tell anyone," I begged Thomas, still traumatized by the night's visitation, fearful that even the mention of Ashbar's name would draw his attention and invoke another attack. Hearing the fear in my voice, Thomas was convinced of the truth of my experience. However, despite my pleas to remain silent, he felt it was his duty to warn the rest of the group that their guru was not the virtuous, humanity-loving being he pretended to be, and he reached for the phone.

Most of those Thomas called were incredulous and told him that I must have simply had a bad dream. But two people told of being sent on missions by Ashbar that had almost gotten them killed. Another said that he, too, had been suspicious of Ashbar, and that he had intended to tell the group at the next meeting. But driving home from the last channeling, he had been run off the road by a car whose driver seemed to be in a trance.

As Thomas repeated my story to more students, I could feel Ashbar's increasing attention, and the knot in my solar plexus ached, and I began to feel nauseous. I could tell he was displeased.

Only returning to the sanctity of my heart, and immersing myself in the love there, protected me from his hostility. The Masters still seemed in abeyance, as if they had said, "You can handle this on your own." So again I visualized a golden sun around me, the center of which was my heart. And I projected a beam of that light from my heart to Ashbar, whose image I pictured before me in black armor, visualizing my light becoming a golden sun in his heart. I held that image as long as I could, intensifying it, still calling on the Masters to take complete command of this being who seemed intent on destroying me, and who was already interfering with the work the Masters had sent me to Hollywood to accomplish. Despite the fact that I didn't feel them around, I knew they heard every thought, and called on them to:

Turn this being to the Path of Light, and bring about the Highest Plan for his evolution and awakening to Divine Love!

During the coming days, it was this love that continued to be my protection. Whenever I would feel his sinister energy coalescing in my aura, I would stop whatever I was doing and consciously generate that feeling. And when I could not feel the love, I would at least say the words,

I AM enfolding you in Divine Love.

And I would ask the Masters to bless and awaken him to the Inner Christ Light. The words of Paul the Apostle came to mind, *Perfect love casteth out fear,* and as I focused on that love, the fear gradually decreased.

Rejoining Thomas, I found that more of the people in Ashbar's group were beginning to believe him and were taking what Thomas told them about as a valid warning. Apparently, I was correct in feeling that this angered Ashbar and that he wanted me out of the way, for the next day after dining at a restaurant in Topanga Canyon, the Inn of the Seventh Ray, as I sped down the tortuous road, I heard a voice claiming to be Saint Germain tell me to pass the lumbering truck in front of me. I floored the accelerator and pulled out, around the truck, into the upcoming lane, where a sports car zooming up the canyon swerved to avoid me and blared its horn in anger. The voice I had heard, I realized too late, was that of Ashbar in the guise of the Master.

A Space Traveler's Warning

Before going to bed that night, and hoping I would catch up on the sleep I had missed during the attack of the night before, I called to the I AM Presence for protection. As I lay with my head on the pillow, I heard a high-pitched humming in one ear, which I associated with UFOs when they monitor those with whom they are working, and remembering the rendezvous I had had with Saint Germain, Semjasse, and my other space traveler friends at Lake Louise, I soon fell asleep.

My sleep was shallow, interrupted by noises downstairs. I seemed to hear doors slamming and furniture being moved in the living room. Finally, I awoke to find a familiar man in a jumpsuit standing at the side of my bed, looking dispassionately at me. His form was outlined in a soft, bluish light, and I recognized my old acquaintance, the space traveler who had fetched me from my room at Chateau Lake Louise before we journeyed in his silvery craft to the Earth's interior. Now he signaled not to talk, and began speaking telepathically.

I have come to tell you that your efforts on behalf of Ashbar have not gone unnoticed. He and other inhabitants of his system have been causing us problems for many ages.

As you are aware, my race and Earth's humanity are related in that we come from the same ancestors. Ashbar and his followers are also distantly related, having migrated here after a galactic war in which we defeated them. While we overcame our selfishness and tendency to aggression long ago, Ashbar's race continues to regard peace as a weakness, and they pursue their desire for dominion through mind control and subterfuge, and if necessary, outright war.

Ashbar himself is only an advance agent in what you would call psychological operations. They do not seek to destroy humanity, rather to enslave it through psychological manipulation, for their own selfish ends—hence their intense interest in the film and entertainment industry, which is the single most effective medium to encourage fear, anger, greed, vanity, and lust. In this way, they seek to control the subconscious, in which they subliminally implant suggestions and associations that act as mind control mechanisms.

We can protect the few who, like yourself, seek to protect themselves by turning to the Source within and invoking the light, and who avoid subjecting themselves to the negative conditioning of the media through which these entities propagate their control. But we can do little to protect the masses who willingly expose themselves to destructive input from the media. Because of our respect for free will, we cannot interfere in the lessons they themselves choose to learn; and we cannot prevent the consequences of those choices, which are a part of the lesson.

There is a battle going on for control of this planet—the forces of control and suppression versus the forces of self-empowerment and liberation—and you are now right in the midst of this struggle. I have come to tell you that we will give you all the protection we can. This does not mean that you can lower your guard, for it is through your own instinct for self-preservation, your own intuition, that we and the Great Masters inspire you to be at the right place, at the right time, so that you come to no harm.

Be warned, Ashbar works not only through his influence over the human mind and his ability to implant suggestions, but also through his influence over astral entities that he controls telepathically, and who unconsciously do his bidding. Since we cannot protect you from your own desires and impulsiveness, I am telling you now—stay centered, and be on your guard!*

Showing no emotion after delivering his silent warning, the space traveler merely nodded to me, then turned and walked out of the room, slamming the door behind him with a loud bang. *For someone who has navigated the far reaches of space to come here, he's awfully clumsy,* I thought. *And how did he enter the house? We lock all the doors before going to bed—yet he seems to have free access to go wherever he wishes.* Thinking I would have to ask Thomas in the morning if he had left any doors open and if he had been downstairs in the living room in the middle of the night rearranging the furniture, I fell back to sleep.

When I awakened, the memory of the space traveler and his warning was still fresh in my mind. Any doubts that his visit had been a dream vanished when I saw that my table, which I always kept flush against the wall, had been rotated 45 degrees into the room, and when I went downstairs, the heavy living room sofa and love seat were both askew, several feet from their normal location. The doors and windows were all locked, as usual.

Coming downstairs, the first thing Thomas and Rebecca asked was why I had moved the furniture. They had not experienced anything unusual during the night, except Thomas had heard the slamming of a door. I kept quiet about the visitor, who had been able to enter and leave the house during the night without a key, and the warning he had delivered. I realized that his apparent clumsiness had been to awaken me to the reality of his visit, so that I would not think it had merely been a dream.

After working on our script for several hours that morning, Thomas and I made sandwiches and took them into the back yard to eat in the sun on the grassy embankment overlooking the Valley. As we ate, I noticed a strange pattern in the tall, dry grass of the terraced hill below us and put my sandwich down to investigate. Although the brown grass was several feet tall, it was matted down in a clockwise swirl, forming a circle about three feet in diameter, as though a huge dog had turned around there many times before lying down. About fifteen feet away, Thomas discovered another swirl, and equidistant from the first two, forming a triangle, was a third matted circle.

We looked at each other in recognition, for we had both seen photos of identical patterns where UFOs had landed. Small shuttle craft had three metallic spheres on the bottom, which made these impressions. Observing these telltale patterns, I then felt I should tell him about my experience with the space traveler during the night. Thomas now said he recalled hearing someone walking around inside the house—but hadn't seen anyone and thought it was me. I told him that the space traveler said we needed to be on guard—a warning that came none too soon.

Returning from buying groceries in Thomas' run-down Datsun the next day, and just as I rounded the last bend of the road that wound uphill to the dead end street where we lived, a car lurched across the road and bore down on me. As I leaned on the horn and swerved onto the dirt shoulder, barely avoiding a head on collision, I saw the blank look on the face of the woman at the wheel as she hurtled by—and realized she was under psychic domination. As I had been warned, Ashbar had controlled this weak-minded person, and used her car like a weapon! Grateful that I had been alert enough to avoid her, I pulled back on the road and drove the remaining few hundred yards to the house.

Unwilling to give in to the fear which his threats had initially provoked, I continued to try to send love in return—still visualizing that beam of light going from my heart to his. Even if the Masters and my Pleiadian friends were ultimately giving protection, it was still up to me to deal with my own emotions and dispel the fear. To free myself from that fear, which came about through living in the ego which was separate from the Source, I also invoked the Violet Consuming Flame. And I continued to call on the Masters to raise this being out of his ignorance, for I knew that eventually all the suffering he caused others would return the same suffering to him, if not in this life, then in future ones; and as a *Bodhisattva* I had sworn to work for the enlightenment of all sentient beings, even ones that appeared in this life as enemies.[102]

In pondering how I had gotten into this battle between warring aliens and psychic forces, I wondered if perhaps I had been around Hollywood too long, with its emphasis on fantasy and use of special effects, if my imagination had morphed into paranoia. But then I felt the pain in my hip where Ashbar had jabbed me with his spear, and I realized that his attack had been very real.

---

[102] Although it is natural to seek out those we like and avoid those we dislike, we often advance more rapidly by seeking out our enemies, or those who oppose us, for it is from them that we learn the most. If not outwardly befriending them, we can do so in our minds, feeling that they are a part of ourselves with whom we need to make peace. We can pray for their well-being and enlightenment, which will advance their growth as well as our own. Since they will show up again, if not in this life then in a future one, we might as well deal with them now. The Four Immeasurables is a foundational Buddhist prayer which liberates the mind:

May all beings have happiness and the causes of happiness.
May all beings be free of suffering and the causes of suffering.
May all beings never be separated from the happiness which is free of suffering.
May all beings be free of attachment to dear ones and aversion to others, and live in the equanimity of all that is.

Ashbar Grants a Boon

Thomas and I tried to put this interference aside and went to work on another script. I found screenwriting to be an exhilarating experience, much like parenting, where the mother and father each assist, yet the child develops its own personality. No matter how inspired the writers of the story, no one contributor prevails, the final movie succeeding only if everyone involved—producers, directors, actors, photographers, agents, and editors and technicians—all surrender their attachment to their own view and learn to work together for the final vision.

We worked almost every waking minute, often while eating or driving on the freeway, and carried notebooks with us, since we never knew when a new idea would emerge that we would want to blend into the evolving story. At least the process kept my mind off Ashbar and the ever-present anticipation of another assault. *Would he attack on the freeway?* He had attacked twice before while I was driving and had plenty of other opportunities, but he was strangely quiet. I wondered if my prayers were beginning to have some effect?

After a ten-day respite, I was driving through the San Fernando Valley to the office supply store in Northridge at eleven in the morning to get an ink cartridge for our printer when I again felt that sickening feeling in my stomach. *Not again!* I thought, feeling Ashbar's approach and becoming nauseous with fear. *Will he attack in full daylight?* If he had been a mere astral entity, morning would have been his weakest time, yet he was not a disembodied entity but claimed to be a visitor from another planetary system.

Pulling into a parking space behind the store, alert for cars that might hurtle out of nowhere, I prepared for whatever trick Ashbar might try. Despite the nausea, I felt no imminent threat, but sat with my hands gripping the steering wheel, waiting. Then I heard his words as clearly as though with headphones:

"I want to ask your forgiveness for what I have done to you," he said, in a softer tone than I had heard him speak before, "and I want to thank you for the work you have been doing on my behalf. To express my gratitude, I wish to grant you a boon. Ask for whatever you want...."

Is this a diversion to throw me off guard? I suspected as much, yet something had changed. Despite his still-unnerving energy, his attitude seemed to have shifted and become almost conciliatory. *Perhaps my effort to send love and my calls to the Masters have done some good? But can I trust him? And what favor can I possibly ask that he could provide? A boon? That sounded like what genies in bottles offered to those who liberated them, or the gift granted mortals who offered their austerities to the Gods in ancient Vedic times.*

I began to think, *What can I possibly ask this hostile alien for, who was my sworn enemy and who had already tried to kill me three times? Is it safe to accept anything from him?*

Since Ashbar had claimed to know Semjasse, the female space traveler from the Pleiades who had taken me to the Inner Earth, and since I had not seen her for a long time and still had many questions to ask about our future work together, I thought it would be safe to ask him to arrange for me to see her. I wanted to meet her on the physical plane, as I had Saint Germain, and to travel with her as had the Swiss farmer Billy Meier, a visit that was well documented.[103] It seemed no harm could come from that request.

After a brief pause, during which I felt his energy depart, then I again felt his presence return, which still put my nerves on edge. He said, "I regret that to grant you that boon is not within my power. Ask for a different boon."

Realizing that my request had been selfish, coming from my ego, I now asked for a boon that I was sure would benefit others.

"I want you to reveal to Grey's group who you really are!"[104]

---

103 Wendelle C. Stevens, *Message From the Pleiades, Volume 1* (UFO Photo Archives, 1988). I have spent many hours talking with Wendelle, a former Lt. Colonel in the U.S. Air Force, who went to Switzerland to meet with Edward "Billy" Meier, and I know his report on the reality of those initial contacts to be accurate. Over several months Billy had numerous physical contacts, some where he was "beamed" aboard Semjasse's craft, and during which he was informed about the Pleiadian mission to help the people of Earth. However, after Semjasse withdrew and the physical contacts ceased, he began channeling supposedly "telepathic" contacts which contain much false information, the validity of which could have been checked by simple historical research (especially with regard to the historical Saint Germain). Hence the need to question all information, regardless of the accuracy of the initial source. See the book of remarkable UFO photos in: Lee Elders, *UFO: Contact From the Pleiades* (Genesis III Publishing, 1979).

104 Although he claimed to be an extraterrestrial visiting Earth from the

"That is what you *really* want?" he replied, thoughtfully.

"Yes, that is my request, and I hold you to your promise, for it is a wish that I know is within your power to grant."

I felt like the legendary, ancient Greek who caught the God Proteus and refused to let go, despite the frightening forms into which he changed, until Proteus had been compelled to grant him a boon.

"Very well, then," Ashbar said, "I will grant your boon. Attend the next channeling, and as you have requested, I will reveal who I am." Then he was gone.

Excited by this surprise contact with the hostile alien and his promised boon, I rushed back to the house and told Thomas of Ashbar's visitation and his promised revelation. He was incredulous—perhaps jaded by the false prophesies and unfulfilled promises he had heard from the psychics he and Rebecca visited every month. Now, when I told him of my conversation with the false guru who had declared war on us, he treated my encounter with skepticism. To test the truth of Ashbar's promise, however, we would not have long to wait, for the next meeting at Grey's was the following night. Neither of us had been to a channeling since my last encounter, but we now planned to attend without fail to see what would happen.

The awaited night arrived, and although Rebecca sat in her usual place on the floor directly at Grey's feet, Thomas and I sat at the back of the room, which was filled to capacity. The night unfolded no differently than usual. After a minute of silence, Ashbar entered Grey's unconscious body, and a discourse ensued. We waited as the voice droned on, but the revelation I was promised did not come, and Thomas looked at me, doubt clearly in his eyes.

Finally came the concluding period of questions and answers, where Ashbar gave personal guidance to his followers, not just in spiritual matters, but about relationship, finance, health, and whatever anyone wanted to ask. Again, his insightful answers impressed on everyone there how clearly he knew the details of their lives—yet they seemed oblivious of

---

future, in a triangular-shaped space ship, the channel said he has never seen this being for whom he has become a vessel. It is quite possible that he is an astral entity native to the Earth, that attached himself to the channel when he first opened his aura to learn channeling in his youth, for when one opens oneself like that, one never knows what will come to stay.

the sinister energy filling the room, which his teachings could not dispel.

Just when I thought I had been duped, and that Ashbar was going to break his promise, a great, winged Cosmic being descended into the room, one whose vast power I had felt from a distance when invoking him in meditation, yet whose awesome form I had never beheld: the living presence of Archangel Michael. I knew that it was a body of projected thought, for had he approached in his true energy body, no one could have withstood that energy. Nonetheless, his presence was breathtaking, and I watched in shock as he pointed a Sword of Blue Flame at Grey's head.

"Now you must keep your promise!" the Archangel commanded.

In obedience to the mighty presence, whose blazing sword hummed like a high voltage power transformer, Ashbar's words slowed, and he began to speak meekly, in carefully chosen phrases. His followers, who were used to his booming voice, now had to lean forward to hear their guru's softly spoken words.

"And now, I would like to acknowledge the assistance that one in this room has been giving me, which has touched my heart, and that has helped me to advance in my own spiritual growth.... In gratitude for that assistance, I would like to keep a promise I made to that person by telling you a little story that will reveal to you who I am...who and *what* I am...and who and what those from my world are who are now visiting your planet.

"Just as every nation has a symbol, an image of what that nation represents, such as the Eagle or the American flag, so, too, do we on my planet have a symbol that represents who we are. On my planet, we have animals that are very similar to your sheep. They are very docile creatures that do not question authority and expect to be taken care of by others. Then there are other beings that resemble your wolves. They put on a disguise that makes them resemble the sheep-like creatures, and they pass among them. When the wolf-like creatures choose, they harvest the docile creatures with such guile, the sheep do not even realize what has happened—not seeing that one of their number is missing. And so, our symbol resembles *a wolf in sheep's clothing.*"

As he finished, Grey's head fell forward on his chest, something no one could remember having seen happen before, and when he raised his face, tears were rolling down his cheeks. Grey shuddered as Ashbar withdrew from his body, and when he opened his eyes, he put his hands to his face. Feeling the wetness, he said, "I feel as though I have been crying."

"You have been crying," a few in front said, amazed, for they had never seen the channel show any emotion before.

Thomas leapt to his feet and began going to those he had warned over the phone, "Did you hear what he said! What could be more obvious than saying he was a wolf in sheep's clothing? Didn't I tell you he was evil?"

"Oh, he must mean something different," they replied, "You can't take what he says literally. Someday we'll find out what he really means...."

We looked at each other in disbelief, concluding that *people will believe what they want, despite evidence to the contrary.* With Rebecca at the wheel, we started home. Although she was puzzled by Ashbar's words, she refused to surrender her adoration of her beloved teacher, who gave her so much special attention. This difference of opinion about their teacher soon opened a rift between these two, and months later they separated. It also caused Rebecca to turn against me, which she expressed by demanding I do more work for her without compensation.

Feeling that my time in Los Angeles was over, I moved out of the house and returned to Mount Shasta. None of our scripts, as Ashbar had threatened, had been produced. At least I felt I had been victorious in my confrontation with this evil entity and had succeeded in beginning to transform an enemy of humanity into a being of light. It had been a powerful lesson, not only in further developing self-reliance, but in understanding the protective power of Love. I had gone through an initiation during which I seemed to have been abandoned by the Masters, and had been forced to turn once more to the Master within—a process that continued the unending transformation of ignorance into wisdom.[105]

---

[105] Some people feel that as they progress spiritually, the path should get easier and their life more comfortable. That is not usually the case, for growth has no end, and in order for growth to take place, there have to be challenges. However, once one has dissolved attachments and aversions and is rooted in the equanimity of the True Self, those challenges are seen not as misfortunes but as adventures, opportunities for manifesting ever-greater Mastery.

CHAPTER 43

Starting Over

When I returned to Mount Shasta, I was broke. No studios had accepted any of our film treatments, and since I had only been working for room and board and Rebecca had been angry at me for turning her partner against her guru, I left Los Angeles almost penniless. At the San Fernando Greyhound station, when Rebecca's back was turned, Thomas had slipped me the money to buy a ticket home. All I could think of doing was to return to doing healing and giving astrology readings. When I had left town, this service had been much in demand, but I had been gone for almost a year.

I was given back the room by the doctor I had worked with, and the adjoining office. He kindly said I didn't need to pay rent until able, but it took a long time to get the practice going again. I sat at the desk in the office and went into meditation, repeating the decree that had previously always worked like magic:

I AM the Commanding, Governing Presence, bringing here those whom I can help, as God's Divine Abundance is now made manifest in my hands and for my use.

But no one arrived. Despite doing every visualization and decree I knew to generate cash flow, nothing happened.[106]

---

[106] Contrary to what books and movies about the power of positive thinking such as *The Secret* (TS Merchandising Ltd.: www.thesecret.tv) would have us believe, we have agreed prior to birth to go through certain karmic lessons, which often prevent circumstances from immediately rearranging themselves according to our will. Once the lessons have been learned, we again become beings of free will. Jesus said, *"If you have faith…you will say to the mountain, 'Move from here to there,' and it will move; and nothing will be impossible to you."* However, when you have that much faith, you will probably also have enough intelligence to realize that the mountain is already where it belongs, and you would be hard pressed to find it a better place. And you will realize that most of the things you wanted before are also not in your best interest.

Apprentice to the Masters

This is crazy; I published a book on the use of decrees and how to alter your reality with your mind. People come to me to learn this, and now I can't get it to work? I redoubled my efforts, enhancing my visualizations and calling on the Masters to empower those visualizations, but still nothing happened. Then one day as I was meditating, I was taken out of my body and found myself among the Masters, their majestic, white-robed forms standing around me, and as my attention became focused in their dimension I recognized not only Saint Germain but the two Masters I had met on the flight to Israel, El Morya and Kuthumi Lal Singh.

"We want to put you through a test," Saint Germain said.

"What kind of a test?"

"We can't tell you that, or it wouldn't be a test."

"I can take anything you dish out," I replied cavalierly, and the three Masters laughed uproariously, as though I had just told the most outrageous joke, and their laughter sparked mine. I was elated that I had brought some humor to that august company, especially pleased that I had gotten El Morya to laugh, whose stern visage always seemed to portray someone beyond humor—though the joke would soon be on me.[107] Then I was back in my body, sitting alone at my desk, their laughter still ringing in my ears. *Wait a minute, why did I say that? What did I just agree to?*

Days passed, and still no clients arrived. I remembered, *When forced to go without food, a wise man will fast,* so I decided to do an internal cleanse. I went on a diet of water and lemon juice, also consuming flax and psyllium to cleanse the intestines and dispel hunger.

I knew that if I told my friends I was out of money, they would have given me a loan, and would certainly have fed me if I was hungry, but I knew that the agreement I had made with the Masters precluded telling anyone my condition. This agreement was with the Masters, and I didn't want to manipulate anyone through sympathy, as I used to do with my mother, calling and telling her pitifully, "I'm out of money."

After a few weeks I found myself becoming spacey, as though my

---

[107] For some reason, enlightenment is almost always portrayed as humorless. Yet, even the Great Ones seem to enjoy a good joke once in a while. Surely viewing the foibles of the human condition must on occasion lend some levity to the observation of humanity's otherwise nearly unremittent suffering.

body was turning into light. *No point in hanging out in my office, since no one is visiting me anyway,* I decided, and wandered out into a large field nearby and lay down in the tall grass, where no one could see me. I took off my clothes and lay down in the sun. I offered myself to the Light and said to the Creator, *I give back to you this body, naked as you gave it. It's yours. I'm tired of taking care of it, trying to make money to keep it fed, clothed, and healthy. Do with it what you want. I want to be free and return to the Source.*

Suddenly I heard a voice above me say, "After the I AM Pageant, your fortunes will change." I opened my eyes and looked around, but saw no one. I knew that the pageant was the one put on every year by the Saint Germain Foundation on the first Sunday in August, which chronicled the life and teachings of Jesus. I used to go every year to experience the Christ energy that came through the performance. With so many people's attention on the Christ, that consciousness filled the town.

How will my fortunes change? I wondered. I suspected that the voice I had heard was that of one of the Masters with whom I had joked about being able to take whatever test they could dish out—one that had become more serious than I had imagined in my moment of joviality.

The Pageant was as inspiring as usual, and the next morning, while sitting at my desk, I saw two women ascending the stairs to the office. They were a mother and daughter, the mother resembling the Madonna I had just seen on stage the day before, and so youthful that she seemed more like a sister to her beautiful daughter.

"We want to work on our health," the mother said. "We have heard of your ability and know you work with Spirit. Although we have only minor health challenges, we want to feel closer to God and do whatever we can to perfect our vehicles and align them with the quickening of the spirit that is happening. Don't worry about money; I can pay whatever you charge or, if you don't charge, I will be happy to make a donation."

At that moment I became aware of being in two places simultaneously, at my desk talking to these beautiful women, and in an etheric realm above the building, with the Masters with whom I had joked six weeks before.

"You have passed the test with flying colors, my boy," one said, smiling. As I became more conscious in that dimension, I now recognized my old friend and mentor, Saint Germain, into whose apprenticeship I had entered so many years before, and under whose tutelage I had gone through so many challenging adventures.

Chapter 44

With Shirley MacLaine on Rodeo Drive

My adventures in Hollywood were not over. One day I heard that Shirley MacLaine was going to do a TV special called "Out on a Limb," about her adventures in consciousness and her experiences with UFOs. As I hadn't yet been able to afford a TV, I talked with several friends who were in the same boat and also wanted to watch the much-publicized show. This desire was soon fulfilled by a friend who was in town on a spiritual pilgrimage and was staying at the Tree House Motel. He kindly invited us to watch the show on the TV in his room.

As Shirley recounted her experiences, I realized that here was a kindred spirit who, although she knew she would be criticized as "wacko" by many, had the courage to reveal her experiences on the edge of what a vast portion of the population consider normal reality.

Part way through the show, I was pleased to see that she had purchased the painting "Moon Temple," by my friend Gilbert Williams, who used to live in Mount Shasta.[108] Gilbert had lived hand to mouth, like many of the rest of us in those days. I had bought one of his small paintings for $15 at a yard sale when he needed to come up with rent. I guessed that Shirley had paid a lot more for hers, and was happy that Gilbert had finally been recognized for the visionary he was.

The longer I watched, the more I began to feel a close connection with Ms. MacLaine, not just because she was a fellow mystic and ready to put herself on the line in the pursuit of truth, but because I felt there was some deeper connection. As I watched, fascinated that her far-out spirituality, which was considered normal in our esoterically-centered community, was being aired to a broad spectrum of the public, I suddenly heard the inner voice say, *You will meet her soon.*

Hardly likely, I countered, my rational mind arguing that since I didn't know anyone in her circle, and I lived eight hundred miles away, there was no way I could possibly meet this celebrity.

To my great surprise, however, a few weeks later, while Karen Carty

---
108 See: www.gilbertwilliams.blogspot.com.

Apprentice to the Masters

(an artist specializing in paintings of sacred geometry) was in my office, the phone rang. It was Sandy, an old friend from my screenwriting days, and a member of the Academy of Motion Pictures. I had taken care of her beachfront condo in Malibu, as well as her dog, also named Sandy, who had played in the film *Orphan Annie*.

"Peter, I got your card."

"What card?"

"The postcard you just sent me."

"I didn't send you a postcard."

"Yes, you did," she asserted, "I have it right here."

"What does it say?"

"It says you know some New Age artists, and that's why I'm calling."

"How do you know the card is from me?"

"Because it has your name signed at the bottom."

I was dumbfounded. I rarely wrote anyone and hadn't talked to Sandy since I had given her an astrology reading months before. I certainly would have remembered if I had just sent her a card.

"Look, I'm putting on a New Age Art show in Beverly Hills with Shirley MacLaine, to raise money to pay off Bella Abzug's campaign debts,[109] and I need your help. Since your card said you know a lot of New Age artists, I thought you'd be the one to ask."

This can only be the work of Saint Germain, I thought. *Who else would have put a card signed with my name in Sandy's mailbox? So, the voice I had heard while watching "Out on a Limb" had been accurate after all.*

"Yes, I do know some New Age artists," I replied, swallowing hard, "In fact, one of them is sitting right here in my office, and there are a lot of Gilbert William's paintings around that friends might be willing to sell." I also knew many other artists who would be eager to have their work displayed at the posh Dyansen Gallery on Rodeo Drive, where the benefit show was to take place.

"That's great," Sandy said, relieved, "I'll tell Shirley that you will be helping us. Just send me a list of the artists, the titles of their paintings, along with the prices, and I'll give it to the gallery. Of course, as agent you will get a 30% commission."

---

109 Bella Abzug was an anti-war, pro-feminist New York Congresswoman who ran for the U.S. Senate, but lost by less than 1% of the vote.

370

After I hung up I told Karen the good news, and she enthusiastically asked me to get her paintings in the show. Suddenly I was an art agent—one more career in my repertoire. I began calling galleries and agents and found that Gilbert's paintings, since Shirley had shown "Moon Temple" on TV, were selling for as much as $20,000. I was sure that my friends, who had not paid more than $300 for them years before, would be glad to sell them at anything in the vicinity of that price. I regretted that I had given away the painting I had bought as a birthday present.

Before long I found myself on Rodeo Drive, carrying Karen's and Gilbert's paintings past Tiffany and Christian Dior, until I came to the Dyansen Gallery. Sandy greeted me inside and introduced me to the manager, who soon began showing me where the works were to hang. She already had the painting's titles and prices printed on neat, white plaques. I was astounded to see that the prices I had listed had been doubled. "We do have quite an overhead here, dear," the manager replied to my surprised comment.

"By the way," I asked, cornering one of the manager's assistants, "What should I wear tonight?"

"It doesn't matter—just make a statement," came her reply, as she regarded what I was wearing with skepticism. "It looks as though you've been in the mountains for the past twenty years."

"I have."

"Well, that explains it," she shrugged.

Walking into several men's clothing stores on Rodeo Drive, I realized that I couldn't even afford to buy a shirt here. In a panic, I called a friend who was almost the same size and who volunteered to bring me a silk shirt and sports coat. Unfortunately, as my feet are huge, he couldn't oblige me with shoes, so I prayed no one would look down at my ankle-high Converses, which at least were black.

As I had very little idea what I was doing at this event, except that it had obviously been arranged by Saint Germain, I began calling to the Master for guidance, and asking for the Great White Brotherhood to send their consciousness and blessings to enfold all who would attend:

Saint Germain, please come forth and take complete command here. Bring about the Divine Plan for all who attend, and show me what to do.

I AM the Commanding, Governing Presence of the Ascended Host of Light, establishing this place as a focus of light.

I AM the Violet Consuming Flame, blazing up, in, around, and through this place, through Beverly Hills, and throughout Los Angeles, forever.

Soon the doors opened, and the celebrities who had been invited began arriving: Zsa Zsa Gabor, wearing a silver sequined dress, made a glamorous entrance, flashing her diamonds for the photographers, and when asked how she was doing, she said in her famous Hungarian accent, "Daahling, I'm just divine."

If she only knew, I thought, *she is far more divine than she realizes. With more faith in the reality of the God Presence within, she would not have to try so hard to stress her uniqueness.* But before I could say anything to her, she swirled around once more for the photographers, and in an explosion of flash bulbs, left in her waiting limo.

Next to arrive was Lyndsay Wagner, star of the TV series "The Bionic Woman," about a woman who uses the superhuman strength of her mechanized body to fight for good. She was also soon surrounded by a crowd of admirers, and after shaking a few hands, soon left. It seemed that the Eight Worldly Dharmas were thriving here.

Just as I was wondering where the host was, Shirley, her daughter Sachi, and Congresswoman Bella Abzug arrived, amid another wave of flashes from the cameras. *At last,* I thought, *the one I have been sent to meet; but what am I supposed to do?*

Shirley walked to a small platform near the back of the gallery and welcomed all the guests. As she began speaking, I was surprised to feel the radiation of the Ascended Masters begin filling the room with light. *That is strange,* I thought, *that the Masters are interested in an art show, and one so dominated by strong egos, but it seems this is why I am here,* and I sent a prayer of gratitude to the Masters for their exquisite radiation.

I visualized the I AM Presence above the gathering, a luminous sun surrounded by rings of rainbow light, sending forth dazzling rays of light. As I felt the Masters amplify that visualization and further empower it with their own energy, I felt those rays go forth, penetrating the night sky over Los Angeles.

Shirley introduced Bella, who said a few words of thanks for organizing the benefit. Suddenly I was brought back into the physical plane by a stabbing pain in my right foot. A heavy, intoxicated woman holding a cocktail glass in her hand had stepped on my right foot, driving her spike heel into the thin canvas.

As I tried to withdraw, she lurched back into a hand-blown glass vase balanced on a nearby pedestal. Still wincing from the pain, I jumped forward and stabilized the vase with my left hand, using my right to keep the woman from falling onto the floor. As we both regained our balance, I found myself holding a vaguely familiar woman, and I wanted to say, "Lady, if you keep drinking like that, you're going to kill yourself."

She looked apologetically at me, then a moment later, as she regained her composure and walked away, I heard people whisper "Geraldine Page," the actress who had recently received an Academy Award, and who Meryl Streep had introduced as "…the greatest actress in the English language." Months later, she died of a heart attack in New York. With all her acclaim, she seemed not to have found happiness, and her fame did not prolong her life by a day.

Soon I perceived Bella Abzug in the wide-brimmed, floppy hat that was her signature, bearing down on me. "Thank you, thank you," she said, gripping my hand and squeezing it firmly. *Perhaps she thinks I'm one of the celebrities buying a painting, or maybe Sandy told her I helped with the show?*

Soon the manager was beckoning. A wealthy businessman wanted to buy one of Karen's paintings. I shook his hand and congratulated him on his excellent choice, and then watched while he wrote out a check to the Gallery.

As I stepped away, I found myself back to back with a flaming red head. As the realization dawned on me that this was undoubtedly Shirley MacLaine, the one I had been sent to meet, she whirled around as though she had also been waiting to meet me, and I found myself face to face with the most engaging, effervescent woman, whose energy seemed boundless.

I was speechless; *Should I call her "Shirley" or "Ms. MacLaine?"* My dilemma was solved when she slipped her hand into mine and gripped my fingers. As I introduced myself, I mentioned that Gilbert, whose painting she had bought, was a friend, and she asked how I came to know him. As soon as I mentioned Mount Shasta, her eyes opened wide, and drawing close and looking me straight in the eye, she said, "I know all about Mount Shasta."

"You do?"

Instead of replying, she gave a look that said more than words, and for a moment I felt a presence like Pearl's—a sense of timeless awareness, and a light emanating between us that spread out through the gallery. I felt a connection had been made whose ultimate purpose had not yet been revealed. Then she winked, said goodbye, and moved toward the door as her car pulled up at the curb.

The radiation of the Masters, which had been pouring through the gallery, now faded, and I felt that the mission on which I had been sent had concluded. I mused that only a few weeks before, I had been watching TV in a motel room in Mount Shasta, with only a *still, small voice* guiding me, not aware that the Masters were going to open the door to attend this gathering in Hollywood, the ultimate purpose of which still remained cloaked in mystery. It was dramatic proof how quickly, when in service to the Masters, life can change—once one has surrendered the illusion of self to the impersonal life of the spirit. In that service, all things are possible—for in the consciousness of *All Mighty God,* material limitation does not exist—space, time, and fortune are but instruments of the Presence that is everywhere.

Chapter 45

Return to Shambhala

In August 1987, seven of the ten planets used by Western Astrologers formed an equilateral triangle in the heavens known as a grand trine—and all in fire signs. This unusual event coincided with what Jose Arguelles believed was a turning point in consciousness long foretold by his ancestors in the Mayan Calendar, which he named the Harmonic Convergence.[110]

Although Astrology has been abused to disempower people, when used properly it can assist in empowerment and self-knowledge. I developed the concept of *Thirteenth House Astrology*, the thirteenth house being the circle in the center of the chart. When conscious of one's own center, the planetary forces can be observed moving through the other twelve houses of one's environment without necessarily affecting the equanimity or well-being of the one living in the center. Seeing the forces that are working in our environment, we can understand ourselves and intuit right action—

---

110 Jose Arguelles, *The Mayan Factor: Path Beyond Technology* (Bear & Co., 1987). Also see: Aluna Joy Yaxkin, *Mayan Astrology, A User Friendly Guide to Mayan Astrology* (Center of the Sun, 1995). See Aluna's highly informative site: www.alunajoy.com. Aluna has a balanced view in harmony with the Mayan elders, with whom she works—not getting caught up in intellectual arguments that try to name the specific day the calendar ends or read in prophecies that are not there. She emphasized in a recent conversation: The Maya continually affirm that cycles of consciousness do not suddenly shift on a particular day, but are ongoing processes with which we can align ourselves. The Maya use calendars based on cosmic time as well as astronomical cycles, which predict 2012 as the end of a 5125 year Great Cycle—a time of transition for humanity. This coincides with the alignment of the winter solstice with the galactic equator and an expected peak in sunspot cycles. This is not the end of the world, as some say, but is definitely a time of major transition, where a way of life that does not work is being replaced by a more harmonious one. This also is in harmony with Hopi prophecies that say we are about to enter from the Fourth World into the Fifth.

much as by observing approaching storm clouds we can decide if we want to go for a walk. If it rains, we don't need to get wet by being caught unaware; we can remain indoors, go out with an umbrella, or simply choose to get wet—but the choice is ours.[111]

I didn't pay the Harmonic Convergence much attention at first, thinking it was another of those New Age events being hyped to further someone's fame or fortune, but when I cast an astrology chart, I saw that this would be a time of spiritual initiation—that for those who had freed themselves of attachments to old emotional conditioning, they would be able to make great spiritual progress.

To maximize this energy for change, as the planets began to converge on the 17th of August, I closed myself in my room to meditate. I sat cross-legged on the bed, eyes partially open and gazing at the floor, spine straight, observing the breath passing in and out as I settled into a calm state of awareness. Suddenly, a man in a white jumpsuit appeared before me. Although not totally physical, his form was quite tangible. Having been trained by Trungpa Rinpoche to disregard all phenomena as distractions that actually block the expansion of consciousness, I ignored the apparition and continued to observe the inflow and outflow of my breath.

"Come with me," the man said. Despite trying to disregard him, I began to recognize by his serene, commanding presence, and the blue-white light that emanated from him, that he was not a projection of my mind, but a messenger that had been sent to contact me. I nodded in consent and suddenly found myself outside my physical body. Looking back, I saw my earthly form continuing to sit on the bed in meditation.[112]

"Do not worry about your physical body," the messenger said. "I will

---

111 William Shakespeare, *Julius Caesar*, Act 1, Scene 2,
Men at some time are masters of their fates:
The fault, dear Brutus, is not in our stars,
But in ourselves, that we are underlings.

112 In one sense, everything is a projection of our mind, yet we must nevertheless learn to function within these various levels of duality in order to realize our inherent nature as creators. It is a mistake to mix teachings that apply to various levels, concluding that "nothing is real," for then we miss the purpose of our incarnation. As Sathya Sai Baba says, "You are the God of this universe. You are creating the whole universe and drawing it in."

put a circle of protection around it, so nothing can interfere while we are gone," and with a wave of his hand, it was enfolded in a shimmering, blue-white light.

My companion then put his arm around me, and I felt my weightless form transported from the room to the side of Mount Shasta. The view of the surrounding mountains and the valley below, though one I had seen many times before, was always inspiring. Turning around, I saw we were at a location my attention had been drawn to for many years, yet without knowing why. I had never visited the location, because it was off the beaten path, but had always sensed that it had some inner import of which I was unaware.

Now we stood before the face of a high cliff, on which my companion placed the palm of his hand. Instantly, the face of the cliff dissolved—as if it had been a holographic projection to hide what lay inside, revealing a cavern containing an underground subway not unlike those in any modern city. However, this one was immaculately clean, and we were the only people there, at what was obviously the last stop on the line. We entered the single car waiting for us, and as an engine began to hum, we moved forward, accelerating inward and downward into the Earth.

"It runs on magnetic pulses," my guide said, in response to my unspoken question as to why the subway car was so quiet and the ride so smooth, "The entire car is suspended, without any metal-to-metal contact."

He then motioned me to join him at the front of the car, where a large wheel was mounted horizontal to the floor.

"Turn the wheel to go faster," he said. I gave it a few turns as he invited, and felt the immediate acceleration.

"That's fast enough," he said. "Our travel time to the center will be about 20 minutes."

Soon we had come to a stop and emerged into a meadow bathed in light. "Just like the surface," my guide said, noting my look of wonder, "only no pollution, and the people live in complete harmony."

I could see mountains in the distance, from which descended a crystal pure stream down through lush, green hills into a nearby azure lake. Instinctively, I followed a path through the flower-studded meadow, encountering people wearing different colored robes. The colors of their robes, my guide informed me, represented their areas of study and their level of advancement. Some stood in groups talking, and as I passed they all gave me a friendly nod as though they knew me. But I did not stop to

Apprentice to the Masters

talk, for I knew that I had been brought here for a reason and sensed that I had an important appointment.

In a few moments my path ended at a small, alabaster temple. It was round, with a domed roof, and its majestic simplicity was breathtaking. My guide held back, and said that I had to advance the rest of the way alone. My heart beat rapidly as I approached, sensing that I was soon to meet some great being, and I knew that this meeting was the reason I had been summoned here to the center of the Earth. As I ascended the steps, a Christ-like figure in a white robe, who had not been there a moment before, stepped forward to greet me. As I reached the center of the domed area, I felt overwhelmed by the love he emanated.

"Welcome, my son," the majestic being said, his luminous eyes looking into mine. "I am Pellour, Lord of the Inner Earth—the place to which many legends have referred as Shambhala. I led our people here many eons ago, prior to the destruction of Atlantis. Certain of us knew of the coming cataclysm that would sink our continent, so we withdrew here to this Paradise. We could have postponed the destruction on the surface, but only temporarily, for until people learn from their own bitter experience that they must relinquish their selfish, materialistic pursuits, there can be no safety or permanent peace anywhere.

"Those who were sufficiently free of negative emotions, we were able to bring with us. Now, Earth is again reaching such a turning point in its self-created destiny. Again, many are choosing to create suffering for themselves by their unconscious attachment to their lower natures, and again there will be those who have stabilized their emotions and overcome selfishness, who will be spared the turmoil of the surface and be transported here.

"You have visited here many times in your Higher Body, but have not been allowed to remember. If you had, you would have found it difficult to continue living on the surface in the barbaric conditions prevailing there. You will eventually come to live here with many of your associates, but for now, you must be content to visit on occasion. We will discuss this more in the future. Now, you must return to the surface. Your guide awaits you."

This majestic being showered me with the love and respect of a father, and as he nodded his head in a slight bow, a wave of exquisite love passed through me, and I bowed to him in return. When I raised my eyes, he was gone. He had disappeared into thin air. As I descended the steps of the temple, the guide was waiting to escort me home.

Soon we were back in the Inner Earth subway, speeding toward the surface, and then I was back in my body, alone in the room and contemplating this unexpected journey. I could still feel Pellour's love—and remembered his prophetic words.

This Shambhala, I now realized, was the place Saint Germain and Semjasse had taken me during my rendezvous with them at Lake Louise. It was this Inner Earth Paradise which Saint Germain had said *holds great import for the future of humanity.* Now I knew why. The time of humanity's transition is fast approaching, and it is to assist in this process that the Masters brought me and many others to Mount Shasta for training.

That great change, long predicted by the seers of ages past, is now at hand. Those who have purified themselves of past conditioning and learned to live in harmony with others—in a state of equanimity, free of attachments and aversions—are being readied, without their conscious awareness, to enter a place more beautiful than they can imagine.

Chapter 46

Released

Soon my worldly lessons took a different form. What had been a core belief and point of reference since I had come to Mount Shasta was about to be withdrawn, as must eventually all reference points on which we lean—for consciousness exists independent of reference to anything. Beliefs, ideas, and spiritual practices are only steps on the path which, once their usefulness is outlived, need to be abandoned.[113] Perhaps that is why so many teachers of non-dualism say that meditation is unnecessary to achieve enlightenment, as their own years of meditation that brought them to that realization are long behind them. But even the Buddha acknowledged that attaining that realization often took many years, even lifetimes, of self-discipline and preparation.

One of my main points of reference for the past seven years had been celibacy—the vow I had made to the Order of Melchizedek. I had asked to know how to deal with the life force, and this was the path I had been shown. The conservation of the life force and its focus on the I AM Presence had made it possible for me to receive teachings directly from the Masters and attain a consciousness that would not have otherwise been possible. However, this fundamental belief was now challenged by no less an authority than the Master himself.

It was New Year's Day, the morning after the conclave that is called every New Year's Eve at the Royal Teton, when students of the light meet with the Masters and are given their instructions for the coming year. So, I made myself a cup of tea and then sat down on the living room sofa to look up at the majesty of the Mountain while I asked the Masters to help me remember what directions they had given the previous night. While waiting for my tea to cool, I stilled my mind, and it was then that I heard Saint Germain's shocking reply, *You are to be married.*

What! That's impossible! I gasped, spilling the hot tea. *What about my*

---

[113] The Buddha was supposedly asked how long one needed to practice the Dharma, and he replied, "Once you have used a boat to cross a river, there is no need to keep carrying it with you."

allegiance to the Order of Melchizedek...the vow of celibacy? Since when is that no longer the highest path?

My mind raced to Elizabeth, the vision I had seen of a possible life together, ending in a painful divorce. *Is that marriage to take place after all, with no way we can change our destiny?* I thought I had been shown that vision to prevent us from getting married, not to foretell the inevitable. Though I had longed for that union, I had repressed my desire for Elizabeth so that I could receive teaching from Pearl and serve as an apprentice to Saint Germain. *Now he is going to give me the relationship he had denied before? Well, if it is your wish, Saint Germain, I will marry Elizabeth.*

Did I say 'Elizabeth?' he replied. *The one we want you to marry is someone else.*

Someone else?

Yes, someone you have already met.

Who could that be? I wondered, as there was no one else to whom I was attracted, and Elizabeth was never far from my mind.

In answer, I saw the etheric form of Dona, a girl I had met at Pearl's many months before, appear before me and walk into the living room. There had been some attraction, but she lived in Berkeley, five hours from Mount Shasta, and after exchanging a few letters about the meaning of Life, we had disagreed about so much that I had stopped writing her. She had read *Zanoni*, my favorite book about how a neophyte Master loses his power through marriage to his student, but her conclusion, unlike mine, was that the spiritual loss was a small price to pay for the love they shared. Furthermore, not only did she not follow my ascetic regimen, she ate meat, liked a glass of red wine occasionally, looked to Tarot cards for guidance, and liked to go disco dancing. Now here she was, walking toward me, and into my life, if I understood the Master correctly.

Dona! I exclaimed.

Yes, he nodded.

What! We don't agree on anything. She's not even on the Path, I protested. *And what about my vow of celibacy? I don't want to be expelled from the Order!* But to these protestations, he made no reply. A look of compassion crossed his face as he said, *Nonetheless, my boy, it is my wish for you to marry Dona—and I expect you to comply.* Then he faded from sight, as did Dona's etheric form, and I realized that my all-too-brief, yet life-altering interview with Saint Germain was over.

Is my mind playing tricks on me, I wondered? Until one is Ascended, it is always possible to be misled by our own projections or by astral beings masquerading as Masters. So I decided to test the guidance, and not call Dona or make any effort in her direction, despite the express command I had apparently just received. If it was meant to be, then it would have to happen on its own accord, without any effort on my part. Not only did I not call Dona, but I decided to actively avoid her.

Despite my efforts, however, Dona soon arrived in Mount Shasta, and I saw her around town. I heard that she had moved here for the summer, so to get away from her I went to Ashland, Oregon, and stayed with friends. To my horror, she had arrived there only an hour ahead of me, at the home of these friends we now discovered we had in common. She, too, had seen a vision of us getting married, and to get away from me had gone to stay with the same people in Ashland.

Seeing that despite our efforts to avoid each other we had come face to face, I said, "We need to talk," and she agreed. That was the first and one of the last things on which we ever agreed. Walking in the rose garden in Lithia Park, we unfolded our stories of how we had each come to believe we were meant to be together—what had transpired in our lives to bring us to this point of contemplating a life-altering union with each other. It was uncanny how similar our revelations were. Since we had both heard Pearl's story about how Saint Germain had come to Jerry while he was driving down the freeway and told him to marry Pearl, we knew that among students of the Masters, such arranged marriages are not unusual. Certainly, in many other parts of the world, most marriages are arranged, if not by the guru, then by the family—as it has been widely observed throughout the ages that if left to make their own choices, young people frequently form liaisons more from short-term chemistry than long-term consideration of permanent suitability.

Since it seemed that we could not escape each other, and that our guidance was genuine, we decided to begin living together in the small bungalow I was renting at Lake Shastina, a community on the far side of the Mountain. Since we were joining together in response to the Masters' wishes, and I had not been told to break my commitment to the Order of Melchizedek, we decided to remain celibate and live together as friends.

News of my sudden liaison with a woman served to deliver one more blow to my connection with Pearl. After berating me to my friends for what she believed was plagiarism, now she felt I had fallen further off the path by breaking my vow of celibacy, though at that point untrue. My rebellion

Apprentice to the Masters

against her and the Masters was complete, she believed. *If only she had known that what I was doing was not my wish—but the Master's command.*

However, one day I was shocked when the Master appeared to me inwardly and said, "Peter, your marriage to Dona is to be a union in every sense of the word." Soon Saint Germain guided me to the tantric practices of the East that teach how to conserve the life force lost in unconscious sexual activity, and how to direct that energy upward through the higher centers to aid evolution and promote health and longevity.[114] I also saw now how that training would not have been possible during my initial work with Pearl and the Masters, which required the one-pointed concentration of the life force on only the three highest *chakras*. Now that I had completed my initial training, other avenues of expression of Divine Love were becoming appropriate. In fact, only through working consciously with all the emotional chakras in a relationship of trust and love could the healing and transmutation of unresolved emotional issues occur. By working with this long-ignored energy, other areas of realization began to open through the catalyst of our relationship. I began to see how the feminine side of life, long suppressed through years of mental discipline, offered the nourishment my soul craved—and caused my heart to open like the blossom of a rose.

This shift manifested as a dream one night, in which I was living in a tall tower on an island in a river. Through the narrow window I could see far into the distance, though only in one direction. Suddenly the tower was struck by lightning, and I was thrown from the window into the river. After pulling myself to shore I stood up and looked around, and I saw the huge world of which before I had only seen a small segment. I had been high, but with a narrow view.

This dream, I realized, showed that my marriage was an immersion in the River of Life, which would expand my wisdom and understanding.[115] Most spiritual teachings, I saw, were male oriented, teaching non-attachment and the attainment of bliss on a higher plane; however, I now began to realize

---

114 Stephen Thomas Chang, *The Tao of Sexology* (Tao Publishing, 1986).
115 This dream was a manifestation of the sixteenth card of the Tarot, The Lightning-Struck Tower, signifying the failure of the intellect to attain Heaven by reason alone—that the next higher initiation can only be attained by the descent of the spirit into matter.

that ultimate liberation could only be attained in duality, not by escaping it, and relationship was the embodiment of that initiation.[116]

Although I would remember with longing my initial days with Pearl, when our close group, gathered together by the Masters in her cozy living room, would sit at her feet to hear their teachings and feel the uplifting purity of their radiation, I saw that my growth had been mostly in one direction, toward the transcendence of the illusions of the Earth plane, and that I still had much work to do integrating that consciousness into my personality—probably the most difficult Mastery of all.

For more than a year, I heard nothing from Pearl. Then one day the door of my office opened and there she was, standing in front of me. She was accompanied by Bill, a student of the Masters who had volunteered to live with Pearl and help her in her advancing years. They pulled up chairs and sat before me, a feeling of expectancy in the air.

"Pearl has something to tell you," Bill volunteered, hinting at reconciliation.

"I feel I have misjudged you, and want to make amends. I would like to republish your book in paperback," Pearl said, refraining from any mention of how she had sabotaged my effort to publish her book, and the derogatory comments she had made about me for the past couple of years.

"I feel that your book is a wonderful introduction to the Masters' teachings, and I think it should be available in an inexpensive paperback edition that everyone can afford. Just tell me what it will cost, and I will write a check."

She held out her hand shyly as an offer of reconciliation, and feeling her sincerity, I took it tenderly. Then the two of them left, Pearl leaning on Bill's arm as he guided her down the staircase. A few weeks later I ran into Bill downtown, and he told me all that had transpired.

Late one night he had been reading my forbidden book, *"I AM" the Open Door,* and had felt the spiritual radiation which he knew could only come from the Ascended Masters. The next morning he presented the book to Pearl, who had condemned it without reading, and suggested she read a few pages. To her surprise and humiliation she, too, felt the Masters' radiation.

---

116 In Tibetan Buddhism, there is the often-repeated statement, *Samsara* (delusion) *and Nirvana* (enlightenment) *are one.*

Apprentice to the Masters

Chagrined, she had said to Bill, "I have to find some way to make this up to Peter. I have done him a great wrong." Together, they decided that the best healing would be to republish the book that she had doubted and that was rapidly becoming a metaphysical best seller.

Gradually, as time passed, Pearl and I began to meet again on occasion—not as teacher and student, but as friends and colleagues. Many others also went their own way, realizing that it was time to apply what she had taught, rather than continue sitting at her feet. The return of her free time allowed her to prepare for her own Ascension, and I watched as she became more and more etheric each time I saw her. After a while she no longer ate food, and for the last five years of her life derived her sustenance almost entirely from the Source—finally passing from her physical body in 1990 and entering the Ascended Master Octave.

Chapter 47

Empowerment at Lake Titicaca

I began to feel the presence of a vast being known as Meru, who maintains a focus of light for the Earth at Lake Titicaca in South America. Often we are drawn to work with beings on inner planes without actually becoming cognizant of what that work is in our outer minds. Although, on occasion, we are able to draw through that energy with which we have been empowered, through the use of affirmation and the focus of conscious attention. Much as iron filings feel the pull of a magnet, I felt drawn to visit this focus that had at one time been the center of a great civilization that was subsequently destroyed by a massive cataclysm that rocked the entire continent. I resisted as long as I could, not wanting to give in to this seemingly irrational desire, without clear guidance. Finally, though, this pull became so dominant that with money I had recently saved I purchased a plane ticket to La Paz, Bolivia. Perched on the west slope of the Andes, this town near Lake Titicaca had the highest major airport in the world.

I had read archeological studies of this area, and although there were disagreements as to the age of the civilization that had created the structures, the archeological and geological anomalies could only be explained by there having been a sudden cataclysm in South America about 15,000 years ago that shifted the entire continent, lowering the east coast and raising the west. Tiahuanaco, the complex of stone temples and piers now at an elevation of over two miles, had been a port that, prior to the cataclysm, had been at sea level. In *Unveiled Mysteries,* Godfre Ray King spoke of this earthshaking event in the chapter "Buried Cities of the Amazon," a book that portrays many civilizations through the ages that have risen to greatness, only to fall into ruin as their populations turned to materialism, forgetting about the light within that was their Source.

The plane first stopped in Managua, Nicaragua. As I had almost three hours until the next flight, I thought I would see something of the country, and decided to go for a walk past the clearing in which the airport was nestled. Inhaling the moist jungle air, I strode toward the lush greenery. However, I had not left the airport grounds before I was overwhelmed by the uneasy feeling that I was being watched—perhaps the same feeling a mouse in the field has the moment before he is snatched by the hawk gliding silently overhead. Glancing over my shoulder, I saw that indeed there was a jeep creeping up behind me with three soldiers, one of them crouched over a machine gun. In that one glance, their icy stares told me to keep walking, to circle back to the terminal. Without looking back, I called inwardly to Saint Germain to protect me, and tried to walk casually, as though out for a stroll. Yet, I could feel their eyes boring a hole into the center of my back, and felt that they would like nothing better than to pull the trigger, as they had been trained. Finally reaching the terminal again, I entered the building and breathed a sigh of relief.

That night we had a layover in Caracas, Venezuela, and I had a taxi take me to the Sheraton. As the itinerary said that the continuing flight did not depart until 10 a.m. the next morning, I fell asleep without setting my alarm. But at 3 a.m. I was startled by the phone ringing next to my head. *Who could that be? No one knows I'm here. Must be a wrong number.* Sleepily I lifted the phone and heard a commanding voice speak in flawless English,

"Peter, your flight leaves at 6:20 a.m. You need to be at the airport at 4 a.m. to go through Immigration. That is in one hour. Make sure you are there on time."

"What! I thought the plane doesn't leave until 10:00?"

"No, 6:20."

"Who is this?" I demanded. No one knew I was there, except the taxi driver who had brought me. But there was only the click of the phone hanging up.

Who was that, and how did he know where I am staying? As I became fully awake, I realized that only Saint Germain could have known my whereabouts. Dragging myself out of bed, I showered in a cascade of cold water and took a taxi back to the airport.

Just as the caller had said, when I looked at the board of outbound flights, I saw that the departure time was indeed 6:20 and that there were no later flights. Herded past one official after another, I acquired all the necessary stamps in my passport and boarded the plane. As it was such an early flight, I hadn't been able to get any breakfast at the hotel, and there were no food concessions at the airport, so I looked forward to eating on board, but the dry roll and jam they served with tea were meager fare. Tired from rising early, I dozed off.

A couple of hours later, I awoke to find the plane descending over the jungle. As we had not yet crossed the Andes, I knew we could not be close to La Paz. My itinerary didn't mention another landing, and I wondered,

Is something wrong with the plane? Yet, no one else seemed surprised at our rapid descent. There were no towns below, only the impenetrable canopy of the Amazon, with wisps of steam rising skyward.

As we dropped into a small clearing, a red dirt runway appeared under the wing, and we bounced to a stop. *Have we been hijacked?* I had the vision of being marched into the jungle by headhunters, a fate I had barely missed on my last visit to South America as a child. Our car had broken down in the jungle at night, where missionaries had been recently killed for refusing the women the headhunters had sent to care for them.

"Exit the plane and go through Customs and Immigration Control," I heard over the speaker, "Take all your baggage with you." *That's ridiculous,* I thought, barely awake, *We're in the middle of the jungle; why take my suitcase, since we'll be getting back on the plane shortly?* So I left my small bag under the seat, and only half awake, I stumbled down the ramp with the rest of the passengers.

In the barren, one-room shack that served as a terminal, we shuffled from one line to another, getting our documents stamped, and then stumbled into another line to re-board the plane—or so I thought.

As I was ravenously hungry, I bought some bananas from a native boy. When I was halfway into the second banana, a man in an exquisite three-piece suit, and wearing a silver tie with violet stripes, walked up and pushed into line beside me.

I thought it strange that he showed none of the weariness of the other passengers, whose clothes were crumpled and faces lined with fatigue. His alert, commanding presence would have drawn respect in any Manhattan corporate board room—yet he acted as though he knew me. As I leaned over to whisper that I didn't appreciate his pushing into line, as the people behind us had begun to grumble, he spoke in flawless English,

"Maybe you didn't know we're changing planes here."

"What! I left my bag on the other plane," I said, suddenly panicked.

"Don't worry, I'll take care of it," he said, bypassing the line and walking directly to the counter, despite more annoyed remarks from those in line. Speaking in fluent Portuguese, he spoke to an official, who glanced in my direction. The commanding stranger beckoned, and waved me to the front of the line, where he escorted me through a security door. Two men with automatic rifles motioned me forward, and I was led to a waiting jeep.

"Go with them and you'll be fine," the stranger said, nodding toward the plane that still held my bag. Then, almost imperceptibly, he whispered,

"Vaya con dios," (Spanish: Go with God), and I thought I saw the hint of a smile flit across his implacable face.

Soon I was speeding out to the plane I had arrived on, the soldiers seemingly preoccupied with other matters. They waited while I re-entered the plane, scurried down the aisle and grabbed my suitcase, and then returned to the jeep. Saying nothing about inspecting my bag, they drove to another plane across the clearing that I hadn't notice before, where the rest of the passengers were now boarding.

I found a new seat, and continued to feast on bananas while I waited for the stranger in the suit to board the plane. I wanted to thank him, for I realized, *Without his help, who knows what trouble I might have gotten into?* Whoever he was, he had arrived in the nick of time, and the officials in the terminal had been most solicitous of his good will, yet, the door to the cabin closed without him. It wasn't until we sped down the dirt runway and the plane lifted into the air that I realized why he had seemed so familiar— that he had been none other than my mentor, Saint Germain, who on a previous flight had assumed the persona of Nick Adams, a traveling Realtor. *No doubt he had also been the one who phoned at 3 a.m. and told me to go to the airport earlier than scheduled.* I gave thanks for his seemingly ever-present umbrella of protection. But he had still not answered the overwhelming question: *What is the purpose of this trip to Lake Titicaca? It is undoubtedly to receive further discourses from the Masters,* I reasoned, *perhaps from the South American branch of the Great White Brotherhood or even from Meru himself?*

We finally landed at the La Paz airport at 13,000 feet above sea level. As I descended from the plane I felt light-headed, probably as much from lack of oxygen as sleep, so I took a taxi into town and checked in to the Sheraton. I had learned that despite the seeming extravagance of spending hard-earned savings, it was usually futile to pinch pennies on a mission for the Masters. They always seemed to make sure that I had what I needed— even if their idea of needs was different than mine.

Having a splitting headache from the altitude, I was unable to sleep. Instead of lying on the bed, holding my head in my hands, and feeling sorry for myself, I went downstairs and ate a small bowl of vegetable soup. Feeling better, I hired a taxi to take me to the ruins of Tiahuanaco at the edge of Lake Titicaca.

Andesite slabs, some over 400 tons, were strewn about like children's blocks, with no sign of how they had been quarried, transported, and placed on top of each other in a structure aligned with planetary constellations. Efforts by a modern engineering firm to restore some of the walls were abysmally inferior to the original craftsmanship. *If modern technology could not reconstruct these buildings, who were these ancient peoples and where did their technology originate?* Recent measurements of the change of the angle between the ecliptic plane (apparent path of the sun) and equatorial plane of the Earth placed the date of construction around 15,000 BC,[117] close to the time that ancient peoples around the world recorded a great flood that destroyed much of humanity.

As I stood before the famous stone archway with the face of the weeping God, I asked myself the same question as others who had stood in the same spot: *Why is the God weeping? Does he know of the coming catastrophe that will destroy their civilization?*

Remembering *Unveiled Mysteries,* I realized that this was the same catastrophe warned of by the Cosmic Being, in the chapter "Buried Cities of the Amazon," that swept an entire empire into oblivion.[118] There have been many such cataclysms that have swept the Earth in the past, and I realized with a shock that we may now be at another such turning point.[119]

Filled with awe to have stood on the ruins of an ancient empire which, at least in terms of its architectural ability, was far in advance of our own, I journeyed back along the dusty roads to La Paz, thinking to myself, *How transitory is life, that an entire civilization could collapse here without enough time to record the event.*

I returned to the hotel, thinking that I would collapse on the bed and sink into the longed-for, overdue rest, but as I walked down the corridor, I was electrified to see before the door to my room the etheric, though electrifying, presence of the Ascended Master Saint Germain.

As I approached, he bowed, indicating with a sweep of his arm that

---

117 R. Cedric Leonard, *Tiahuanaco, the Mysterious City*: "Thus, I think it likely that Tiahuanaco was originally built at sea level c. 15,000 B.C. as an Atlantean seaport," citing research by Prof. Arthur Posnansky (www.atlantisquest.com/prehistcity.html).

118 Godfre Ray King, *Unveiled Mysteries* (Saint Germain Press, 1982).

119 See also: *Science Daily* (April 15, 2008), *"California has more than a 99% chance of having a magnitude 6.7 or larger earthquake within the next 30 years, according to scientists using a new model to determine the probability of big quakes."*

Apprentice to the Masters

I should precede him into the room. As I passed I couldn't help noticing the jeweled Maltese cross on his chest and feel the purifying effect of the energy that emanated from him. He followed, and I closed and locked the door behind us.

With his jeweled sword hanging from his waist, he was the image of splendor and dominion that, in past centuries, had dazzled the courts of Europe. He smiled at my obvious admiration and then motioned me to a chair. I waited to see what his visit signified. *Is he going to give me the records that tell what befell this lost civilization? Or are he and other Masters going to give me further discourses, as they did the previous year in New York?*

Instead, I was surprised when he said, "Peter, the age for channeling is over. Our visit to you last year was an exception. You have been brought here, not for us to give you discourses, but for you to give your own discourse, your own message."

"What message?" I asked, amazed. "I have nothing to say."

"Yes, you do. Look within your heart, and you will find the message inside you. Describe what you have just witnessed at Tiahuanaco, how it made you feel, and the message will follow. Call on your I AM Presence and you will know what to say." Then he stepped back, and I knew that this great friend, who so tirelessly watched over me, and to whom I had become apprenticed many years before, was about to depart.

"By the way," he said, with a twinkle in his eye, "Next time you are told to change planes, don't take shortcuts; for on the path to Mastery there are no shortcuts." Then his form dissolved into a pillar of violet light, and he was gone.

With great effort I grounded the euphoria that I was feeling, and, no longer tired, grabbed the yellow pad I always carried in my suitcase, and moved to the desk. Observing my breath, the natural rise and fall of this unending mantra, I soon felt a calmness descend. Turning my attention inward, then upward to the I AM Presence which I knew was awaiting my call, I decreed,

I AM come forth in and through my mind and being, and write what I AM meant to write—Thy words, not mine, come forth now!

As I turned further within to the Source, I felt the Presence answer those calls, and I became infused with insight. Gradually, I became aware of that magical Presence, a sun surrounded by rainbow rings, which was the origin and sustaining power of my being. And as I became immersed in that radiation, the lower self merging with the Higher, the message that the Master had asked me to deliver began to flow:

I am writing this in my own words. It is not a "channeling." The time for channeling the messages of others, be it even from the Masters, is drawing to a close. We must be the message. We must be the Masters. The truth must be known for what it is, not because of the person from whom it comes.

I wish, however, to express my deepest gratitude to those Masters who have helped make me what I am, and what I and those others who are receiving their assistance are rapidly becoming—through self-discipline, meditation, and dedicated service: Master Presences in this new age striving to be born.

"What is to become of me?" people are asking, as they view the world around them and see the ancient prophecies being fulfilled.[120] Do not despair. These words are not meant to cause fear, rather Hope. Even if the masses seek destruction, still the individual may seek his salvation. And as he seeks, he is not alone. To the sincere call of the individual, the Presence of God is always manifest. If the masses choose not to seek that Presence, what is that to you? True, the ancient prophecies are being fulfilled, but remember also the prophecy: "Where there be prophecies, they shall fail...."[121]

A prophecy is a trend, a stream in which the individual swims. If he heeds the call from the shore, the call which the Masters are continually giving, he or she may still arise and emerge from the stream in time to avoid being carried over the falls.

I must speak what I have seen, and hope that people will awaken. Arise! Exercise your Free Will that has been yours always. Arise! And go unto the Father-Mother Presence that is calling you to the Home that you once knew, and from which you wandered so long ago.

Exercise your Free Will! It is the key to existence. It is by our own choice that we entered the world of human experience. Now, it is by the exercise of that same Free Will that we must leave the world of human experience, though there may be many who do not wish to leave—that choice is theirs.

For those who seek a higher world the question to be asked is, "Am I ready?" There is a Life More Abundant, a world of far greater Peace, Love, Happiness,

---

120 Prophecies regarding the year 2012 abound, as any search of the Internet will reveal.
121 1 Corinthians 13:8.

and Light than can be known through the five senses—a world some are entering even now through self-conscious application of Divine Law. But not until a person has learned why they are in the world can they be ready to leave the world. Not until there is nothing more here that one wishes to experience, not until one has set straight what once they made crooked, and brought the light of understanding where once they were in darkness and confusion, not until one has overcome all human weakness and become a harmonious Sun of Perfection radiating the Light, Love, and Wisdom of the God Self to all one's brothers and sisters—not until then will one be ready to live in that next world—the Kingdom of Heaven.

"What do I still need to work on?" should be the question everyone is asking him or herself every day, every moment. "How can I be better, closer to God?" As sincere as you are with God, will God be sincere with you. And if God will answer these questions, then will not God also help you to attain that for which you ask? At least ask to know that for which to ask, and to have the courage, strength, and understanding necessary for its attainment. Ask to become that Master Presence that you wish to be. Do not punish yourself for past wrongs—if your lesson has been learned, you are forgiven, and can at any moment arise and go unto the Father-Mother God. Did not Jesus say, "As I have overcome, so shall you overcome...what things I have done, so shall you do, and greater things than these shall ye do." And there is no time like the present for these greater things.

The Truth is simple, though those who do not wish to follow the Truth make it complicated, so that it is easy for them to find loopholes. But that is their own funeral. Let it not be yours. There are many false prophets today, those prophets of doom giving forth more information than we know what to do with. What good is all that nonsense? Certainly there are enough theories floating around without propagating more. We don't need more theories and information; what we do need is more self-love, self-discipline, and obedience to the Truth that we already have, the Truth that we have always had—the Truth of the One.

The One is the key to all Truth. If you would know the truth of a thing, ask, "Does this correspond with the Truth of the One? Does it reflect the One Eternal Consciousness that is manifest throughout the Universe? Or is it rather the product of the limits and fears of the human intellect?"

Energy travels in a circle. What you create returns to you. And thinking is creating. Had we better not watch our thoughts, then? And since feeling is the energy behind our thoughts, the power by which thought is brought into manifestation, then we must, of course, control our feelings as well. Then you will always be feeling well and not wondering any more why you feel a certain way, because your own creation has returned to you. For then you will be Master of your own world, and have the understanding and wisdom to create only that which is good—which is what you yourself wish to experience. So, you see there is really only One—not many. And the Consciousness that is within us is that One—that light of Universal Consciousness, a common thread, making the necklace on which each individual's being is a Divine bead. There is only One energy, One force, One consciousness, and the sooner that each one realizes the meaning of this and begins to attain this God Consciousness—accepts the responsibility for the use of this Divine Force—the easier will it be for each to progress in Mastery, and the sooner will humanity enter the New World that is waiting.

As you want assistance attaining this consciousness, call on the Masters for that assistance. But remember, Mastery is something you achieve for yourself; for if it were something that someone achieved for you, it would not be Mastery, would it? The Way to Mastery is through mastering yourself.

When you see something within you that needs working on—and you will—instead of pretending that it isn't there, or that it doesn't matter, because you feel that you are going to be saved regardless of your bad habits—be happy that you have found something to work on, an opportunity to call God into action and rid yourself of that thing. Be glad that you have been honest with yourself, and then say, "Now I'm going to enjoy watching how God works, and feeling God's Love in action."

And you will be helped, for your God Presence, the "I AM THAT I AM," is a real, tangible being. Though you may lifetime upon lifetime have completely ignored It, your God Presence has not ignored you—for it lives for you alone. It is you.

You are a Ray, a spark from that Presence, sent forth into the world, and as you become conscious of that Rayship, then you move into that Presence and return to that God Consciousness again. Only this time you are on a higher level, have attained a greater degree of evolution. There is involution and evolution. Light descends into darkness. Then light brings order. Having expanded and learned from its experience, light dissolves darkness and becomes a greater light. Resistance is the food of growth. From the struggle of overcoming comes understanding; from understanding comes Love—the perception of God in all things—and from that Love comes Victory over all things, even Victory over the illusion of death.

It is the very resistance that all who have Ascended have had to overcome. Jesus said, "In the world ye have tribulation, but be of good cheer; I have overcome the world."[122]

"Before Abraham was, 'I AM.'"[123]

Before the creation of all material universes was that cause which was, which is, and which always shall be:

"I AM."

And only in understanding, applying, and becoming that "I AM," and in calling that "I AM" forth into action in one's life and world, can one become a conscious creator.

God is an Intelligence—a Living Presence that permeates and gives rise to the Universe—a presence that one can experience and become. And that Intelligence, in all Its Infinite Wisdom and Love, has provided humanity a faculty by which it may stay in continuous contact with its Source. And that is the faculty of feeling. It is at the very center of your being, near what some call the Heart, wherein is that Sacred Flame, the focus of the "I AM"—a Presence you can feel and with whom you can communicate. It is not the mind, but the Presence which gives rise to mind.

The Seed of God is within your heart—the rest is up to you. Will you water that seed? Will you tend that seedling and protect it as it grows? Will you accept the responsibility for becoming a Divine Creator? A Son or Daughter of God? Or will you choose to ignore that Seed and go on about your way from birth to death, age upon age, seeking only the fruits of human pleasures with their consequent sorrows? The choice is yours at every moment.

Do not be afraid. Do not fear that you are not strong enough to overcome. God is strong, and God is within you. If you dwell on your shortcomings, you strengthen them. Rather, call to God and put your attention on that Presence which you wish to become. Affirm within yourself that which you wish to manifest—and you shall. All is already within you as a seed—and with your attention upon that seed, you feed it the light of your being, the Water of Life—and you will feel it grow and blossom into flower and bear fruit within you. "As a man thinketh in his heart, so is he."[124] *"The Kingdom of God is within you."*[125]

---

122 John 16:33.
123 John 8:58.
124 Proverbs 23:7.
125 Luke 17:21.

It is so easy; why do more not practice this? Ask the Presence to awaken all God's Children to the Presence of God they have within them—the Presence they are. How beautiful all will then become.

When all realize that there is only One, that they are that One, then will individuals stop trying to "get" at each other's expense. What one is deprived of, all are deprived of, what one suffers, all suffer. When humanity learns that, then will the dominant desire be to give rather than to get, to bless rather than to be blessed, to give Love rather than to be loved. And when that Love rules, then the New Age will begin.

But we do not need to wait for others to learn to Love; we can Love now. Only in Love is Mankind's salvation. The time has come when those sitting on the fence must move. No longer will individuals be able to say, "That is what I want, but I'm too busy." An age is drawing to a close, another age is beginning. Those who have not learned their earthly lessons, who still cling to their human desires, those who are still sitting on the fence when the last Angel sounds its trumpet, will go through the great ordeal which mankind has created for itself.

Soon the fence will be shaken and will fall. And then where will those sit who have not yet found the courage to stand?

There are many schoolrooms in God's Universe, many mansions in which all God's Children may find room, where they may continue the lessons where they left off; however, Earth is no longer going to be the schoolroom that it has been, for on the Earth is to come forth a New Heaven and a New Earth. The Earth is becoming a Sun, a creative center of God's Light. It is the fulfillment of God's Plan, and it can no longer be delayed. Day by day the light increases. Day by day the Inner Light grows within the Hearts of those who have turned toward the Light, who have sought It, who have asked that Light into their Lives.

The very center of the Earth itself grows and breathes with the rhythm of God's Breath more powerfully with each passing hour. And the Radiation of that Light is causing, and will continue to cause, many changes. The changes have just now begun, and will be felt in all human affairs and in the Earth itself. These are the pains of growth.

Those who are in tune with the light, who have found it within, will grow in harmony with It and will experience greater Understanding, Enlightenment, and Love than they have ever imagined possible. While those who have not found It, or who turn away from It for one reason or another, will experience this energy as discord, suffering, and despair.

People, O people, I beg each of you, to turn within to the Light, to dwell in the Light, to seek only from the Light all that you require. Overcome human desires and habits that hold you back from the fullness of that Light—which is what you really desire—the only thing that will truly make you happy.

Seek, and you shall find. Knock, and it shall be opened unto you. Strive, and you shall overcome—but you must make the effort. You must seek, you must knock, you must ask, and you must overcome. It will not be done for you. As much as the Great Ones would do it for you, still it is your lesson. You are the one who must grow and become strong. Follow in the steps they have prepared. It is a narrow pathway, indeed, beside the many wide pathways that lead to ruin.

"What is it that I really want?" each must ask. All the assistance in the universe is available to you, if you will only ask.

Age upon age, this same message has been given. Some have heeded, most have not—and age upon age, civilizations have gone down in ruins. We are now at such a time in this age, in our present civilization. Still, there is much that can be done to change and divert influences that are at work, to save many who might otherwise be lost, and always there is the opportunity to express more light. The darker that things seem to become, the more manifest is that opportunity—and a great opportunity it is now for those children of Earth who wish to take their firm stand in the light—and realize, "*I AM the Light!*"

Chapter 48

I Am With You Always

I found marriage to be the ultimate proving ground for Mastery, a crucible for self-purification, where one's spirituality and wisdom are tested and refined. *You may feel liberated, but can you share your life with someone twenty-four hours a day, with the mirror of their awareness in your face constantly reflecting where you are deficient?* Hopefully there is also the unconditional love and understanding to heal those wounds—a process which can only take place when each partner takes one hundred percent responsibility for their own feelings.

I realized that Dona and I saw only a fraction of who we were, that we understood very little of what the other was thinking and feeling, and that this failure caused the miscommunications that fed our strife. Even the Violet Consuming Flame did not dissolve the problem; rather it brought everything to the surface—the first step in real healing.

But the greatest pain was the absence of the Masters and lack of connection with the I AM Presence, that left me feeling abandoned in outer darkness. In the midst of this emotional turmoil, they could not approach, for their energy would only amplify the struggle. I could not believe that after all the years of apprenticeship with Saint Germain, and the adventures I had been through with the Masters, I was now in a marriage, the purpose of which seemed to be to learn the basics of relationship—the most difficult task yet, and one which I would not learn entirely in this relationship. Because our union had been directed by Saint Germain, I assumed that our marriage was for life; but within two years we had separated,[126] and

---

[126] Dona returned to Berkeley, where she entered politics as "Dona Spring" and was elected to serve on the Berkeley City Council. She was a staunch crusader for animal rights, the physically challenged, the homeless, pure food, and the environment, and became known as "The Conscience of Berkeley." An opposition candidate who tried unsuccessfully to win her seat said, "Running against Dona Spring is like running against Mother Theresa." She passed away on July 13, 2008, after a life-long struggle with rheumatoid arthritis that, for the last thirty years, kept her confined to a wheel chair.

after a long period of solitude, I was directed by the Master to again enter into relationship—this time with someone who brought different aspects where I was deficient to the surface.

One night I was awakened by a light in the room. My body seemed on fire and sweat ran from every pore. I looked up to see a ball of light brighter than the sun descending into the dark room. *A meteor is falling on the house,* I thought. Then, *Two airliners have collided and exploded overhead.* The night sky was illuminated, and as the light fell through the roof, a searing heat penetrated my body, and, certain I was going to die, I sat up in a panic.

"No, no," I shouted out loud, as the heat in my body became unbearable.

Suddenly the light was gone. I was sitting wide awake in the darkness, wondering why my girlfriend, asleep on her futon across the room, had not heard my cries. Exhausted, I lay back and tried to purge the fear—apprehensive that this terrifying chimera might return. Lying in the darkness, I dared not lower my guard.

As I had feared, the light began to return, and I realized that this was a light that could kill. I broke out in a sweat, every cell blazing as if from an inner sun. This time I saw that the light was surrounded by rainbow rings, and I realized that the intruder was none other than my I AM Presence, the Source of life.

"No, no, I'm not ready to go," I shouted, feeling every cell was dissolving into its constituent elements. *Am I going to complete the Ascension now that was begun years before in the Atomic Accelerator?* There would be a flash of spontaneous combustion, and the physical body would be no more. Yet, for some reason, my ego still clung to the precious form, wanting to continue the human existence which, I felt, had not yet completed its assigned mission.

"Stop!" I shouted, "What do you want?"

"I want you to know beyond the shadow of a doubt that I AM REAL," came the astounding reply. "I AM the *Alpha* and the *Omega*, the beginning and the end of your being. Without me, you would not exist. It is by my Grace that your heart beats, that you draw breath, and that you think every thought.

"I come now to remove all doubt as to WHO and WHAT I AM, so you will know I AM GOD—that you exist only because of ME, and that nothing can happen in your life but through MY WILL. I visit you now to give you the consciousness and energy you will need in the days ahead, so that no matter how dark and challenging your life becomes, you will know that I AM REAL and that I AM WITH YOU ALWAYS."

As those words penetrated, accompanied by rays of light pouring into my mind and body, I fell on my knees, trembling, knowing that the physical presence I called "myself" was no more enduring than a cut blade of grass before the morning sun, but which had been allowed to endure a while longer. As the light faded, the heat diminished, and once more I was alone, filled with the shock of realization that, as the Masters had been trying to convey all along—

I AM GOD.

Postscript

Many crave the excitement of adventure written about in this autobiography, but how many are willing to sacrifice the material security and comfort, and undertake the rigorous training required? And how many have the innocence to follow their guidance with absolute trust?

This is the example of one person living the Master's teaching: *Ye must become as little children before ye can enter the Kingdom of Heaven.*

I have known Peter for over twenty years, and I feel this account to be truthful—because he lives that truth.

—Diane Evans

Acknowledgments

I would like to thank those who encouraged me over the years to write down these experiences so that others might benefit. Though I cannot mention everyone, I would especially like to thank Nancy Marriott for her initial encouragement to complete this book, and for her editorial ability in helping organize these experiences, written haphazardly over the years, in more or less chronological order. I am also grateful to Carl Marsak for his kind Foreword, detailed editing, and numerous suggestions based on his deep understanding of the spiritual development of the West—a vision possessed only by those with an open heart. I also am thankful for his friendship and constant encouragement to persevere through all challenges. Thanks also to Beverly Harlan and Prof. Robert Manis, who provided detailed editing and made invaluable suggestions; also to Robert Rose, former publisher of *Halo Magazine;* and to Victoria Baldini and Jonathan River Wolfe, both of whom knew Pearl and whose encouragement and support has been a blessing. Special thanks to Lama Tony Duff, who helped clarify the subtleties of consciousness described by various Tibetan and Sanskrit terms. I am also grateful to my former wife, Diane Evans, for her heartfelt Postscript, and to all those over the years who encouraged me to continue this account of my experiences despite the turmoil in my personal life.

I would especially like to thank Aaron Rose, whose editorial and graphic design ability have greatly improved this latest edition, and for whose unflagging friendship I am deeply grateful.

Appendix I

Who Are the Masters?

An Ascended Master is an enlightened being who has raised his or her vibratory rate to a higher frequency, and from that higher dimension they serve as *Bodhisattvas,* assisting human evolution. In Tibet this process is called *Jalus,* attaining the Rainbow Body; in the West, *Ascension.* This book is an account of my training under those Masters who, on occasion, materialized in visible and even physical form, and who sent me on missions which to most would seem like fantastic adventures—although their first rule is to shun phenomena.

Those secret teachings on how to attain human perfection, long held guarded in the Far East, are being released today under the Masters' direction. As humanity awakens from its slumber of materialism to become aware of the inner light, experienced in the past only by isolated mystics, this knowledge is being revealed ever more openly.

Previously given by the most recent Buddha and other great adepts of India, these teachings were taken by the great master Padmasambhava to Tibet, where they were taught in secret to the initiated few. They could not be taught more openly, because many years of austere practice in seclusion were required to realize their fruits, and to speak of them would be to open them to distortion, dilution, and possible misuse. Similar teachings were known in China prior to Communism.

It is with the hope of transmitting these teachings in a new form more easily practiced in today's society, that the Masters are now giving these core truths and practices through diverse avenues. Although studying the teachings is of profound benefit, the essence can only be transmitted by the student merging their mind with that of the teacher. However, without the teacher being physically present, this can only take place on the inner planes where the Masters dwell—where the student's mind is never separate from theirs—a transmission taking place now on a vast scale for those who are aware, and who choose to pursue this path of initiation.

Some of the obstacles to this transmission have been the fact that many terms do not translate from Sanskrit or the language in which they are written. In Tibetan, for example, there are many words for *consciousness,* defining various subtleties of meaning with great precision. Also, there are few realized teachers in the outer world capable of giving these transmissions, and students are prevented from having the necessary intimate contact with them, either because the teacher is constantly traveling or because the student has to devote so much time to survival.

Nonetheless, the Great Ones who watch over and guide the destiny of humanity began transmitting a simplified form of these teachings to the West in the late 1800s. They used Madame H.P. Blavatsky as their messenger and guided her to found the Theosophical Society in 1875 for this purpose.[127] Her first step was to prove the existence of other planes than the physical, and that such beings as Masters did in fact exist. This, in itself, was quite a feat in the prevailing culture of materialism, but few were ready for the actual spiritual teachings. When the teachings were given, they were of such a mental nature that it took decades for more than a handful to understand their import and how to apply them. The English initiate, Alice A. Bailey, was also instrumental in this work of making some of the inner teachings known in the outer world. She introduced the Aquarian concept that there is now on the Earth a group of Christ Conscious beings known as the *New Group of World Servers,* actively engaged in service to humanity.

More experiential aspects of the path to self-perfection were given to the West in the teachings of meditation and yoga, first introduced in the United States by Swami Vivekananda in 1889 at the World Congress of Religions in Chicago. Following him was Paramahansa Yogananda, whose book *The Autobiography of a Yogi* revealed to the world the great yogis of India and their miraculous feats, and popularized the concept of *self-realization*. Meditation was more fully introduced to the West by Maharishi Mahesh Yogi, who taught it as a science, without religious connotations, that would open the door to higher consciousness. This strategy attracted many celebrities in the '60s and '70s, such as the Beatles, and made *meditation* and *mantra*[128] household words.

---

127 Daniel H. Caldwell, *The Esoteric World of Madame Blavatsky: Insights into the Life of a Modern Sphinx* (The Theosophical Publishing House, 2000). An abridged version can be read online for free at https://www.theosophical.org/online-resources/online-books/1726.

128 Mantras are words and phrases usually in Sanskrit, a language of great vibrational purity, which stimulate the various organs and spiritual centers of the body, and which invoke different aspects of consciousness.

The concept of working on oneself, a cornerstone of the subsequent New Age Movement, was introduced in the first half of the twentieth century by the catalytic and syncretic Armenian mystic, G.I. Gurdjieff, who synthesized ancient teachings that dealt with the perfection of the self. He used the confrontational tactic of juxtaposing people with discordant personalities in order to bring up their emotional *stuff*, so they would have to look at their neuroses and work on them, rather than hide them under a veil of spirituality and psychological escape mechanisms. This eventually led, through the work of Oscar Ichazo, Claudio Naranjo, and others, to the development of the *Enneagram*, a method to help people understand their personality type so as to gain insight into their unique evolutionary path and remove behavioral and psychological obstacles to their spiritual development.

During the '60s and '70s, when drug use opened public awareness to the possibility of alternate realities, attention turned to the East for explanations of what people were experiencing. Foremost among these seekers was Harvard Professor Dr. Richard Alpert, who traveled to India and found many answers in the Himalayas at the feet of his guru, Neem Karoli Baba, with whom I also studied. Transformed by his experiences with this yogi, who demonstrated that he knew the innermost workings of Alpert's mind, he returned to the U.S. with the new name Baba Ram Dass. Then he wrote *Be Here Now*, a seminal work containing a distillation of the Vedas, the ancient Hindu religious texts, that became what some referred to as the hippie Bible. The secret teachings suddenly began to permeate the mass consciousness. Many came to realize that drugs, while giving a glimpse of alternate (although not necessarily higher) realities, actually blocked or sedated the will to attain true spiritual growth.

However, the transmission of the core of the secret teachings—awareness of the I AM Presence and the creative use of the expression I AM that calls that God Presence into action—was given to humanity

---

Repeating a word or affirmation in one's native language also has an effect by invoking the aspect of consciousness on which one is focused. However, in the latter case, the words need to be repeated slowly, with full awareness, rather than rapidly, as is often done now by those attempting to combine the teachings of the East and West.

by the Ascended Masters in the 1930s through Godfre Ray King.[129] Under the guidance and tangible radiation of the Masters,[130] he taught that each of us has a Higher Self which is the Source of our being—a focus of consciousness that is a sun surrounded by the rainbow aura that is the accumulated wisdom and merit of our many lives. From this luminous Self a tube of light descends into the physical body, anchoring the God Flame near the heart. By meditating on that light, we ascend in consciousness and become unified with our source—regaining union with our Rainbow Body. When we say the words "I AM," we call forth that light of our God Self and bring into manifestation whatever quality we associate with those words.

I have seen that God Presence on several life-altering occasions, and I hope in this book to have shared the simple key of that I AM Presence, which unlocks the most esoteric Eastern practices and grants access to the realms of the miraculous.

---

129 This individualized focus of God which is the source of our being, known as the Monad in some esoteric writings, is called here the I AM Presence. In its octave, it is a sun surrounded by an aura of rainbow light, which projects a ray down through our seven levels of being, finally anchored in the chest near the thymus gland, sometimes called the heart center. The Higher Mental or Causal Body is an intermediary being existing between the I AM Presence and the human self, and aware of both worlds, sometimes called the Soul. Children sometimes see the Presence above them and think it is a Guardian Angel. It is, in fact, the God Presence that is above and within us always. Having granted us free will, however, It usually only makes Itself known when we are willing to submit to its Direction.

130 See Appendix II for an explanation of the seven rays and the Masters who serve as *Chohans* of those rays.

Appendix II

The Seven Rays and Their Chohans

As Lao Tzu said, *The Tao that can be written is not the Tao,* so take the explanation below as only a sign by the roadside, pointing out the general direction. It is not essential to study this esoteric philosophy unless it is your path, and I doubt you will be tested on it at the gates of heaven. However, it is important to understand that we are composed of different energies, each of which must be honored and developed. By analogy, in order to cook a good potato soup, it is not enough just to have potatoes; one must also have other ingredients, such as onions, celery, carrots, and various spices. Likewise, the activity of the rays must also be combined, and we must assimilate all the energies which the seven Masters—who are *Chohans* (heads) of the rays—embody.

Despite the many books written on the subject of the Masters and the rays, there is much confusion on the subject; this is largely due to the impossibility of conveying a multi-dimensional reality in two-dimensional print. The difficulty is analogous to explaining the ocean to one who has never seen it, saying it is like a glass of water, only bigger. Thus, I would suggest using what is said here only as a point of meditation to begin exploration, not as a definitive explanation.

The seven rays are not beams of light originating from a localized source, such as a spotlight in space, but are aspects of consciousness which permeate creation. To understand the rays and how they work together is to understand oneself. These seven aspects extend to every living cell, each of which is made up of seven basic components. Seven endocrine glands act as foci for the psycho-spiritual centers of the body known as *chakras*—represented in the Book of Revelation as The Seven Churches. These churches must all function in cooperation and harmony to form the complete body of the Christ, as must all the emotional and spiritual centers of the human body function in harmony in order to function as a Master.

These rays and the Masters associated with them may roughly be characterized as follows:

First Ray, El Morya, will and power, conscious self-awareness of one's basic identity as "I."

Second Ray, Kuthumi, love and the wisdom which comes from the first ray going forth into the world of experience and being reflected back on itself, the feminine and magnetic awareness surrounding the electronic first ray.

Third Ray, The Venetian, patron of artists and writers, the active intelligence of the first two rays exercised in conscious thought.

Fourth Ray, El Serapis, the first three rays manifesting in a body, consciousness of form, space, and etheric substance, physical and energetic development as in yoga, struggle and conflict leading to harmony, self-discipline.

Fifth Ray, Hilarion, the "Master Mechanic," the study and understanding of how the previous four rays work together, science, the manipulation of substance.

Sixth Ray, Jesus, devotion, the acknowledgment of and surrender to the divine spark that animates and is at the heart of all life, the animating and cohesive force central to the previous rays.

Seventh Ray (the primary subject of this book), Saint Germain, freedom through forgiveness, and the conscious understanding and mastery of the previous six rays in action. Ritual alchemy and ceremonial magic by which dross is transformed into gold. Occult transmutation. The New Humanity.

Each of us throughout the day, consciously or unconsciously, exercises the activity of all seven rays. For example, in the morning we awaken and become aware that we exist, and will ourselves into action (First Ray).

Then we become aware of a significant "other" in our lives—a partner, pet or occupation—that impinges on our awareness, and we start to see ourselves in terms of others (Second Ray).

Then we start to think about who we are, what we did yesterday, and what we are going to do during the coming day (Third Ray).

Next, we get up and become aware of the body and take care of its needs, stretch, do yoga and Qi Gong, nourish ourselves, and try to harmonize our energies and activities (Fourth Ray).

Now we are ready to analyze what we want to do and how we can accomplish those objectives in the best manner (Fifth Ray).

Next, we become aware that by ourselves we can do nothing, that the spark that keeps us alive is the real doer, and we acknowledge that same spark in everyone—hopefully dedicating our actions to a higher cause for the benefit of others (Sixth Ray).

Finally, we see what effects our actions are having on others, and see how we can improve ourselves through heightened awareness. Before we go to sleep, we recapitulate the day and glean the wisdom we have gained. We invoke forgiveness for all thoughts and actions that may have caused suffering, and realize the transitory nature of all phenomena. By changing ourselves, we change the world (Seventh Ray).

Appendix III

Recommended Reading

U.S. Andersen, *Three Magic Words*

David Anrias, *Through the Eyes of the Masters: Meditations and Portraits*

Joseph Benner, *The Impersonal Life*

Dr. Raymond Bernard, *The Great Secret, Count St. Germain*

Sir Edward Bulwer-Lytton, *Zanoni, a Rosicrucian Tale*

Isabel Cooper-Oakley, *The Comte de St. Germain*

Pearl Dorris and the Ascended Masters, *Step By Step We Climb* (3 volumes)

Will L. Garver, *The Brother of the Third Degree*

Elizabeth Haich, *Initiation*

Virginia Hanson, *Masters and Men, The Human Story in the Mahatma Letters*

Herman Hesse, *Siddhartha*

Godfre Ray King, *Unveiled Mysteries*
——*The Magic Presence*
——*The I AM Discourses*

Phylos, *A Dweller on Two Planets*

Mipham Rinpoche, *Turning the Mind Into an Ally*

His Pupil (Cyril Scott), *The Initiate Series* (3 volumes)

Baird T. Spalding, *Life and Teachings of the Masters of the Far East*

Chögyam Trungpa, *Cutting Through Spiritual Materialism*
——*Meditation in Action*
——*The Myth of Freedom and the Way of Meditation*
——*The Path Is the Goal*
——*Shambhala: The Sacred Path of the Warrior*

Discover Other Books by Peter Mt. Shasta:

"I AM" The Open Door

Fourteen discourses given by ten different Ascended Masters, who appeared to Peter Mt. Shasta in their light bodies to teach how to contact your inner God Self and bring its mastery into daily life.

"I AM" Affirmations and the Secret of their Effective Use

How to make affirmations work through the practice of meditation. Contains many affirmations for use in different areas of life, from spiritual development to business, parenting, and planetary service.

I AM The Living Christ: Teachings of Jesus

Profound teachings of the New Testament edited in light of the Gnostic Texts, teachings that are highly applicable in today's tumultuous life. Jesus's own use of the I AM is highlighted.

Lady Master Pearl, My Teacher

The biography of Pearl Dorris, to whom the Master Saint Germain sent many of his students for training in how to contact the I AM and bring its Presence into daily life. She was an assistant to Godfrey Ray King, and director of the "I AM" Sanctuary of San Francisco.

Search for the Guru: Apprentice to the Masters, Book I

First part of autobiography of Peter Mt. Shasta, describing his spiritual awakening, journeys to India, adventures with Ram Dass and his guru Maharajji, as well as many other saints and sages—including profound experiences in the US with Trungpa Rinpoche, Chagdud Rinpoche, and Joseph Sunhawk (Taos Pueblo).

Step by Step: Ascended Master Discourses

Discourses by various Ascended Masters, given to a group led by Pearl Dorris in Santa Rosa, California in the 1940s. Re-edited for clearer understanding. The power released through these talks is amazing.

My Search in Tibet for the Secret Wish-Fulfilling Jewel

Further adventures of Peter Mt. Shasta as he goes to Tibet at the request of the Sixteenth Karmapa. He is given Buddhist teachings that Saint Germain instructs are to be incorporated into the I AM teachings to make them more effective in developing expanded consciousness and compassion.

To connect with the author, please visit his website and blog at www.i-am-teachings.com.

CPSIA information can be obtained
at www.ICGtesting.com
Printed in the USA
LVHW110210220822
726518LV00016B/47

9 780692 570449